LINCOLN CITY FC

A SEASON REVIEW

2020/21

BY GARY HUTCHINSON

For my Patreon supporters:

Tom Williams, Stuart Wilson, Stuart Borthwick, Steve Empson, Simon Butler, Shaun Symons, Shane Wakefield, Sean Wattam, Sean Hunt, Robert Townsend, Robert Hipworth, Richard Harvey, Richard Coy, Rachel Ward, Pete Robinson, Peta Leggatt, Pauline Ward, Neil Carlton, Mark Torkington, Mark Taylor, Mark Armstrong, Mark Churchill, Jane Churchill, Maria Horner, Margaret Watson, Marcus Needham, Liam Scully, Liam Forrester, Lee Vasey, Kiwipuskas, Kevin Williams, Kev Barwise, Keith Fletcher, Jon Kempton, Joanna Manning, Ryan Whelan, Jom Olsen, Jeremy Chappell, Jay Shemenski, Jason Wright, Jane Chamberlain, James White, Ian Dovey, Henry McMunn, Harry Winkworth, Gavin Andrews, Felix Richardson, Emma Crellin, Drew Hird, Dom Clarke, Dean Wagstaff, David Ward, David Larder, David Johnson, David Drewery, Dave Wilkinson, Dave Potter, Dan Shinn, Dan Rawson, Colin Green, Clive Wetton, Clive Smith, Clive Nates, Chris Wray, Chris Laming, Chris Konrath, Charli Chmylowskyj, Carole McPhail, Jon Buckthorpe, Ben Daniels, Antony Foottit, Andy Helson, Andy Bulley, Andrew Pearce, James Barnatt and Amanda Slater.

Introduction

The 2020/21 season was the second to be affected badly by Covid-19 and the associated fallout. The season started late, and financial restrictions meant that hard decisions had to be made before a ball was kicked. Players were released and City were stripped back to the bare bones. Our squad churn was the highest of any team in the division and that meant lots of new faces.

New players bring expectation and uncertainty, excitement and apprehension. Would they gel in time? Would a large enough percentage of them perform to our expectation, and help us become established in League One. That really was the key focus ahead of the campaign – sustaining our position. Such was the uncertainty around fans being in stadiums, and thus income, simply surviving the season would have been an achievement. Quietly, Michael Appleton and the team worked hard behind the scenes, only suggesting we 'might surprise a few people'. Boy, was he right.

From the very first kick against Crewe, Michael Appleton's aspiration squad impressed supporters. Quickly, we established ourselves as a promotion contender, and managed a run in the League Cup too. That brought the joy of the seeing the English champions at Sincil Bank, and the agony of fans not being allowed in to witness it. In fact, for every positive that occurred, there seemed to be a negative.

We quickly climbed into the top two, but lost our backup striker, Callum Morton to injury. When Joe Walsh came back to fitness, we lost Adam Jackson to suspension. Every good result seemed to bring another obstacle for the club to get over. By Christmas, fixtures were falling due to Covid and injuries were mounting up. At one point, seven or eight senior players sat on the sidelines and still the Imps maintained a promotion push.

The EFL Trophy brought additional minutes we could have done without, but it also delivered another run towards Wembley and the agony of a penalty shoot-out defeat in the semi-finals. After that, our league form dipped as Jorge Grant, Tom Hopper, Liam Bridcutt and Joe Walsh all missed out, along with a handful of others. Our youngsters battled bravely, a collection of players borrowed from other clubs, and those brought in by ourselves.

In the end, the slide was corrected and Lincoln City made the League One play-offs for the first time ever. That meant another semi-final with Sunderland, and a possible Wembley date with either Oxford or Blackpool. Could we erase the memories of 9182/83, when a single game sat blocking our route to the third tier? Or, would history repeat itself and a wafer-thin squad be torn in the second half of the season, resulting in agony at the final hurdle?

Sadly, you know the answer to that question, but the final twist of the knife should not detract from what has been a sensational season, the fifth in a row that Lincoln City have bettered themselves over a 12 month period. The big question now is can we do the same in 2021/22? Rest assured, in twelve months' time, I'll bring you the answer.

This is the story of the 2020/21 season, as published on my site Staceywest.net week by week. In some instances, it may be obvious that this was written for the internet, penned with certain dates and times in mind. There might even by a typo or two, but it wouldn't be the Stacey West without that, would it?

Enjoy.

Summer 2020

Bostwick To Leave Imps As Retained List Announced
May 28, 2020

I'm a few minutes behind the official news but, credit to the club, I did get the press release early.

Instead of taking to the keyboard, I went to walk my dog in the calm evening sun and ensure I had a clear mind. The big news on the retained list is that Michael Bostwick, arguably my favourite player in the current squad, has left the club.

The Imps are releasing all but one of the out of contract players; Charlie Andrew, Michael Bostwick, Neal Eardley, Lee Frecklington, Akeem Hinds, Jamie McCombe (oddly), Tom Pett, Jason Shackell, Alan Sheehan, Grant Smith and Josh Vickers. Ellis Chapman is the only player to be retained, or rather to continue in talks with the club.

Interestingly, the wording around Ellis is this; 'prior to Covid-19 we engaged with representatives of Ellis Chapman and conversations remain ongoing'. That clearly indicates that the current financial climate has made it impossible to retain players whom I think we all wanted to see stay. Further on in the official statement, it also says; "Due to the unprecedented situation we find ourselves in, it has made making any positive decisions around out of contract players impossible at this time. The club would like to express our sincere thanks to all those players who will leave us in the coming weeks and wish them a successful future."

Right now, I find it hard to be critical or positive about the list. There is a sense that if this were the actual retained list, put into place at the end of a full season and with the summer to recruit as we wished, we might have kept one or two of these players. However, with the pandemic and financial uncertainty, I guess the club couldn't offer new deals to players. We don't know where the market will be in two months time, what constitutes a fair wage in the 'new normal'.

The club added a nice thank you at the end; "To Michael Bostwick, Neal Eardley, Lee Frecklington, Tom Pett, Jason Shackell and Josh Vickers – thank you for being an integral part of one of the most successful periods in the club's history and helping to create such wonderful memories." Perhaps for the likes of Lee and Tom, woefully underused post-Christmas, the thank you might ring a little hollow.

For now, I'm going to step away and consider the reaction of others. I can't summon up the right emotions to be fair and just. I know the club are operating under the most unusual of environments, where survival is simply the only goal right now, and this retained list makes it all the more real for me.

I could help think back to the article I wrote at the beginning of the day about the end of an era as I finished this one. Seeing Gain, Butcher, Yeo and the rest leave 15 years ago was tough; seeing Eardley, Bozzy, Freck and Vickers leave does feel very similar. I suppose the only difference is every team is in the same boat and we are in the third tier.

Please, try not to get too angry with the club on this one, the mitigating circumstances really are challenging.

Imps 'lead the race' for 24-year-old midfielder
July 6, 2020

You wait all summer for transfer news and suddenly, you get two lots back to back.

Yesterday, Alan Nixon reported we were looking at three players, with Cheshire Live adding a fourth name to that list this morning; Crewe Alexandra midfielder James Jones. Jones is a Scottish central midfielder and he's a little older than some of the other target we have been linked with. He's 24-years-old and in August 2017 he was close to a £300,000 move to Preston North End, but that was curtailed through injury. Indeed, injury seems to have blighted his time at Crewe, but he has still turned in some impressive stats.

He bagged ten league goals from central midfield in the 2016/17 season, and in total has 185 outings for David Artell's side, including two seasons as a youngster in League One. Last season, he added two goals and two assists to their charge towards promotion and he was offered a new deal when the Railwaymen were confirmed as being promoted. However, he looks set to turn down that deal and join us, with Gillingham also in the hunt but reportedly unlikely to snatch him at last minute.

Jones is a former Scotland Under 19 and Under 21 star who would not command a fee as he is now over the age of 24. It would be a big blow to Crewe to lose him after he has come through their youth system, but it would also be a coup for us to secure his services. If he is able to steer clear of injuries, he is exactly the sort of player we want in the door; plenty of senior experience, some at this level and with potential to move forward in his career and maybe bag a bigger move quickly. Jones is a cross between potential and experience, someone who we might not have to wait two years to see develop.

After scoring in a 2-1 win against Oldham earlier this season, Jones gave a little insight into his favoured position after waiting for a chance at Gresty Road.

"It's been a case of biding my time, working hard and waiting for my chance," he said."I know I am capable, and hopefully I've taken my chance. It was a bit of a scruffy goal but I'll take it, and know playing that higher role I can get into the box and get chances. It was a good feeling."

Usually, if a local paper reports a story like this, it is based on some facts and that makes me think we could be close to this deal. I like the sound of Jones, he hasn't stood out for me in our clashes with them but his record is decent and he fits the bill. It is hard to judge any player we haven't see and even one with a record behind him could change in our system, or with a move, but I feel this is more along the lines of the type of player fans will be happy to see linked.

Shortly after this article, James Jones became the first in at Sincil Bank over the summer.

Imps Make Dutch Defender Second Summer Signing
July 14, 2020

Michael Appleton has bagged the second signing of the summer for the Imps, bringing in Dordrecht defender Lewis Montsma on a three-year deal.

The 22-year-old is described as a 'ball-playing defender' who has joined the club following a successful spell in the Dutch Eerste Divisie. Lewis, who was born in Amsterdam, started his youth career at AFC Amsterdam before moving to Eredivisie side SC Heerenveen featuring for their U17 and U19 sides.

Following his four-year stint there, he signed for SC Cambuur making his mark in their U21 side but not breaking into the first team. However, his stellar performances attracted the attention of FC Dordrecht and he moved there in the summer of 2018. Standing at 6ft 3in tall, the centre half has been a regular in their first-team squad ever since.

He made 23 league appearances for FC Dordrecht in the 2018/19 season, as well as a further 23 this time out and he cannot wait to get started with

City.

"I'm very happy, I think it's an amazing club and I'm delighted to be here. From the National League to League One in four years is amazing and I think it's the perfect move for me to play games and gain some experience in England."

Lewis added, "The style, the people, the supporters, everything is so good over here. I'm a footballing central defender and I can't wait to play in front of our fans".

Michael Appleton was really pleased to sign Montsma, "Lewis is a very versatile defender who can play either side at centre half. He is a physical specimen and I'm thrilled to have signed him. He uses the ball really well and is comfortable with both feet in possession whilst being very aggressive out of possession. I'm sure he'll be a real asset to this club".

'I think we'll surprise a few' – Michael Appleton talks upcoming season on new podcast

July 22, 2020

Michael Appleton has been speaking to podcaster Joe Citrone about the upcoming season, and it's a great listen, it always is when Michael speaks as he is very candid, and he's certainly opened up a little about his mission here, and the future. I haven't transcribed it all because you really should listen, especially when Michael talks about the crowd response to the final few games of last season.

However, I did find his comments about the reasoning behind joining Lincoln to be relevant, and perhaps a little more candid than we got when he first came. The change of direction and budgeting has been discussed in great detail, but I think these comment perfectly compliment the future direction and pour some real scorn on some of the more outlandish claims after Huddersfield sacked their management team recently.

"I knew it was going to be tough at Lincoln because they had three years of success with Danny and Nicky," said our boss. "They did it in a certain way which isn't my style and I knew they spent a lot of money in gaining success.

"They (the board) knew they couldn't compete budget-wise in League One with some of the big clubs. They felt that they overspent on certain players who were at an age where there was no resale value at all. They knew when Danny and Nicky left, they had to change their way of thinking and that was music to my ears."

Whilst being open and transparent, Michael isn't the type of person to name names in this respect, but you have to wonder if alleged club-record signings such as John Akinde fall into this bracket?

"They said they wanted to improve value on the pitch and develop their own players as well as other people's young players. You go into any job and as an individual, you have a certain way of doing your job. I think I have a reputation for developing young players in a certain brand and a certain style. Everyone has got a USP and my USP is developing young players. It ticked a lot of boxes, what they wanted and what I enjoy doing came together."

"We did it in January, we got rid of a lot of players in January and took a calculated risk on players, young players. At the time we went through a spell where we had a poor run, six or seven games where we lost a few and drew a few. All of a sudden, we came good again just before Covid kicked in. You could tell the belief was in the dressing room and I think it has stood us in good stead what happened in January. I think now, all of a sudden, I have got a young group I'm going to add to and bring more players in of a similar sort of ilk."

Michael hints a little at the future direction of the transfer business; it doesn't sound like the likes of Liam Bridcutt will be coming in on big wages, because that would ape the situation of the past. Let's be clear; there is no criticism of the strategy which brought us to League One here, just an acceptance of change and a new direction.

However, if you're concerned that leaves us in a potential relegation battle, Michale believes we're going to be dark horses for a decent finish, if not a promotion challenge.

"I think we'll surprise a few this year. We will be competitive, we'll certainly not be near the big dogs in the league, expecting to be in the top six, but you never know. If you get a group of young players like we have got, and their belief grows, and they start winning games...

"The biggest thing you need to do with young players is winning close games. I know on any given day I've got a group of players who could win a game five or six nil, like Oxford did against us before I arrived. I know I have. Belief grows more when you win a game 1-0 or win a tight game against a top side.

"Let us see how it goes. There is going to be no massive expectations on us as a club, but we can be really competitive and surprise a few people."

The future could well be exciting, Oxford fans certainly think we've got a good man and personally, I'm intrigued and hopeful that the mission Michael is on will lead us to a continued stay in League One, unheard of during my time as an Imps' supporter.

City make 17-year-old third summer capture
July 23, 2020

The Imps have offered a first professional contract to 17-year-old Irish defender Sean Roughan, who has impressed in the academy.

Roughan is very highly thought of at Sincil Bank and he has now penned a professional contract with the club, after featuring not only for the academy but also the Eire Under 17 side last season. He has been with the club for a year thus far and said he is now delighted to have turned professional.

Sean said he's felt right at home. "When I first came on trial, I really enjoyed it and felt really good. I was offered a scholarship before I went home, which was just before Christmas, and a really nice present at the time.

"I came over a couple more times before joining full-time and was getting used to playing football for Lincoln, I really enjoyed it and felt right at home. Since I've been here as a Scholar, it's been nothing but good for me. The club has wanted the best for me both on and off the field and I really want to pay them back."

Sean's arrival was something of a coup for the club, which even arranged for a tutor to help academy players achieve their leaving certificate, the Irish equivalent of 'A' levels. The Irish market has been kind to us in the past with the likes of Gareth McAuley and Jeff Hughes, with Roughan reportedly showing as much promise as both would have had at the same age.

Indeed, chatting to people behind the scenes, there is real hope the youngster can progress to be a part of the first team setup, although there is also a desire not to heap too much pressure on his shoulders early. Either way, Jez George revealed how delighted he is to have been a part of delivering the first professional contract for the youngster.

"This is a fantastic moment for Sean and a proud one for his family, who have supported him brilliantly since he left Ireland to join us last July. Sean made great progress throughout last season and we feel that he is a player of real potential, hence offering him a professional contract at the earliest possible opportunity."

"We are absolutely delighted that he has trusted us with his continued development and committed his future to Lincoln City."

I've been very aware of Roughan all season, not least because he played in the first team friendly against Sheffield United back in October. Even then, there was an element of excitement around his potential and recently, when discussing the arrival of Lewis Montsma, it was also mentioned that Sean Roughan had similar qualities that Michael looked for in a centre back.

This signing won't make or break our season, but it is another reason to be positive about the direction the academy is taking. I know some sceptics will point to the Ellis situation and question the commitment to bring through our own youngsters, but I have little doubt that we will keep seeing players coming through, not necessarily ones from Lincoln, but hopefully players with international youth honours like Sean, who can go on to become either key players for the club.

City land 6ft 5in former West Brom stopper
July 24, 2020

The Imps have bagged 6ft 5in stopper Ethan Ross this afternoon, the first of two keepers expected at Sincil Bank.

Ross arrives on a free transfer from Colchester United, with whom he has spent the last two seasons. He's experienced the Sincil bank atmosphere before, he was in goal the afternoon we lost 3-0 but were presented with the League Two title.

The 23-year-old began his youth career with Arsenal and Cambridge United, before joining West Bromwich Albion. During his time with the Baggies, he gained senior experience n the non-league with Worcester City and Redditch.

Following his release from the Hawthorns, Ethan joined Colchester United, and had a short spell with Maidstone in the National League, returning to make his professional debut in a 1-1 draw against Yeovil Town. He made his full debut the week after, keeping a clean sheet in a 2-0 win against MK Dons, before keeping a clean sheet against us on the final day.

This season, the young stopper has appeared just once in the league, keeping a clean sheet as the U's turned over Carlisle 3-0. He also appeared in all four of their Leasing.com Trophy matches, with a clean sheet again, this time at home to a strong Ipswich side.

On his move to the Imps, Ethan said, "I'm over the moon, once I found there was interest from Lincoln, I was really excited to see what that beheld."

"I felt like a fresh start was something I needed and jumped at the opportunity straight away, it's a step up in league and a new challenge which is something I really wanted. I'm looking forward to kicking on and working really hard across the season and seeing where it takes me and the team."

It appears that Ethan isn't the only keeper we're going to sign though, Michael Appleton has explained that someone else is going to be coming in to compete for the number one jersey.

"I'm fully aware that I won't be the only goalkeeper at the club and I know they're not going to bring someone in who doesn't want to play football. I know I'm going to have to compete and fight every day. When you work with good people you can bounce off each other and learn from each other, so I'm really excited to get going and see where it takes me."

Of his appearance at Sincil Bank last May, Ethan added; "It was brilliant, I remember walking out and seeing a big display in the Coop Stand, the 617 Squadron also in the corner made loads of noise. I remember defending the first corner and hearing the siren go off as well."

"When you hear just under 10,000 Imps going mad it makes you feel ten-foot-tall, I can't wait to get out there in red and white colours soon."

Ethan is a big keeper, he has a good pedigree in terms of his upbringing and he's young enough to be classed as potential, rather than being established. His lack of first-team action at Colchester would make me wonder if he is going to be our backup stopper, with a view to playing cup matches and challenging for the starting spot. That would be my gut feeling, but having not seen the lad play, it would be unfair to class him as a second-choice from the off.

If that is the case, it is a role he is used to, having played second fiddle to Dean Gerken at Colchester this season. He spoke in October about his role as back up, saying: "When you're not playing, it's not so much about yourself – it's more about the team. If you've pushed the goalkeeper who's playing and he goes out and plays well on the Saturday, it's a win-win for everybody.

"For me, there's a little bit more focus on training now as well, trying to show the gaffer and the management staff here what I can do every day in training."

Ross' arrival means that the club do now have eleven players who could form a first-team, so hopefully the 'need a keeper' comments can stop, even if we do still need a second keeper!

Confirmed Deal: Imps bag 24-year-old attacking midfielder
July 27, 2020

The Imps have moved to secure the fourth permanent deal of the summer, landing MK Dons midfielder Conor McGrandles on a free transfer.

McGrandles was under contract at MK Dons, where he was named Young Player of the Year in 2018/19, but he's fallen out of favour with Russell Martin, who agreed to a termination, allowing City to swoop in. He joins James Jones, Lewis Montsma and Ethan Ross as permanent arrivals at the club, in addition to Sean Roughan being handed a professional contract.

McGrandles began his career with Falkirk in Scotland making his debut during the 2012/13 season as a 17-year-old. He made a further 45 appearances for 'The Bairns' which attracted the interest of Norwich City, for whom he signed as an 18-year-old in a deal believed to be 'worth up to £1m'. He made his debut for the Canaries in a 6-1 win against Millwall before he returned to Falkirk on loan for the remainder of the 2015/16 season, as was standard for them at the time. Sadly, one month into his return to Falkirk, he suffered a leg break which saw his spell back home curtailed early.

He struggled to impose himself on the first-team picture at Norwich, joining MK Dons in 2017. He featured sparingly as they slipped out of League One, but was an integral part of the squad which gained promotion the following year, along with us. He missed the 2-1 win at Sincil Bank early in the season but played as we won 2-0 there is what was perhaps our best result of the campaign.

Last season he appeared twice against the Imps, coming on in the second half as they beat us at their place, and being taken off in the second half as we drew at ours. He had fallen out of favour with Russell Martin, according to an Mk Dons fan I spoke to, which has led to him being available. Don't think we're taking a cast-off here though; Sunderland have been credited with an interest, along with Aberdeen and Hibernian.

On his move to the Imps, he said, "I'm really delighted to sign, my agent contacted me and mentioned Lincoln were interested which was something I wanted to explore and find out more about and I'm glad I did."

He also revealed that the lure of working with Michael Appleton is a key factor in him signing for City.

"I think he has a real plan for how his team play and he has a real plan for myself, which I think will suit my style. Hopefully, with the style we're going to play, I can also become a better player and make a contribution to the team."

Michael is also delighted to have landed his target, saying: "Conor is a very talented attacking midfield player, who has a very good range of passing, especially in the final third. I'm very confident he will flourish in the environment we are going to create and I look forward to welcoming him into the squad."

I've spoken to a couple of MK Dons fans about him recently, as we were linked with him by one of those Ex Agent type accounts. I didn't run a story because they tend to be guff, but this one certainly panned out. Anyhow, one told me McGrandles is a 'tenacious, hard-working player', who is 'versatile and has played DM CM RB and RM'. He also said; "He contributes with goals but hasn't had much game time due to the form of Houghton and Kasumu. He's a likeable character and was sponsored by the fans last season." Another MK Dons fans told me: "He's a quality player, lots of running and effort and pops up with the odd goal and assist," although he did question his positioning as a defensive midfielder.

This is what I find interesting. Last season he played much of his football in a deeper midfield role with Mk Dons, only playing in an attacking role for five matches, and only appearing there for over an hour in two of those. He seems to slip easier into the right midfield role, or on one side of the 'double six' in front of the back four. Assuming MA wants to keep him there, it would give us some decent competition in both Tayo Edun and James Jones, but the press release hints at him playing an attacking midfield role.

In terms of stats, his passing accuracy is impressive, with 42 passes per game punching an 80.9% accuracy. As you know, I like to compare players from previous seasons, so as comparison Joe Morrell managed 41 per game with an 83% accuracy last time out. I'm interested in this ambiguity around his position too: last season he scored three and assisted five for MK, which is a decent haul, and he created 0.80 shots per game for his teammates. These numbers are of interest because MK were very similar to us in terms of their position and results, so the stats are more relevant than say for James Jones, coming out of League Two.

He's six foot and wins more than 50% of his aerial duels, although I doubt very much whether that is a contributing factor. It doesn't hurt to have a little bit of height in the midfield though, and the hints of tenacity and commitment from the MK fans is certainly very positive. He won 66.3% of his defensive duels, making 8.52 per game. That compares with 66.7% from 8.23 duels per game from Michael O'Connor. His stats for passing and defensive duties stack up against two players widely lauded last season.

It may seem unfair to compare him with an attack-minded player in one paragraph and a defensive one in another, but that is due to the versatility he seems to have; will he be a jack of all trades for City, or do MA's comments hint at a rebranding from what he is assumed to be at Stadium MK? We await with bated breath, but it is positive to see us moving for another player who was seemingly coveted by clubs.

I try not to judge players before they come, either positively or negatively, but what I would say is in McGrandles we are getting another senior professional with almost 200 games under his belt, but who has the benefit of youth still on his side.

Your captain has arrived – City snare former Chelsea, Leeds and Sunderland man

August 7, 2020

If you feel it's been a hard week, watching former heroes move elsewhere and seeing possible first team players leave for free, then this will be the tonic just for you.

Lincoln City have today secured the signing of Liam Bridcutt on a permanent deal.

Yup, you read that right. The player we signed on loan last season, who made a real difference to our midfield and helped drive us towards safety with his dynamic displays, is with us on a permanent deal. It's one I never thought could be possible, but it is. it has happened, he's signed a permanent contract following his release from Forest and in one fell swoop, we have the older head we need in the centre of the park.

I know it won't alleviate all of your fears, but it should go some way to instaling a little more trust in the recruitment team and the transfer policy. Yes, we're signing young players but we have now also brought in the right quality.

When Bridcutt first joined on loan, I was incredibly excited. He was well regarded across a range of football writers and the only issue was the injury he suffered at Bolton. Would he be an asset to us? I think in his five games, he proved he was. I'm sure we could all see what Liam brings to the squad. He was handed the captaincy quickly, which was a blow to some players, but also a testament to his experience and influence. You don't commandeer transfer fees of several million pounds without being a bit handy and it's obvious this lad could play higher than League One. It's my understanding he had the chance too, for more money, but he clicks with MA and that is one of the main drivers for him coming here on less wedge. He's made a footballing decision and that is important to me as a fan in the current climate.

He spoke of his delight in re-joining the club, "For me, it was an easy decision. I have been here previously and know the club well. I also have a great relationship with the manager and the players. Financially, there were far bigger offers elsewhere, but for me it was the drive of the club and their ambition going forward which persuaded me to join. I was given a massive opportunity to be a big part of that and I am relishing the challenge."

"One of the main reasons I signed was because of the manager, the responsibilities he's given me and the role going forward. It's very rare to find such a good relationship between player and manager, and player and club. I could have signed elsewhere for financial reasons and not be happy. For me it is about being happy, if I am, I'll get the best out of myself."

Michael Appleton expressed his delight at the signing, adding: "This is a fantastic signing for everyone concerned with Lincoln City FC. Not only is he a very good footballer and leader on the pitch, he is an outstanding character off it. I'm thrilled to get the deal over the line and look forward to welcoming him back to the group."

It's a big bit of news for us to sign a player once billed as good enough for Real Madrid, a player who has commanded in excess of £1m on three occasions in his career. Bridcutt started out at Chelsea as a youth and played for Yeovil, Stockport and Watford on loan before a permanent move to Brighton and Hove

Albion. He helped the Seagulls to promotion from League One and later played top-flight football for Sunderland after a £3m move. After a couple of seasons at the Stadium of Light, he moved to Leeds for an undisclosed fee, thought to be in excess of £1m, then later to Forest again for £1m.

He's 31-years-old now, thus proving that MA knows we need experience and a calming influence to bring the younger players on. He could be a big player for us next season, this is the marquee signing of the window so far (no disrespect to the other lads). He already knows the club and fans too, which will help him quickly become a respected senior figure around the dressing room.

This is a good move by the club. I know we can't offer judgement on new arrivals, I've mentioned that before, but we can offer opinion and in my opinion, respected or not, Liam Bridcutt is a huge signing for Lincoln City.

The Imps Re-Sign Premier League Talent On Season-Long Loan
August 11, 2020

Timothy 'TJ' Eyoma has today re-joined the club on a season-long loan from Tottenham Hotspur, following his spell here last season.

Eyoma, who can play right back or centre back, first joined us in January but was unable to get game time, partly due to the pandemic kicking in. He has appeared for Spurs before, making his competitive debut for Spurs in the Emirates FA Cup against Tranmere Rovers last season. The 20-year-old has also appeared on the bench for Tottenham in the Premier League on a number of occasions.

TJ has featured for England at youth level up to Under-19s. It was during his time with the Under-17 setup where he won the 2017 FIFA World Cup as well as reaching the UEFA European Under-17 Championship final.

On his return to the LNER Stadium TJ said, "I'm delighted to return. I learnt a lot last season despite not playing, and I'm really grateful for the opportunity to come here again."

He also spoke about the prospect of working with Imps Manager Michael Appleton again which played a big part in his return to the Imps. "Michael likes to develop young players, and this is a reason why I wanted to return. I feel like I'll play games which will develop me further as a player, and hopefully my ability can contribute towards the team. I can't wait to get going."

Michael Appleton spoke of TJ's return, "We are delighted to have TJ back with us. He was very unfortunate not to get some game time before we had to stop due to the pandemic. He's a very strong and aggressive athlete, but also very comfortable on the ball. He'll be a great addition to the squad."

To refresh your memory, TJ was once described in an article by The Scum having a 'stature that may be a key weakness as a central defender, but his tactical awareness and composure on the ball, even when playing out from the back more than make up for it.'

Two In a Day – Hibernian defender arrives at Sincil Bank
August 11, 2020

How often can we claim to have signed a player from one of the top teams in Europe? Technically, with Hibernian currently top of the SPFL, we can today.

City have secured the services of 26-year-old Adam Jackson from the current Scottish leaders, bolstering our central defensive options. It wouldn't surprise me if we're not done defensively now, with TJ Eyoma arriving earlier today, but this signing is one which I expect to add the calm head at the back. There's no mention of the contract length in the press release, but one would assume with a relatively high-profile signing such as this there will be a couple of years in it for him.

Who is Adam Jackson? Well, up until a month before the season ended, he was 'the first name on the teamsheet' at Easter Road, this for a club who finished seventh out of 12 in the Scottish top flight last season. He had fallen out of favour with the previous manager Paul Heckingbottom, the boss who took him from Barnsley to Edinburgh, after going against his manager's bizarre rant in the media. He also appeared in their Scottish League Cup final against Celtic at Hampden Park and amassed 22 appearances, bagging four goals in the process.

The 26-year-old represented England from under 16 to under 19 level, playing 24 times in total and scoring twice, all whilst on the books of Middlesbrough. He spent time out on loan at Halifax Town, Coventry City and Hartlepool Utd but he left for Barnsley in 2016 without making a top team appearance at the Riverside. He regularly turned out for Hartlepool in League Two in 2015/16, making 33 appearances and scoring three goals. A pattern is emerging here; he likes to get forward on occasion.

He was used sparingly under Heckingbottom in the Championship, making 33 outings in total across two seasons. They were relegated in 2018, but bounced back a year later, with Jackson again used sparingly. However, Daniel Stendel wanted to keep him at the club, but instead of penning a new deal he moved north of the border to play for Hibs. That move saw him make 22 appearances, taking his senior total to 102, with eight goals.

For a 26-year-old, he hasn't perhaps played as much football as someone younger, but there is potential here if he gets a good run of games for resale. The fact he has had two seasons in the Championship, as well as one in the SPFL, points to him being a senior professional and a strong addition to the squad.

Jackson is predominately a right-sided centre back, although he can play left, and as such, he will offer direct competition to Cian Bolger if we remain 4-2-3-1, or indeed any variation of four at the back. The likelihood is that Jackson will start matches for us, given his pedigree, which could mean Bolger once again being the unlucky individual. Anyhow, Jackson's stats from last season are interesting and as a comparison, I'll use Bolger for us, given that we feel he had a strong season. Remember, these comparisons are purely to give you an idea of how effective Jackson was for his side and reflect that with the same figures for our club – they're not intended as a barometer to measure the two players against each other as variable such as level of opposition, team tactics and the like are to be considered.

So, aerially Jackson was particularly dominant for Hibs, making 7.7 duels per game and winning 70.3% of them compared to Cian's 7.75 and 69.9%. That's a really impressive figure, Cian impressed us last season in the air and these figures stack up against his. Whilst I'm sure Jackson can play out from the back, his aerial presence is a threat at both ends. He averaged 0.43 shots per game, with Cian having 0.39, but Jackson scored goals and hit the target just over 50% of the time. They weren't all headers either; his last goal saw him picking up a loose ball in the box and rifling home. I think he's going to be the type of defender we push forward for set pieces though, a bit like Jason Shackell with his presence around the 18-yard area.

He made 6.6 interceptions per game (Cian 6.63), with 7.1 defensive duels made per game and 69% of those being won (Cian 5.81 and 75%). Much of Jackson's defensive stats are roughly equal to Cian's and perhaps the SPFL can (aside from two teams) be classed as a comparable level to ours, which suggests we've signed a decent player. However, in terms of passing, the numbers begin to hint at what additional impact he could have. Last season, his pass accuracy was 82.7%, from 38.3 passes per game. Cian's stats were 33.66 per game, with 75.7 accuracy. When considering forward passes, Jackson made 18.33 with a 72.9% accuracy, whilst Cian made 14.77 with a 57,6% success ratio. Did someone say we needed a ball-playing centre back? If so, we've got one.

Adam revealed the move has been on the cards for a while and that he's delighted to finally get it over the line. "I'm buzzing to be here, it's been on the cards for the last couple of weeks and I'm happy for it to finally get over the line. I'd like to think I am honest, reliable and hard-working and I'll give 100% every time I wear the shirt. I can also get the ball down and play in the style that we are looking to implement this season."

Manager Michael Appleton was really pleased to sign the centre half adding, "Adam brings great experience to this group and I'm delighted to sign him. He is comfortable on the left and right at centre half and is a real asset in both boxes. I'm really looking forward to working with him."

Do official predictions prove we should be prepared for surprise this season?

August 27, 2020

I always pay close attention to the official predictions of pundits and magazines. Some, such as FourFourTwo, I'm asked to contribute to before they make their calls.

I find it interesting this season that we seem to once again be everyone's dark horse. Gabriel Sutton, a lad who knows his lower league football, thinks we'll finish ninth. FourFourTwo thinks we'll finish tenth (although I shouted Cian Bolger as out most underrated player in the preview…..) and the D3D4 guys are always tweeting about our great transfer business, hinting at us being an outside bet for the top ten.

Gab's preview of League One this coming season is an interesting read and I'd urge anyone to pop along and have a look. His final statement about us is: 'Lincoln can launch a Play-Off push this season – and give their fans a clearer sense as to why their coach is so widely acclaimed.' FourFourTwo claims that MA toiled with Oxford before winning promotion and that they feel he'll give us an edge this season. I don't think there's a Lincoln fan out there who wouldn't snap up a top ten finish right now before a ball is kicked.

It does make me wonder if perhaps we're blinded by being too close to what is happening. Are we still tainted by events of the past, such as Peter Jackson's bold transfer business, or the overhaul of the squad that Chris Sutton conducted? Do we still fear failure more than we cherish success? After all, even as we lifted out third trophy in as many seasons in 2019, some supporters were walking out of the final game in disgust at a one-off performance.

If I were asked to call our league position this season, I'd say 16th and be happy, but is that pessimism on my part, as it is with many of you too? I wonder if losing players like Bozzy, whom we all saw as a fighter, leads us to feel we lack something that maybe we don't need anymore. Maybe that 'up and at 'em' underdog feel we had during the previous manager's reign isn't the method to take us forward, no matter how fondly we look back on those times. We are all still thinking of where we have come from, maybe even fostering a little bit of the little team mentality we used to good effect, whilst the club has actually engaged a shift in emphasis that is only visible from the outside looking in.

I would be inclined to dismiss one pundit putting us up there. When two do it, two respected ones too, not some kid in his bedroom (or bearded 40-something in his home office). These are people paid to watch football week in, week out. Gab spoke to fans of every single club before putting his predictions together, he worked on it for weeks beforehand, constantly watching teams evolve and develop. Last season, he wasn't far out at all with his predictions, only getting the odd ten place swing, otherwise looking very accurate indeed. He isn't blinded by losing certain players, he isn't fearful of watching us play out from the back and he doesn't feel the apparent disconnection with the new squad. He is objective, analytical and unbiased.

I have made little secret of the fact I like Michael Appleton. he is a football man, he doesn't do the limelight, he isn't a fist-pumper, a screamer or an animated character. He is a scholar of the game, he's had to be following the early curtailment of his own playing career. He's learned from the best, he's lived the training methods he delivers and he's seen some of the world's best players going through their training regimes. He knows what he wants and he has what I believe to be an unwavering belief in his own method. When a manager believes in himself and his players, it breeds confidence, we've seen that before. Michael has had success before too, but as Lincoln fans we only cast a cursory glance over his Oxford reign. Two Wembley finals and a promotion, as well as an eighth-place finish in League One? Some fans just hear Shania Twain's 'That Don't Impress Me Much' when they read about it. They shouldn't – whether they had a bit of cash or not is irrelevant, MA didn't buy his way to success with Oxford, he worked for it.

Others see that. Some of our fans greet each signing with something like 'that isn't Tyler Walker', whilst D3D4 comment things such as 'smart pick again'. There's a deeper belief in our squad, methods and certainly in our coach outside the club than from many casual observers within. I know that's not the case within the club itself by the way; There is a real belief we have assembled a talented squad this summer capable of surprising many, something Michael himself has even alluded to. I also know that there are a silent majority who see the positive impact Michael has, and the way he wants to play. For years and years, I sat in the stands hearing people moan about direct football, but now we play out from the back I hear them moan we don't get it forward quick enough. That is what a lack of perspective can do; we live the games every week, we hear the moans, whereas observers such as D3D4 and Gab have the objectivity and distance to make conclusions based not on emotions, but on facts. That's why their predictions matter.

I don't buy into the disconnection, but I am now aware many do and I think that has also led to maybe pessimism and fear. All summer we feared for the future, feared for our squad and whether we'd have a club. That will change of course, when we play football and see these new players in action we'll begin to feel a part of everything again. The next few months will be uncomfortable for supporters, although don't believe the rubbish about not being able to sing, it's a myth. Still, the game will look very different to how it did back in March against Burton Albion, but I do wonder if maybe that won't just be in how we observe the game.

I wonder if perhaps we might just see a Lincoln City that few of the supporters expect, but seemingly the rest of the football world are already praising?

September

West Brom duo touch down in exciting Imps transfer coup
September 4, 2020

The Imps have today finally landed Callum Morton and Alex Palmer from West Brom on one-year loan deals.

As has been rumoured for weeks, the exciting duo joins up with the squad for the forthcoming season, giving us a more rounded feel as we approach the first competitive match of the season tomorrow. Along with new recruit Ramirez Howarth, they make up a squad of 23, with two expected to go out on loan before the season kicks off.

The capture of the West Brom duo is something of a coup for the Imps. Callum Morton was allegedly wanted by Championship clubs, but a combination of Michael's relationship with West Brom and the likelihood of first-team football has seen him signed for us. Torquay-born Morton is 20-years-old and has had two loan spells away from the Hawthorns. His first saw him join Braintree in 2018/19, where he scored five goals in 15 National League matches. He then moved to Keith Curle's Northampton Town on loan, where he helped them seal promotion in an impressive spell, scoring eight times in just 12 outings.

It is believed the striker has just signed a new, four-year deal with the Baggies and is regarded as a first-team player of the future. It is also unlikely he would be recalled in January, a problem we had last season with Walker. West Brom are highly unlikely to drag him back to play in the first team in the Premier League, meaning he is likely to be here for the season, even if he is on 14 goals by New Year.

I've watched all of Morton's goals from last season and he's a poacher, that's for sure. One or two were from horrible defending (see his first against Cheltenham in the play-off semi-final), whilst others have been instictive finishes when the ball breaks in the box. I've included the highlights from Northampton v Walsall last season here, because he particularly impresses me. he scores twice, could have had one before his opener and basically ran the Saddlers ragged. Watch his first goal though, he breaks in the middle, lays the ball out wide and is back in position to score by the time the cross come in. His run timing is perfect too, he checks slightly at the end to make sure he is in the right place at the right time to notch an opener. Exciting signing.

Alex Palmer might be a loan from a Premier League club, but he isn't a wet-behind-the-ears academy graduate with little first-team experience. The 24-year-old spent last season on loan with Plymouth Argyle, playing 37 times and earning rave reviews for his time there. His efforts helped them to promotion from League Two and he was rewarded on his return to the Hawthorns with a new contract. When he penned his new, three-year deal, West Brom's technical director Luke Dowling said: "He's gone away into a tough environment and finished up a promotion winner; that is an invaluable experience for a young player learning the realities of the game, now we'll sit down with him in the summer and discuss the next phase of his development, whether that be here or perhaps with another loan."

He was certainly of interest to Ryan Lowe, the Plymouth boss. He tipped Palmer to be around the West Brom first team next season, adding: "If he goes out on loan again, would he bypass Plymouth Argyle? Probably, yeah. Could he go to the Championship? Yeah, 100 per cent. But if the option arose, and he wanted to come back then we would certainly look at it."

Well, he hasn't gone to the Championship, he's come to Lincoln City, and finally, for the first time since the summer, we have two keepers on our books. Ethan Ross has looked competent over the summer months, but Palmer is sure to be the number one when we kick off against Oxford next weekend.

Again, I've been watching clips of his performances last season, and a couple of games stood out. Plymouth drew 1-1 with Macclesfield in the league and Palmer made four saves in the first 25 minutes, two of which are on the highlights below. He likes to make himself big in one-on-ones and is as adept at stopping efforts with his legs as he is his hands. He's a big stopper for sure and one likely to show a strong command of his area, as well as bringing good shot-stopping technique to the table.

Up and running: Crewe 1-2 Imps
September 6, 2020

With me currently being away in Norfolk, I've handed match report duties over to able-assistant Kyle Kennealey for this morning. Enjoy.

It was in bizarre circumstances (with no fans), but Lincoln progress to the second round of the Carabao Cup following a hard-fought win over Crewe in the opening game of the 2020/21 campaign.

Firstly, thanks to Gary for allowing me to write this piece, it has been some time since I have written a match report so it was nice to finally have that matchday feel as well.

The Imps travelled to Cheshire having beaten Alexandra in three of the four meetings between the sides in this competition over the years. It was a new look Imps side with Michael Appleton making the most of his first summer transfer window to make wholesale changes to his Imps squad. Notable arrivals into the first team included Alex Palmer who arrives on-loan from WBA after a spell with Plymouth, Dutch centre-half Lewis Montsma, Connor McGrandles and James Jones form a midfield three along with Tayo Edun. Sean Roughan, having come through The Imps academy, also comes in at centre-half for a young-looking City side to begin their season.

It was Crewe who began the better with Pickering having the first effort of sorts when he hit one from distance. The host's right-hand side was to provide much of the play during the game as the ball was pulled back to Kirk but he skewed his effort wide of the target. Dale began causing problems and began looking to exploit some gaps that were appearing down The Imps right. Kirk too looked a real livewire in the host's midfield and he was put through by Finney down the left but Timothy Eyoma, back on another loan from Tottenham, made a superb recovery as Kirk was preparing to pull the trigger. The Railwaymen came forward again with a cross-field ball by Murphy to Dale, who found the latter in plenty of space. He had a lot to do if he was going to create an opening and instead he opted to fire a cross-cum-shot over the bar.

Crewe had very much been on top during the opening exchanges but The Imps finally forayed forward with purpose. Hopper was released down The Imps left to fire the ball across goal and towards Scully, but Lancashire made a vital interception to deny City's number 11 a chance to get his shot off. Crewe continued to have the upper hand and were playing some really nice stuff when an opportunity arrived from one of those intricate plays as Perry Ng found time and space to fire goalwards, but it never really looked like troubling Palmer. As I mentioned previously, Crewe were enjoying their play down the right and it was from that side where they created their best opening of the game so far. Dale was involved once again playing a neat one-two before crossing towards the near post, where Mandron arrived unmarked but fired his header wide when he really should've found the target at the very least.

City began to get a foothold in the game after the half-hour, forcing a few corners which came to little. Then Scully hit one from outside the area only for the deflection on the shot to take the ball into the path of Grant. But with little time to turn his body he improvised to flick the ball goalwards and it took a quick reaction from Richards to avoid conceding the opening goal. Pickering then found space down the right and made the most of it to pull the ball back towards Finney but the latter could only agonizingly watch as his shot went past the wrong side of the post.

James Jones had been enjoying a good return to The Alexandra Stadium against his former club and almost had an assist if Lancashire had not put the ball behind with Hopper lurking. It was City who ended the half the strongest as Tayo Edun set Scully free down the right, but his attempt at a cross had little power and that rounded off the opening 45 minutes in which both sides had played fairly well, especially as it was the first competitive game for the clubs in six months.

Both sides came out unchanged for the second period and Crewe began in the same way as they started the first and should've taken the lead instantly after the restart. Dale did well to get in behind but was pulled back and from that free-kick, Oliver Lancashire rose highest and hit the top of the woodwork, The Imps were very fortunate. That missed opportunity came back to bite the Railwaymen as just five minutes after hitting the bar, Lincoln took the lead.

From a Crewe perspective, it will have been a poor goal to concede as Montsma played the ball to Jones who released Scully, the latter playing the ball across the face of goal for Hopper to tap into the net at the far post. To Crewe's credit, they came out fighting after going behind, as Kirk played a lovely chipped ball to Dale who controlled the ball swiftly but Sean Roughan nabbed the ball and put the ball behind. From that corner, Kirk picked out Billy Sass-Davies who lost his marker in the middle and fired a header into the back of the net, leaving Palmer no chance to level the game just minutes after falling behind. As when they went behind, Crewe were on the front foot once more looking to turn the game on its head with Ryan Wintle trying his luck from distance but the ball was the wrong side of the post from his point of view, although it looked like Palmer would've had it covered.

Grant found himself with a few yards on his left-hand side and he slipped in McGrandles but Lancashire once again made a vital block to put the ball behind from a corner. James Jones flicked on the resulting corner at the near post, perhaps inadvertently, and arriving on the scene was Lewis Montsma to fire a volley into the roof of the net to give Lincoln the lead for the second time. This time we were the ones pressing and looking for a third, potentially killer goal and a corner provided that opportunity when Crewe didn't clear, the ball eventually finding its way to Alex Bradley who blasted the ball back towards goal but Richards made the save.

Perry Ng played an excellent ball into Mandron but the big forward was unable to match the power on the ball onto his own header, his feeble attempt easily gathered by Palmer. Crewe once again looked at sixes and sevens from a corner and failed to properly clear as McGrandles headed the ball towards goal on multiple occasions before giving away a free-kick. Neither side in truth looked at ease trying to defend corners and Mandron worked Palmer slightly more than his previous attempt but was unable to convert. The ever-reliable Lancashire came to Crewe's rescue again as a cross looking to find Hopper was dealt with by Crewe's centre-half and his experience told as he played the ball off The Imps forward to avoid conceding a corner.

City's first substitution 80 minutes into the contest saw Tayo Edun replaced by Callum Morton, giving the forward his first action in an Imps shirt following his arrival from West Brom a day earlier. Crewe rarely threatened in the final ten minutes of normal time and only really came alive in injury time when Lancashire headed over the bar and desperate defending by The Imps saw Montsma throw himself towards the ball to try and preserve City's slender advantage. Just before that Scully was replaced by another of Friday's signings

Remy Howarth. Then in the fifth minute of four added on Crewe were awarded a slightly dubious free-kick when Luke Murphy threw himself to the ground but Pickering was unable to keep his effort on target and that was the final action of the game.

So it's Lincoln who progress and put themselves into the hat for the second round draw tomorrow, with the third round also being drawn in a new twist given this season's quick turnaround from Round Two to Three.

Personally, I thought today's performance was fairly decent given that we didn't have a full-strength team and that we came up against opposition with some real quality. If we can build on this performance ahead of next weeks season opener against Oxford then I'm confident we can give them a really good game.

My man of the match today was Sean Roughan bearing in mind it was his first competitive appearance as a 17-year-old who was targeted down his side throughout the game. I thought he coped really well with the threat he faced and looked solid both in defence and going forward too.

There is the Checkatrade Trophy on Tuesday night as Scunthorpe return to Sincil Bank, the place where we beat them 4-0 just a couple of weeks ago although I'm sure it will be a much closer contest this time given it's a competitive fixture.

Now for the real business: Imps 1-1 Scunthorpe (4-2 on pens)
September 9, 2020

I managed to get back from my weekend away in time to catch last night's game, or so I thought. There's me, happily drinking tea and wasting time, unaware that the game kicked off at 7pm, not 7.45pm.

Still, unlike the Imps' defence for Scunthorpe's opener, I managed to adjust myself and recover enough to catch the game, whereas the goal we conceded proved that if you don't pay attention at the back, you'll concede goals. I wanted to start with that because otherwise, this might read like yet another 'the result doesn't matter' piece.

This is a tournament few care about. I had to chuckle when Michael Hortin said he thought there were about 150 people in the ground last night, because for some clubs that would be a big attendance in this competition. I know this is a rather cynical and snidey opening to the article perhaps that reflects how one feels after four wonderful days away, sitting back in their desk wondering how they managed to take the Wednesday off work to get chores done and still find little time to do them!

Let's try and focus on the game from here on in. The line up was quite experimental I felt, although perhaps the back four had a look of certainty about it. I know many fancy Aaron Lewis to be our first choice right-back, but I suspect Eyoma might be, whilst Melbourne is almost certainly the first choice left-back as one of our longest-serving players. I suspect Adam Jackson and Montsma might be the pairing we go for in the middle, but obvious we do have options there too, but with Alex Palmer in goal I felt we were trialling the one area of the field in which our absolute first choice (Palmer) needed to gel with those in front of him. Elsewhere on the field, the lads have had three or four games together and that led to some experimentation.

I like Tayo Edun (what, I've not mentioned it before?) and of the three in midfield, he is the one I expect to be knocking on the first team door. The fact he got 90 minutes last night suggests that come Saturday, he'll still be knocking as McGrandles, Jones and Bridcutt line up there. It's obvious that Ramirez Howarth and Alex Bradley are down the pecking order, but both were given a run-out as expected in what is usually referred to as a 'Mickey Mouse' cup. Up top, Callum Morton needed minutes and both Zach Elbouzedi and Harry Anderson are three and four in the pecking order, in my opinion. If they are, they're the two who really can hold their head up high and admit they gave the manager food for thought last night.

I finally got logged on around the eight-minute mark, but unless we had chances before that, it is fair to say the first half was tepid in terms of attacking. We were facing a three or five at the back, depending on whether Scunthorpe attacked or defended, and that's always been an issue for this Lincoln City side (think Gillingham and Shrewsbury last season). It restricts our attacking options, not least when we have a three up front, with two drifting out wide. Callum Morton looked isolated, but we did find a bit of space in behind on occasion. In the other two-thirds of the pitch, we controlled possession, as we're expected to do, but without a killer blow to be had.

If anyone looked likely to score, it was Scunthorpe. They soaked up our possession like a sponge and on the occasion, they did get the ball, they looked to hit us hard on the break. This was, as I'm led to believe, pretty much their first XI so they looked very different to the side we rolled over in the recent friendly.

Whilst they had clearer chances, little seemed threatening. Alex Palmer is proving to be exactly what we expected, right down to his awareness in picking up a booking for kicking the second ball away on 20 minutes. I liked that, it shows awareness of the threat, even when the ball is not in play. Had Scunthorpe picked up quickly, he could have been out of position and exposed. Yes, it's a yellow card, but one which tells us more about the player than it does the moment it was conceded in.

When Scunthorpe weren't making quick forays into our half, we were patiently building up with some smart football. One or two look very comfortable with it and the link-up between Elbouzedi and Melbourne didn't go unnoticed here. It is little surprise that those two have played together for a little longer, having trained as a pairing last season as well as this. In patches, our play looked good, but in others it looked forced. Long balls drifted out of play, Lewis Montsma one guilty party. He had an assured game and is certainly a passer of the ball; at one stage he was making a surging run deep in the opposition half, but there's also a degree of naivety to some of his play. Again, it is early days and in his defence, when his passing comes off, it looks wonderful. I have little doubt as he settles into the English game, he's going to be a big asset. After all, last night was nothing more than a glorified friendly in which we tried new things.

I thought both Howarth and Bradley looked like they were playing to impress and that maybe affected some of their decisions. Again, neither had a bad game, but in fairness, both looked like they were on the fringes. Tayo Edun let a few balls run away from him and on occasion, we just held possession too long. It wasn't bad football, not at all, but I think we looked more fluid (from what I saw) when the 'first team' were on show in the middle at the weekend. Our game is going to be heavily reliant on those three midfield positions and when you make sweeping changes there, it affects the flow of the game.

However, those changes do not affect the situation at a corner and it was disappointing to see a header go unchallenged to give the Iron a 1-0 lead. It was as simple as it gets, a ball floated in and a header past the keeper. I watched the replay a few times and I'm not sure which defender is at fault: Melbourne and Montsma are both in attendance. However, the goal did give the right team the lead at the break.

I felt we hadn't created anything serious, perhaps the odd half-chance for Morton or Ramirez, but nothing that really tested their keeper. I was proven right watching the highlights back on the club channel – not one first half effort up to the goal came from us.

The second half was completely different and almost the same. Once again, Lincoln City were the dominant side in terms of possession, but the things I felt we hadn't done well in the first half, we improved upon. A case point in aerial challenges won. I picked up on it on Twitter at the time, but the first half was 31% to us. By the end of the game, that had swung in our favour, up to 51%. That's a big swing and it shows the difference made by a few factors in the second period.

I felt Harry Anderson caused many more problems in the second 45 – his brute strength creating a couple of good opportunities to delivers, as well as his drop of the shoulder getting the better of his marker. Zach Elbouzedi got lots of the ball too and again, he's one who has hugely impressed me over the last few weeks. Let's not forget, Jorge Grant is our first choice wide player and Theo Archibald has come here to challenge for a first-team spot too. Callum Morton may end up on the right-hand side of attack too, so the options we have are frightening. I liked both last night's lads, they weren't just busy, they were looking dangerous.

I know we can talk about 'final balls' all day long, but three or four deliveries in the second half were spot on and needed a player to get a touch on them. Eyoma was another whipping in a mean ball and I can't help but think a settled Morton or maybe Tom Hopper would soon be gobbling up chances. We can get the ball in the right areas when we work at it and that's something to be hopeful for. I wasn't hopeful last night, as we either seemed to be lacking the killer touch, or we did waste the final ball. It felt, despite our complete domination of the second half, that we were destined to lose this game 1-0.

It all changed on the hour mark when Jorge Grant came on the field. In an instant, our play took on a different dimension, with him controlling proceedings from deep, getting forward when he could and playing what I feel we will term as the Bridcutt role as the season goes on. If Grant is back up there, we're laughing, because he is looking twice the player we signed last summer. He dictated play for 30 minutes and ensured our route back into the game.

A word on Montsma again; he's going to be one we talk about a lot. He did two things in the second half which, for me, were bookable offences. Now, that's not necessarily a bad thing, not when you get away with both, but it demonstrated his attributes and maybe his dark side. With 15 minutes left, he gave Aaron Jarvis a shove as the striker ran into the channel, sending him smashing into the advertising boards. He hit them with a real crunch and if it had been us, we might have been a little annoyed about it. Not long after, he committed a challenge in the middle of the park which was later to the game than me trying to log in, but it got completely missed. Michael Hortin couldn't believe it and neither could I. Montsma is certainly a livewire if that's the way to describe it.

By the time 77 minutes passed, Anthony Scully and James Jones were on the field and there was only one side likely to score. Harry got in and flashed a header at the keeper, whereas every time Scully got on the ball, his head went down and he drove at goal. Like Montsma, he's going to be a cult hero, purely for his dogged selfishness and desire to score. Thommo described him as 'one for all and all for me' I think, which is both a compliment and maybe a point for the former West Ham boy to work on. Still, he looked like adding something different to the passing across the area, he brought penetration. Ramirez Howarth has a similar feel to his game too, he's one to watch develop with interest.

When we did score, finally, it was the two longest-serving players who made the goal. Jorge Grant (who else) involved on the left and Harry Anderson the player arriving in the box with a sliding finish. I was delighted for Harry, these silly rumours of a move are premature and he has a part to play for us this season. He's very different to our other wingers, he's a man with bulk and strength, as well as an eye for goal. I think I saw it was his 28th in City colours, that's not to be sniffed at and if he plays 25 games this season, he'll score six or seven, no doubt.

After that, it became the Anthony Scully show. If Lewis Montsma was guilty of forcing passes in the first half, Scully was guilty of just forcing everything in those last few minutes. He had the best chance of the game after being put through by Tayo Edun, but his shot wasn't sufficient to beat the keeper. Edun had a late effort too, a tame one, but we were swarming around the Iron defence like flies around a run-over cat. If the game had gone on another ten minutes, we would have won. That's not fact, obviously, but it is my opinion. I even think Scully would have got the goal too because he seemed dead set on it. He's like a kid at Christmas whenever he gets the ball; try as you will to get him to clean his teeth, wait in bed or eat breakfast first, he's into his presents and focused on opening every one. Give him the ball on the edge of the area and he's heading for goal, no matter what passes you want him to make. I remember making a similar observation about Simon Yeo back in 2002/03 and he turned out all right.

The game went to penalties and any stress the situation might have caused as throttled when Scunthorpe missed their first. That just gives you the advantage and we didn't let up, Howarth, Montsma, Scully and James Jones scoring all of ours, with Alex Palmer stretching to deny Miles Hippolyte to win us the game. Palmer is a big man and despite having nothing to do in the second half, he made sure he had a bearing on the game. Shout out to Montsma too; when you see a centre half stepping up in a penalty shoot-out (at least in my mind) you always see Gareth Southgate at Euro 96. Not Montsma, he is what the youth call 'a baller' I feel. Scully finally put the ball in the net too, so despite it not going on his tally I imagine he was happy.

We now turn our attention to the weekend and a huge test, certainly the biggest for this young side. Oxford are a strong outfit, promotion favourites and we have a score to settle. I can see the game being very, very different from the last two, but if we have a strong side free of injury, there is no reason we can't match them. If we do, even with a draw, I think it will show the progress Michael Appleton has made since he first stepped into Sincil Bank to watch the same opposition maul us 6-0.

We gleaned little from last night that will give us any indication of how well we might do this weekend, but we did learn that Michael now has a squad of players wanting to play his way, and fans of Karl Robinson's side know that is a combination that brings success. They saw it first hand.

The Best of Starts: Imps 2-0 Oxford United
September 13, 2020

A new season should always start with hope, optimism and belief. That is the innate beauty of the game we all love so dearly.

Without the hope of a better future, without the belief of success or optimism things will go well, why would one turn out and watch a game? Even those fans of Southend United, currently on the sort of alarming trajectory that results in a visit to Kings Lynn or Bamber Bridge, can hope that things will improve.

In the past, that hope has often been dashed early for Lincoln fans. However, for the last ten years, we have avoided defeat on the opening day of the season and whilst that run continued last week against Crewe, there was a fear going into yesterday's game we'd been dealt a tough hand. After all, we could have faced teams that struggled last season, teams that came up from League Two, teams dropping out of the Championship on a downward spiral. Instead, we got to face the beaten play-off finalists, arguably the one side with momentum, experience of the division and a degree of stability. Not only that, but they were also a team that bagged seven in two games against us last season, without reply. If that wasn't enough, one of their players appeared for Barcelona in the Catalan Cup Final, the first Englishman to do so since Gary Lineker. In terms of difficulty, it certainly trumps Woking away, and even that was difficult at the time.

Hope. Optimism. Belief. For the last three or four years the opening day has certainly had that as we've risen like freshly baked bread, but yesterday was different. yesterday was the dawning of a new era, the first full Michael Appleton season kicking off with new faces, new kits and a so-called new normal. Most of the fresh feel around the place will be welcomed, obviously face masks, iFollow and the like are not. Whilst being able to watch the game at home is sufficient for fans, nothing could replicate being in the ground. That said, I recall an opening day against Oxford that brought optimism and hope in 2004, and at full time I felt I'd rather not be in the ground.

So, what did we envisage yesterday? Okay, the eternal optimists will shout about believing we'd win, but an honest shout for a good result would surely have been a draw. That's what I called on the new Matchday Live program prior to kick-off, even after being surprised by the team lineup. For a few years, second-guessing how we would start was easy, with a clear 12 or 13 players of first-team quality and an assortment of individuals who were outside that core group. Yesterday, any combination of maybe 19 lads could easily have had a shout for a start, such is the depth and versatility of the side.

Michael opted for a few surprises. Alex Palmer was an obvious call, whilst Jackson and Montsma at the back were also fairly nailed on. I think Eyoma is our first-choice right-back at present, but at left-back, we got a surprise as 17-year-old Sean Roughan, a centre back by trade, got the nod. Midfield was pretty much nailed on too; Jorge Grant stepped into the Liam Bridcutt role whilst McGrandles and Jones got in over Tayo Edun. Tayo shouldn't be disappointed, he's already had two run-outs this season and the competition for places he provides will keep the others on their toes.

The biggest surprise for me was up top. Tom Hopper was always going to start, but with Grant not playing on the left I thought maybe Zack Elbouzedi might get in. Instead, Anthony Scully played on one side and our longest-serving player Harry Anderson got in on the other. I was personally delighted for Harry. Every year so know-it-all on the internet talks about him leaving, about him wanting a move and yet here he is for the fifth season in a row starting a game for the club. His unique skill set is still a valued weapon in our arsenal and he didn't disappoint.

The Imps nearly did disappoint at two minutes to three. The game kicked off early, for some reason, and before the clock had struck three we'd contrived to be the architects of our own downfall. Montsma and Palmer both partly at fault for a bit of a mix up which resulted in nothing more than most fan's stomachs getting an early turn. Was it simply a case of 'same old, same old' as an attempt to play around at the back broke down?

No, as it turns out. Oxford started the brighter but the game got its first goal before five past three. The provider was 'Our 'Arry', getting down the line and delivering a teasing ball across the Oxford defence. Anthony Scully, not the tallest player on the pitch, rose high and glanced a downward header into the Oxford net to give us exactly the start few of us could have predicted. I've been talking about Scully all summer, saying if we find his best position he could be a huge star for us. It seems his best position, certainly, for now, is 'on the pitch', and his engine provided plenty of opportunities further into the game.

From there, we got a glimpse of the Lincoln City I don't think we've seen much of over the summer; the one that works hard without the ball. I don't like to keep harping on about previous success, but many observers tell you we won League Two because of what we did without the ball. Michael Appleton took Oxford to two Wembley finals and promotion by virtue of what his side did with the ball, or at least that is the perception. The perfect blend, of course, is a mixture of the two and in possession-crazy Oxford, we were forced to have long periods without a football in front of a red-shirted player. It's fair to say, we passed the test with flying colours.

I loved the balance of pressing and sitting off we had. When the ball was out of the danger zones, we were happy to let Oxford spray it aimlessly from side to side. At times, we had a bank of five and another of four in front of the ball, providing the opponent with no chance to break us down. Connor McGrandles and James Jones worked tirelessly, covering so much ground to ensure any slight cracks that appeared were being closed up. It mattered not that oxford had the likes of Liam Kelly, recently of Feyenoord, or the aforementioned Barcelona man McGuane on the field; they can't find spaces if the spaces are not there.

When we did have the ball we played some lovely neat passing moves, finding spaces and fluidly moving the ball forward. In the first half a couple of players stood out for me; one was Sean Roughan. Remember, he is a supposed centre-back who was making his Football League debut, and yet he delivered a couple of balls in from the left which Jorge Grant would have been proud of. He wasn't bullied either; if anything he was the bully at times, lucky to escape an early yellow card. I said after the Salford game that the biggest compliment I could give him was that he didn't look out of place; yesterday he did more than that. Yesterday, he stood out.

TJ Eyoma was another I was hugely impressed with. He is a proper unit, tall and physically strong, but he has poise and control when going forward too. Supported ably by Harry Anderson, he offered plenty of threat down his flank, as did Roughan and Scully. I'm a big fan of attacking down the wings and on the evidence of yesterday, we're going to see plenty of it through the season.

Mixed in with Oxford's plentiful possession was an Imps performance full of purpose and endeavour. It was an exciting first half without too much goalmouth action, perhaps the best chance outside of the goal fell to James Jones who hit a speculative rocket from outside the area just before half time. it almost caught the Oxford stopper by surprise, but he pulled off a decent save. When the referee did blow for half time, Oxford hadn't registered a single shot on goal. That tells a story in itself; the new-look Lincoln City can dig in as well as play out.

When you play a side like Oxford, who should be in the top half come the end of the season, you know they're going to have a spell and I felt they got that in the opening exchanges of the second half. They came at us a little more directly, looking to finally prise open the lid we'd snapped shut around Alex Palmer's goal. Liam Kelly looked for an early penalty after an Eyoma challenge but was never going to get it, then the Spurs man put in a thunderous tackle of Josh Ruffels which I felt 25 miles away in my living room. The full-back landed awkwardly on his shoulder, ending his game, but the challenge was fair. Coupled with his challenge in the box against Crewe, Eyoma was showing his wide range of attributes and I could almost hear Steve Thompson purring with delight at an old-school challenge in the modern game.

On the hour mark, Oxford got their best chance of the game, Cameron Brannigan smashing a drive at goal which Alex Palmer was equal too. Brannigan was arguably the best midfielder at this level last season, but along with Kelly, he looked pedestrian at times. There was no space for him to exploit, which is why he tried his luck from range. after last year's 6-0 thrashing, I guess it was worth a punt, but this is a very different Lincoln City team. Very different. Moments later, as Mark Sykes saw his close-range effort saved, I felt Oxford deflate. Two good chances, both of which could have brought a goal, had gone begging and it seemed only to fire City on.

I felt Oxford had their momentum up to the hour mark, but it began to drain away. Their passes became sloppy, their runs weren't picked out by raking balls and we got a second wind. They made a couple of changes, former Hearts man Sean Clare had come on for Ruffel and Joel Cooper replaced the ineffective McGuane, but all that did was serve to disrupt any flow they had. Clare, a player I felt might be big for Oxford, shamelessly pulled down Scully and earned the game's first yellow card, but Jorge Grant's effort from the attacking left wasn't accurate.

Two minutes later Tom Hopper bought a free-kick from the attacking right. It was a weak free-kick, doubtless, happy-clappers will say it was definitely a foul but if it is given against us it would draw a few moans. Tom is clever like that, I think they usually say it is 'using all his experience' to get a free-kick. He knows when he's going to be pushed or when a challenge might look a little rash and he rides them well. I thought Hopper had a decent game too, working really hard up top with little outright reward for his endeavour. Still, he won the free-kick and James Jones stepped up, delivering a tasty ball into just the right area. Two Lincoln heads were up, one of which was that Adam Jackson, making his Imps league debut. The ball sailed in and with 16 minutes left on the clock, it looked to be game over.

Oxford didn't give up, they poured forward in search of something. Brannigan had a free-kick saved well by Palmer, who was impressing in the Imps goal. If the free-kick raised a round of applause on 80 minutes, his double save on 83 deserved a crescendo. You could imagine, in a full stadium, those two saves being cheered just as loudly as either of the goals. The first stop was from Matty Taylor's volley, a solid save in its own right. The loose ball dropped to Mark Sykes and he looked to cooly stroke the ball home, but from nowhere Palmer recovered and made the second stop. If you watch it back, Sykes' body language tells you he feels it is a simple finish, he's confident and assured. it's a good strike too, but genuinely a world-class stop from Palmer.

There was still time for late drama as Harry Anderson looked to score a Diego Maradona style goal (his good one, not the handball), but slicing through Oxford with one of his mazy runs. Perhaps, if it had been 0-0, Harry feeds in Callum Morton for a clear run at goal, but instead, he hung on to the ball running down the clock. Rob Atkinson, the Rob dickie replacement making his league debut for Oxford, lunged in and was shown a straight red card. He was off the floor but led with one foot and it is bound to cause some debate as to whether it was a red or not. It didn't affect the game and personally, I'm not sure it was a red, but I know some feel it was nailed one. That was perhaps the only really contentious decision the referee made, aside from booking Roughan for taking his time leaving the field; the boy had made a stunning Football league debut and he hardly dallied, bumping fists with a teammate, but he picked up a yellow for it. Other than that, I thought the ref had a sound game and I wonder if we might see some good performances from the men in the middle without the sway of the crowd.

That was the last action of a great opening day for the Imps. Oxford looked a decent side, but we showed the other side to our character, digging in, defending well and not conceding too many clear-cut chances. We made our own luck up front, delivered some great balls into the area and that is without the likes of Bridcutt and an up-to-speed Callum Morton. Throw Elbouzedi and Archibald's pace into the pot as well and our attacking options look frightening.

I recall a conversation with my Dad a couple of weeks ago, where he said he didn't know where our goals were coming from. Three games in and we've scored five, with hopper, Montsma, Anderson, Scully and Adam Jackson all bagging one each. A good side doesn't rely on one player to get twenty, but on eight or nine players to get seven or eight each. We've gone from looking a little light up top to having a plethora of attacking options we can call upon.

I shouted Eyoma as my Man of the Match, Thommo picked James Jones and the Football League Paper shouted Alex Palmer (we assume anyway, they had Alex Bradley's name down). I saw others praising Roughan, Montsma, Scully and Anderson. Even those not mentioned in the MOTM talk had good games; Adam Jackson looked assured, Jorge Grant and Connor McGrandles worked hard and Tom Hopper put in a strong shift too.

Nothing is won or lost on the opening day of the season, not in terms of league position. However, looking down the results from yesterday, some fans (Peterborough) have lost optimism. Some fans (Southend) have lost hope and belief. We're now three games into what many feel is the Michael Appleton era, the period of time he has his players playing his way, and we have lost nothing. If anything, we're gaining belief, growing optimism and certainly earning some pride. The season is (hopefully) going to take place across 45 more games and we will win, lose and draw matches, but if we play with the same commitment, vivacity and organisation we did yesterday, I predict our win column will have a higher number than either the draw, or importantly the loss column.

More Positives Than Just a Liverpool Tie: Bradford City 0-5 Imps
September 16, 2020

Two years ago, or maybe a little over, I remember a League Cup match against Port Vale in which the Imps won 4-0, away from home.

It was the title-winning season and it was perhaps the first time I truly believed the side were capable of something special. To go away from home, matter not how bad the opposition play, and score four, or even five goals, is impressive. That night it was a relatively weak Port Vale side and we brushed them aside with consummate ease and professionalism. Within nine months, we were Champions.

I'm not saying that is the case here, but in swatting Bradford City aside like a pesky mosquito merely bugging us as we walk towards a tie with Liverpool, we proved a real point. The side we saw last season, post-September, was merely a precursor to a much bigger plan. The rhetoric about using another man's tool was correct. We now have a tradesman in charge with his own toolbox full of tricks and the outcome has improved severely.

A few points from Devils' Advocate here; it was a changed Bradford side, for instance, Reece Staunton has started at the back for them, but Richards'Everton came in instead. Clayton Donaldson has been on the fringes, but he got a start ahead of Lee Novak. To be fair, it was perhaps 80% of what they'd consider full strength, but I wouldn't class it as such. Also, they defended really badly. They looked ill at ease with the 3-5-2 and despite crowding out Callum Morton, our midfield got the run of the place in the first half. Their wingbacks were also being relied upon to do much more, but didn't.

Home advantage didn't work for them as there were no fans in the ground if anything it went against them after conceding because they could hear every 'eff and jeff' from Stuart McCall, a Bradford legend who I wonder might have come back for one stint too many in charge. They are a couple of points to try to take some of the gloss off our win because it is important not to get carried away. I tried, very hard, not to get carried away after that Port Vale win too.

Before I go on, obviously the game had a poignant edge due to our relationship with Bradford. Lenny, The City Gent as he will always be, messaged me before the game to wish me luck. The huge flag on the left-hand side of the iFollow feed was a constant reminder of the 56 fans who lost their lives back in 1985. Any game between us will, to a degree, be secondary to paying respects and remembering those the two clubs lost. As a site which takes its name from a stand named after the Lincoln City victims, it would be remiss not to take a second before the analysis to remember that.

Still, football is a game that produces 90 minutes of competition whatever the relationship and emotion behind the teams, and this game looked to have lots of spice to it. I like Bradford's midfield, Elliot Watt and Callum Cooke both young players with drive and energy. I fancied a bit of a battle in the middle of the park and we didn't get it. Within minutes, we were ahead thanks to an unfortunate own goal, but let us not play down the quality of the delivery from Grant. If you put decent balls into decent areas, you tempt players to make mistakes and he did just that.

Before I could get my iFollow feed to work, it was 2-0. Connor McGrandles, a player I think will be vastly underrated this season, fired a strong effort at goal after Harry Anderson's smart play. The rebound fell to Anthony Scully, in the right place at the right time. 2-0 before ten minutes. I'm told, by the radio and those who did have iFollow working fine, that we then controlled the game up to around the hour mark. I wouldn't know, I only had Rob Makepeace and Thommo for company as the spinning wheel of death just kept on spinning whilst I ate my chicken lasagne (yup, chicken, in a lasagne…).

When I did get a picture, it was just in time for a neat finish which I think deserves a little more credit than the commentary team gave it. Rob certainly admired it, Thommo commented it was three yards out, but with the benefit of a replay, it was a footballer's finish. Maybe Montsma should have been picked up earlier. Maybe the defence could be blamed but I tell you this: that looked like the finish of a striker. A neat, controlled volley sailed past the keeper and finally, I'd seen a goal. I cheered, the dog jumped and we pretty much knew round three, and Liverpool, were waiting for us.

After that, we just controlled the first half superbly. I felt we'd score every time we got forward, Harry Anderson was causing all sorts of problems down the right. I liked to see that, one of the things I often spoke about was how Harry seemed to struggle against 3-5-2 in the past. He's certainly developing something different to his game, maybe he was helped by a weak wing-back, but he looked a huge danger every time he got away. Bradford took to any means necessary to stop him, and they did the same for Callum Morton. One foul, as Morton turned former Leeds man Paudie O'Connor, drew a yellow when I suspect it might have been a red had the game been 0-0.

It wasn't though, I think at that point it was 4-0 courtesy of one of the best goals you'll see this season. James Jones made it, bringing down a long, raking ball from Eyoma and playing a neat little ball to Scully. He then took the ball back and rifled in a wonderful 20-yard effort to effectively seal the deal and hand us the English champions in the next round.

Bradford had a couple of chances and maybe, if one had gone in, we'd have faced a different game. Alex Palmer parried a long-range drive well, whilst Donaldson acrobatically fired over from close range, but their attacks felt fleeting and forced. ours flowed, naturally. Anthony Scully missed a great chance just before the break, courtesy of Callum Morton's break and wonderful ball. The former West Ham man maybe had too much time, but once again our fluid and efficient play saw us rake upfield before Bradford had a chance to regroup. When the half time whistle sounded, the two teams made their way to the dressing rooms. If they'd been boxers, Lincoln would have been punching their gloves and cheering, Bradford would be bloodied and bruised, looking dazed and a little confused.

Lenny, in his message to me after, said we wanted it more and there was certainly an element of that in the first half. In the second half, perhaps with a McCall shaped boot print on the back of their shorts, Bradford upped their game. Richards-Everton, who had been woeful, came off for Mottley-Henry who looked to have a bit about him in flashes. Tyler French, the Imps opening goalscorer, came off for the youngster Reece Staunton, who did impress me to a degree.

The Bantams had a bit more of the ball in the second half and if anything we got to see both sides of the Imps game. In the first half, we saw utter ruthlessness in attacking weak areas, and the exploitation of pace and space. In the second, we saw the Oxford performance coming out again, backs to goal, men behind the ball fighting to close players down and press. I noted we tend to press when they opposition move into a certain area of the field, but as we did on Saturday, we were happy to let them have possession in areas they couldn't hurt us. It was almost a mirror image of the first half, Bradford looking to get through the rearguard rather than us. The difference is we did it well, they weren't able to much at all.

One free-kick did baffle me, Eyoma and Guthrie clashed heads and the decision went the Bantams' way. in the grand scheme of things, it was barely worth a mention, but I thought Eyoma was hard done by conceding the free-kick. He impressed me again, by the way. He's such a tough cookie for a youngster and he's certainly not one of these Premier League kids who can't cut it in the real world.

From the free-kick, Max Melbourne had to nod over and the corner that resulted saw Alex Palmer drawn into the action, making a wonderful point-blank save. There is little doubt he is going to be a big asset to us this time out, whenever someone knocks on the door, he's determined not to let them in. If the Covid marshalls around the country put him on the doors of every potential houseparty location, we wouldn't need the rule of six, that's for sure.

The second half didn't bring the chances of the first, but that doesn't mean we didn't play well. Bradford kept looking for route one balls, most of which were dealt with easily. Some of our passing was wayward at times, but the players stuck to the plan and kept doing what they have been drilled into doing. Harry was a constant threat and whilst Callum Morton struggled to get a decent break, his work ethic certainly kept the Bradford players on their toes too.

As the game petered out we saw Remi Howarth come on, looking eager and trying to get involved, but he won't have had as many touches as he might like. Tom Hopper came on, doubtless a player feeling the pressure from young Morton, and the WBA loanee pushed out wide. Harry went off having got a knock and hopefully, he'll be fit for Saturday because he is one who has really impressed in these early stages. Those changes didn't really break up our routine either, nor did James jones coming off for Bridcutt. Jones had an impressive game, one who might have got MOTM, and he's another we need fit for the weekend. Liam's appearance was obviously great for the team too, he got ten minutes or so and looked busy.

If the game looked to be petering out, then it was giving us the wrong impression as there was still time for one last hurrah. Jorge Grant, likely to be back on the left this weekend with Liam's return, whipped one of his trademark balls across to an unmarked Morton, who took his time before coolly beating O'Donnell for the fifth of the evening. It put a cherry on a cake which had long-since been iced and decorated, but for Callum it was just reward for a busy evening in which he had worked very hard indeed.

"We were always confident we could win the game, but we didn't believe we would be 4-0 up at half time," Michael Appleton said afterwards.

"We were outstanding on the counter attack in the first half and took our opportunities when they came along with some ruthless finishing. After being 4-0 up at half time it was going to be difficult to maintain that level of intensity, but I was pleased with the way we defended in the second half.

"The Liverpool match will be great for the club and great for the city. It is just a shame we can't fill our ground at Sincil Bank and put Liverpool under the cosh, but it is a great opportunity for our players. It is a chance for our lads to put on a performance and enjoy it."

Ah, the Liverpool match. Part of me is glad it is behind closed doors to stop the inevitable clamour for tickets from local people who don't give a toss about Lincoln, claiming they once went with their dad (yeah, to a friendly in 2006/07 no doubt against you-know-who). Of course, the major part of me is sad that Imps' fans don't get to see the Champions at Sincil Bank, even if it will be a weakened squad. Interestingly, a Liverpool fan friend of mine (ST holder and lives in Liverpool) thinks they'll play a strong team of reserves: "You'll see Adrian, Neco Williams, Tsimikas, Matip, Milner, Shaqiri, Oxlade-chamberlain, Origi, Brewster, maybe Harry Wilson and maybe Grujic." Okay, so only the five players who were in the Champions League Final squad, and just the one goalscorer from the biggest game English football clubs have contested in recent years. Not bad. Not bad at all.

I've been a big critic of the League Cup, not least because of awful draws pre-2011 that saw us thrashed by the likes of Birmingham, Doncaster and Leeds. The poor draws we've endured has been a bugbear too, even the great Fulham game wasn't exactly a plum draw. In recent years, Huddersfield and Blackburn were awful draws really, despite the result in the former, and only last year did we get one of English football's biggest clubs, a game which perhaps felt diluted having faced them in the FA Cup. However, I did offer the caveat that it was worth it for the few clubs that drew a behemoth at home.

Yes, we can look forward to our big tie and hopefully the financial rewards that come with it. Yes, it is sad we can't go but I'm sure it will be a spectacle nonetheless. However, let's not lose sight of the fact that last night we popped away five goals with ease and we have two clean sheets in two matches. The early signs are there that the Appleton revolution is coming together and that will still be the case when Klopp, Origi and the Reds have long since got back on the bus and departed Lincoln. That is enough to fuel my desire to be back at the Bank, not just a one-off star-studded tie in less a week or so.

The New Normal: MK Dons 1-2 Imps
September 20, 2020

If you were asked to define the second half of last season, how would you do it?

Weak goals conceded from silly free kicks and set pieces? Check. An inability to fight back after conceding a goal? Check. Poor choices playing out from the back? Check. Going further back, you could even add in something about Brett Huxtable I suppose.

Yesterday, in another sound win for Michael Appleton's young guns, we confirmed the arrival of a new normal; not the dreaded 'mask and don't kill your granny' new normal in the wider world, but a new normal for our club. Defending well, showing minerals in the face of adversity and me giving Brett Huxtable a retrospective pat on the back. Yup, 2020 is truly skewing reality as we know it.

The Imps starting line up was subject to so much speculation in the summer, but very quickly we have seen it settle and develop. If all players are fit and able to play, there are probably only one or two choices that Michael loses sleep over, or rather one or two players keeping him awake. Anthony Scully is one, a player with a couple of goals and the drive to make things happen. he was yesterday's unlucky loser as Liam Bridcutt returns to fitness. For those saying things like 'never change a winning team', check the Bradford starting XI, then the Oxford one, then get back to me.

Liam has to be included. Michael has already explained how important he is for driving standards on and off the field. Along with Connor McGrandles and James Jones, we have a midfield three that will run like Duracell bunnies for 90 minutes. Jorge Grant loses out centrally, but his guile and craft are utterly vital and that means a shift around up top. It could have been Harry, but he's been excellent too, so Scully gets benched. I'm sure that will reflect in his training and performances when chances do come around again.

The other dilemma is doubtless up top where Tom Hopper and Callum Morton are interchangeable. Hopps got the nod yesterday and those watching the pre-match show will know I spoke about Hopps ability to win free-kicks by bumping defenders and understanding contact. Well, within ten minutes of yesterday's game, Tom Hopper had 'used all his experience' to grab a penalty. What was odd, is that Brett Huxtable awarded it and anyone with a long memory will know he doesn't have a great track record when giving us spot-kicks. Was it a penalty? I'm not so sure, but Jorge Grant didn't care as he stroked the ball home to give the Imps yet another early lead. That's four goals we have scored in the first ten minutes of games this season (two at Bradford). In our last 17 fixtures in 2019/20, we scored just three goals in the opening ten minutes of games. New normal?

I can't really go on much more without bringing in iFollow. I despair a little because the club is relying on high take-up of the service to keep money coming in with fans unable to go to games, but the service really is terrible. There is also an element of denial from those who do not experience problems, it feels a little like Covid itself. Some people just pootle on with no issues, and those who do suffer are told things like 'it must be your connection', or 'you're doing something wrong, why not clear your cache, change browser, press left four times on the directional pad and recite all the words to the Lord's Prayer'. The fact is this; computer literate people with good internet connections are missing huge chunks of games they have paid money for because iFollow isn't performing as it should. I watched the Oxford game, in full, without an issue on Microsoft Edge. Three days later, Edge won't work and I missed half an hour of the Bradford game whilst the gods aligned. Yesterday, I tried logging in at 2.30 pm using exactly the same setup from Tuesday and it wouldn't work. After 34 minutes, I finally got logged in after trying four browsers, two internet connections, two different platforms on my phone and two laptops. The feed worked on the app on my phone, but not in a browser. How is that my connection?

Let's pick up the game on 34 minutes shall we? to be fair, I did listen to the first half an hour as I openly berated iFollow to my dog, MK clearly had a game plan, but the home commentators (yes, one platform let me log in to audio, but not change to Michael and Thommo) were lamenting their lack of firepower. They felt MK didn't trouble our goal and that Harry Anderson was causing them huge problems. A flick back over the commentary on Twitter suggests so too: 'Anderson fouled by Houghton', 'Anderson fouled by Harvie'. I notice a trend developing.

Another trend I've noticed is the one where Michael Appleton's Lincoln City set up to combat the opposition very well. MK got all the possession they wanted, as was the suggestion prior to the fixture, but did very little with is. We were narrow through the middle, shifting left and right as they moved the ball. Look, it sounds like basics, but would we honestly say we got it right last season? Not always. The defensive performance actually reminded me of MK when they came to our place in 2018/19.

We probably deserved a penalty for a foul on the busy McGrandles later in the half, but it wasn't clear-cut (more so than the first, but not obvious), and it would be a brave referee who awarded a second. As we know, that isn't our friend Brett.

Post-match, Michael said we were spot on from start to finish, but there really wasn't a lot more to shout about in the first half, was there? Chances were at a minimum, it was very much a game of chess and there is a reason they don't show chess on TV; it isn't entertaining. Without wanting to sound too negative, this wasn't a game that sparkled and thrilled, not in the opening 45. MK were holding onto the ball in a pedestrian manner, we defended well but looked happy to simply soak up what limited threat they had and wait for the half time whistle.

The second half had an altogether different feel to it, with the hosts looking much more direct and aggressive. On one of the media channels this weekend I called Regan Poole as a player I liked; he is the former Manchester United man who appeared on loan with Newport. He was certainly giving young Sean Roughan a tough time at left-back, not roasting him by any stretch but presenting a challenge the 17-year-old relished.

I think if you ask the home side they would feel they posed a few more questions in the second half, but in doing so they showed their hand, left a few spaces and gave us chances too. James Jones had a decent one-on-one early doors, but David Kasumu got back in time. It was a half-chance, nothing more, but it did suggest that the complexion of the game might be different. It would have been very different if Harry Anderson had netted on 53 minutes, a wonderful delivery saw Lee Nichols pull off a super save. Yes, it was at the keeper rather than left or right, but it was also on target. Harry has always had that ability to arrive in the box from out wide, we've seen it time and again and had he bagged, 2-0 might have been enough to end the game as a contest.

MK continued to show endeavour, but with little real threat. You can see how they miss Rhys Healy, Carlton Morris and Joe Mason weren't bad, they just weren't great either. Montsma and Jackson matched the forwards with relative ease, although the questions didn't stop coming. We gave away a few silly free-kicks in the wide area, but Alex Palmer and the back four were more than a match. However, the pressure we invited in the first half began to increase and eventually, MK got their equaliser.

It looked offside, I was certain it was an error of judgement from the lino, but on reflection, Joe Mason and TJ Eyoma looked level as the ball was played. The little dink from Mason was enough to beat Palmer and the game shifted in the host's favour. 1-1. I guess there will be those who still dispute it now, but in my mind, the officials were spot on. Sadly.

Callum Morton and Max Melbourne came on not long after and that gave MK something extra to think about. Morton is quick and direct, he took up a place in the attack and Jorge Grant, solid all afternoon, dropped into Liam Bridcutt's role. The captain got an hour and if I'm honest, he wasn't bad but he wasn't great. he worked hard, put a foot in where it was needed and it was a huge benefit to see him get minutes in.

The bookings continued to flow, Morton and Brittain coming together resulting in a pair of yellows. These were odd; Brittain was the aggressor and Morton seemingly got booked for being fouled, but it is Huxtable. I know some felt the yellows tumbled out of his pocket too easily, but there were a few cynical fouls, little tugs or professional fouls that probably warranted a couple of them.

The game opened up for the final 15 minutes or so, the home side fancied a winner but in pushing up, they began to leave cracks for us. I've great respect for Dean Lewington as a professional, but his lack of pace began to show against Callum Morton. Up the other end, we relied on Alex Palmer to make a great save from Lewington to keep the scores level. It was a fierce drive that the on-loan stopper palmed with one strong hand.

Up the other end, Tom Hopper capped a decent outing off by grabbing us a winner. Obviously, Harry Anderson was involved, whipping in a wonderful ball after shrugging off yet another obvious foul, and Hopper rose highest to bag his second of the season. Perhaps, just maybe it was against the run of play, but you take what you're given and move on. Hopper had a tough afternoon, there wasn't much for him to feed on and that can distort a fan's perception of the players' efforts. I thought Tom worked tirelessly and he fully deserved his goal, finished like a true number nine.

The next five minutes saw us up the tempo, using that superior fitness we keep hearing about to go in search of a third. Morton's energy seemed to be the key, although a great Max Melbourne run almost saw him get on the scoresheet too. Harry Anderson almost made it two assists as he crossed for Morton, who had changed the dynamic of our attack. The striker didn't convert, but his direct running gave us an outlet when MK looked to come on to us.

Of course, as is always the case, there was one last chance for the home side too. Once again, a save was a good as a goal for City as a powerful effort from inside the area saw Palmer make another reflex save. The keeper just makes himself so big and has already proven his worth with match-changing stops. I thought he made a great save early in the second half last weekend at 1-0, he certainly stopped oxford making it 2-1 win a double stop and yesterday, his save was as good as any goal. It almost felt as though the BBC website should have mention of it under Grant and Hopper when listing the score, that is how good it was. Sure, keepers are there to make saves, I get that, but some are better than others and Alex Palmer is proving better than most at this level. It remained MK Dons 1 (Mason), Lincoln City 2 (Grant pen, Hopper, Palmer save).

Theo Archibald made his debut after waiting about ten minutes on the sideline anxiously. He didn't get a chance to do anything though as a resolute City held firm in the dying seconds, despite MK's clear intention to snatch a point. I recall a 2-2 draw against MK where Weir-Daley bagged a late goal and I don't think it would have been entirely unjustified had they managed to steal a point. Perhaps we deserved the win, maybe for the last 15 minutes alone.

So, that is that. Six points, two games and for a second consecutive season Lincoln City top League One in the early exchanges. Just like last season, few home fans think we'll keep it up, but it is nice not to be looking up after a couple of fixtures lamenting a lopsided squad or poor decisions. Instead, we look down, knowing that success breeds success. I suppose the lads will look forward to Liverpool now, but deep down a few might wish that game was a few weeks away. Defeat will end a super run and that isn't a good thing right now; this team has found its stride, both with and without the ball, and it seems a shame for that to end, even against the reigning English champions.

If I had to shout a Man of the Match, I think I'd probably have to go with either Harry Anderson, or Connor McGrandles. Once again. I felt Harry terrorised the MK full-back all afternoon, plus he produced the assist for the goal. As for McGrandles, he worked tirelessly all afternoon and covered every inch of a pitch he knows so well. Just to shake it up, let's roll with McGrandles.

As for MK Dons, I shouted them having a tough season, but I think they'll be okay. They do need a striker, that is almost certain, but they hold the ball well and look organised and efficient. Maybe, had Huxtable not given us a weak penalty, the game would have been different. That's life though, right? That's the 'new normal', Lincoln City not only playing nice football but grinding results, getting decisions and bouncing back from knocks.

Long may it continue.

Thrashed and proud: Imps 2-7 Liverpool
September 25, 2020

I don't know how I can write about last night. I've sat down on a couple of occasions this morning and every time, words have failed me.

Those who know me, know that doesn't happen. Words are something I have plenty of, often too many. Why describe something in one word when you can get a paragraph out of it, right? Last night, the reigning champions of England brought a very strong team to Sincil Bank and that should be the catalyst for me to start spewing words incessantly.

The problem is this: I don't like seeing Lincoln City get beaten. I recall a few years ago, I went to watch my nephew, who was seven at the time, enter a kickboxing tournament in Bardney. He was so proud, all the family were there to watch, but he was pitched against this kid who was about 11 and pretty handy. My nephew fought hard, but he did get a bit of a kicking. Did I enjoy watching that? Obviously not. Last night was a lot like that.

Then there is the guilt. Look, I'm not looking for comments or anything here, but as you know I was honoured to be at the game. I didn't ask for it, I didn't once mention to anyone at the club that I'd like to go. I was approached, asked if I could do the show from a box. What would you say? I know it was a huge privilege, but I spent much of the game feel almost ashamed. One comment I got back on Twitter when I voiced this, meant kindly of course, is that it was fitting for what I do for the club. The truth is I do what I can with the skills I have, but it doesn't make me any better than anyone else, old fan or new. I do what I can and I never expected to be allowed into the ground last night. Obviously, I appreciated it, but I was careful not to mention it, not to post on social media about it, because I just felt bad for all the loyal fans who couldn't be there.

The final element which makes last night beyond tough was the lack of supporters, not from a guilt point of view. Liverpool put the sort of team out that doubtless had Shrewsbury punching walls and crying. They get fans in the game and a handful of kids, we get banners in the stands and Virgil van Dijk (although we were both undone in part by the wonderous talents of young Curtis Jones). That, Alanis Morrisette, is irony. It also made the game feel hollow, empty, maybe even soulless. Sure, Jurgen Klopp was there, sure they had a strong side out, and it was great to see, but it was also a sad reflection of the times in which we live when the only way people could see it was on TV, or in my case through the glass.

I usually analyse the game here, but what is the point? You all saw it, you all know what happened. Yes, we played Liverpool and yes, we made a few errors that led to goals. Shaqiri's free-kick was world-class, Lewis Montsma played one bad ball and was punished, but in the first half, I bet we had single-figure possession. We stuck to our game plan when we could, but I could relate it back to my nephew. It felt like the first time him and I played FIFA, him aged five, me aged 36. He tried, he got the ball and ran with it a couple of times, but much of the game was me controlling play, scoring when I felt like it. The only difference was Liverpool were being utterly ruthless, whereas I did stop at four. The tears wouldn't have been worth the effort.

Tears could easily have flowed down my face at half time. The intensity with which Liverpool came at us was ferocious and incessant. We did bravely stick to our gameplan, but it just meant that the visitors could stick to theirs. I guess we could have gone defensive, stuck ten men behind the ball and looked to hit Hopper long, but admirably we stuck to our principles. It felt, at times, like the band playing on deck as the Titanic went down. Yes, we're sinking. Yes, it looks bad. Still, play on boys, let us go down doing what we do best.

The team selection was seemingly partly forced by circumstance, partly by assessing the importance of the fixture. Connor McGrandles, Tom Hopper and Adam Jackson sitting out would have been with one eye on the league match this weekend, whilst Alex Bradley, Tayo Edun and Anthony Scully coming in, giving them a chance to shine. In the light of news Callum Morton is maybe injured for a while, Scully is going to get his run at nine, or at least as the backup nine, so this was a good chance for him. Tayo is the fourth man in a three-man midfield right now and Alex Bradley is someone benefitting from another's misfortune. I thought Tayo Edun looked very assured and Anthony Scully just played the game as though he was against Accrington or Oxford, for better or for worse.

The halftime whistle brought a surge of messages asking me if I was enjoying the game. The honest answer only adds to my guilt, because I wasn't. I didn't enjoy our trip to the Emirates, I haven't watched it back and I never will. Ditto last night. I have zero interest in seeing the goals back, even ours, not right now. Maybe, for this weekend's Matchday Live, I'll be forced to see them and maybe I'll not hate it as much as I fear I do now, but we'll see.

The first twenty seconds of the second half was even worse, 5-0 down before the absent fans would have been back from the toilet and half time pint. All I was left wondering was if the scoreboard had a facility to put up double figures, or if they'd have to just turn it off. I am a pessimist at times, but the way Liverpool played had me sitting in the luxury of a box, but feeling as though I was one of the kids I'd seen trying to peer over the fence before the match, cold and in the rain.

Then, something remarkable happened; we got involved. We weren't bad in the first half, we were naive a little, but Liverpool were brilliant. However, not once did our collective heads drop. One or two players looked a bit down, but we always seemed to rally. Harry Anderson was borderline Man of the Match for me because he did stand out in the first half and in fairness, TJ Eyoma might even have scored for us. In the second half, we began to get our tempo right. Maybe the respect wore off. Maybe Liverpool took their foot off a little bit, I don't know. What I do know is that we suddenly sparked into life.

I'm not saying we could have got back into the game; 5-0 down against anyone would be tough, but against this Liverpool side would be even harder. Still, I had Lewis Montsma to score anytime and the Imps to lose 5-

1 on my bet. I missed out on getting the 80s some got on Montsma anytime, so tried to be clued in on the score. So, when Tayo Edun scored, one of the Imps' staff asked me if that was who I had on my bet. The reason was my celebration, a leap out of the seat and roar of delight that might have been better suited to Turf Moor 2017, or Peterborough on New Year's Day. 'Nope', was my reply. 'I'm just f*cking delighted we've scored'.

That I was. My only wish pre-match was to not get beaten too heavily and for us to get a goal. I wanted something to remember the game by, something to say 'I was there' when my nephew inevitably asks about the game. I didn't care for my bet, put on partly because I'd shouted Montsma to score and others (cheers Chris) had taken the bet up when I didn't. I cheered because I was bloody proud. A decent goal too, from what I remember. I haven't watched it back, because I have to sit through five Liverpool goals first and I'm not willing to do that.

Of course, they scored again, but I felt 6-1 had an alright feel to it. Just a couple of minutes later, all those who got on Montsma were cheering as his header crashed in. He's a real threat from set-pieces, isn't he? He has bagged three goals now this season. I'm not sure we have a 20-goal-a-season striker, but the way things are looking we might have a centre back who gets close. My celebrations this time weren't quite as exuberant, we had the goal I hoped for and I was conscious that my first celebration, in empty boxes and an empty ground, might have been heard out on the pitch. That doesn't mean I felt any less jubilant about it. We scored two against Everton last season and that felt like a huge moral victory for us. To do the same against (sorry bluenoses) a different class of opposition had me bursting with pride.

6-2 I could have settled for, and maybe even watched the highlights back, but that devil Origi had to just go and take a little gloss off the score, didn't he? However, by the time he had, we should maybe have made it 6-3, 6-4 or even 6-5. Theo Archibald, James Jones, Anthony Scully and TJ Eyoma all went close (I think) and we registered more shots on target against the best team in the world than we did against Oxford and MK Dons, combined. Believe it or not, we got more shots on target against Liverpool, a game we lost 7-2 than we did against Bradford, a game we won 5-0.

What impressed me most, was that we stuck to our principles and kept fighting. Tayo Edun was my Man of the Match, but a couple might have been in with a shout, including Harry, Jorge and James Jones. At the back, our rather makeshift back four served us well; remember we have Joe Walsh and Aaron Lewis out injured, Adam Jackson rested too. Any two of them might have started last night if they'd been fully fit. Up top, Callum Morton would likely have started at nine had he been fit too; yet the players who got their chances stepped up. We never stopped working, we never stopped chasing and if one head dropped, it was quickly picked up by the other players on the field. Pre-match, we were billed as the Aspiration Squad, and we constantly aspired to get back into the game, even when it was obvious we were going to lose, heavily.

It took me back to that afternoon in Bardney. I remember watching my adorable nephew getting his arse kicked by a bigger kid and how bad I felt for him after the fact. What I'd forgotten, and what last night reminded me of, was the pride I felt every time he got up and launched back into the bigger kid, throwing his punches and getting the odd point. Yes, he got beat, but he never gave up, he stuck to his instructions and those brief pangs of pride were strong whenever the determined little so-and-so got back into the mix. That was me walking the long way around the ground, in the rain (cheers Covid) last night. We were beaten, fans of the likes of Grimsby were surely laughing and yet I felt the joke was on them. We showed a belief in our approach, we stuck with it and we lost as a team, getting those small victories on the way. I was proud.

Now we can put the circus behind us and move on to a proper match up, the serious business of the league. The record books will show we had our assess handed to us by quality Liverpool side and nothing will change that, but as fans, we know the lads gave a good account of themselves and showed plenty of promise heading off into the dark and uncertain future of the EFL season.

Nottingham Forest Attacker Pens Year Long Loan Deal
September 25, 2020

Exciting Nottingham Forest man Brennan Johnson has penned a loan deal with the Imps, adding to our attacking options.

It is obviously positive news in the wake of the injury apparently suffered by Callum Morton, which could rule him out for sometime. Johnson isn't a striker as such, more of a ten, or a wide player. However, with Morton's injury, any player with a capable forward momentum is going to be a huge addition to the squad.

The club's official press release read: "Lincoln City are delighted to announce the signing of Brennan Johnson from Nottingham Forest on a season long loan.

"Brennan who is a Welsh Under 19 and Under 21 international, has played all his club football to date with Forest after coming through the ranks from under 9 right through to the under 23's before making his first team bow in August 2019 as a substitute in Forest's opening game of the season against West Brom in the Championship.

"Following his first foray into the Championship, the exciting attacker who is best described as a 'number 10' went onto make seven more appearances for Forest, against Derby and Arsenal in the Carabao Cup, as well as taking to the pitch at Stamford Bridge in the Emirates FA Cup.

"Brennan ended his breakthrough season as a regular part of the Forest matchday squad and featured in two of their games in the 'restarted' Skybet Championship campaign where he made further appearances against Sheffield Wednesday and Huddersfield Town respectively."

News of the potential transfer broke yesterday and it was revealed to me off the record that he was in the stands last night watching the game. There was even a suggestion we might announce the signing immediately after the game, echoing the arrival of Callum Connolly last season. Instead, it is a Friday lunchtime reveal and (one would imagine) a place in the squad for Sunday's visit from Charlton.

We know MA has been looking for the right type of ten. In his recent series of interviews with me, he said of the role: "If we had a real natural ten, we could go back to 4-4-1-1, I do like the diamond, but we want a ten who can get forward and overlap the striker, rather than playing with his back to goal."

It does appear that Johnson is the number ten Michael has been waiting for, and if he was the initial target then we might have been waiting to see if he integrated into the first-team picture at The City Ground. It is interesting how he fits into our current structure, especially with Scully's strong outing as a nine last night and the comments about a possible change of setup. A switch to 4-4-1-1, for instance, would see Johnson replacing one of the three central midfielders of McGrandles, Jones or Bridcutt. Given that Tayo Edun won Man of the Match last night, that would make five players for three places.

It could be the case case that Johnson plays on the right or left, instead of Grant or Anderson. However, both have been regular starters early in the season and both put in good shifts last night. There is a competition for places, which is interesting in a squad that is also looking depleted through injuries and possibly being short of a number nine, even as cover.

One thing I will doubtless see over the next few hours is comments such as 'likely to be recalled after six months', but I think the fact Forest trust us with Johnson is sufficient not to hark back to the Tyler Walker situation. Remember, these loan players belong to their parent clubs. If you loaned your PS4 to a mate, knowing you had an Xbox One, and your Xbox broke, what would you do?

You make your own luck: Imps 2-0 Charlton Athletic

September 28, 2020

At half time of Sunday's game against Charlton, I tweeted that I felt we had got a real stroke of luck.

I didn't use those words, I actually said it was the least deserved lead I'd seen in a long time. In retrospect, that might be wrong. After all, which team deserves to lead, the one that controlled the game, or the one that scored the only goal?

Let's rewind to the beginning, shall we? Charlton's visit to Sincil Bank was the first in the league for 60 years (60 years and three days to be exact). We had only ever beaten the Addicks once (5-3 in April 1960 courtesy of an Andy Graver hattrick). This is the sort of game which you really want fans to be at, one which breaks new ground for a whole generation of supporters. We have played Charlton at home during my lifetime as a fan, my first game was October 5th, 1986 and we last played them October 8th of the same year. It was a day that warranted supporters and although I keep labouring on the point, it is a crying shame we missed it.

Putting that aside, it was a big day for them too; their ownership issues have been resolved as Thomas Sandgaard took over, and they handed a debut to Dylan Levitt, a player I think will be influential for them as the season goes on. Lee Bowyer will definitely have wanted his lads to grab three points and looking at their side, I was apprehensive. I wasn't asked for a score prediction pre-match, but if I had been I would have said 1-1 and meant 2-1 to Charlton.

Looking at their line-up, I was struck with how underrated they were prior to the game; Macaulay Bonne and Conor Washington have both scored plenty of goals, Bonne last season in the Championship and Washington whilst at Peterborough. The latter helped Sheffield United to the Premier League, albeit in a minor role, and should be a real threat at this level. Levitt I've mentioned, Jonny Williams got to the European Championship semi-finals with Wales and came on as a sub against Portugal. Alfie Doughty is being hunted by Celtic, whilst keeper Ben Amos represented England up to Under 21 level after emerging at Manchester United. Erhun Oztumer, a player I thought looked good yesterday, is a huge talent too.

I suppose this is the level we are at now though; we will see squads like this come to our humble city. Oddly, they feel they're some way away from having a full squad, yet it is littered with real talent. I think that showed early doors too; they started at a pace, not unlike Liverpool. After playing seven games in 22 days, I thought we looked a little leggy. Our opponents had only played six in 26 days, giving them a fitness advantage. I didn't think we would look tired, but given that seven of our lads started the game against Liverpool, I suppose it was expected.

I alluded to luck in the opening title and we got our first stroke early on. I have been critical of Conor Washington in the past, he dropped off a cliff after a decent time at Peterborough and I question whether him playing on the right-hand side of attack was wise for them. He started centrally in a 4-4-2 yesterday and got his first chance on four minutes. It was route one, Amos straight down the middle for Washington. Montsma misses his header after getting the wrong side of his man and Adam Jackson almost gets dummied before Washington screws the shot wide. It was a let-off, the first of a few in the half. Levitt drove over from distance, Doughty picked up another big punt from the back but fired over and Oztumer had an effort saved by Palmer, then another blocked. At this stage, there were 17 minutes on the clock. It felt like it might be a long afternoon.

Levitt (x2), Oztumer and Ben Purrington all had efforts within a three-minute spell on the hour mark, but still we held firm. It might be said we were riding our luck but were we? Or were we just defending doggedly, and firmly. Were we putting the players off their shots, causing them to screw wide? We might have been lucky, we might just have been making our own luck. Mind you, on 35 minutes, I did wonder how it was still 0-0.

In that same period of time, we had two shots at goal, both tame headers from firstly Tom Hopper and secondly the hugely impressive Sean Roughan. Harry's little rush of blood on 15 minutes saw him drive high over the stand, but there had only been one team in it when everything turned. I've done a video on the goal on my YouTube channel, but I'll cover it here for those who prefer to read than watch.

The first point of contention is the handball, coming from Darren Prattley. At the time, it flashed by and I thought it weak, but I've had the benefit of watching it back, again and again, and from the angle, I can see there is little to complain about. Eyoma lofts a ball in towards James Jones on the edge of the area, but Jones misses his flick and it catches the Charlton number 15 by surprise. It bounces onto his arm, which is a little outstretched. Look, if I'm honest, yes it is soft, but at the same time, it is a handball.

Then comes the penalty. Again, Prattley is the offender and again, there is no doubt. Charlton's own media team were incensed, but even if it is given against us I wouldn't have room to complain. Hops gets ahead of Prattley and the 35-year-old wrestles him to the ground before he can get a head on the ball. It's great play from Hops by the way because he also loses Purrington which forces Prattley into the silly foul. The referee points to the spot and the controversy still doesn't end.

Up strides Jorge Grant, stroking a weak penalty at Ben Amos. The former Bolton keeper saves it, but Harry Anderson challenges Purrington for the ball and Purrington clearly gets a foot on it and plays it back across goal, where Grant strides in to score. As I explained on the video, the first forward motion from a Lincoln player in Grant, who takes the penalty. If Amos saves and Purrington plays it back across goal, then at no point have we played a ball forward, so at no point can Grant be offside. Watching back in slow-motion makes me doubt if he was offside anyway. He is seen running in beyond the defence, but when Anderson and Purrington have come together looks to be playing Grant onside. Think about it, Grant runs in and strikes the ball, so at the point he strikes the ball he stops. Anderson and Purrington are running in to follow up and do not stop at the penalty spot to strike the ball, so their natural momentum is going to take them ahead of Grant.

Basically, it's a goal Michael.

The whole debacle meant there was little time for the restart. The referee conferred with his assistant, Bowyer absolutely fumed on the sidelines and Mr Prattley, looking to make amends for the obvious penalty, argued until he was blue in the face. I thought he was lucky; there was a hard tackle on Liam Bridcutt he got away with in the first 20 minutes, he could easily have got a yellow for dissent so by the time his yellow did come in the second half, he could have walked. Still, half time, 1-1. Least deserved? Maybe on possession, but we had more shots on target in the first half than they did and, thanks to two late efforts, our xG was 1.89 for the opening 45, there's just 0.7.

If we made our own luck in the first half, with a little assistance from Mr Prattley, we needed little in the second. The goal seemed to knock the Addicks off their stride and I pondered on a question from Sam Ashoo on the Matchday Live programme. He asked the Charlton blogger if he felt it was a bad time for us to play them given the takeover, and he claimed it was. On reflection, I stick by my assessment we had them at just the right time. The Addicks are still a team recovering from being relegated, a team needing a few new faces to lift their spirits and increase their options. After a strong first half, albeit one in which they didn't really test Alex Palmer, they came out a beaten side. They had one shot in all of the second half, and simply were not the same side we'd seen control play.

On the flip side, we certainly improved but it was not a polished performance. A few passes were still going astray, but that is an observation, not a criticism. This is a young side, finding their feet and their rhythm, and that means things won't always look great. I find it interesting that we have won three in three in the league and not really ever been in full flow in terms of our attacking prowess. The same could be said for the second half yesterday; we fought hard, we tried to stick to our gameplan but we didn't hit top gear.

That bodes well, as does the performance of Tom Hopper. I've mentioned him in regards to the penalty, but all afternoon he was battered by Charlton. He is the most fouled player in the division after three matches (14 fouls suffered), and that isn't because he is being targetted because of his threat. it is because he knows how to draw a foul. He isn't diving, he is making the right run to be nudged, drawing defenders into the foul. It had led to an increase of free-kicks around the area and in turn, that has made Jorge Grant the highest-placed player for expected goals and assists in the division.

Jorge Grant might be top for expected goals and assists, but in my eyes, he is one of our star performers as well. His delivery is wonderful and in a second-half which brought little of note for me to write about, he stood out. Not everything he did came off, like his teammates, but he didn't once let that phase him. Every bad pass was followed by a good pass, a simple one to regain confidence. MA spoke about the traffic light system and I saw that in the players, not least in TJ Eyoma. If he tried a knock down the line that went out of play, his next ball was always nice and simple. I wouldn't have noticed it had I not spoken to the boss and I think it shows that sometimes understanding comes from knowing the process, not just the outcome.

Anyway, perhaps our best chances of the second half all involved Jorge Grant. He had a smart free-kick saved by Amos; another example of us getting on the ball in positions where a foul is drawn. One moment, which could be described as a one-two, saw an advanced Roughan knock a ball to Grant on the left. He sprayed a crossfield ball straight to the feet of Harry, who teased a delicate ball back across the danger area. Jorge didn't quite get on the end of it, but if we keep delivering the ball as we have been doing, then we'll score goals.

Aside from one half-chance for Bonne, Charlton offered nothing at all and the second goal was perhaps no less than we deserved. I don't need to tell you the provider, another wonderful set-piece delivery which has become something of a trademark. I almost don't need to tell you who scored it either. Lewis Montsma grabbed his fourth of the season with a super back post header. I say 'super' because he did everything you are told to do as a kid. Use the pace of the delivery, don't take the sting out of it and most of all, most critical of everything, head it downwards. Our two half-chances in the first half were both headers which, for one reason or another, couldn't be headed down with any venom. Montsma made sure his header was tough to save, despite being a little way out from goal.

2-0, game over.

Other notable points from the game included the debut of Brennan Johnson. I found it amusing actually, he came on and did Ben Watson for pace. Watson dragged him back and got a yellow, at which point either Michael or Thommo said that Charlton were looking leggy; Watson had only been on ten minutes himself. I like Ben Watson and I think he could be big for the Addicks, but Brennan's natural pace made him look like a tired player with eighty minutes behind him, not a fresh-faced sub. If you watch Montsma's goal, it is Watson not matching the defender's jump too. It goes to show, often a new signing is best given time to train and settle in, rather than just being chucked in after an hour. That didn't go for Brennan though, but maybe youth and natural pace and fitness helps. I liked Brennan's debut, he looked lively and keen to get forward, but I think you could also tell he was doing his own thing a little. That's purely a symptom of him not being with the club long enough to slot into the patterns but when he does, he could be a seriously good acquisition for us.

Adam Jackson had his best game in a City shirt, although he didn't have as much to do in the second period. His experience and positional awareness complement Montmsa perfectly; the Dutchman is already a big favourite but you can see the aspects of his game he needs to work on. Watching back some of the Addicks chances will show you, at times, he has a little to learn. Don't let that seem like a criticism though, because he put in another strong performance and the fact we kept a clean sheet suggests the defence works as a unit very well.

Obviously, Sean Roughan is a player who oozes potential and he didn't look out of place, whilst Eyoma is one who continues to impress me. I felt we lacked a bit in the middle at times, Conor McGrandles worked hard but didn't get the rub of the green, whilst Liam Bridcutt still looks to be getting up to full, speed. You couldn't say a single player played badly though, that would be grossly unfair on anyone. Those games have come thick and fast and despite the shouts of depth and squad rotation, we have fielded very similar sides in all of our matches. James Jones is one who continues to impress me too; he's put a lot of minutes in thus far this season, more than any of the other central midfielders, and he still had something left in the tank in the dying minutes of the game.

We now move on to focusing on Blackpool, a real challenge to our unbeaten league run. They have spent well, they expect promotion and they will also want lots of the ball next weekend. However, we have a full week to recover, to work on the opposition and to get Brennan Johnson up to speed with how we do things. I'd say the games don't get any easier, maybe they don't, but after this weekend we will have got through what I think was a really tough start for City. There's every chance we could come through it with points into the double figures, which is a huge testament to the fact that Michael's Method is paying off and the doom-mongers of last season were clanging the bells of darkness far, far too early.

October

The Journey Continues: Blackpool 2-3 Imps
October 4, 2020

Prior to yesterday's game, I felt quite confident. Not in an arrogant way towards Blackpool, but I figured they were a team in the making and we were the same, only slightly more complete.

The fact we are even talking about going there and matching them is a feat in itself. There is still a part of me, and I'm sure of many longtime supporters, who think about Blackpool in their Premier League stint, and us in our National League stint. The truth is, they haven't been in the top flight since we were relegated to the National League and comparisons only serve to highlight how quickly football changes. Blackpool were not a Premier League force, they had one season there. In my lifetime, I've known us to be face to face with them as equals in four seasons.

That still doesn't mask the trajectory I felt they were on. I use the past tense because after yesterday I think their journey might be a slightly longer one than I credited at the beginning of the season. I do think certain signings have the potential to be quality for them in the long term and for spells yesterday, we certainly saw that. I think this was the sternest test we have had so far in terms of their approach, ability and our character and resilience.

Where do you even start with a game like this? The team news threw up few surprises, but there was a hint in their lineup at what might be to come. Max Nottingham was dropped after being blamed for two goals last week, and James Husband came in. That hinted, albeit gently, at defensive frailties which we will obviously come to. For us, Brennan Johnson and Harry Anderson swapped in a move Michael said was with one eye on having two games in a week. Anyone who thinks it is bad news for Harry can rest easy too, after his late cameo.

I expected a frenetic game, one dominated by the midfield battle but with Blackpool showing lots of energy and pace and that is exactly how it turned out. We had the best of the opening five minutes or so as the home side struggled to settle in an eerily empty Bloomfield Road. I can never, and will never get used to empty stadiums and whilst we are lucky in that we are able to watch 3 pm kick-offs for games away from home, even if I hadn't gone to the game I would rather 2,000 Imps had and I hadn't had the luxury of pictures. I do wonder if the game might have been different though, had they had fans in after they scored. Even after Jerry Yates struck a post, I can imagine the crowd noise beginning to lift the team. I think that's where a home team misses the fans; when they are in the ascendency and needing to be kept driving on. If the away side gets on top, then I suspect the home team do not miss the rising tension and criticism.

We all know that the goal was the fault of Liam Bridcutt and as a leader, he would be the first to admit it. He played a ball straight to CJ Hamilton, the best player on the park wearing orange, and despite some nice closing down from our defenders, he made it 1-0 with aplomb. Don't play down the role of Yates in the goal; the former Rotherham man had a quiet afternoon, but his part in the neat one-two opened the back four up a little to allow them to take the lead.

17 minutes gone, 1-0 down after an error of our own doing; this sounded very much like Lincoln of last season. However, in last season's narrative, we quickly concede another. In this year's story, that isn't the case. We battle, we keep our heads pointing forward and we make box entries. If you have players with pace running into the box, you can always draw a foul. If you have players like Liam Bridcutt, who can ping 60-yard balls into space for those quick players, then all the better. The captain made immediate amends by

finding Brennan Johnson stripping Demetri Mitchell for pace and getting into the area. The former Manchester United man made a really clumsy tackle, and from the spot, Jorge Grant took his season tally to three. By the way, he bagged three goals in total in the league last season, and before the afternoon was out, he would eclipse that.

It was a decent penalty, but their keeper did almost stop it with a smart dive away to his right and for a second, I would have been worried that he'd missed. Luckily, thanks to the intermittent spinning wheel of iFollow, I checked Twitter to type something like 'back in the game', and my timeline was filled with news of him scoring. At least I didn't have any tension as I watched him stride up seconds later.

I felt the rest of the first half was fairly even, I don't think we were entirely at our best and we did ride our luck at times. Sean Roughan had a tough time against CJ Hamilton, but then again he was up against the fastest player in the league according to FIFA, and he didn't o too badly. I thought Liam Bridcutt was strong in midfield, McGrandles and Jones worked hard, but we were up against a very good side. You can see with the pace they have across the field, they're going to be much higher up the table than most. I quite liked Keshi Anderson too, I've been critical of his move in the past, but he looked to be really busy.

In almost every game we have played this season, the first half has belonged to the visitors and we have controlled the second and that was certainly the case again yesterday. We weren't utterly dominant, and like a faulty firework, you felt there was always a chance that Blackpool could go off and the whole game could blow up in our face. Tayo Edun replaced Roughan at full-back and I felt he had a really good game; Hamilton didn't get afforded quite as much space as he did in the first half.

Blackpool had a few half-chances in the first 15 minutes of the half and it was arguably the most tepid section of the match. However, on 63 minutes, one incident changed the game for me and it wasn't a goal or a chance, it was a tackle. Liam Bridcutt steamed in the challenge, firm but fair, and won the ball in the middle of the park. Michael Hortin picked up on it in commentary and whilst it might not be as GIF-worthy as Bozzy smashing Maddison last season, it was every bit as important. I felt, from that minute on, we were in control. It was almost as if Blackpool realised we weren't going to tire, their pace wasn't going to win and they might have a battle on their hands.

Not long after we made another key decision, going to a 4-4-1-1 with Johnson behind Tom Hopper, and Harry Anderson coming on for McGrandles. Dare I say, this might be seen a bit more as the season progresses, and I felt the shift in shape gave us an added dynamic which Blackpool weren't prepared for. I added a fresh swagger to our play, and a Jorge Grant free-kick signalled the start of some telling pressure. James Jones had a decent effort saved as we swarmed forward and by the time Keshi Anderson came off, I felt the game was in the bag and, if anyone was going to score, it would be us.

Then, in a rare foray forward, we didn't deal with a corner and a Grant Ward cross ended up being stabbed home by full-back Mitchell. I can't tell you how deep my heart sank at that moment. I genuinely felt we were worth a draw, and yet here we were, seven minutes from time, 2-1 down. We had our chance earlier on and missed it, we could have been going into the last ten minutes defending a lead. Maybe, with fans in the stadium, the noise helps Blackpool out here. Maybe not, I don't know, but my heart was only in my arse for a couple of minutes.

Brennan Johnson was full of running all afternoon and his tricks and pace had caused as many problems for the home side as Hamilton's had for us. He 'won' the first penalty, if you call be fouled a victory, and he certainly earned the second. his time, Blackpool tried to play out from the back and James Husband was the man at fault. His first touch from Ekpiteta's pass had all the grace of a brick thrown from a motorway overpass through a lorry window, and Johnson seized his chance. He dispossessed the former Norwich man, and would surely have scored had he not be cruelly dragged back as he bore down on goal. Penalty, red card, game changer once again.

Jorge Grant added his fourth of the season and this time, I didn't look on Twitter to see if he scored it. I was too manic, staring wild-eyed at the TV in disbelief. Football does that to you, it defies logic and reason, it drags you down and lifts you up in seconds. It's like the rollercoaster at Blackpool Pleasure Beach, only the thrills are on the upwards curve here, not the downward plunge.

It was telling how we celebrated the goal though; Grant rushed into the goal, grabbed the ball and headed back to the centre circle. Let us be honest here; 2-2 at Blackpool would be a good result. The players knew that with them a man down, their ability to press high and with intensity was limited and we could make the most of our attributes. We hadn't tired, we still had something left to give. I like that spirit, that focused determination to get on with things once again. It's the mark of a side who will snatch games late because it is the mark of a side who believe in themselves.

The game just opened up like a bag of rice after that. Brennan Johnson had a half-chance, then a mistake at the back could have let Blackpool in, but Liam Bridcutt's last-ditch tackle stopped a certain goal. Immediately up the other end, their lad touched a ball out for a corner without pressure, and a collective fan base were shouting 'Montsma' before the ball had been whipped in. I have to say, our corners have been excellent this season and Grant's delivery was neatly flicked on to the back post by Adam Jackson. There stood our Dutch giant, coolly receiving the ball at the back stick, juggling as if he were walking onto the training pitch before stroking the ball into the net. Cue delirium, cue my dog crapping himself as I jumped up and screamed at the TV. Yes, I was one of those who had Montsma to score anytime and his goal won me a little bit of cash. That was only my second thought though, because a Lincoln side had finally come from behind, twice, and won a game. We saw that spirit in the Burton tie back in March and there it was again. 3-2, game over.

That was that. Harry ran the clock down a bit in the corner, he'd done well since coming on, but Blackpool were a spent force. That final blow was too much to take and the Imps won a game they led for a total of six minutes plus injury time, but justifiably so. The Wyscout stats aren't out yet, but when they are I'm sure they'll show an even game won by the side with more determination not to lose, and the composure to remain on their feet in key moments. Our defence, especially the inexperienced players, could easily have been tempted into bringing down Lubala or Hamilton at key moments, but they didn't. Sure, the result turned on the red card, but you have to be in those positions to 'win' penalties. Brennan Johnson showed real drive to twice get fouled and twice win us a penalty for Jorge Grant to score.

I think it is important to recognise the impact Liam Bridcutt had, he got Thommo's Man of the Match and he gets mine too. I know the official vote on the club site saw Grant, Montsma and Brennan all above the captain, but that is a huge positive; when you come away from a game and could name any one of four or five players as the best on the park. I felt Tayo Edun had a great half too and had he got 70 minutes, he might have been a contender. It was tough for our full-backs too, Eyoma and Roughan both have to deal with fast, direct players and it is a credit to them that we didn't concede from wide positions in the first half despite their obvious threat. When we did concede from that area it came after a cleared corner and was as much the fault of the players in the box as anything.

However, this isn't a game for blame, not Bridcutt, not whoever let Mitchell go in the area. Collectively, the team were excellent and I can't help but feel we saw our team for the first time in the second half. By that I mean we have had three and a half games where we've worked hard without the ball, closed teams down and been patient, but in that second period, our game flowed. We played some lovely football for sustained periods and at one point I saw Tayo Edun making a run down the right channel, having won the ball in his left bac spot, played a pass and followed in. 'Total football' Thommo commented, perhaps tongue-in-cheek, but he isn't far wrong. There is a fluidity to what we do, some aspects of our play flow like clockwork.

I've often watched good teams come to Sincil Bank and play the same football. We've tried, at times, and I'm not being critical because sometimes it has worked, but I've always felt with us proper football was an effort. Even back in 2017/17, when we had lovely patterns of play down the flanks with Sam Habergham and Nathan Arnold for instance, it felt like that was one part of our game and some of the other elements were a little more direct or forced. For the first time in my life, I see a Lincoln centre back with the ball and I don't think 'just whack it up top', I genuinely believe we can pass comfortably and with purpose through the thirds. I see players seemingly penned in and lofting a ball fifteen yards between two players to a free man. I see patterns, just like 2016/17 and just like 2006/07, but these are not individual patterns, they all connect to form a whole tapestry of slick football that spans the whole park. Then, when we don't have the ball, we see the tough and hard-wearing underlay that tapestry sits upon, the blood and guts tackling, the incessant harassing and the character and attitude all good sides have to keep in their locker.

I know it is four wins from four, I know there are 42 more matches to go (or I hope there are), but this is our best start to a third-tier (or above) season since 1935/35. I can't help but feel that this new era in our history is a hugely exciting one and it might just end up taking us to the sorts of heights a generation of Lincoln City fans dared never, ever have dreamed. £1m player sales, genuine top ten potential in the third tier and the sort of football others watch and say 'I wish we could do that'.

City seal loan agreement with West Brom talent
October 6, 2020

The Imps have announced a short-term loan deal for West Brom forward Jamie Soule from West Brom.

The move comes after another fellow West Brom loanee, Callum Morton, picked up an injury ruling him out for a couple of months. The deal seems to have been fast-tracked too, with no official photograph or quotes from our new arrival, who is eligible to play in this evening's EFL Trophy tie at Mansfield Town.

Soule is a former England U17 international and a player we first mentioned on here a year ago as a possible recruit. He has come through the West Brom academy setup, signing a new three-year deal with the club last year ahead of a short loan spell at Barrow, where he appeared just twice.

The 19-year-old scored seven goals in 13 Premier League 2 appearances last season, adding a further six assists, showing the sort of form that once had German giants Borussia Dortmund linked with him. He will come in as a straight like-for-like replacement for Morton and although the duration of his loan hasn't been specified, one would imagine it covers the duration of Morton's injury.

Whilst many of the stats available are from Premier League 2 matches, he does seem to be a promising prospect. he's 6ft tall, so should offer a little something in the air, and he appeared for West Brom U21s three season on the spin in the EFL trophy. His first outing came in a 2-0 defeat by Gillingham in 2016/17, where he got ten minutes late on. The following year, he added 18 minutes to his tally against Coventry, whilst in 2018/19 he played in a 2-1 defeat at Accrington and again in a defeat by the same margin at Macclesfield Town.

Wyscout only seems to track the Under 18 or Under 23 fixtures of big teams, such as Liverpool, but Soule is noted as having scored against Manchester United at both age groups, once in a 4-3 reverse in 2018 and again in a 3-1 defeat in 2019. In those games, plus one more against Liverpool. he averaged 2.39 shots on target per game and appeared to like a dribble as well, looking at the highlights. His goal in the 3-1 defeat by the Red Devils was the opener and saw him arriving at the back post after a wicked-looking cross, not unlike the ones we've been delivering of late.

It is hard to read too much into this move at this moment in time, Soule is very much a young and unproven prospect, but I have a sneaky feeling we might be getting a really good young player here. When I spoke about him before a West Brom mate of mine messaged and said we had 'no chance' as Soule was the brightest young thing in their academy.

He might just be the unknown, unexpected youngster that comes in and writes headlines for himself. A winning goal in the 90th minute against the Stags tonight would be very nice, thank you.

Done and Dusted: Mansfield 1-3 Imps
October 7, 2020

On another good night for Michael Appleton's Imps, a routine victory against Mansfield Town has ensured qualification for the next round of the EFL Trophy with a game to spare.

The EFL trophy gets a lot of stick, rival managers seem to think it is a distraction, and yet Lincoln City take it seriously. Whatever your politics, I think it is encouraging that our club wants to win every match, instead of having a Steve Evans style 'I don't care' attitude. Our desire to win football games was evident last night in a game we completely controlled for a good 75 minutes.

The benefits of such a win are multiple, from the £10,000 prize money to the chance for some of our fringe players. I cannot fathom, for one second, how clubs apparently 'suffering' from Covid restrictions are happy to say they'll take the fines incurred for fielding weakened teams. For me, that is a gross affront to the very fans they are supposed to serve. I know some of those EFL trophy detractors will welcome the stance, but right now finance is important and I would be appalled if my club would rather payout £15,000 in fines than collect £10,000 in prize money.

This is a competition that both The Imps and Michael have a bit of a love affair with. It delivered our first shot at Wembley glory, a memorable day for those who chose to attend and a day which provided the sort of income that allowed us to win the league title the following season. Michael has been there twice as a manager, losing on both occasions, and I suspect he sees this as a chance for some silverware to add to his growing reputation as a manager. I say 'growing', he already has a good pedigree from Oxford, but a second spell with a League One side at the right end of the table will be just the job for him, as would a successful Wembley appearance.

I think our team selection represented two sides to the competition. We had to play some senior players and the ones we saw appear were ones who perhaps haven't had injury issues. Jorge Grant, Connor McGrandles, Harry Anderson, TJ Eyoma and Sean Roughan are all what I would consider first-team players and they all got 90 minutes last night. In addition, some of the exciting players just outside the first XI had a great chance to shine, none more so than Anthony Scully, Remy Howarth and Theo Archibald. If this was a test for them, they certainly passed it in my eyes.

The biggest news was probably the inclusion of Jamie Soule, which meant the game broke new ground for a number of reasons. It is probably the fastest transition from rumour to the first team we've seen for a new player, and almost certainly the youngest centre-back pairing we have ever put out in a competitive fixture. The team certainly had an 'EFL trophy' feel to it, but the game had anything but.

The Imps started with intensity and vivacity that hasn't been seen for some time in my opinion. We've often given our opponents respect, letting them have their cake and waiting until we can snatch a piece and eat it. Last night, against an experienced looking Mansfield side, we took the cake and ate it right in front of them. The Imps passing game was slick, our possession always seemed to be with purpose and the players who had a point to prove looked eager to do just that. In the early stages, Connor McGrandles impressed me for his harrying and hard work, whilst you could see glimpses of Theo Archibald's unique talents. We have some great wide players, but Theo is markedly different; he takes players on with skill and a sharp turn of pace, as well as being naturally left-footed. When we need to drop Jorge Grant back into the midfield, I expect the former Celtic man to be our first choice on the left.

We knocked on the door a bit and whilst I'm not going to dissect the whole match, I'll talk about the goals. The first was created courtesy of Remy Howarth, a driving run into the area saw him have an effort at goal which fell to the feet of Soule, who calmly poked home. It was a striker's goal, instinctive and natural. The youngster had a good game too, he faded towards the end but certainly didn't look out of place in the first-team and that bodes well for the future. He did get thrown around by the big lump Menayese at the back, a player I quite liked up until his second-half howler.

I always felt from there the game was in the bag and I went into half time wondering if we might score again, or might have scored again, given that iFollow froze just as Anthony Scully was preparing a shot. Thankfully, it froze for everyone, so I couldn't be accused of having bad internet or whatever else the iFollow people tend to blame substandard service on. At least all we missed was a bit of the halftime break.

The second half was very much like the first, with us on top. Jorge Grant was simply outstanding, pulling the strings from deep, pinging passes around like he was David Beckham down the park with a bunch of local kids. Our wide players were lively too, Anthony Scully bullish and strong, Theo graceful and elegant. I tell you who Archibald reminds me of a bit; Peter Gain. He has that natural ability that I always love to see. He was working hard for a goal, a little too hard at times, but he wanted to make his mark.

Anthony Scully wanted to do the same and he seemingly squandered a great chance to do so in the second period. A sumptuous ball from Archibald sent the former West Ham man free, he went one-on-one with the keeper and maybe just had too much time. His effort was well saved by young Aidan Stone, with Soule not quite able to steer the rebound in. Minutes later he got his chance to make amends.

This time it started with McGrandles winning possession well, and finding Tayo Edun. The left-back surged forward, made up plenty of yards and then slid another great ball through the defence for Scully, who finished a harder effort than moments before with aplomb. With service like that, our strikers should all get fifteen goals or more. We seemed to just have a killer pass for every occasion and although they didn't all come off, not one player made two or three bad ones in a row.

Scully then turned provider, with another great example of our football philosophy. Mansfield's attack broke down and TJ Eyoma nodded out to Scully on the right, deep in his own half. He chested the ball away from his marker, moved fifteen yards forward and lofted a sixty-yard pass in the direction of Archibald. The winger gambled, and Menayese got in a horrible mess with Stone, leaving Archibald with a cool chance to loft home. 3-0, game over, turn out the lights when you're done, Mansfield.

To be fair, the Stags had a decent period after that, Nicky Maynard and Stephen McLaughlin came on and added something to their forward line. Couple that with a few tired Imps legs, and you have the recipe for a comeback. Mal Benning's drive needed turning away by Ethan Ross, who had a solid night on his full Imps debut, Menayese made amends for his earlier mistake by arriving for a free header in the area to make it 3-1, but that was the sum of their endeavour. I do wonder is Harry Anderson lost his marker watching it back, but overall Harry had a solid game at right-back.

It could have been four, a great ball from Eyoma, another forty-yard ping into feet, saw Remy Howarth get free, but he couldn't quite find the space for a shot. He worked his way across the area before laying it off to Soule, who saw a smart snapshot saved. It was the last meaningful action of a really solid outing for City.

Let's be honest, Mansfield have something missing (something BIG according to their blogger, Mansfield Matters) but you have to beat what is in front of you and whilst they were poor, they weren't utterly woeful. However, the players we had all showed their qualities. The first-teamers starting showed fitness and application, the hungry fringe players showed they could do a job in league action and those out of position (or in position I suppose for Eyoma and Roughan) all adapted really well. Jamie Soule settled quickly too, providing plenty of positives for Michael to enjoy.

We now face Man City's kids with nothing to play for other than pride and £10,000, both of which are hugely important to this Lincoln side. We are now nine games in, boasting seven wins, one draw and one defeat, which is a phenomenal start to the season. Last night probably told us more about the side than a league game, because it turned the stone over and showed us what is underneath, those knocking on the door, and the capabilities of those in other positions. I liked what I saw and if five or so of those lads are the so-called back-up brigade, we're in a great spot.

Also, huge kudos to Hayden Cann for coming on and making his debut. this tournament is where the young lads often get their debuts and it was in the EFL Trophy we first saw Lee Frecklington, Shane Clarke and Ellis Chapman for the Imps. All progressed to the first team and hopefully, young Hayden can do the same and keep the flag flying in the academy for local talent, as well as those we bring in from further afield.

Reality Bites: Imps 1-2 Bristol Rovers
October 11, 2020 0

I always seem to find it hard to write after a defeat like yesterday, which is in sharp contrast to many on social media for whom criticism comes as a default setting.

Let's be honest, looking at the fixture list this looked like the most winnable game of the opening five, and with them having won something like three in thirty before the encounter, we had to feel confident. Maybe, on reflection, we should have been concerned about our depleted team; Callum Morton's injury has been a big blow, Max Melbourne missing disrupted the left-hand side and of course, Brennan Johnson would have allowed us to change to a 4-4-1-1 which might have been more effective in those final minutes.

We can also moan a bit about the penalty decision in the first half, where McGrandles didn't get a penalty he clearly deserved, but that would be hypocritical, would it not? We are happy to say 'that's football' and move on when we get the rub of the green (MK Dons anyone?), so to then start shouting blue murder when things go against us isn't fair. It is the second year I've mentioned an incorrect penalty decision in the game against the Gas, but that is really where the similarities end.

There was little surprise pre-game with the team selection. Sean Roughan, who had a tough time against CJ Hamilton last weekend and who played 90 minutes in midweek, dropped to the bench, whilst Tayo Edun came in. Edun had looked decent at left-back over the previous 135 minutes of football and deserved his place in the side. The rest of the back four looked sound enough, our midfield was as expected as were the front three. It felt like 'business as usual' and after the often thrilling display against Mansfield in midweek, I fancied a game in which we created a few chances.

As for the visitors, they got a win last weekend but I didn't see them as a significant threat as, say, Fleetwood will be next week, or Ipswich the week after. Nope, this was definitely a golden chance to break that 100-year record of five consecutive league wins at the start of the season.

The first half didn't really give us much to talk about in terms of action. I didn't think we played badly if I'm honest, no worse than in games against Oxford or Charlton. At times, our approach play was laboured and passes went a little astray, but it was an even game in which neither side deserved a lead. We perhaps had the best clear-cut chance with Harry Anderson's close-range effort being smartly saved. However, the Gas were strong opponents and perhaps played the better football. They were restricted to a couple of long-range efforts which didn't really trouble Alex Palmer, with fans not exactly being served up a treat by either side.

I do think the Gas had some steady but forced build-up play, whilst we tried to move forward quicker, but again everything felt forced. After being treated to some really slick football in midweek, it was hugely disappointing for us as fans to see the method not working in a big league game. Remember, if we'd won, we would have been clear top of the third tier for the first time in many, many years. This was the type of game where we needed fans in the stadium, not least to maybe sway the ref when a stonewall penalty shout comes up.

I've watched the incident back and the foul on McGrandles is 100% a penalty. If we score that, I feel the game would be different from how it went with us scoring just after half time. Plus, there's every chance if it is a penalty, then it might be a red card too; still, as I've said, we can't complain. The weak penalty against MK Dons changed the game and I'm not sure we entirely deserved it. I think the saying is 'swings and roundabouts' and that certainly applies. We didn't lose the game because we didn't get the penalty shout, there were 96 minutes and 59 seconds outside that incident we could have crated chances to take all three points.

The first half wasn't really inspirational, but it wasn't awful either. There were few chances, little to shout about and in all honesty, not a lot to dissect. Yesterday was my Dad's birthday and he came over to watch the game, insisting we'd lose 2-1. I must confess, I didn't feel entirely confident before kick-off either, the big occasions always seem to derail us and as the lads trooped off at half time, I felt no better. With Dad still proclaiming a defeat, I made another brew and hoped for better.

Games do turn on moments, and this one turned on two immediately after the restart. Within seconds, we were ecstatic as an Imps set piece, once again, resulted in a goal. The Gas had the better of the corners in the first half, but a free-kick from a corner-like position caused trouble at the back for them straight away. Who else, but Lewis Montsma steamed in to claim the goal. I think it has gone down errantly as an own goal, but my understanding is if the touch from our player is taking it in, he should get the goal. It wasn't that on which the game turned on for me though; it was the fact Montsma collided with the post. He hurt his shoulder, received treatment and had to go off before coming back on.

Naturally, that left him out of position as he raced back on the field and he had barely got back to the centre of defence before the best goal of the game made it 1-1. A deep cross from the right wasn't cut out and in swooped Daly with a header to draw things level. It wasn't a great goal to conceded and I ask if Montsma hadn't gone off, would we have had him in a better position to defend the ball in? I think so but again, it is one of those things. I suppose all you ask is for consistency, which as you'll know we didn't get later in the half. Still, even with a couple of minutes of the second half gone, 1-1 was a fair reflection of the game I think.

Had we not conceded immediately, I believe the game would have been different. The Gas might have had to come on to us more and we would have been able to bring pace on from the bench in Archibald and maybe even Soule. As it was, with an immediate retort, the balance remained as it was and that Rovers to stick to their game plan. They weren't necessarily defensive, but they had no reason to come on to us having hit back straight away.

Within ten minutes the final goal of the game arrived from a penalty, and for me, there are no complaints. It looked like the Lincoln players felt Adam Jackson's foul came outside the area, but it didn't. It was a foul, it was inside the area and they Gas rightly got a chance from 12-yards, which they took. Alex Palmer wasn't far away from the save, but he didn't quite make it and City trailed 2-1. Oddly, the Gas scored the first goal against us at Sincil Bank in the league last season, and the first penalty against us at home in the league last season too, an honoured they have once again secured for themselves. Did someone say bogey team?

The game changed after that, they went from three at the back to five and were happy to defend their lead. We needed a change and the first surprised me; TJ Eyoma for Remy Howarth. I can see the logic, Harry Anderson dropped into the full-back position which made us more attacking, and I guess with Howarth ahead of him we hoped to push further on to the Gas. I'm not sure it worked, Howarth had a tough afternoon and struggled to make a serious impact on his full Football League debut. The same has to be said for Anthony Scully, he came on up top for Hopper and wasn't able to affect the game. Hopps had a slow afternoon, dare I say he didn't look like scoring and had Callum Morton been fit, he would almost certainly have given us another dimension. Maybe, in that scenario, Scully comes on in the right-hand side of attack too, but again, that's football.

The one change I felt that could make us more potent was Theo Archibald coming on and if we were to get a leveller than I felt it would come from the left. Jorge Grant hadn't had much joy out there, but when he dropped into midfield I felt we began to look a little more threatening thanks to Archibald's pace. It was harsh on McGrandles coming off though, for the first time this season I thought James Jones was a little below-par and might have been the man to make way. The midfield trio just didn't work in those latter stages and the intricate passing we enjoyed in midweek was replaced by a misfiring machine that looked ill-at-ease with what they were being asked. We know they're not, they've done it before, so the only conclusion I can draw is either Rovers pressed and harrassed perfectly, and we were having as close to an off-day as we've seen this season.

I do have an issue with an incident not long after the subs. First, Harry Anderson drove a decent ball across goal in what was probably a better chance than it looked before a scramble almost saw us grab the leveller through Montsma. In the panic, two Gas players went down with head injuries as we looked to mount another attack. Now, I have no problem with that, but both required treatment and the game was rightly stopped, but afterwards, they were not required to leave the pitch, why? Montsma was, so why was the ruling different here? It wouldn't have made a difference though, because this ridiculous drop ball rule meant that Rovers were actually able to mount an attack from the incident, instead of us getting the advantage we clearly had. Again, it wouldn't have changed the game, but surely we are due a little consistency from officials? Maybe, because we lost, I'm inclined to pick at these little moments more than if we'd won the game.

Adam Jackson's sending off came not long after and again, I have a bit of a complaint. I'm not sure why he was so far forward bursting into the box anyway, it looked like us trying far too hard to force an attack, and as he was on a yellow he was always at risk with a wild tackle, if that is what it was. Now, I've watched it back a few times now and I don't see any contact at all with the Rovers man. My gut feeling is, in an attempt to wind down the clock, the defender feels he wants to go down and in doing so, inadvertently draws what looks like a straight red Jackson barely deserved. Again, it had no bearing on the result, but it is a really weak yellow, let alone a red, considering some other challenges (from both teams) that went unpunished.

That effectively ended the game, even though another fifteen minutes elapsed. Our approach then went to getting lots of balls into the box, but having nobody on the end of them to finish. By the time the final whistle came, Dad had already left (I've seen enough he said), and I was sat there more in blind hope than belief. The whistle went, we were beaten and that was that. For the first time in a while, I almost let the result ruin my Saturday evening, which is a mark of how much I believe in this side. Even for those successful three years, I didn't get down after a defeat as I expected us to lose matches, but this one I really didn't.

It is hard to be critical though, at least scathingly so. Some players will know they didn't have good games, others were playing another 90 minutes after midweek and we were missing some key faces. The fact we lost meant we dropped one place to second, a position I would have snapped your hand off for at the beginning of September, so it really is about the bigger picture. Michael said we'd lose games, go on bad runs and staying together was important and that is definitely still the case. What will I add by saying 'this player looked off it' at the end of my article? Sure, some of the lads have had better games, but these are the same players that put us top in the first place, so I won't be scathing, I'll leave that to social media.

What I will highlight are some of the positives. I thought Eyoma was unlucky to come off when he did, but I felt Harry had a better game at full-back than he had out wide. I thought Jorge Grant was consistent throughout, and probably borderline Man of the Match again. Personally, I thought McGrandles worked really hard all game and was unlucky to be taken off when he was, plus it would be harsh to blame Alex Palmer for either of the goals; he had a confident game in goal and claimed a few crosses, as well as making no fuss stops from long range when called upon. I feel Theo Archibald is closing in on a start very soon, especially if we choose to mix up the midfield a bit, as I think we might do for three games in eight days coming up in a week's time.

I also thought it interesting we saw Michael take very decisive action as soon as it was needed. Last season, some were critical that he sat with his bench unused until late in the game, but we certainly tried to change things and that is promising, even if it didn't come off.

I do try to see positives in negatives, just as it is important to see negatives when everything is positive. In terms of the season, this is a result we won't cherish, but I don't think it was a terrible performance (woeful I heard from someone on social media. Woeful? You were at Oxford at home last season, right?). I didn't quite work for us, but we now have seven days to prepare for three matches that, if they yield five or six points, I'd be delighted with. We're still in good shape, I still feel a finish of between 10th and 12th is achievable and I still believe in this exciting young side. Sometimes, you lose matches when that is what you deserve and yesterday, despite my referee moans and squad depletion groans, that is exactly what happened.

The First Ten Matches – How the Michael Appleton Era is Panning Out
October 16, 2020

I think it is fair to say that whilst Michael has been in charge of the club for over a year, his 'era' has only really started this summer.

It was this summer we began to see his players coming into the club, and the ones he previously targeted settling in. His style has been evident for a while, but this summer was when we first saw round pegs in round holes, in terms of the squad's attributes. I mentioned when I spoke to him earlier this year that he was firmly settled into the EPC and felt like he was now driving his vehicle, not one recently vacated by someone else.

So, with our incoming transfer business seemingly concluded, how has the MA era started, and what can we expect from the future. I thought I'd break this down into three parts, on the field, off-field and the future potential. I feel a bit guilty as I've not been well the last couple of days and I missed yesterday's ins and outs, aside from this analysis video, and I wanted to provide something worth reading before tomorrow's clash with Fleetwood.

On The Field

Even including this weekend's defeat, if someone had told me during the last week of August that after ten matches we would have lost twice, once to the reigning English champions, I would have snapped your hand off. Football is not all about results of course, despite what you might think. Eight wins (seven and one on a penalty shoot out) certainly seems impressive, but performance is also hugely important. Anyone who tells you otherwise only need think back to the final day of the 2018/19 season, where the Imps were booed off despite winning the title, to realise performance is important. If you win a few games, there's a chance you are getting lucky; Plymouth did this back in 2017/18, registering rubbish xG but finishing well. That was unsustainable and the next season, as expected, they were relegated after the problems they had managed to mask with hard work eventually got through the papered-over cracks.

Is that the case with us? Have we had the rub of the green? The short answer is (and you may not like this), but yes we have. The penalty which turned the game at MK Dons wasn't a penalty. Against Charlton, we were second best for a long period before grabbing another penalty. At Blackpool, we were 2-1 down with seven minutes to go and maybe with supporters in the ground the result would have been different. This does not mean we'll 'do a Plymouth' of a couple of years ago though, not one bit. Those result, whilst fortuitous, also showed some signs of real promise. Blackpool away was a lesson in remaining focused, applied and adhering to your own game plan. We won that game through our attitude as much as anything, although Lewis Montsma's juggling skills helped. Charlton, and to a lesser degree Oxford, were not fluke wins, but victories born out of letting the opponent have the ball and ensuring that on the occasions we got it, we did better than them. Even MK Dons, a game were conceded a lot of possession, we ended up on the right side of the result on the balance of play, even if the penalty was fortunate.

Then there have been the games in which I have been mega-impressed, namely Mansfield and Bradford. They were matches in which we showed a ruthless edge, a hunger and desire to play football the right way. My hope is that those matches are a hint of what to expect in future league matches, once the team find a rhythm and continuity. There is no reason why the free-flowing attacking football we displayed at Field Mill won't make much more regular appearances in the league, but for now, we have to accept that our four league wins from five maybe doesn't tell the whole story. Perhaps, if we had ten points instead of 12, it might reflect our endeavour a little more accurately. I'm not being controversial or cutting here at all, the start has been superb, but I think losing the Bristol Rovers this weekend has tempered expectation slightly and, being brutally honest, that isn't a bad thing. Here's another statement which might not win me many friends: I can see us losing a couple more in the coming weeks, maybe starting tomorrow. It s no reason to panic, no reason to be over-critical because the first ten matches have shown me that this team is bursting with potential and that the passing of time will only serve to improve us and make us stronger.

Off The Field

This is really the squad, more than anything. Is our current squad a serious improvement on the one which Michael inherited a year ago, and then on the one that broke up in May? The short answer, and I'm sure this will be echoed by many, is yes.

The medicine hasn't been sweet though. When you have a team that has seen strong levels of success, as ours had over a three-year period, then key figures departing is always going to bring about uncertainty, and not knowing is as much a part of genuine fear as anything. Seriously, when you watch your favourite horror movie, what is the scariest bit? the unknown? Not quite realising what is going to happen? Football is the same. When we lost Michael Bostwick, in particular, I got that fear. I know many felt the same about Josh Vickers and Neal Eardley, even as far back as when Toff left too, but that is football. At the time, I didn't see it as clearly as I felt that Bozzie would be a big influence on a young squad. Could you see those players in this squad though? I'm not saying they're not good enough for League One, but in the style and setup we have, would those players have a significant role to play? I'm afraid, the answer is probably no. Plus, when you consider that both Bozzie and Eards are injured for Burton Albion, a real fear as players enter their thirties, we may have ripped a plaster off in the summer; taken a short term hit of discomfort for the greater good.

I'm not saying our current squad is perfect, but it is exciting and MA has shown he will react to developing situations as well. prior to Jamie Soule coming into the side, we didn't expect another new face, but the youngster came in from West Brom and obviously, Robbie Gotts landed from Leeds too. Throw Brennan Johnson into that mix, a player we have seen for one full game, and the latter transfer business looks impressive. I know loads of people are raving about Gotts, but being objective they are doing so because of what they've heard or seen on a computer game, not because of what they have seen. He sounds like a great capture though, both flexibly and full of youth and potential. That describes more or less everyone we have signed over the summer.

I've done plenty on our squad over the last few weeks so won't go into the finer points, but I feel we have a squad that is far more rounded than any previous season. It is a young squad and we must not heap too much expectation on the shoulders of TJ Eyoma and Sean Roughan, for instance, but we can also be excited by their potential. Those two individuals could be key going forward; our current system relies heavily on full-backs being able to get up and down, play it short and neat as well as beat players and deliver into the box. Whilst a three-man midfield is always going to be the heartbeat of a side, our success will depend on the effectiveness of the full-backs. Sure, if they do well then the attackers need to finish chances off, but if we falter at full back, we are far less effective. That was evident on Saturday, especially down the left, where Tayo struggled and Bristol bagged from a delivery from the right and a penalty earned from a run in the right-hand channel. Blackpool hit us from that area in the first half too; food for thought.

Overall, I'm happy with the squad. In a perfect world, I'm sure we'd have another striker, but for now, Soule and Hopper will share the load, with johnson and Scully able to play there. The difference in this squad, compared with say 2018/19, is the flexibility. When we have only had three strikers in the past (Green, Palmer and Rhead for instance), other players couldn't fill in and the ones we had were either a nine or a ten, not both. MA's squad is like an intricate steampunk contraption, where all the different parts switch and change, making them functional in areas that you didn't think they could be.

Even with expected departures today, we're in a good place squad wise, although a couple of injuries would test that, as we saw at the back this weekend.

The Future

The key now is playing matches and getting time on the training field, and once the transfer circus closes its doors at 5 pm tonight, we have 18 games to find the rhythm and be happy with our lot.

I think the next few weeks could be challenging. Fleetwood tomorrow is a big game I suspect we could struggle in. Ipswich don't worry me, despite being top, because I think our style and their style could lead to an exciting game, as we have seen with Oxford and Charlton. I have a feeling we may see challenges in matches we shouldn't – Wimbledon, Accrington and Gillingham are all sides with different styles of football that we should perhaps consider ourselves capable of beating. They will be the big tests, sides that want us to play our game (Wimbledon), sides that have much smaller budgets than us, but a huge spirit (Accrington) and bullies (Gillingham). Portsmouth are up in the next few weeks too, another side I feel we can more than matches.

The fact is there are no easy games at this level, no games we should feel we have a right to win. What we are going to get is a rocky ride, we will lose matches we think we were better in, we'll win matches we should have lost. I think that shows the journey we're on is heading in the right direction though; last season after DC left we were losing matches we were okay in (Coventry, Oxford away), losing matches we played away (almost all) and losing some matches without really putting up a fight (Southend, Gillingham). Now I feel that there is enough around the squad to ensure that our good start can be built upon. The key is staying together, especially off the field, Sure, fans are not in the ground so the players won't hear a moan if things don't go our way, but I think this squad has earned the right to have fans backing even if we lost two or three on the spin. Earlier this week, the words 'Project Big Picture' had people frothing at the mouth, but if you applied the wording only to us, it is worth backing. Our own personal 'Project Big Picture' is eventual Championship football and after last season's bump in the road, I think that destination is still programmed into MA's sat nav. Arrival time might be 2022/23, or beyond, but at present, we are definitely on the right road.

Impressive point for solid City: Fleetwood 0-0 Imps
October 18, 2020

I'll begin today with a confession: I thought we'd lose this game.

I felt maybe last weekend was the start of one of those bad runs the manager tells us will happen. We were average against Bristol Rovers and I wondered if still have Max and Callum out, as well as Adam Jackson missing, might cause us to stumble at Fleetwood, who were on a high after hammering Hull.

On Matchday Live I enthused about the home side's squad, their potent threat going forward and their style of play, whilst secretly being concerned at our ability to bounce back. Last season, after losing at Wycombe and missing out on the chance to go top, we crumbled. I know there were other circumstances there too, but in my mind, I still feel we have no right to be in the top six and eventually, we'll get found out. I know, shoot me for being more pessimistic than a certain Mr Pearson, but that's how I feel.

Maybe, Michael Appleton's Aspiration Squad are turning the tide of Gary Hutchinson's Pessimist Persona. Make no mistake about it, yesterday's game was our best performance of the season, bar none. Better than Mansfield, better than Bradford, better than any of our home fixtures. It came against yet another side I thought would be top six this season (Blackpool, Charlton and Oxford all tough fixtures) and yet we controlled the pace of the game, outwitting some very experienced players at the same time. I suspect that as he sits down to his Frosties this morning wearing his Teddy Ruxpin pyjamas, Joseph Barton will be more than happy to have come away with a point.

The Imps line up gave us plenty of interest pre-match. My first feeling, and the right one, was that we'd line up 4-3-3, with Grant in the middle and Johnson on the left. The more I looked at the players, the more I was convinced we'd be in a 4-4-1-1, with Grant and Anderson wide and Johnson behind Hopper. What that demonstrates is the versatility within the squad; even with a first XI named and in front of us, we don't know how the lads will line up. That is a big advantage for the Imps, because if we don't know, fans who watch every game and study the side, how on earth do the opposition know how we're going to approach the game? Then, halfway through the game, Harry Anderson takes up a place on the left-wing and Johnson on the right, further bamboozling Fleetwood. I keep using words like 'fluid' and 'organic' when talking about our approach, and that covers everything from our style of play to how we line up tactically. It keeps everyone on their toes, not least a 'pundit' who has to formulate an opinion on the team within seconds of seeing it. if in doubt, make three claims and then when one is right, forget the others. After all, isn't that what these ex-agents do on Twitter?

The first five minutes or so had me a bit worried. Fleetwood looked like a side packed with dangermen. I know Harvey Saunders is the man of the moment, but I would have been more fearful had they started with Josh Morris and Barrie McKay over Madden and Saunders. After a couple of slightly worrying moments where Evans got in between Montsma and Walsh, we settled down and got into our flow.

Oh boy, what a flow it is. I think the game was made even more exciting by Mark Hone purring his way through it, throwing superlative after superlative at the side. Genuinely, you would have thought the stand-in pundit was watching Barcelona, such was his admiration for our play, and in fairness, maybe we don't see it. I think it is like when you see a picture of you and your partner form ten years ago; you go 'wow, how much have we changed?', but day to day, you don't notice that change. When Mark commented on how different this side played compared to Danny's teams, that struck home. Here is an expert who hasn't seen us for ages, watching with fresh eyes and he sees the development more acutely than fans who watch every game.

One of the defining moments of the game came on eight minutes and seemed topical after Jordan Pickford's horror-challenge on Van Dijk earlier in the day (yes, Premier League references. Come on, it's been bigger in the new than bloody Brexit and Covid today). Alex Palmer rushed out of his goal and seemingly took out Harvey Saunders. It was a big call for Anthony Backhouse, but he isn't a referee who usually makes the big calls. Palmer seemed to have got away with a challenge, not unlike Schumacher's collision with Battiston in the 1982 World Cup. Looking back, the incident wasn't as bad as it looked in real-time and although some referees would have given it, Palmer's challenge wasn't intentional, nor as severe as the other two mentioned here.

On 15 minutes the game turned in our favour and I think it is fair to say it stayed that way for the whole half. Harry's cross-cum-shot should really have been turned in by Tom Hopper, who was agonizingly close to tapping home, but it wasn't to be. We raided dow the right with an impressive looking Harry, we marauded down the left with the (at times) sensational pace of Brennan Johnson, but we could quite find the clear-cut chance or the killer ball. Harry stung the keeper's glove with an effort that was more dangerous than it looked, whilst James Jones had an acrobatic volley fly over the bar. Fleetwood played their part, they weren't woeful like Mansfield were, but they often had to let us play our game; this is what I've wanted to see. It is the first time in the league I felt we have gone to a game and played our game, more or less from start to finish, and we were all the better for it. Maybe the tweak helped too; Grant playing in the centre of midfield helped with our creativity as he was able to play balls left and right as he wanted. He had a superb game by the way, but when are we not talking about how good he is these days?

I think the indication of City's dominance came just before halftime when Sam Stubbs came off for Charlie Mulgrew. It was a big call to hook a player on 38 minutes, but it reflected how dangerous we were looking going into the final period of the half. Only one team looked likely to score at that point, and that was us (in case you were wondering). Even a Lewis Montsma run just before half time had me off my seat, the central defender going on a Maradona-esque dribble before just losing out.

If I were Mr Pessimism at 3 pm, just like Mr Hyde's Dr Jekyll, my optimistic side had surfaced by the blow of Backhouse's whistle.

The way these games usually go is that we play well one half, and not in the other. Usually, it is a weak first half backed up by a strong second, so I expected the home side to really come at us during the second period. Again, as with the first 45, that wasn't the case. Fleetwood had their moments, it wasn't all one way, but that contributed to a truly thrilling game of football.

We had our chances again. Brennan Johnson switched to the right-hand side, had a good effort stopped by Leutwiler, who was the busier of the keepers. James Jones had a good drive from distance that was parried and Tayo Edun, looking solid on the left, couldn't quite get on the rebound, In truth, you couldn't pick a single Imps' player who wasn't having a good game. Joe Walsh had settled in as if he'd played 100 games for us, he looked calm and assured and it is likely Adam Jackson was watching on a little worried. As I've said, I thought Tayo bounced back well after getting some stick for his performance last week. It was a big call to play him at left-back again, but I thought he coped really well against a pacey Harvey Saunders, as well as involving himself in positive play further up the pitch.

The real superlatives must rain down on Jorge Grant though. He makes the game looks so easy and it is clear he is thriving for us. He skips away from challenges, pirouettes around opponents and smashes 30-yard passes around like he's playing FIFA on easy mode. I've been a vocal supporter of playing him on the left, but alongside Jones in the attacking midfield role, he made a huge difference. I'm not sure where we go from here in terms of our midfield, McGrandles is a workhorse, but Grant put in a real claim for a more central role. Where does that leave Robbie Gotts? Right-back? It would be hard to drop TJ given how excellent he was yesterday. These are big decisions that I'm sure a manager loves to have. However, we talk about Montsma and Roughan when mentioning bigger clubs having a look at our lads, but on this form, there will be a host of suitors pulling up Jorge Grant's videos on Wyscout and liking what they see.

By the time the hour mark rolled around, it seemed a case of if, rather then when City scored. Fleetwood had lost their grip on the game and the midfield of Coutts, Whelan and Camps was looking ragged and overrun by our boys. Joey made a like-for-like change bringing on Morris and McKay for Saunders and Madden and I felt that changed things a little but not before two very big moments. There was a great chance for City as Jorge Grant got free in the area, but couldn't find space to shoot. We might have been guilty over overplaying it a bit, but Harry's effort was eventually saved and Fleetwood cleared. Harry was also fouled in the area, a second stonewall penalty that we should have got, but didn't. Still, given the ambiguity over the Palmer foul, I suppose we have nothing to really complain about. Genuinely, I'd rather be writing about a 0-0 draw than a 1-0 win from a League One game blighted by VAR.

For the last ten minutes or so the game opened up and, in fairness to the home side, we began to ride our luck a bit. I almost pooed myself (that's a proper professional journalistic term) when we gave a free-kick away on the edge of the area and Charlie Mulgrew stepped up, but the wall did its job. That fear double minutes later as Fleetwood rushed clear, one-on-one with Palmer, only for our keeper to produce a great stop to keep the score at 0-0. He rushed off his line and made himself huge, 'doing his job' people would doubtless say, but it had me celebrating almost as excitedly as if we'd scored a goal.

In between Anthony Scully added some energy to our forward line, testing the keeper from range twice. It all added up to a scintillating 0-0 draw, which likely disappointed nobody once confirmed by the shrill burst of the whistle. I was glad too, having listened to Mark Hone saying 'losing this would be terrible now' for fifteen minutes. Mark is a great pundit, but he has to lay off the prophet of doom vibe during matches. I do enough of it pre-match without him adding to the tension when we are doing well!

So, there we are. 0-0 at Fleetwood, a great point from a tough match and we remained third. Our next two matches are against sides in the top six, which means things are getting no easier, but if we play as we did yesterday then we should bring home four points in my opinion. I don't believe we have anything to fear right now, except ourselves. If we have an off day or misplaced a pass as we play out from the back, then the malaise will be of our own doing, but there is nothing I have seen from any side thus far that makes me think we are out of our depth or heading for a big fall. You see, yesterday was a huge test for us. How do you respond from a disappointing defeat? How do you cope with suspensions and injuries at this stage of the season? The answer, it seems, is just sticking to your guns and do what you are told by the manager. There wasn't a bad player on the pitch yesterday, not one who you could say 'wasn't up to it'. I have seen some criticism of Tom Hopper, and maybe he could haves cored early doors, but he worked hard, occupied the centre backs and that in turn allows our wide players a bit of freedom. That isn't to say when Callum Morton is back that him and Hopper won't alternate a bit more, but criticism of Hopps isn't entirely fair as he is a part of the overall machine that is doing very well at present.

We forge on to Plymouth and Ipswich, little time to recover for the players but with the squad we have, it isn't such a big deal. For instance, Theo Archibald would drop into the first-team picture with ease, as would most of the bench from the weekend. Robbie Gotts has yet to appear and he is likely to be around the first XI, Joe Walsh showed us exactly what we've missed thus far with him and frankly, we are probably in as good a position squad wise as we have been during my entire time as a Lincoln fan. I can't recall us having such depth from the bench and even into the fringe players before and to use a phrase I role out every week on Matchday Live, it bodes well.

In fact, it bodes very well.

Pilgrims sent packing: Imps 2-0 Plymouth
October 20, 2020

There are few things in life that are certain, death and taxes are the famous ones, but it seems at the moment me talking positively about my football club is another.

I felt tonight was a big test for us, coupled with Ipswich this weekend. We battled to a draw with Fleetwood and should have won, but it was one point from a possible six and the start of a possible slump. How we progress over the next four matches will go a long way to setting us up for the season. With six games gone, the season is in its infancy, but with ten gone you are almost a quarter of the way through. Plymouth, Ipswich, Crewe and Doncaster are four matches from which seven points upwards would be a really great haul. Well, one game down, four points to go.

I still have my pessimist head on ahead of a game at the minute, but going to watch it with my Dad tonight reminded me how a real pessimist thinks. Not being in the ground has meant I forgot how my Dad gets before a fixture, worried and constantly saying 'I don't know about tonight'. He said it against Bristol

Rovers and once again, he was on it this evening. Still, it was nice to watch another game with him, seeing as that has been cruelly snatched away by Covid and inadequate governance.

I'll leave politics in the first paragraph though, this is all about football. I can't say I hold the belief Plymouth will be up there this season, but I do think they're a good side who play football in a manner which will see them win more than they lose. Ryan Lowe has built his Plymouth side in the image of his Bury promotion winners, and we know what that means; 3-5-2, playing out from the back and usually through Danny Mayor. Not a lot has changed, which hinted at an open and exciting game.

In the first fifteen minutes, both sides had chances. There's no doubt we should have been 1-0 up, Brennan Johnson's shot not quite sitting up at the back stick for Jorge Grant, but his flashed return effort should have been turned in by Tom Hopper. Our forward endeavour was smart, but Plymouth had a constant air of menace, like a dodgy backstreet inner-city boozer, you never quite knew when they might flare-up. Danny Mayor was the focal point, his effort saved by Alex Palmer in an evenly-balanced opening 15.

After that, I felt we began to let them control the tempo, not unlike matches with Charlton and Oxford. One effort from a free-kick drew a superb save from Palmer, who wasn't aware their forward was offside. It came at the start of a good spell of pressure for the visitors, and if anything I felt we began to retreat into ourselves a bit. Nobody was playing that badly, but there were too many loose passes. Conor McGrandles, in for Harry Anderson in one of two changes, didn't have a great first half, but his constant work rate made up for being a little sloppy in possession. Brennan Johnson looked a threat, but he drifted in and out of the game. when he was in it, he was a real livewire and posed a constant threat, but when we couldn't get the pattern right in midfield, it left him looking isolated, Jorge Grant too for short spells.

However, when Grant did get on the ball, he teased and tormented Will Aimson. He had another effort across goal late on which, once again, it looked easier for Hopper to touch than avoid. Sadly, he didn't get on it and twice we should have scored but didn't. Those two chances were more or less the sum of our first half though and when the whistle blew for half time, my Dad the pessimist said he didn't know where a goal was coming from. Part of me could see what he meant; we had played some nice football, in patches, but at the same time we'd allowed Plymouth to do the same. It wouldn't be over the top to liken the first half to that of the game against Bristol Rovers. We weren't bang on it, a couple of lads were misplacing passes and when that happens, the machine breaks down. On the other hand, despite having a little more purpose in possession, we hadn't really looked like conceding.

In the second period, things certainly swung the other way. I had called a possible change at half time, maybe Harry for McGrandles, but to his credit, Michael stuck to the same XI that started the game and I felt it paid off. McGrandles came out rejuvenated and from the first whistle of the second period to the last, we were the better side.

Brennan Johnson was once again the main source of the threat, and within three minutes of the restart he had a solid penalty shout turned down. Good work saw him released down the flank and as he jinxed into the area, he seemed to be tugged back. The honest player in him stayed on his feet, the effort was cleared and it seemed we had faced an injustice. We didn't have to wait long for balance. McGrandles lashed a superb effort against the post and when the rebound fell to Johnson he was seemingly bundled over for a spot-kick. I wouldn't possibly suggest a referee has the earlier one in his mind, but the second looked weaker. Still, it doesn't matter, he pointed to the spot and at that moment the game was won and lost.

Jorge Grant continued his fine run of scoring with a well-taken spot-kick and Plymouth's heads dropped. Now, when Bristol Rovers conceded around the same time, they got straight back at it and scored, but the Pilgrims didn't have the same focus or drive. In fact, straight after the restart, we went back up and almost added a second, Johnson and Grant the architects once again, this time James Jones with the effort that their keeper turned away. Minutes later, Sean Roughan went through on the keeper and had to be denied quickly.

If there was a lesson for us in being on the front foot after scoring from our last home game, it is safe to say it has been learned, 100%. I felt we looked more dangerous in just ten minutes of second-half action as we had in the first half. James Jones had an effort deflected for a corner as the visitors looked to run out of ideas. They didn't get the ball to Danny Mayor at all and the threat he posed us in the first half was non-existent. Instead, they started to go a bit longer, with both Walsh and Montsma having decent evenings.

The change I thought might happen at half time came just after the hour mark, Harry Anderson (who still hasn't cut his hair) coming on. For six minutes, he barely had a touch, with my Dad saying just as much. As he finished the sentence 'we haven't seen much of Harry', he laid a smart ball out wide to Tom Hopper. His cross was deflected and up popped Brennan Johnson to settle our nerves with a classy header. It was a good finish too, he didn't have a lot of pace to work with on the ball and had to add direction to beat the keeper, rather than power. Whilst he will take the plaudits, I also spotted Harry's run to try to get on the end of Hopper's cross too; in the first half when Hopps drifted out wide, we didn't seem to have the option in the middle. That is what Harry gives us and even though he didn't score, his presence added to Johnson's gave the Plymouth backline too much to think about.

Once we got to 2-0, there was little to do other than safely see the game out. Plymouth were well beaten, there wasn't any chance they were going to get a second wind unless it was of our doing. Their best chance came when a tired-looking Walsh lost out on the attacking right, but it as a half-chance, little more. I've got to give a big shout out to Roughan and TJ Eyoma though. Roughan certainly catches the eye and his performances are perhaps under a microscope because of his age, so he is unlikely to get overlooked, but he had a good game. TJ however, he is the new Sam Habergham, in that he is a seven or more every week and rarely seems to earn plaudits. This is a young man just seven matches into his Football League career who plays with the calm assurance of a senior professional with 200 outings under his belt. He was strong and stable again tonight, rarely giving the ball away and rarely being beaten by a runner. He has power, he has pace and I think as the season progresses, he might even chip in with a goal or two.

In the middle of the park, I felt we got more balance with Grant alongside Jones in the later stages, but it could have been the tired Plymouth legs making it look that way. I'm leaning towards preferring Grant in the middle, which poses problems of the positive kind for MA. I also wonder if Anthony Scully might get off the bench every week, because his introduction always inspires a second wind of sorts. He must be a frightening prospect for tired legs, a player with a lower centre of gravity and plenty of running in him. He torments and teases when he comes on; he isn't always orthodox, but he isn't afraid to shoot either. He should perhaps have scored late on as he had a late effort, as did Theo after coming on (a wild one) and Harry too.

In the end, it was a comfortable win from a game that could have proven to be a banana skin. That's two clean sheets on the bounce now, four points from six and the ghost of Bristol Rovers has been well and truly exorcised. Plymouth will be alright, they're a good footballing side who I think are maybe one or two components shorts of a top ten place this season, but they won't be troubling the bottom four either. They have strength up top in Nouble, but was he ineffective, or did our young defence just deal with him really well? He came up against Roughan a couple of times and the 17-year-old dealt with the issue, something that scouts will take note of. The worry with youngsters is not being able to mix the physical, but Roughan, Eyoma and Montsma have all proven they won't be phased by so-called robust forwards.

We move on to Ipswich now, knowing they've been hammered 4-1, and maybe thinking there could be something in the game for us. I wouldn't rule it out either, this Lincoln City team are unlike anything I have seen before. We play football the right way, we are not intimidated or bullied and we have options all over the park. It's going to be an exciting few months, that is for sure.

We're together, they're apart, we're detached – Imps 1-0 Ipswich Town
October 25, 2020

At around 4.45 pm yesterday, I should have been stood in Upper 3, Row J, Seat 80 screaming 'we're top of the league' with my Dad stood behind me.

I should have been hoarse for, rather hypocritically, shouting all variations of 'ginger rat' themed abuse at Jon Nolan, despite obviously being ginger myself (the last bastion of seemingly acceptable political incorrectness going, by the way). I should have come away from the ground hoarse, frantically enthusing about another win, another exciting journey and increasing expectation. I don't doubt, for one second, my Dad would have had a dig at fans calling for Appleton's head after a month or two of his rein had passed either. That's what we do.

Instead, I stood in my living room with a lukewarm beverage on the table, screaming 'we're top of the league', as well as a bit of 'ginger rat' themed abuse, and of course issuing a manic laugh as Paul Lambert got sent off for his little show. I'd say happy days, and they are, but for the first time since this whole pandemic began, I really did feel a genuine, gut-wrenching upset at not being there. Sure, it was sad fans couldn't watch us play Liverpool, or win against Plymouth, Oxford and Charlton. It was a real shame the Blackpool weekender was ruined and that we couldn't celebrate the insane ending to that game, but at 4.45 pm last night, I felt it as bad as at any other point.

We're not just joint top, or top after four games, we are clear top, having played the side previously top, and having bounced back from an apparent blip. Maybe, just maybe, we are in the top ten to stay this season. Who knows?

In amongst it all yesterday, there was a game of football that was just the same as any other; 90 minutes long, officiated by one man and contested by two teams who both wanted to win; or at least that's the theory. For the first 45 minutes, dare I say only one side really looked like they wanted to win. As you all know, I'm a stat man. I love a good stat and xG is one of my favourite, something many lambast me for (hope you're well Jack), but xG is a damn sight more of an indication of a side's performance than possession. The opening 45 minutes show Ipswich had more possession, but like money, it is only useful if you do something with it. Ipswich frittered theirs away like Viv Nicholson (look it up), whilst we invested ours wisely, not quite seeing the returns perhaps it deserved. In terms of xG, the best team won by the way. In fact, it should have been 2-0 or 3-1, according to those stats.

I wasn't particularly worried about the game, I'd written before that I felt they would be a team we could play our game against, but I hadn't been expecting quite such a laboured and lethargic Ipswich. They played the ball around with little purpose, looking perhaps more like our side of a year ago, with players uncomfortably trying a style not suited to them. It would be unfair to taint all of their players with that brush, of course, some are clearly comfortable and much better than their style allows them to display. Jack Lankester and Gwion Edwards certainly wouldn't look out of place in our squad, but Hawkins, Nsiala, Nolan and Wilson, amongst others, wouldn't get on our bench. It's sad for Ipswich fans to see, but most can see it, as demonstrated by the reaction to the result on social media.

This isn't an Ipswich site though, it is a Lincoln one, and I'm pleased it is. Instead of vitriol and anger aimed at our manager, we get superlatives and plaudits across the whole squad. There is still a lot to come from our side, but we attacked with real verve and intent yesterday. Dropping Hopper for Brennan Johnson was a big call, one that MA has shown he isn't afraid to make, and it changed the dynamic of our attack. I do wonder if it was done with Ipswich's defence in mind; there wasn't as much space down the wide areas due to their setup, so we seemed to be a bit more direct running into the channels. When we did get forward they tucked in and closed space down in the middle, which I think meant a pacey attack was always going to be the better option.

We could have had a couple in the first half, Jorge Grant blazing over after some superb work down the right, then not long before half time Brennan Johnson's shot was touched away by Holy's outstretched toe. Our best chance fell to Grant, a deflected shot bouncing up and off the bar with the keeper stranded, whilst Ipswich's only really dangerous chance fell to Hawkins, whose looped header beat Palmer, but not McGrandles, who nodded away calmly to keep the scores level.

All in all, the first half was a joy to watch for Imps' fans. Last season, we played Ipswich twice at home, in my opinion dominating both matches but losing one (FA Cup replay) and winning the other. I think we were better yesterday than in either of those, far more assured in possession, but just lacking that final moment of magic that would have unlocked the Tractor Boys defence.

It seems a little weird to be thinking I have a lot to write about from what was a pedestrian second half, For long periods, neither side really threatened and the pace went out of the game completely. It would be easy to say we were 'dragged to their level', but that would be me taking a leaf out of the Paul Lambert Book of Excuses, looking to deflect. Yes, the game lost its pace, but I felt conditions didn't help, nor did the number of games we are playing at present. With one eye on next week, Michael made only one change and that didn't come until late, and I do wonder if maybe he would have been happy with a draw on 90 minutes, not that he'd admit it. After all, I said four points from those two home games would be great and having done the job against Plymouth, maybe even I would have been happy with the point.

Gwion Edwards could have made it an open game after he nodded a decent chance over, proving the danger Ipswich had in the squad, even if that danger was only occasionally demonstrated. We lacked a cutting edge for much of the half, something that wasn't made easier by a relatively poor performance from the referee. Or, should I say, a perceived poor performance.

Yes, Kevin Johnson was picky. His use of the drop ball rule was to the letter and much to the ire of supporters at home. His call of offside against Oli Hawkins looked bizarre, but without the benefit of cameras in all areas of the ground, it is hard to gauge. The ball was played forward and looped up and over the defence, where Hawkins came around from behind a player to control it. Palmer made a save anyway, but the striker was given offside, much to the anger of Lambert and his pals on the bench (and those in the Portakabin actively trying to influence the official). I get that it looked dodgy, but even as a fan I am now ambiguous with such decisions, for or against us. I always say this; we could have VAR and the game be ruined. These decisions go for us, and against us every week and sometimes you just have to accept that. I don't believe, for one second, that the linesman was so far behind play he didn't spot the infringement, it is more likely that everyone was watching play, whilst he had his eye on the line and spotted what we all failed to see.

The referee also gave an offside which led to a free-kick inside our half, something lots of people picked up on and hammered him for. I'm told the law is now that the free-kick is taken from where the offending player touches the ball, not where he was called offside from. Funny, how so-called experts often do not know the rules. I'm just as guilty, crying foul when the two Bristol Rovers players didn't go off with head injuries, but Montsma did with his shoulder injury in our 2-1 defeat. I was wrong then, and a lot of people were wrong yesterday.

It wasn't a great afternoon for the official, but I think he got the big calls right, and those who read regularly will know I'm happy to say if I feel we've been handed one (Plymouth and MK Dons stick in my mind). The really big moment, on 77 minutes, has led to plenty of discussions, with some Plymouth fans still moaning from Tuesday. The facts are these: Brennan Johnson got on the ball, tore Nsiala a new one as he got to the touchline and was fouled by the defender. Did Johnson move a leg across and initiate contact? In slow motion, it looks that way, but can you really say a player running at his pace has time to think 'I'll put a leg out here'? It may be instinctive, but if Nsiala makes no contact, it isn't a penalty. Johnson, labelled a cheat by Pilgrims supporters, stayed on his feet for the first incident on Tuesday, a definite penalty, and didn't get one. What's he to do to be right? I do think he went down easily for our penalty the other night, I do think this was a clear penalty.

Jorge Grant did what John Akinde used to do best, and scored the penalty. Unlike the Gillingham striker, it capped off yet another wonderful afternoon for a player I will comfortably label as one of the most skilful I've ever seen in a Lincoln Cty shirt. Genuinely, I think you could play Jorge Grant at right-back and he would still glide around the pitch like an Under 18 captain playing for the Under 13 side for a laugh.

The game opened up a bit after that and we almost added a second when Holy raced out of his goal, only to get back and toe-poke James Jones' effort away at the last second. Jones had a good outing for us, his industry and endeavour ar excellent (something you could say about the whole squad) and his performances will surely bring him another goal soon; I wouldn't be surprised if he doesn't bag against Crewe on Tuesday night. I felt he popped up more in the channels than usual yesterday, complementing Anderson and Eyoma on the right-hand side in a real potent area of the field for us. By the way, TJ Eyoma; what a player he is. Seven or eight every single week and as strong as a reinforced, eight-inch-thick steel wall. Luckily, he is incredibly mobile too and for me, is showing signs of a player that might just appear in the top flight on a regular basis by the time he is in his early twenties.

I also want to mention Conor McGrandles, a player who runs more than Mo Farrah. His energy was exceptional and he plays (in my eyes) almost as a six and an eight. Very rarely did Ipswich pick up possession and McGrandles not suddenly appeared from nowhere to harras and cajole. He won't ever seemingly get the plaudits as Man of the Match, not with so many eye-catching players around him, but his work is absolutely essential to the cause and the main reason we probably haven't seen Robbie Gotts as yet.

The second major talking point from the game came at the death, as City looked to close the result down. I thought there was a foul against us on the edge of our defensive area, but the referee didn't give it and we broke upfield. Harry Anderson streaked away at pace, heading for the corner and showing all the energy of the first minute, not the 93rd, with a trail of players in his wake. Jon Nolan, a player we know all-too-well, showed the same energy (something he hadn't shown all game) to lunge across with an atrocious challenge. It was cynical and the actions of a frustrated and niggly player. He wasn't saving the game with a professional foul, he hadn't just been fouled himself but he stuck a studs-up challenge in on Harry which could have easily caused serious injury. It was petulant, nasty and exactly what we eventually came to expect from Nolan (remember Eastleigh away). It sparked scenes that some would say 'marred the game', or were 'disgraceful', but that Michael Appleton had a begrudging respect for.

'You take one of us on, you take us all on' he said after the game, and the fact Tayo Edun stuck himself in amongst much bigger men, and that Alex Palmer ran the length of the pitch to be a part of showed that. I know some will condemn it, but I've been saying nice footballing sides have to be built on tough foundations. We have to be able to work without the ball, we have to be able to win ugly and we have to be together. I try to shy away from comparisons with the past, but remember these triumphs: GMVC 88, promotion 98, title 2017 – what did they all have? Great team spirit. As the game wound down and players exchanged their frank views, you saw that togetherness in this side. Another lesson we learned, another aspect of MA's Aspiration Squad to love.

That ended the game and before we could (metaphorically) stand on our seat and sing we're top of the league, Paul Lambert gave us another wonderful moment to enjoy, as he blasted the referee and earned a red card for his troubles. Of course, his post-match reaction has given everyone a laugh, both Lincoln and Ipswich fans, making the result even sweeter.

In my living room, as the iFollow feed cut out and my afternoon's joy was ended far more abruptly than I would have liked, I lamented our exclusion from the ground with a deep, sickening sadness. Sometimes, a 1-0 win is unremarkable (Tranmere last season, Bristol Rovers in December 2006) and sometimes a 1-0 win sticks with you forever (yesterday, Swindon in 2006, Burnley). Sometimes, a result is much more than a goal and three points, it is incident-packed and something you want to be a part of. Sometimes, it sends you to the top of the league and on the very rarest of occasions, it means you are the top-ranked team when the FA Cup draw is made. This game will be one that Imps fans will almost certainly never forget, and is likely to be a quiz question on this very site in ten year's time, if we last that long!

There are even occasions where a 1-0 win is still making you tweet and sing 24 hours later, maybe even 48 hours later. I know, right now, as he goes downstairs to get ready to walk his dog, Radley, my Dad is singing 'we are top of the league' to himself. I just wish, deeply, that I could have heard it for real from the seat directly behind mine in Sincil Bank yesterday, rather than imagining it now.

Still, at least we can all go to the circus this week, eh? Or, if you're an Ipswich fan under Lambert's control, every week.

The Beat Goes On: Crewe Alexandra 0-1 Imps
October 27, 2020

Throughout my life as a Lincoln City fan, I was taught to take the small victories when they could.

Good starts weren't rare, winning six and drawing one in 1989/90 had me dreaming of promotion, but it never materialised. Sometimes, those runs of six wins came at the end of a season, or on occasion, the result was just a win against a top side, like Preston in 1995/96. You know, deep down, that there are teams better than you out there, no matter what sequence we put together, That is what being a Lincoln City fan is all about.

Arguably, 2016/17 changed that to a degree, and of course we on the League Two title, but those were one-offs in a long run of acceptance. It's not a terrible place to be in, at least we have those runs, right?

As Lewis Montsma rattled a 35-yard effort against the bar, I began to wonder if maybe this season was different. Not just because we reacted to our defeat, but because we are in the third-tier of English football and are not only the best team I have seen this season, but apparently the best the Crewe commentators have seen to.

Okay, the last paragraph had a minor lie in it. I would have thought that if iFollow had done its job. I paid for the feed at 5 pm, but after coming in from doing Matchday Live, I was greeted with a message that read something like 'you don't have access to this video'. I paid again, got access and settled in to watch the game. Two minutes before kick-off, it cut out and again I got 'access denied'. then couldn't log in to the Lincoln City site, I kept getting a bouncing ball, so in the end I registered as a new user with Crewe Alexandra and paid for their service instead. Seriously, when is the EFL going to address this problem? It took me about eight minutes and I was logged in by the time Tom Hopper hit the post, but once again I missed some of the game due to the awful service. it wouldn't be so bad, but we're paying £10 a time, and not I have to wait to see if iFollow takes the other £20 off my card that seemingly went through, but then cut out. Madness.

Maybe I had my thoughts about our brilliance when Hopper hit the post, although I distinctly heard my dad say 'for f*ck$ sake Hopper' when he did, even though I wasn't in Wragby tonight.

The first half saw an Imps side with just one change play some of the finest football Imps' fans have seen in years, if not ever. We ebbed and flowed with a real purpose, tested both flanks with eager running and in reality, we should have been five nil up after 20 minutes. When someone says that about a game, I often treat it with scepticism, but we really were rampant. Crewe weren't awful, Beckles looked a bit suspect, but they didn't crumble. Instead, we were just good. Another aspect of being a Lincoln fan is having the opposition claim to be woeful and off it when you play well, diminishing your efforts. Not today. Also, David Artell won't be lamenting a referee either, I think there was one booking all game in a match that flowed really well. Nope, no blame, no excuses, just a really, really good Lincoln City performance.

I'm not sure what my highlight of the first half was, up to the goal. Brennan Johnson' purpose and poise are coming to the fore more and more, he teased and terrorised Perry Ng, a top young full-back. Every time Johnson gets the ball, you wonder if we're going to score. Every time Harry got the ball in the first half, you knew we'd attack with purpose. James Jones looked eager to get a goal, Connor McGrandles was like a reality TV celebrity (he seemed to pop up everywhere), and Jorge Grant was just Jorge Grant. It was a very good performance indeed, but it lacked one thing.

May I offer a tiny bit of criticism? We must start putting the golden chances away. McGrandles, Montsma, Hopper and Johnson could all have scored long before Harry put us ahead. Mind you, when we did get a goal, what a strike it was. Harry showed great awareness receiving the ball on the edge of the area, turning smartly before firing a low finish past the keeper from the edge of the area. I thought Harry was our Man of the Match, and his goal was just reward for the Imps complete and utter domination of the opening 45 minutes.

I think had our next great chance gone in on 50 minutes, we might have got four or five. Johnson's effort was palmed up into the air by the Crewe keeper, and somehow he scooped it away from goal as Tom Hopper came steaming in. The ball seemed to defy gravity as it twisted away from goal, bouncing out for a corner. I felt that we were a sure-fire bet to go on and get more, but gradually, Crewe got back into the game.

This isn't a poor Crewe side, not one bit, and I guarantee you they won't trouble the bottom four when the dust settles in May. They showed that by forcing themselves into the fixture as we looked to tire. Charlie Kirk started to get on the ball a bit and the game slowed down as the rain made the surface slick and slippery. We did occasionally tease forward, usually through Johnson or Anderson, but the balance of power shifted.

With 20 minutes left, Crewe brought on Chris Porter and Daniel Powell and that brought about a massive change in emphasis. Gone was their passing game, which to be fair had brought them little, instead, Beckles started pumping it forward. let us be a bit harsh here; the lad wasn't getting much joy with his passes on the floor, but when he started pumping it into the big man, it worked much better. Maybe a bit of his Shrewsbury experience coming through there. Porter and Mandron came to life as the big balls kept coming in, and instead of waxing lyrical about our forward, I got a chance to see our defence in action.

Joe Walsh has started four games for City now, and has amassed four clean sheets, which is a fair reflection of how well he has done. As an attacking force, Lewis Montsma grabs the headlines and don't get me wrong, the young Dutchman was excellent again, but with Walsh alongside him, we do look very, very solid. Montsma has to be up there as a possible Man of the Match too, he got in to turn a Powell cross out for a corner when another second would have seen it turned in for a goal, and either him or Walsh got their head to anything and almost everything that Crewe threw into the box. Almost.

Crewe did get a couple of half-chances, Mandron could have done better after a cross from the left, whilst Powell caused problems on the rare occasions they got the ball out to him. Eyoma and Edun both knew they'd been in a game by the end of proceedings, as did McGrandles who prominently featured at the back in those dying minutes. It was backs-to-the-wall, all-for-one defending that showed that firm foundation I keep talking about. We're pretty when we attack, but we can be ugly at the back as well. I've said it before and I'll say it again: successful teams don't just play nice football, but are rock solid and dogged at the back. Right now, we have both of those attributes.

As the minute ebbed away, you did wonder if maybe fresh legs would be an option, but instead, every player got 94 minutes, including stoppages, under their belts. Credit to each and every one of them, they battled hard for a 1-0 win that should have perhaps been much more comfortable than it was in the end. I always praise players for getting in positions to miss chances, and we proved in 2018/19 that even without a 15-goal striker, you can win titles, but I do feel we just need to be better in the eighteen-yard area. Yes, we have kept four clean sheets in a row, but in those four matches we have only scored twice from open play. Look, I'm not taking anything away from this side and I firmly believe we will keep getting better, hopefully that will manifest itself in us achieving our xG, because when we do, a bunch of poor buggers are going to get one hell of a thumping.

The evening ends with us still top of the table, 20% of the way through the season. Nothing is won and lost in October, not when the season kicked off three or four weeks late, but for many of us, finishing outside the bottom four is the first aim. Unless something goes catastrophically wrong, that will be achieved, and if we keep playing as we are, we might even be genuine play-off candidates.

Yep, you heard that right. That's how good we are looking right now, and when you consider the players we have to bring in (Archibald, Gotts, Roughan, Jackson, Morton, Scully….) as well as the fact Bridcutt was missing, there is no reason why we can't keep winning games, why we can't keep more clean sheets, why we can't hold our own right up there. The only two sides I am genuinely looking at with concern are Hull City and Peterborough, but I'm sure a whole load of clubs are looking at us and thinking exactly the same.

Remember, we're the best side Crewe have seen this season, and we're nine games in. Look what Michael Appleton has achieved with this squad in such a short space of time. His players, playing his tactics, have got us all on the edge of our seat, dribbling in anticipation like I do when they lay that sirloin steak out in front of me at the Bluebell in Belchford. Even some of the critical voices on Twitter are purring with delight. Maybe, just maybe, those preconceptions that I held as a Lincoln City fan are being brushed to one side.

Maybe, this really is the dawning of a new era. On tonight's evidence, it might just be.

My apologies for the unusual optimism and perhaps outlandish talk of the top six, but the honesty shout is I'm finding it hard to keep my feet on the ground, as a lot of you will be too. Michael Appleton's boys are the real deal. Oxford fans told us so, and they might just be right.

November

Fear and Loathing at the Keepmoat: Doncaster 1-0 Imps
November 1, 2020 0

I can't help but think about a whole host of other things as I write this article. I know we lost a game of football and fans of the site will be expecting the usual analysis and dissection, but I'm finding it hard.

Thanks to the calamitous way in which the impending lockdown has been announced, I spent most of yesterday's game with one eye on Twitter, wondering how it might affect us, as a club, and of course Fe, Charlie and I as a household. My Dad was due last night, could he come over? What about my trip to see my brother next week and give my nephew a gift for passing hid 11+? Can I do that? I had hoped to join the media team for Match Day Live at Sincil Bank over November as well, could that happen? With my birthday coming up as well, I hoped to go for a meal with five other members of my family, but I guess that's up the swanny now as well.

You will all have your problems and worries around the lockdown. I heard a blog reader's father is currently in hospital with the virus, and I wish him a speedy recovery. These are challenging times, for each and every one of us, but please remember this: someone's always better off than you, and someone is always worse off. The time to be kind is now, the time to debate and be divisive is when the handling of this pandemic is analysed once it is over. One day, it will be over.

I guess the news of a 4 pm announcement (contempt for football fans again) really disrupted everything pre-match, then as it moved towards 7 pm it just dragged out the inevitable. It was hard to watch the game of football without other things on our mind. What made it even worse was seeing the video of the 617 boys during Match Day Live too. For the first time since March, I felt sick at what we were missing. This 'life' we have now, masks, restrictions, fear, it is pure George Orwell. Watching block 7, upper and lower, bouncing to their own rhythm, made me misty-eyed for the past. Hearing the entire Coop joining in, seeing just how good it was, I'll be honesty (and you can call me what you want) I wanted to cry. I don't do crying, not for much at all (unless I step on a plug or pull out a nose hair with roots like a tree), but as the VT ran yesterday, with the imminent spectre of restrictions hanging over us like the ghost of 2020 past, I could have cried. I didn't though, I'm a pro.

In the middle of all this was a football match against the best team I have seen us play this season. Pre-match, we heard from 18Dapper and he told us how losing the likes of Tulloch, Gomes and John-Jules to injury hadn't been a reason for them not winning games. As I watched Okenabirhie fail to get on the end of at least two clear-cut chances early doors, I wondered if he might have been wrong. Look, I spend a lot of time talking about Lincoln but yesterday, I owe it to Doncaster to talk about them. In midweek, we blew Crewe away and David Artell suggested it was them being poor which made us look good. I know we didn't help ourselves yesterday, but credit where it is due, Donny are a good side.

I may have underestimated Darren Moore on the podcast. His side were superbly organised and found a way to counteract our approach with a high press and fast-paced harassing. They balanced that by being steadier when they had possession, so their energy was spent chasing us and they seemed to conserve it on the ball. I know it led Michael and Thommo to mention they looked slow in the build-up, but it was part of the plan I think. We break quickly, but we were forced into making bad decisions. How many times did McGrandles, Edun, even Eyoma and Montsma, give the ball away? A fair few, because they were closed down in packs, twos and even threes, shutting off any option. It doesn't matter if Harry Anderson is on for a thirty-yard switch pass if the view is restricted by some very talented midfielders.

Both sides had chances, theirs were perhaps better than ours. I thought it was an engrossing first half in which we defended well against their slow build-up, but they throttled our quicker approach, suffocating us on the ball. Dare I say, for the first time this season, their midfield was better than ours. Ben Whiteman is a hell of a player and his work ethics was undeniable. He had plenty of say in the first half, before the goal that ended up winning his side the game.

For us, I might get shot down here, but I thought Tom Hopper was probably one of the better players in black and red. He worked really hard all game, dropping back to defend as well as running channels and dropping out wide. The only problem it caused was that vacuum up front, which became evident later in the game. He played the lone striker role well, apart from not popping up in the areas where you want to lone striker to be. That might sound like he didn't do his job, but he did 95% of it. The 5% we might have needed, he couldn't do, but to be fair given how choked the 18-yard area was whenever we did break, it isn't a surprise. The big chance came from Brennan Johnson's shot, palmed away by their keeper. It went behind Anderson, but Hopper hadn't got himself into the area after getting back to defend. Five yards further forward and he sidefoots into the net, but instead it was cleared as he arrived late. I'm not pulling him down too much here, his work rate is unreal, but when Callum Morton is back I can see him being used as much as Hops in a 'horses for courses' scenario. Some games we need a target man, others we don't.

Shout out to the Doncaster defenders too, former Imp Tom Anderson and Joe Wright. They were never isolated against Johnson's pace or Anderson's power, due to hunting in packs and hard-working midfield. Johnson clearly terrified them, but the Forest man was marshalled very well. In truth, this Doncaster side reminded me an awful lot of us. They were functional, organised, stuck to their plan and after they got their goal, happy to keep it tight at win 1-0.

What a goal it was though. I know they say things like 'you don't stop those', and from Alex Palmer's point of view, you don't, but the midfielders might be disappointed not to have got in front of the shot. I'm not being critical here, it was a wonder strike, but there is always something you could do better. I don't doubt Michael will look at it today and have some suggestions, developmental ones of course, ahead of Pompey. If you watch the replay, Jorge Grant might feel he should have blocked the shot. Again, that's not me calling Grant out, but it is the sort of thing a diligent manager might pick up on and discuss on Monday.

The second half flew past, perhaps because I kept thinking about the 5 pm press conference, but I didn't ever feel we were going to get back into the game, even though we weren't out of it either. I just felt Doncaster had their 'refuse to lose' head-on and, as we pushed more men forward, they were more likely to take the win. It was entertaining, but something at the back of my mind stopped me becoming too invested in it.

We weren't getting mauled, but Jon Taylor's pace did have Tayo Edun on toast a time or two and he could easily have made it 2-0, but for a great stop by Palmer. Johnson, by far our most potent threat, could have levelled as he fired across goal not long after as the game opened up a bit. I think what disappointed me the most was our threat from set-pieces; we had plenty of corners and a couple of free-kicks in good areas and I don't recall us getting one effort on target from any of them. Given how good we looked with Montsma and Jackson earlier in the season, it's another area I feel Doncaster had tied up nice and tight.

Being honest, it was a tough afternoon for a few players. TJ Eyoma had a rare 'six' at full-back, and Tayo Edun certainly struggled against the pace thrown at him. Lewis Montsma's passing was awry, as was Conor McGrandles in the middle of the park. There was no ebb or flow to our approach, but we kept on pushing and pressing where we needed to. I felt we might get one chance that we'd rue missing and we did, Theo

Archibald coming on and firing his first touch into the side netting. In Theo, I see a bit of the Brennan Johnson, a maverick winger with skills to pay the bills. If that touch is his third or fourth, I think it goes in, but having come straight on and having it as his first sight of the ball, he just didn't catch it right.

That was more or less that. I'm not sure what was more unwatchable, bumbling Boris and his circus clowns on the TV in the late evening, or the iFollow stream which was woeful for different reasons from normal. I got on fine, nor spinning wheel at all, but I missed half the game due to incessant replays, often going over the top of proper action. At several points, there was a chance and immediately the replay came on, whilst the chance was still alive, leaving us to rely on commentary as we got to watch what had just happened, rather than what was happening (which is what I pay for). I've said it before, I'll say it again, iFollow is awful. Sadly, it is critical to the club and it is a great way to watch every minute of Imps' action, but it is head-scratchingly bad at times.

When the final whistle did sound, signalling our first away defeat of the season, I felt miserable and down, but not for the defeat. Being honest, the better side won. No complaints, it was a game in which we competed, but didn't quite reach the levels we have of late. To play Devil's Advocate, we should be happy that we're going to the Keepmoat as equals and when the home side win, they're delighted to have done so. In 2007, we went there in the Carling Cup and were thrashed 4-1, with the two clubs never so far apart. This result, whilst not ideal, is part of a bigger picture in which we seem to be an established League One side capable of sustaining top ten football. I'll take that, even if we can't be in the ground to give our players that little push they need, and to create memories of our own.

Lockdown is now imminent, the future of the club, and others like us, is still up in the air and we are living in such unprecedented times, driven by fear, uncertainty and division. When you consider the bigger picture (not the nefarious power-grab Big Picture pedalled by the big clubs), the wider problems and the environment that is 2020, it makes a narrow 1-0 defeat at Doncaster seem almost insignificant.

It isn't, but it seemed that way for a while last night, more or less until I sat down here to write about it. We're back on the horse this week with the first of four home games in a row and you know, 100%, that when the whistle blows to start the game on Tuesday we'll be bang at it, again, doing what we do best, again.

Alex Bradley Departs Sincil Bank
November 3, 2020

Alex Bradley has joined National League side Yeovil Town on a loan deal which will run until January 10th.

The midfielder, who has also been deployed as a right-back, spent much of last season out on loan with Harrogate Town, who he helped towards their Football League promotion. He joins a Glovers side in a very different position, second from bottom of the table, having played more games than the two sides they are level on points with.

Yeovil's hierarchy are clearly delighted to have secured Alex on a temporary basis, as they explained.

"Firstly, Lincoln were great to deal with and we thank them for allowing us to have Alex for the foreseeable future," said Yeovil boss Darren Sarll. "Terry and I watched Alex last year for Harrogate and were always impressed and that was backed by the number of our football confidents that recommended Alex to us.

"Alex has a power and energy that is vital to the way we play, he adds real depth to the right side of our defence and midfield and I have been really pleased with his character in the first few days. He's another player that comes off of a winning experience last season and I am really looking forward to seeing him play for us."

Alex has appeared three times for the Imps, in the EFL Cup against Crewe and Liverpool, as well as the EFL trophy draw with Scunthorpe United. He has slipped down the pecking order at the Bank, with MA seemingly seeing him as more of a right-back, which puts Robbie Gotts and TJ Eyoma ahead of him for a first-team place.

Time to reflect, not react: Imps 1-3 Portsmouth
November 3, 2020

Tonight's defeat will have surprised few, and whilst supporters may be disappointed, it is just a reminder of where we are at the moment.

Being forced not changes is never ideal, and with Montsma, Morton, Walsh and Bridcutt injured, as well as Melbourne only just on his way back, there was a makeshift feeling about the side. This, against a side bang in form and boasting a £2m striker, as well as two other players in Curtis and Harness who would command seven-figure fees right now. That's where we are though, League One, a division packed full of haves and have nots. For me, this was the final game of our horrible start, and whilst the result wasn't a big surprise, we have to take stock of where we are on the whole journey, not just this one encounter.

Pompey are the only side to beat Michael Appleton's Lincoln on a Tuesday night, and they've done it three times since he joined, but they are a side who operate in a financial sphere far in excess of our own. That was evident in the names that appeared on the scoresheet, one of which was the excellent John Marquis.

Four minutes in and the Imps trailed, which asked a real question of our young side which wasn't answered. Marquis was the scorer, curling a wonderful shot into the back of the net with Alex Palmer stranded. Being a little critical, TJ Eyoma's challenge was weak in trying to block the effort, but overall I thought Eyoma had a decent game. The sad thing to see was it wasn't the first chance the visitors had, in an early spell of dominance. When a visiting team comes out of the blocks early, and gets something to defend, it doesn't bode well.

Not that Portsmouth went defensive at all, the Imps just couldn't find a flow, Pompey looked in complete control as the makeshift right-hand side lacked the potency usually seen Eyoma and Anderson. Jorge Grant's endeavour was as consistent as usual, but there just wasn't the space to exploit against a good, organised defence. The long, sweeping balls were not effective, and it appeared that the Imps needed to be patient. Still, half-chances did come.

The Imps first real opening came from a corner, but it was the efforts of Pompey keeper Craig MacGillivray that led to deep breaths from his own bench. He flapped at the delivery, but a red shirt couldn't take advantage of the loose ball and the chance went away. The keeper was back in action on the quarter-hour mark, Robbie Gotts looking to get a shot away from the edge of the area from Johnson's lay off. It was a half-chance, but it signalled that the Imps were trying to get back in the game.

How I've missed you, spinning wheel. Anyone who says it is my internet ought to note I can film matchday live in my shed on the same connection. Damn you, iFollow.

Roughan turned provider a few minutes later, after work from Tom Hopper. The 17-year-old's ball whipped across the six-yard box, where Anthony Scully's header wasn't quite enough to test the keeper.

With little space to exploit, it was the best the Imps could hope for, a quick delivery into the area. Whilst the Imps were grabbing half chances, the constant threat of Marquis loomed large. His movement is excellent, and it is clear to see why he is so highly rated.

The final fifteen minutes of the half were best described as tepid. Anthony Scully looked hungry and created two corners for the Imps, but neither posed a problem against a side comfortable in dealing with balls in from wide areas. Eventually, Brennan Johnson and Scully began to come inside looking for the ball, but with little space and plenty of congestion, it seemed to be a blocked route. Whenever the Imps did lose the ball, Pompey were potent in pressing forward, looking to move through the thirds at pace. Sean Roughan was certainly having a tough time against Marcus Harness and for every good action he did, such as a pass or a cross, the youngster also had an adverse action, such as selling McGrandles short on a throw which led to Adam Jackson furiously remonstrating with the pair.

That's not to just criticise Roughan though. Robbie Gotts had a suspect first half, looking easily barged off the ball by a strong and physical Portsmouth. Our midfield trio just couldn't get going, Grant's creativity was coming from too deep and neither McGrandles nor Jones looked capable of creating space for the wide players. Much of our approach was relying on Johnson and Scully getting on the ball and causing problems, but both were choked out by three or four players. When we did manage to get into decent positions, there seemed to be a lack of presence in the middle.

Still, at half time despite the obvious shortcomings, it was only 1-0 and Portsmouth certainly hadn't handed us our arses as we did Crewe a week ago. Instead, a Lincoln who were not quite at it had weathered the storm against a side packed with quality and players arguably worth seven figures. Would the second half see the exciting young guns of Lincoln back to their best?

In a word, no, not at all. Ronan Curtis had the first effort of the second period after once again getting the better of Gotts, who had a thoroughly uncomfortable debut for City. When City did break Hopper either tried to buy a free kick, and failed, or was caught offside. The former Southend man certainly puts the yards in, but being blunt, he didn't look like scoring a goal at that stage. John Marquis did though, and before we hit fifty minutes the game was over. A great cross went over Jackson's head and there was Marquis to nod home. 2-0 down and having not looked like scoring from open play, the writing was on the wall.

Instead of us looking like scoring, an excellent Portsmouth kept the pressure on. Most of their good work came down the attacking left, Marcus Harness and Ronan Curtis both looking very lively indeed. Palmer's save from the former on 58 minutes kept the score at 2-0, but only for a couple of minutes. Incessant Pompey pressure saw a shot across the goal just evade Marquis, but in the same attack, Ronan Curtis lashed in the third. Two minutes later, another Palmer save kept the score mildly respectable. Mildly.

Robbie Gotts came off just after, he had a torrid debut and with Lewis Montsma out, Harry Anderson slipped in at right-back. Harry's introduction did seem to put a little stability onto the right side of the Imps' attack, but it was never going to be enough. When it isn't your night, it just isn't. To be fair, we weren't woeful, we were just poor in key areas and they were ruthless in possession. The enforced changes to the starting XI just didn't work, this time. When Joe Walsh was forced into the side, he settled quickly, but as I've mentioned, Robbie Gotts struggled and Anthony Scully looked positive in flashes but just never got going. Roughan, who has been out of the side, was inconsistent in possession and although he showed some good moments, he also struggled at times to contain his man on the attacking right.

One thing this Lincoln side do have is spirit, and on 72 minutes we did get a goal from open play. James Jones and Anthony Scully broke on the right, and the ball ended up at the feet of Harry Anderson. He worked a great cross into the six-yard box and finally, Tom Hopper got his head on the ball to give the Imps a glimmer of hope. Hopefully, that will give Hopps some confidence going into to next few matches, because up until that moment I wouldn't have bet on him being the Imps to get on the scoresheet. Brennan Johnson, maybe, but few of the other players really looked like being rewarded for their running.

It was the introduction of Harry Anderson which changed the emphasis, and if we were going to get anything from the game, it was coming through Harry on his 150th league game for City, despite Brennan Johnson believing it would be him. The Forest man had another shot straight at the keeper after good work from TJ Eyoma, but he may have been better feeding in James Jones, who needs a goal just as much as Hopper did.

The game just petered out after that, and we can have few complaints. Pompey always looked dangerous, from the first minute to the last. As for us, we can complain about the players who were off it, if we want, but the truth is we have outperformed expectation and if you'd offered my fourth and 22 points at the stage, I would have taken it. We must remember to never be too high when we win, and never too low when we lose, not against a side who expect to be in the top two, and who really should be. This wasn't a disaster for City, we were outfought, but we stuck to our ethos and had a decent closing half-hour, even if the game was largely over by then.

We know how high the bar is now and without a £2m striker, we're not going to get there, yet. However, there is still plenty to be optimistic about and sometimes, you have to accept where you are, where you're going and that at times, the route might not always be easy going. There is no point in supporters reacting badly to one result when the overall play-off picture is one you never expected to be a part of in the first place.

Irresistible City progress in style: Imps 6-2 Forest Green
November 7, 2020

On paper, it looked tricky for the Imps this afternoon as we hunted a place in the second round.

The pre-match build-up was all about ghosts of the past; that FA Cup run in 2016/17, the previous wins against Mark Cooper's men that are timeless and iconic. With injuries and other circumstances building up, this could have been a banana skin, a game which we wouldn't look back on so fondly. Whilst the win might not result in a quarter-final appearance, and it might not turn around our entire season, it was a masterclass in attacking football from Lincoln City 2020, the next chapter.

In terms of team news, there was plenty for fans to digest. Out went TJ Eyoma, James Jones, Conor McGrandles and Tom Hopper, in came Max Melbourne, Harry Anderson, Theo Archibald and Tayo Edun. That didn't tell the whole story though, with a major reshuffle seeing only Adam Jackson keep his place in the back four from Tuesday, with Roughan shifting across from full-back. The midfield saw Robbie Gotts join Tayo Edun and Jorge Grant, whilst Theo Archibald's first Sincil Bank start against his former side.

Interestingly, Forest Green made a number of changes, with Jamille Matt, Jordan Moore-Taylor and former Imps trialist Eboue Adams all dropping out of the side. It meant an unpredictable game, one that was hard for so-called pundits such as me to call.

The first half-chance of the game came courtesy of Theo Archibald. His run down the right stretched the Forest Green defence, but a teasing cross just evaded the onrushing Brennan Johnson. Minutes later, the visitors got their first chance, a ball from the attacking left splitting Jackson and Roughan, neither of whom could recover to stop Bailey's effort. Luckily, Alex Palmer didn't need to either. Whilst the early exchanges hinted at a tight game, we did need a little slice of luck to go our way.

Should Tayo have walked before the ten-minute mark? His tackle drew the first yellow of the game, but it was late, high and if it came against us, we'd be screaming blue murder. Again, luckily for us, the ref pulled out a yellow. Two let-offs in a minute or so.

It was a slow start from the Imps and little hinted at what was to come. Max Melbourne certainly found it tough with a few stray passes, before giving a cheap free-kick away on the edge of the area. Luckily, again, the Imps dealt with a poor delivery, but the pressure continued, mostly down the right-hand side at Melbourne. With him and Theo appearing with each other for the first time, there did seem to be a lack of cohesion, earlier on in the game at least. Max grew into the game though, and once he had got rid of the cobwebs, he looked much more composed and argubaly by the time the clock struck 90 he had one of his best games in a Lincoln shirt.

One player really standing out for City in the first 15 was Harry Anderson, composed at the back but offering plenty going forward too. You do have to wonder if wing-back might be his position in a year or two, he has all the right attributes, pace and power which he uses well.

16 minutes into the game, the breakthrough came. Jorge Grant picked up a loose ball just inside the attacking half, drove forward ten yards and released a vicious drive past the keeper. It was arguably the best goal we have scored this season so far (maybe just better than Jones against Bradford), a truly wonderful strike that would be worthy of winning any game at all. It had shades of Ronnie Radford's famous FA Cup goal according to Michael Hortin and it is hard to disagree. That gave us something to defend and gave them a reason to come out and attack us, which opened the game right up. It certainly left some space for us to exploit, and the midfield looked consistently dangerous. Jorge Grant threaded a ball through to Johnson who was marginally offside and not long after, Edun's sumptuous ball almost cut the defence open again, but a last-ditch challenge stopped a clear Johnson chance.

On 22 minutes, Anthony Scully's usual dogged persistence saw him get away in the area and the Forest Green defender was left with no option but to haul him back. It was blatant, and right in front of the referee. There was no other choice for the referee than to point to the spot, and that was that. Jorge Grant might have bagged a worldly to open the scoring, but it was business as usual from 12 yards as he stroked home the spot-kick to make it 2-0 with less than a quarter of the match gone.

Forest Green looked unsettled after that; they still looked hungry in attack, but Cooper was getting angry on the touchline, whilst the players seemed to be arguing amongst each other after the odd wasted chance. That's the way we've beaten FGR before; get them to self implode. They're a good side, there's no doubt about that, but the Imps looked better and they didn't like it, not one bit.

City looked likely to score whenever they went forward, with the opposition keeper in a real mess. One of his clearances was cut out by Harry Anderson, who dropped a ball into the path of Scully to fire wide. Their defence looked terrified by the Imps' pace and running and Scully was one of their main antagonists. He was dropping deep, despite playing out wide, and fed in Brennan Johnson just past the half-hour mark. The Forest man scooped his lob into the keeper's arms, but it was yet another good move from the Imps. It should have been 3-0 just before halftime, Scully again the provider for Johnson, who timed his run perfectly but his shot was parried. It fell to Robbie Gotts who couldn't quite get a clean strike on it, but the young midfielder was close. He had a strong first half, shrugging off the disappointment of Pompey.

Within a whisker of it being 3-0, it should have been 2-1. Sean Roughan played a loose ball out which caused momentary panic, leading to a corner. The corner was nodded back across the area and should have been touched in at the back stick. It wasn't, and a glorious chance to be back in the game slipped past the opposition. Even as injury time approached, Brennan Johnson created a chance for himself, charging the keeper down and dispossessing him, but the ball just ran too wide for him to have an effort at goal. It was still a great piece of closing down from Johnson, who had been as dangerous as ever the whole half.

It had been a good first half from the Imps, with the three midfield players having a strong game. Tayo Edun was looking very comfortable on the ball and found some key passes, playing what I would call the James Jones role. On the other hand, Robbie Gotts was perfectly emulating Conor McGrandles, covering every blade of grass and looking really busy. As for Jorge Grant, he was just doing what he does. Owning it.

The early pressure in the second half, much like the first, came from the Imps and the result was never really in doubt.

Harry Anderson's pace clearly still frightened the visitors, even after a half time regroup, and he was fouled twice in quick succession, the second time by Elliott Whitehouse. That led to little, but Forest Green still looked on the ropes, often being chased back into their own half. When they did compose themselves they were playing some decent football, Matt Stevens firing wide after a rare foray forward courtesy perhaps of Roughan's physical presence. It was all very pedestrian though, they lacked the cutting edge that we kept hinting at, laboriously coming forward with little purpose or energy.

Theo Archibald came close in a second half that, at first at least, seemed slower as it progressed. He got on the end of a lovely Jorge Grant pass that split two defenders, but the former Celtic man pulled his ball across goal and wide if the far post.

The game may have slowed a little in the opening 15 of the second period, but it accelerated after the hour mark into a fine spectacle once again. It was Archibald again who started the move that effectively finished the tie. This time he split two defenders with a through pass, finding Brennan Johnson. His finish was excellent, he dropped a shoulder, beat a man and bought a yard as he drove forward before he slotted the ball into the keeper's right-hand side. 3-0, get our name in the hat. It was just reward for Johnson too, who has been lively for weeks now and has come close on plenty of occasions. We would have missed him had we had to face Gillingham, he could be this season's Tyler Walker, such is his impact. Given the Wales connections, he almost like a cross between his former teammate and Joe Morrell.

On occasions, the Imps found themselves watching the game from the defensive third, but not being threatened. When the ball changed hands, the transition was swift as we swept up the pitch with speed. Theo Archibald, who certainly worked hard on his first home start, lashed over after a quick break involved Johnson and Scully. It was certainly impressive stuff from the Imps, who did look like the League One side. There is a danger for the higher level team to be matched in cup ties and for neutrals to say stuff like 'you couldn't tell which side was from the lower league'. Well, on this occasion, you absolutely could. I wondered if the two styles would produce an entertaining game and it did, but one side did it much, much better than the other.

Another of our young guns, Zack Elbouzedi, got fifteen minutes at the end of the game, joining Conor McGrandles and James Jones as subs for the Imps. When changes are made it can upset the flow of a tie, but within seconds of the Ireland Under 21 coming on it was 4-0. Scully, another of our international prospects, found Wales all-up Johnson with a pass. He knocked it to James Jones, who flicked a neat backheel into the path of the advancing Scully who angled his effort again past the keeper's right-hand side. It was a typical Lincoln move, and it killed off the visitors once and for all. Time and again this season, we have threatened to run riot without doing so, and this was the perfect way to sign off for ten days or so.

Everything went a little crazy after that, Forest Green finally went gung ho and left lots of space at the back. On 82 minutes, Elliott Whitehouse got the goal he will have been keen to get, sneaking in to give the visitors a little bit of pride. It was disappointing for the Imps to concede, but six minutes later our four-goal lead was restored. Anthony Scully, another who had an excellent game, received a pass from Thommo's

Man of the Match Harry Anderson to lash the ball past the keeper. That came just as the board went up for injury time, and by the time the clock struck 90, it was 6-1. James Jones' cameo might have been brief, but he added a goal to his assist, and a smartly taken one at that, twisting in a tight spot to hook a left-footed effort into the net. That will do Jones' confidence the world of good, he's been solid throughout the last month but to chip in with a goal and assist should give him a big boost.

That wasn't the end of the goals either, Jake Young managed to get a late consolation after finding space in the Imps' area. It was far too little, far too late, and the last action of an exciting cup tie.

I don't know what was more pleasing; the fact we won 6-2, the fact we finally made good on the goalscoring promise we have shown against the likes of Crewe, or the fact that some of our fringe players stepped up and played well. Even the established first team player sin different positions played well, another huge boost. Finally, and perhaps the most joyous of all for some, it is seven wins in seven matches against Mark Cooper's Forest Green. You could almost take the words Forest Green away from the end of that sentence and it still be just as pleasing to read.

Thommo picked Harry Anderson as his Man of the Match, but there were so many contenders. Brennan Johnson would be a very close second, and Anthony Scully would have to be around the top three as well. I thought Gotts and Edun were superb as well, and Max Melbourne returning with such a solid performance is a big boost. It is hard to call anyone out when you have won 6-2 though, and from Alex Palmer to the last sub Zack Elbouzedi, everyone came out of it positively.

On Monday, we go into the hat for the second round, a good achievement for the club. Not only do we get a stab at progression, but the £17k prize money for winning today will be a big boost for the financials, and hopefully a favourable tie in the next round can set us up for a bigger payday. There isn't a bad thing to say about today, another good chapter in the Michael Appleton saga.

Ok, so it might not yet have the storyline of the DC trilogy, but this isn't a tale of the underdog rising up, not yet. This is the next level, the next phase and one might say the MArvel universe, a very different one to the 2016/17 season. This is slick football, exciting and goal-laden. It is perhaps best summed up by two comparisons – this is the first time I have not felt like we'd lose going in to play Forest Green, and it is the first time I have seen us beat them so utterly comprehensively by playing football the right way. There is nothing Cooper can moan about tonight, other than simply being outclassed by a much, much better football team.

Meaningless workout brings penalty joy: Imps 1-1 Man City (4-3 on pens)
November 17, 2020

Let us be honest, tonight really was a non-event. The Imps needed a win to top the group in a tournament which isn't seeded.

All that was really at stake was £10,000, the possibility of a home te and potential injuries. Topping the group gives you a home te, unless you draw an Under 21 side, then the opposition will be at home. One wonders, what if two Under 21 teams draw each other?

Anyway, with Zack Elbouzedi, Brennan Johnson, and Anthony Scully on international duty, plus Lewis Montsma, Joe Walsh, Callum Morton and Jamie Soule all injured, the key was just to get through the game unscathed. In one bit of good news for the Imps, Liam Bridcutt returned for his first match back after a short spell out.

As for Manchester City Under 21s, their squad numbers went up to 96, which reflects youth hoarding if ever there was one. They started brightly too, looking to play a strong, possession-based game. On the other hand, the Imps struggled to settle in the early exchanges, with the best chances falling to Man City through mistakes at the back. An early slip by Ethan Ross almost led to a goal for Felix Nmecha, but his effort was wayward. Not long afterwards, Sean Roughan's errant pass led to a break for the boys in blue, with Remy Howarth came back to help resolve.

City's first chance of the half also came courtesy of Remy Howarth's work. He broke down the left, checked back and found Max Melbourne, whose cross was good for Tom Hopper, who headed meekly into the keeper's arms.

Keyendrah Simmonds had a shot well saved by Ross, who looked to grow in confidence after the early slip, before the first real blow of the game for City. Howarth chased a ball into the channel, pulling up clutching his hamstring. That was the end of his evening, replaced by McGrandles.

The change forced City into a major reshuffle, Robbie Gotts heading to right-back, Harry Anderson going wide right, Theo Archibald wide left and McGrandles dropping into the midfield. It didn't majorly change the complexion of the game though; the Under 21 side still dominated possession even if they didn't create clear-cut chances.

The first half was punctuated by a 'busy' referee, Carl Boyeson, who didn't get any big calls wrong, but was very precise over where throw-ins should go from, as well as perhaps handing a harsh yellow out to Liam Bridcutt early doors.

Tom Hopper was almost in for City's opener midway through the half, Melbourne and Archibald combined for the latter to put a telling ball into the danger area, but the defender just got a toe in as Hopper looked likely to meet the cross. From the resulting corner, Robbie Gotts almost made a real name for himself with an inswinger that was punched away as it looked to be heading straight in.

As the half wore on, it was Man City's U21 side that looked more likely to take the lead. Jaden Braaf showed unbelievable pace to get between Melbourne and Roughan, firing a shot at goal which got blocked. The loose rebound dropped to Nmecha, who always seemed to be in good positions, but he fired over.

Their next chance came from Oscar Bobb, he turned Robbie Gotts inside out and laid a lovely ball into the path of Simmons who fired over. It seemed the visitors were getting the upper hand, but there was still time for one last Imps chance.

Tom Hopper hunted a long ball on the left, which keeper Slicker came out for. He tried to dummy Hopper and win a goal kick, but instead saw the striker come away with the ball with him stranded. Hopper took his time to place the ball into the path of Edun, who was disposed at the last second with an open goal gaping. It was an excellent piece of defensive work from Man City's number 81, Claudio Gomes.

The Imps could have taken an early lead in the second half, a great Crossfield ball from Bridcutt found Archibald. He took his time to deliver a great ball in for Max Melbourne, who just collapsed onto it under no pressure all. It wasn't as bad as I made it sound, Max was caught by surprise and just looked like a defender being taken aback a little.

Archibald certainly looked better in the second half, putting in a quality ball not long after from good tenacity from Tayo Edun. Sadly, as has been the case for much of this season, nobody could get on the end of it.

At the other end, great work from Adrian Bernabe saw a wicked delivery which Ross claimed, but he caught a boot to the face in the process. Could that have been a reason for what was to come because he barely touched the ball after that until the final minutes.

Connor McGrandles had two shouts for a penalty, the first he looked to lean into their player before going over, but the second was certainly a decent shout away to the attacking right. Neither were given, but the yellow cards kept coming from Boyeson.

Man City could have taken the lead after great work from Bobb, but Bernabe fired over when he should have scored. It was a busy evening for Bernabe, who was one of the offending players for McGrandles penalty shouts.

Sean Roughan almost opened his account with a great effort after some good work from City, but his goalward bound shot cannoned off Tom Hopper. Hopper eventually came off, not before a booking for going in late on the keeper, with Archibald moving up top.

It was the Scot who created the Imps' goal, pressuring Gomes and Slicker into a mistake. He collected the ball, took his time to find Harry Anderson who fired confidently from the corner of the box to put the Imps ahead.

After that, City should have scored again, McGrandles seeing his excellent effort saved after some good football from the Imps. Harry Anderson combined with sub James Jones, who delivered cutely into the area. It seemed at that point as though the Imps would top the group and take the £10,000. Instead, City contrived to give the game away. Sean Roughan's weak header out dropped to Nmecha, who drove a shot straight at Ross. The keeper got down to it, but it slipped from his grasp and bobbled behind him. Before he could recover, Simmonds drove in and slammed it into the net, 1-1. Despite four minutes of injury time, little else happened and we went straight to a pointless penalty shoot out, the outcome of which meant absolutely nothing at all.

Archibald took the first penalty, firing a good penalty to the keeper's right., which Bernabe replicated afterwards to make it 1-1. Anderson took the Imps' second, striking with power and again off to the right-hand side. Nmecha then brought it level with a Panenka straight down the middle, whilst Gotts made it three in a row for City with another to the right. Lavia repeated the feat making it six from six as he fired high to Ross' left.

Sadly, James Jones saw his penalty saved as he went to the right as his teammates had done, but Slicker saved. Gyabi had a chance to make it 4-3 to the visitors, but he 'Chris Waddle'd it' over the bar to leave the scores level. Jorge Grant, who has had a bit of practice, bagged his penalty to make it 4-3, leaving Simmonds the goalscorer needing to score, which he didn't. Unlike normal time, Ross managed to stop the Man City man scoring, to give City the pointless win.

It wasn't a great spectacle, being honest. Five yellow cards for the Imps with one bad tackle all match. A penalty shoot out with no purpose at all, an empty stadium against a soulless Under 21 side and an injury to add to the growing list. However, if you put that aside, Liam Bridcutt got 60 minutes, whilst players such as Robbie Gotts, Theo Archibald and Tayo Edun all got a full game.

Harry Anderson and Liam Bridcutt certainly stood out, whilst Robbie Gotts was busy after having to change position early. Theo Archibald impressed in the second half, but he looked a little rusty in the first 45. Tayo Edun gave a typical performance too, often looking to have the ball at his feet for a little too long. There is no doubt the Imps settled once the likes of James Jones got on the field, and Harry looked strong on the right flank, showing strength and pace against some similarly quick young players.

It is hard to be too critical towards players in a meaningless game, but there is no doubt Ethan Ross will be disappointed after making two relatively big mistakes at either end of the game. Sean Roughan had a couple of dodgy moments too, but he seems to bounce back quickly with his following touches, It isn't easy for a keeper to bounce back as quickly and Ross will now have to wait until the next round, where he will almost certainly get a game.

All in all, it is a game that we got through, relatively unscathed, but we pretty much knew that already. The biggest plus will be the return of Liam Bridcutt, a player who looked energised and on form, which is what we need going into a tough game this weekend.

No VAR, No Problem: Accrington Stanley 0-0 Imps
November 22, 2020

The Imps came away from the Crown Ground with a decent draw this afternoon, but it could have been all three points with two key decisions changing the game.

Both decisions have split the fanbase and it is likely that both decisions, had we been unfortunate enough to be in the Premier League, would have been overturned immediately. That would have led to a 1-0 Imps win we wouldn't have deserved, and Sean McConville's comeback after ten months out not being ruined. We don't have VAR, thankfully, and hand on heart I can say I'm happier with 0-0 and something to debate than I would have been with a 1-0 win and constant breaks in play. I know the VAR debate doesn't touch League One anyway, but this encounter was the perfect example of 'what if'.

Michael Appleton made six changes to the team that faced Manchester City U21s, with Lewis Montsma, Adam Jackson, Jorge Grant and James Jones amongst those returning to the starting line-up. Accrington came into the game on the back of a three-game winning run, without conceding a goal in the process. They started the game four points behind the Imps, but with two games in hand have lost matches through the Covid-19 pandemic. A win could have put the Imps top of the table, if Ipswich, Hull and Charlton all drew, and Peterborough not only lost, but conceded a four-goal swing. Unlikely, but it is nice to be halfway through November and still in touching distance of the top two.

It was also the debut of the third kit, which looked really smart. I do wonder, how many times have the Imps had three kits all emblazoned with the same main sponsor? I suspect never, which really should result in fans giving Peregrine Holdings a nod of apprecation, no only for their support, but for have a subtle and succinct logo which complements all three of our kits this season.

The game started at a frenetic pace, and it could have been 1-1 before five minutes were up. Matt Butcher and Joe Pritchard testing Alex Palmer at one end. Up the other, Jorge grant seized on a poor back pass from the hosts, with Connor McGrandles seeing his effort smartly saved.

After that, things slowed down a little and despite the early hint of an end-to-end encounter, it never materialised. In those early exchanges, McGrandles was right in the middle of the action, involved in a couple of tussles with Chelsea loanee Joe Russell. It was McGrandles on the receiving end of a rather cheeky elbow from Matt Butcher too, which led to a bulk of the three minutes added on time at the end of the half.

The Imps looked disjointed at times, with Lewis Montsma sporting a new tattoo, but guilty of giving the ball away on numerous occasions. Still, despite not being at our best, it could have been 1-0 on the 20-minute mark. Harry Anderson set TJ Eyoma away on the right, and the Spurs' man whipped a great cross over everyone, only for McGrandles to struggle with adding power to the ball, heading straight at the keeper.

The last fifteen minutes of the half belonged to the home side, who were giving the Imps no time on the ball. Bridcutt was harassed into losing possession on 28 minutes, but the resulting shot was fired over. Within seconds of the goal kick, McGrandles fouled Jon Russell, but the free-kick was fired over from 30-yards out.

When the Imps did get a corner, it seemed to be a platform for the home side to launch a counter-attack, with one such instance on the half-hour mark seeing them break quickly up the field. Accrington certainly seemed quicker in the tackle, and willing to break at pace. For all our possession, 62% at one stage, we had struggled to create anything too meaningful on goal.

As the minutes ran down, Accrington threatened more. Dion Charles got the better of Melbourne on the flank, but his cross was stabbed wide by Colby Bishop with Montsma shadowing tightly. Jon Pritchard, scorer of a stunner in the 4-3 reverse last season, lashed a powerful effort wide from 25-yards out, whilst just before the whistle a comedy of errors almost let the hosts in, but they again fired over.

The Imps did have one more half chance, Eyoma's cross was flicked extravagantly, but harmlessly wide by Grant. Despite the hosts looking more likely to break the deadlock, Michael Appleton would doubtless be the happier of the two managers.

Michael made a big call at half time, bringing off Harry Anderson, arguably one of the better players over the last few months, with Brennan Johnson coming on after his debut for Wales last week. I did wonder if Brennan's fitness might have been in question, had he got a knock whilst on international duty? Maybe, maybe not, but he certainly added something to our approach in the second half, which was remarkable for two moments, both of which put the referee centre stage. In the end, neither changed the scoreline, but certainly both had the potential to.

Before all that Accrington were once again looking most likely to score, with the disjointed approach from City evident at the start of the half. Immediately from the restart, City played out from the back, which eventually led to Palmer passing straight into an Accrington player, which in turn led to a corner. It wasn't a chance, but it was unnecessary pressure of our own doing. The resulting ball saw the attacker look for a penalty, running across Bridcutt and going to ground but the referee had none of it. In terms of consistency, if it is a dive, it is a booking, but unlike the Forest Green game, the ref was trying to keep his cards in his pocket.

On 50 minutes the home side had another good chance, with Jon Pritchard again the provider. They instigated a quick counter-attack up the field, with the midfielder eventually looping an effort over the top of the goal to Palmer's left-hand side.

The first fifteen minutes of the half were scrappy, which both sides contributed to. The Imps were their own worst enemies, with loose balls and errant passes often conceding possession instead of anything the home side had to offer.

Just before the hour mark, the game's first major incident occurred. Brennan Johnson made his usual probing run into the area, with Christian Burgess chasing across to cover. The defender seemed to go to ground early, but instead of winning the ball, he appeared to play the on-loan Forest man. Johnson went down in what looked like a stonewall penalty, but maybe a reputation has followed him because instead of a spot-kick, the referee drew a yellow card. Given their players dive from the corner in the early exchanges of the second half, it was a frustrating choice. Looking back, both at the replay and the stills, there was a shout for a penalty, perhaps 95%, and maybe if it had been in the Prem it would have gone to VAR and been given. We're not, and thankfully so, despite us coming out on what seems like the wrong side of the decision.

The Imps began to assume control and Johnson was again the dangerman not long after his penalty. Lewis Montsma, who had an erratic game on his return to the side, surged forward and pinged a wonderful pass through, which Johnson delivered into the area with real quality to earn a corner. City had several corners during the game but rarely threatened, this one perhaps the most dangerous, although it ended up back with Grant who made a cross-cum-shot that went straight into the keeper's arms.

The game began to open, and rather than end-to-end it was counter-attack to counter-attack. With none of the play resulting in chances, it seemed for a while as though neither side would get a goal. One scary moment for City saw a corner lifted into Palmer, who took it cleanly but dropped the ball as he landed. The loose ball was quickly cleared, but the hosts were back not long after. Max Melbourne gave the ball away cheaply on the left-hand side, with Dion Charles opening his body and firing a shot which Palmer saved well.

Accrington brought on Sean McConville, a player who loves scoring against City, but his contribution was a little less direct. A ball forward within five minutes of his entry, after ten months out, saw him go in to challenge Montsma just inside the D. McConville's studs looked to be up and he caught a stooping Montsma at an awkward angle, with the referee drawing a straight red. It looked nasty on the first viewing, and slow-motion replays didn't do the midfielder any favours, although there was little malice. With the home side down to ten men, the complexion of the game change almost immediately.

This decision may well have been reversed had the referee had the benefit of VAR. It looked nasty, and even after a second viewing I felt red, but it was borderline. I couldn't help but think of Billy Knott back in 2017/18 when he caught a player high against Notts County. If the card was for a high boot, it is harsh. If the ref thinks the challenge was dangerous, maybe it is a red. The real threat came not from McConville's challenge, but from Montsma's position, much like Ellis Champman on Gary Deegan back when we played Cambridge in 2018/19.

After that, you felt there was a winner in it for City. Johnson and Hopper both got in down the right-hand side, but couldn't get telling balls across. Anthony Scully, on for McGrandles, had two chances, one after Montsma's ball-juggling from a corner, the other a break down the left which cannoned off the post. The hosts were on the ropes, but still posed something of a threat on the counter, but the Imps were certainly in the ascendency.

On 79 minutes, a historic moment occurred, as City brought on Tayo Edun and Robbie Gotts. Gotts was the second to come on the field, making him the first-ever fourth sub for the Imps, as he replaced TJ Eyoma. Gotts then had a strong ten minutes, with lots of involvement as we pressed for the winner. On the other flank, Tayo Edun came on for Melbourne and he worked the ball well down the left, finding Liam Bridcutt 20-odd yards out, but the captain fired a rash shot over the bar. Gotts and Johnson also looked a threat, working a chance to cross down the right, with the Leeds' man's delivery fired wide by Adam Jackson. The referee awarded a corner oddly, but again City couldn't do anything with it. Grant was next up, he broke into the channel on the left-hand side but fired wide, whilst the final chance of the game fell to James Jones. Grant was the provider again, his whipped free-kick was met by the glancing head of the former Crewe man, but it struck the post and came back out.

Sadly, with four minutes of injury time, Accrington did enough to claim the draw which, if we're being fair, their play deserved.

On reflection, the Imps' best spell came against ten men, which isn't surprising. I felt the game was there for the taking and had we put something meaningful at their keeper, we might have had some joy. Despite it being a decent point, I can't help but think there was more there for a ruthless side to exploit. We've been hit hard with injuries and I think we're seeing some settling in the division now, with those early shouts of possible top six being examples of us getting carried away, a little, as fans. In my mind, teams in play-off contention win yesterday's game, team looking to finish seventh to 11th get a credible draw against a good, organised side, and team due to finish in the bottom half lose the game. That's my take, and I think we got a great indication of where we are. Yes, we are a little short up top, mainly due to injuries, especially that of Callum Morton. Losing him is a huge blow because he's a very different nine to Tom Hopper and sometimes, that is what we need. I think we needed it yesterday, despite Hooper's hard work, and if there is any scope in the transfer window than I think MA will focus on that.

However, this is a young team, a team which is developing and learning all the time, and there is little doubt that a draw at Accrington will be more than a lot of teams get. Of course, had the key decisions both gone our way, we could well have had all three and be joint second now, but that's football and you have to be pragmatic.

On to Swindon next week, who got an important 1-0 win against Bristol Rovers, with Brett Pitman the scorer. He will be a real handful for our defenders in another tough encounter.

We're going back – plans finally afoot for a return to Sincil Bank
November 23, 2020

261 days. That is how long it has been since I have sat in the open air at Sincil Bank and watched a game in the Football League.

By the time we play Sunderland, it will be 280 days, but there is a real possibility that on that day, the 280th in exile, fans will finally start getting back into the ground. I know I got to watch the Liverpool game, courtesy of doing Matchday Live, but like all fans, I haven't known the exhilaration of a goal going in, surrounded by 8,000 like-minded supporters. I have missed that rush, so much. 've missed meeting friends, having a drink and walking up the stairs and seeing the green pitch reveal itself as the curtains go up on another game.

I genuinely didn't think we would get back in the ground this season, but today the government have announced that we could start going back as early as the end of lockdown. The country comes out of lockdown on December 2nd and is to return to the confusing tiered system. It seems a return to the grounds is lined to the tier system, with the number of fans allowed in based on the tier level of the location.

Reports suggest that 4,000 fans, or 50% capacity, could be allowed back into grounds that are in a tier-one location. The lower of those numbers would apply, so the maximum supporters we might see in the ground come December 12th is 4,000. In tier two, which Lincoln were approaching when we went into lockdown, the level would be 2,000 supporters. Sadly, if our area becomes tier 3, then fans will not be allowed back in.

This is obviously a fluid situation and we could see 2,000 one week, and none the next, or 4,000 one week reduced to 2,000. One would hope, given the infection rates in Lincolnshire at present, that we will at least remain in tier 2, meaning 2,000 lucky fans could well be in the ground to finally witness Appleton's Army on their quest for a top ten finish.

Of course, this is great news for the Shed Light on the Plight campaign, as well as the Save Our Clubs campaign, but it is a tentative start and by no means a clear pathway to watching games again. With around 4,300 existing season ticket holders, it will pose some logistic problems, but the fact is the club will have lots of work to do around not only allocation but also people management, traffic flow and the like.

Still, it is nice to finally get some good news around the possibility of getting back home, to where (and I'm aware this is very Faithless-centric), We Come One, to the church where I heal my hurts... Sincil Bank.

After a fairly rotten weekend, this is just the tonic. Hopefully, it will put a smile on a few of your faces too.

It's a win, but not as we know it: Swindon 0-1 Imps
November 24, 2020

Michael Appleton's side made it four points on the road in four days, with successive clean sheets and a leap up to third in the table.

It wasn't always pretty, it wasn't always attractive, but sometimes the result is more important than the process. That was the case this evening, as we avoided defeat at Swindon for the fourth meeting in a row.

The Imps made four changes from the team that drew at Accrington, Robbie Gotts and Tayo Edun coming in at full-back, whilst Anthony Scully and Brennan Johnson came in up top. That meant Jorge Grant dropped into midfield, playing alongside James Jones as part of Michael Appleton's 'Golden Triangle'.

The first proper chance of the game fell to Swindon, but it as a half-chance at best as a header was flashed over from a corner. Within seconds Adam Jackson's errant ball fell to a red shirt, but the drive from Caddis was poor and Palmer was able to control it with his feet and get the Imps going again. Swindon looked to be brighter in the opening stages, a slip by Tayo Edun saw a swift move upfield ended by Matt Smith firing wide with Bridcutt adjudged to have got the defensive touch.

The Imps first real attack came after 15 minutes, with Brennan Johnson the culprit being a little greedy. He strode into the left channel with Edun on the overlap, but instead of looking for the former Fulham man, he drove over wildly. In his defence, fans on the pre-match show were saying we should try our luck from range more, but it felt like a panicked effort.

The next two Imps chances fell to James Jones, as City finally got a foothold in what was a tepid first half. A Tom Hopper flick-on found Jones in a little space, but he fired over and wide to the keeper's left. Two minutes later, Johnson bullied the Swindon full-back in a footrace from Liam Bridcutt's excellent ball, stabbing to Jones who again fired a shot wide. The Imps were knocking on the door, but just as suddenly as the chances came, they dried up again.

Swindon seemed to have more possession, but neither side were stringing passes together in a frustrating watch. Mathieu Baudry had an effort deflected over from a corner courtesy of Lewis Montsma, who was looking increasingly comfortable at centre half.

With seven minutes left in the first half, City finally got a shot on target. Adam Jackson switched play intelligently and found Anthony Scully. The former West Ham man had struggled to produce an end product for much of the half, but his sweet first touch brought the ball down well and he worked a shooting chance, but his effort was weak and rolled into the arms of Kovar.

One moment that did make me smile came just before half time. This season, I have screamed at my screen as opposition players have made their way up the line with ball in hand, stealing ten, fifteen yards a time before releasing the ball. We do it and, to be fair, I don't scream as much. The whistle of Graham Salisbury screamed at Akin Odimayo as he went a little too far, and again when he failed to return to his position. It looked fussy, but Salisbury had a thoroughly unfussy game in the middle and rightly pulled the player up for it.

There was still a chance for a shot at goal from Swindon as the half drew to a close. Hallam Hope, who had been quiet, found some space on the edge of the area, but he released a tame effort at Alex Palmer's goal, although a late touch on the player from Montsma might have had something to do with it.

Thus, ended a first half of football that I will struggle to remember in two weeks' time, such was the lack of excitement, flowing football or incident. My gut feeling was changes might be needed at half time, with a little more dynamism needed on the flanks. Personally, I would have been tempted to take off Anthony

Scully and replace him with Theo Archibald, but if I go on about Theo much more, people will start to think I'm his Dad (which, tragically, I'm old enough to be).

A stat which summed up the first half succinctly was the passing accuracy – 59% for the home side and just 69% for us. It was a disjointed first half which bore little relation to the Imps of earlier in the season. We found it hard to get Johnson on the ball, hard to find Grant in decent positions and when balls did go forward, it was often easy for the defence to mop up. That said when the ball did go well, and when the run was well-timed, we looked like scoring.

The Imps came out for the second half all guns blazing, with two great chances in the first minute or so. Michael decided not to make any changes, and as Jones rasped an effort at Kovar, which was tipped just wide, it seemed like a wise move. Not long afterwards, Brennan Johnson picked up the ball 25-yards out, drove a little towards goal before hitting a great drive which seemed to clip the crossbar.

That proved to be a false dawn in terms of the spectacle, whilst we certainly looked busy, little happened in terms of clear-cut chances. Swindon did attack at speed at times, but never truly looked like breaching the Imps' back four. Anthony Grant did get a drive off at goal, which palmer held with relative ease. Immediately afterwards it was the turn of Matt smith, another relatively weak effort saved by Palmer without fuss.

Just before the hour mark, tom Hopper was fouled to draw the fifth yellow card of the evening for the home side. They hadn't been cynical as such, but going into the last half hour the whole back four were on cards. It might have been tempting to get pace on to run at them, but instead, Michael went for guile, with McGrandles swapping places with Anthony Scully and Jorge Grant pushing out on the wide left.

That certainly brought some balance to the Imps attack and for the first time since those early chances, we sprung into life. Grant played a smart ball to Edun whose cross was lashed out for a corner – from that corner a loose ball dropped to Bridcutt who fired well over Kovar's goal.

Finally, with 16 minutes left to play, the deadlock was broken. A nice move down the right saw a teasing ball evade Hopper and Grant and get touched out for a corner. Grant's delivery had Kovar rush of his line with a weak punch, and the loose ball dropped to Lewis Montsma, who headed at goal. Kovar recovered and tried to claw the ball out, but it had already crossed the line and the Imps had the lead.

Credit to Swindon, after that they pushed hard for a leveller. Liam Bridcutt gave away a free kick on the edge of the area causing some panic, but Dion Donohue fired well over. Shortly after, a move down the right-hand side saw a ball flashed across goal where Jordan Stevens saw a rebounded effort go wide.

There were no chances left for City as we looked to close the game down, a couple of corners were kept in the corner to wind down the clock, whilst Robbie Gotts took plenty of time to come off as he was replaced by TJ Eyoma.

There was still a little late drama, and typically it involved former Imp Jack Payne. He whipped a cross in as we entered injury time, which Tom Broadbent flicked on. His header found Baudry, all alone in the six-yard box with the whole goal to aim for, but he headed over.

In truth, it should have gone in. In truth, it would have been no less than the home side deserved in what was an equal encounter. However, they didn't get the goal and the game finished 1-0, pushing the Imps into third.

Michael Appleton was happy with the result, if not the process, as he spoke to BBC Radio Lincolnshire. "We were far from our best tonight, it wasn't a particularly eye-catching game from both sides really," he said.

"To come here and get the three points is the most improtant thing. Don't get me wrong, the players are frustrated and expect us to be better, but there is more than one way to win a game of football. We didn't look like we were going to concede again, but we lacked a bit of quality in the final third and we have to get better."

That said, another clean sheet on their travels is impressive, which Michale was impressed with.

"It's great. It's really pleasing the amount of clean sheets were getting. We're in a really good position, we have given ourselves a great platform to work from."

On reflection, it was a tough watch at times. Passes did go astray and Swindon operated a high press which forced one or two players into bad decisions. That said, a clean sheet is great, two in a row is superb and I always maintained four points from these two games would be a good haul. It has proven to be, and whilst individuals might not have impressed some supporters, the overall outcome was more than satisfactory.

I think that, more than anything, should be the take-home this evening. It might not have been free-flowing, it might not have been easy on the eye, but the facts are indisputable. 1-0 win, third in the table and ending a three-game winless run in the division. There is now a seven-day break with the FA Cup game, before a crucial double-header against Wigan (24th) and Rochdale (20th), which could well set us up for a tasty tie against Sunderland, maybe in front of fans.

We're not going back – plans for a Sincil Bank return dashed as country left in tiers

November 26, 2020

Covid-19 decimated our game in the 2019/20 season, leaving points per game to relegate Tranmere, helping to promote Wycombe and leave others crying foul.

From next week, that disparity will be back with a vengeance as some clubs can welcome supporters into stadiums, whilst others cannot. As I'm sure you already know by now, Lincolnshire, as a whole, has been placed in tier 3, meaning that until December 16th at least, there will be no supporters back at Sincil Bank. Indeed, those headline figures of up to 4,000 supporters going back were essentially people-pleasing fiction, as the only areas to be in tier one are those without elite football clubs, Cornwall, the Isle of Wight and the Isles of Scilly.

In our league, 12 of the 24 teams will be permitted to have fans in attendance, namely Wimbledon, Charlton, Crewe, Ipswich, MK Dons, Northampton, Oxford, Peterborough, Plymouth, Portsmouth, Shrewsbury and Swindon Town. Only one of those teams affects us, that being Shrewsbury in the EFL Trophy. The first away League One game we may see fans in the stadium is Northampton on 19th December, with Wimbledon, Shrewsbury and Portsmouth all to come after the new year.

Of course, the tiers are subject to change, so we may even see a return to fans at Sincil Bank for the visit of Burton Albion on Boxing Day, which would be rather ironic given they were the very last visitors to the ground. That would hinge on our county being hauled out of the bag in the Covid-19 lottery happening every two weeks from now on, hosted by the comedy double act of Johnson and Hancock (Jancock anyone? No?)

I understand that we want fans back in the ground across the country and there may not have been another way, but knowing that some clubs will have home supporters cheering them on, whilst other clubs cannot, does stick in the throat a bit. Having supporters is a big boost to players and given that there will be no away fans, obviously, it means some very partisan trips for some clubs with the benefit at their home ground. Bristol Rovers will suffer in the first instance, playing away at Charlton and Wimbledon with fans in the ground – the Wimbledon game being especially tough as it will be the first back at Plough Lane with paying customers. Burton have it tough too, facing both Ipswich and MK Dons, whilst Fleetwood also have two trips to grounds which can admit supporters.

I applaud the return of supporters and can offer no alternative to the rules, other than a blanket approach to football matches. Genuinely, in the grand scheme of things, how can it be safer to go to a gym every night with different groups of people there, than sitting in a football ground, no matter what tier your area is in? How can it not be safe to go to a football ground in a tier 3 area wearing a mask and taking precautions, but going to the supermarket, or school, or college is fine?

Last season, the Football League was unfair, especially in League One. Some teams played Bolton's kids, others did not. Some teams got long breaks thanks to Bolton and Bury's troubles, others had to play twice a week for what seemed like forever. Ultimately a team was relegated without actually being one of the worst three teams in the division over 46 games. I guess I shouted that was the 'only fair way' back then and have to swallow that down now, but this is not about clubs surviving, it is about people surviving. Not just staying clear of Covid, but mentally too. I think it cruel that they dropped headlines of a possible return, knowing full well a huge section of the country could not.

This year was always going to be the same as the last one to a degree, anyone playing away at an empty Stadium of Light was going to have it easier than someone going there later in the season, but tying football into the tier system just creates disparity. Yes, I am bitter and yes, this is perhaps me only seeing one side of the coin, but Covid doesn't stop at a county border and think 'I can't go across there', just as it doesn't knock off on December 23rd for a few days. We are told that wearing a mask, washing hands and not licking each other's faces is a good way to steer clear of catching it, so why tie football into tiers? If it is safe for your kids to go to school in tier 3 if it is safe for my brother to go to the gym, or for people to queue outside Primark, why oh why can 2,000 supporters not file into a 10,000 capacity stadium with masks on and not rub their hands on each other in the process?

Congratulations if you are one of the areas in which football has returned (widely known as 'the South'), it is genuinely good news that some fans will be back, I just find it hard to comprehend how one minute we're being given hope, only for it to be cruelly snatched away. It feels like torment, bullying even, which you just don't expect from the government.

Whatever they have said, the current lockdown does continue past December 2nd, because if something smells like a fish, looks like a fish and swims underwater, it doesn't matter what you call it. It is still a fish.

Out, but not down: Plymouth 2-0 Imps
November 28, 2020

City went out of the FA Cup at the second round stage, despite more than matching Plymouth Argyle in an exciting game on the south coast this afternoon.

In a game which should have brought three or four goals, we drew a blank, and were shown why being clinical is so important. A cup run, whilst hugely important in financial terms, went begging but many will surely say league wins are more improtant. Perhaps, judging by the team selection, Michale Appleton felt the same. He made a raft of changes to the starting XI, with Theo Archibald getting a start on the left, Harry Anderson on the right and Anthony Scully in what he would surely deem his best position, the number nine.

It saw the Imps line up in a 4-4-1-1 formation, with Brennan Johnson playing the ten role and looking to get in the box where possible.

Before the game could start, we had a minute's silence for Diego Maradona, impeccably observed by the empty stands. It was FIFA directive which has been seen across the game and it wasn't the only hold up prior to the game – Plymouth had to remove some dark green under armour and Brennan Johnson having the wrong colour tape on his wrist. It suggested the referee might have a picky afternoon, but in fairness, it was the only aspect of his performance worth commenting on.

When we did get underway, it was the Imps on the front foot with the first half-chance on three minutes, which came from a quick counter. Robbie Gotts dispossessed George Cooper, drove forward and fed in Brennan Johnson, who picked out Anthony Scully. He cut back inside before curling an effort over the bar.

Sadly, on six minutes, Plymouth took the lead from a set-piece. Alex Palmer punched a free-kick out for a corner, but the resulting delivery was inch-perfect, Luke Jephcott flicking a header past the former Pilgrims stopper. It was an early blow which didn't reflect the balance of play, but it may have induced memories of our last FA Cup game here, a 5-0 thumping. In some respects, it might have been easier to take the resulting defeat if the home side had been rampant from there on.

The Imps quickly got back into the opposition area, a break started by Joe Walsh found Theo Archibald, who found Scully and then Anderson. His effort was parried away, but Johnson couldn't quite get a touch on the saved effort despite taking up a good position. We had a great chance to get back level on 16 minutes, with Johnson cleverly winning a corner after pressuring the full-back. Sadly, instead of cleverly waiting for players to get into the area, he took it short and quick to Scully, who had nobody to aim for and the chance went away much to MA's fury. Whilst it was wasted, the Imps were looking much better than Tuesday night, attacking down both flanks with plenty of success in terms of opening the opposition up, but not in terms of troubling their keeper. On 23 minutes it was the Imps again knocking on the door. Archibald found Gotts with a lovely ball, and he delivered a deep cross which Joe Walsh nodded back across goal. McGrandles arrived in the six-yard area but couldn't quite get a decisive touch on the ball. In fairness though, only one side was showing any attacking intent at all.

Theo Archibald was looking lively, both on the left and centrally. He tried one of his long-range efforts, which we have yet to see pay off, but it flashed wide of the post. That shot came after three or four minutes of Imps passing, completely uninterrupted. Plymouth almost looked happy with their goal lead, even 28 minutes into the tie. Even a regroup from Ryan Lowe after an injury to the keeper didn't help, City creating another chance on 36 minutes, but Harry Anderson's shot from a tight angle was easily gathered by the aforementioned stopper. On the right, Gotts and Anderson were linking up well, whilst Melbourne and Archibald were the same on the left. Through the middle, Johnson looked frighteningly dangerous, whilst Scully was also working hard. Even Edun and McGrandles looked like they wanted a goal, the former firing wide from 20-yards out on 37 minutes.

The Imps came closest to levelling on 44 minutes, with Leeds man Gotts again the key man. Johnson, a constant threat in the ten role, found Gotts out to the attacking right. He had an effort from 20-yards which had the keeper scrambling across to make the save, with the rebound falling to Scully. The former West Ham man couldn't find his feet with his back to goal, but it was as close the Imps came in a one-sided 45-minute spell. Somehow, as the man in lime green blew for half time, City trailed 1-0, despite utterly dominating from five minutes onwards.

The problem, and it is one becoming increasingly apparent as the season progresses, is the lack of Callum Morton in the squad. There simply isn't an out-and-out centre forward available to us, not even Hopper, who wasn't involved today. Anthony Scully puts himself about, but he won't pop up on the end of a cross, or a corner, nor will you find him lurking on the penalty spot for a loose ball. We talk about flexibility within the squad, we talk about how well the players are playing and yet we just don't have the clinical striker who could (and in my opinion would) have put us level. It's no good having a bag full of bullets if you don't have a gun to fire them and despite our very best efforts, we just didn't have enough to kill off Plymouth, for all our great football.

The first fifteen minutes of the second period saw the game won and lost. The best chance of the opening exchanges fell to Plymouth, coming from Melbourne's slip, which allowed Joe Edwards spring a three against two attack. He found Nouble in a bit of space, but the Imps were able to close down quickly and get the ball out for a corner, which came to nothing. It was a let-off for the Imps, who had looked bright in the opening couple of minutes. Plymouth continued their early pressure, playing a bit more football than the first half and certainly looking like the side I feared they would be. A lovely curling effort from the right-hand side went wide, but inside seven minutes they offered more than the whole first half. It began to look like perhaps, the Imps had missed their chance in the first half.

Joe Walsh was very lucky, in my mind, on 54 minutes. He followed through in a challenge on Fornah with studs showing but received only a yellow. Had it been against us, we would have definitely been in uproar. Niall Canavan also picked up a yellow in the incident for his reaction, which saw players confronting each others, pushing and shoving (not sure how to term that). Plymouth had the last laugh from the incident though, from the free-kick, Nouble looped a ball into the path of Ben Reeves who lashed a stunning volley past Palmer for 2-0, effectively ending the game.

Reeves grabbed himself yet another shot with 15 minutes of the second half gone, lashing a drive to the left-hand side of Palmer's post, with the complexion of the game had completely changed. It didn't look like the same City side which dominated the first half, with possession hard to come by and passes going astray akin to the midweek game. Michael Appleton had to do something to shake it up, and he did just that, Joe Walsh coming on the hour mark, which would seem like the pre-match plan. Liam Bridcutt got an hour on his return to the team in midweek and Walsh, lucky to be on the field, had an otherwise decent game in his first game for some time. Jorge Grant came on and had a positive impact immediately.

The Imps kept pressing and finally created a chance. Tayo Edun's intelligent ball didn't quite drop for Anderson, but the loose ball was backheeled into the path of the captain by Johnson, with the defender touching wide. Shortly after the corner, Grant played a ball into the box which Nouble touched into his keeper's arms. From that, another glorious Grant ball found Harry, who drove at goal and drew a save from the keeper. Was it too little, too late? Yes, but not if Grant could help it. He jinxed into the area from the resulting corner and tried to play a ball across goal which was stabbed wide for yet another corner. In one move, Michael Appleton had changed the entire approach once again. Sadly, with a two-goal deficit to overhaul, it would take a Herculean effort to restore parity.

The game had become much more competitive, unlike the one-sided first half. Edun outmuscled Nouble on the attacking right but was not backed up and Edwards picked up the ball, feeding in Reeves. His effort got deflected wide, but the home side had certainly come alive, which prompted the second change of the gáme for City, James Jones replacing Archibald. The Scot had a sound first half, but never got going in the second.

Jones got his customary effort on goal on 73 minutes, strong work from Edun on the left saw him keep possession when the Pilgrims felt they deserved a free-kick. The former Fulham man was having a strong afternoon and he found Jones who curled wide to the keeper's left post. McGrandles was the next to have a gifted chance, a wonderful ball into the area saw him struggle to get the connection, and then the loose ball wouldn't quite drop for Edun. The Imps were knocking on the door, with Melbourne rasping a drive high and wide on 75 minutes in a wasteful moment. Sadly, it did feel as though City could play all night and not score, which proved to be the case (not playing all night, obviously).

It wasn't for a want of trying though, and the fifteen-minute spell at the start of the half was well and truly in the past. Edun had his best game in a City shirt for me, helping the Imps to win corner number eight of the afternoon. For the eighth time, the corner didn't bring a chance, and not long after the same could be said for corner number nine. Combinations of poor delivery and no physical presence meant that our set-pieces came to nothing and, if you take away Kovar flapping at the ball on Tuesday night, it is something I think we have struggled with.

The last chance to make a contest of it fell on 85 minutes. if we'd scored at that point, the home side might have panicked. Harry Anderson earned a free-kick on the right-hand side, and finally, we saw a delivery and contact which brought a chance – Grant's delivery nodded down and just wide by Anderson. It seemed there was a shout of handball, but it would have been harsh on Plymouth, and I think they still feel a little aggrieved about a penalty at our place.

The Imps kept pressing, to their credit, but anything after that point would have been a consolation. They hunted anyway, Jones driving into the keeper's arms with two minutes of normal time remaining. Plymouth kept hunting too in an end-to-end finish, Nouble headed over when it was easier to score, then Palmer made a super save to keep the score respectable. City immediately went up and saw a Johnson effort saved, then the same player, a constant threat, saw a late, late effort hit the side netting. In terms of shots and chances, the Imps must have had more in this tie than the last three or four league matches combined. Shots and chances, like possession, don't win you games though, goals do and aside from the Forest Green game, the Imps have only scored five in the eight games played between the two Plymouth matches. That, for me, is a real concern for Michael to address, but given the limited resources available, all he can do is press on and hope January brings some joy in terms of either Morton's fitness, or a favour from a friend at another club.

It isn't like we didn't create today though, but when it isn't your day, it just isn't, and it wasn't for City. I felt we played better than last weekend against Accrington and better than in midweek, and yet we got a much worse result. I didn't feel the defence played badly, certainly Gotts at full-back was as good as he's been in the Imps' shirt and for me, was Man of the Match, just shading it over Edun. Tayo looked strong in the middle of the park and, in spells at least, we looked excellent on the flanks. What we lacked, without a doubt, was a presence up top. So many balls came into the area without a touch when players did pop up in danger areas it was almost always a midfielder getting on the ball.

The FA Cup is gone for another year, and it hasn't brought a third-round tie, which is a sickener as I felt we were the better team today. Still, the team with the most goals wins the game and that's something we can't seem to do at the moment. We're all bark and no bite in front of goal right now, which makes our league position of fourth even more remarkable. Being honest, I don't know how to feel tonight. I'm hacked off we didn't go through, I'm down because we lost, but oddly in the aftermath of a 2-0 defeat, I don't feel gutted. We played well, really well in patches, as well as we've played since Forest Green and perhaps as well as we have played in the league since beating Plymouth. If you do the right things, in the right way, then success will come and today's defeat might show us where we are now, and what we need, but it also shows me we are doing the right things. Michael journey is not that of a single season, and I'm confident as the squad builds, finances settle and the budget increases, we'll find that elusive striker, the man who would put efforts away and ice the cake which, even without icing and without an FA Cup run, is looking tasty.

December

Take Time To Appreciate The Moment – Imps 2-1 Wigan Athletic
December 1, 2020

The Imps moved into second in the table as another challenging test was passed at Sincil Bank.

We keep hearing that good teams when they don't play well, and at the moment that seems to be the order of the day at City. For sixty minutes or so, City weren't second best, but they certainly weren't in good form. A Jorge Grant stunner and Tom Hopper's predatory strike were enough to see us jump to second in the table.

If we're not ruthless enough, if we're not at our best and if we do have key players missing, imagine what we might be able to achieve, seeing as we're second in League One right now. That sort of perspective is important.

Still, each game of 90 minutes is judged on its own merits and the truth was, for at least 45 minutes, those merits were not obvious to anyone watching on iFollow.

As expected, the Imps made five changes from the team which lost at Plymouth, although one of those was no captain Liam Bridcutt. He missed out after picking up a strain in training, meaning James Jones, Conor McGrandles and Jorge Grant made up the midfield three. Tayo Edun, who had a strong game against Plymouth, dropped to full back with Robbie Gotts keeping his place. Lewis Montsma and Adam Jackson returned to the side, whilst Tom Hopper came in up top for Theo Archibald.

In a tepid first half, the Imps seemed to struggle to get out of first gear, but dominated large chunks of the play. The first effort fell to the Imps, a Jorge Grant corner found Conor McGrandles who scuffed an easy shot at the keeper. The lack of attacking intent was underlined byt the next chance not coming for 11 minutes, despite Wigan looking to be there for the taking. McGrandles was involved again, he found Johnson out wide, but a heavy touch took him further away from goal than he would have liked. He did get a shot on target, although not one to challenge the keeper.

It took half an hour for Wigan to get going, but when they did they had the best chance of the first half hour. A deep ball saw Montsma slip, allowing for a knockdown for Curtis Tilt to drive at goal, but luckily his shot was deflected wide for a corner

It was the blue shirts who next pressed for a goal, a deep corner was flicked on at the near post, but the balls dropped for Chris Merrie on the edge of the area whose long-range drive went well over.

The ball just wouldn't fall for City. A quick break by Johnson saw him cut inside, make up yards and look to lay a ball into the path of James Jones. Sadly, either Jones' run was mistimed or the ball was poor and it rolled away harmlessly. For every bit of good play, the Imps saw it break down as they approached the 18-yard box. Adam Jackson made a surging run from deep, arrived on the edge of the box and no idea what to do next.

Sadly, for the Imps and Adam Jackson, he pulled up on 24 minutes with an injury and had to come off the Joe Walsh.

Finally, on 41 minutes, the Imps had a chance that looked like it might result in a goal. Tom Hopper outmuscled Curtis Tilt midway in the attacking half, which Johnson picked up. He made his customary surge to goal, turned the defender inside out, but stabbed the ball narrowly wide. It was certainly the best chance of the game for either side, but the score remained 0-0.

That seemed to fire the Imps as two minutes later Johnson spun on the ball in the centre circle and found Jones. He had just been caught in two minds and fumbled an effort seconds before, but he hooked a strong effort at goal which went agonisingly wide of the keeper's left post.

Even after that, poor passes were the bane of our attacking intent. Grant spread a weak ball into a defender when we were in a good position, then moments later Jones spread a ball from right to left behind Gotts for a throw. At times, we looked nervy, as if maybe the pressure of expecting to do well was weighing on the player's shoulders somewhat.

If that expectation weighed on their shoulders at the end of the first half, it threatened to bury them early in the second. The Latics came out all guns blazing, creating a great chance in the opening exchanges, but a ball across the area found a man in all sorts of space, unfortunately for them, offside. It did look ominous though as the visitors came out full of life.

On 52 minutes, Wigan took the lead in a game which seemed to have 0-0 written all over it. The Imps were on the attack, a Crossfield ball found Edun who took it down well, but was dispossessed. Wigan quickly played a ball into the feet of former Rangers man (and their most dangerous player) Kai Naismith, who struck a shot at goal. Without a touch, Palmer saves it, but it took a horrible deflection off Montsma and dropped into the back of the net.

The Imps were suddenly shocked into life, the impressive Robbie Gotts had a cross blocked, but the loose ball fell to Grant who lashed over the bar from an impossible angle and distance. It wasn't an obvious chance, but it was a danger. However, with half an hour left, bottom club Wigan led 1-0 and chances had been at a premium.

The best managers make changes that influence games, and just before the hour, Michael proved his credentials with a tactical change. The Imps went to a 4-2-3-1, Harry Anderson coming on for McGrandles and going out wide on the right, Scully going to the left and Brennan Johnson sitting in the ten role behind Hopper.

The change gave the Imps a more attacking impetus, and on 66 minutes, Anthony Scully found some space in the area. Tayo Edun, who I think had a good game, took a pass from Joe Walsh and played it neatly into Scully's feet 16 yards out. He turned in space and had a shot at goal, but didn't catch it right and it crept towards the keeper with little danger.

The former West Ham man, who had a tough first half, then had a couple of opportunities within a minute. One ball trickled towards him on the edge of the area, but he couldn't quite meet it before the defender hooked away. The ball came back to him quickly, but his shot was blocked. It doesn't always work for Scully, but he always makes himself available and shows the right application in pressing forward.

Ten minutes after the change, the Imps got a deserved equaliser. It started with a free-kick away to the left, 35-yards out. It was whipped in, cleared and picked up by Johnson, who held off his defender well before going to ground. The referee gave another free-kick, on the edge of the area to the attacking right, not ideal for Grant. That didn't bother the captain, who strode up and sent a wonderful dead ball past the despairing keeper to get City level.

The goal put a fresh wind in the Imps' sails and it could have been two almost immediately, Johnson almost getting away. Grant then played a smart ball into Harry Anderson, a willing runner after coming on, and he fired at the keeper, drawing another save. The Imps kept knocking, hoping to be let in, with Anderson having a second effort blocked on 73 minutes.

It was the attacking right that provided another chance on 74 minutes, Anderson slipping a ball into Gotts, who saw his effort blocked by the keeper. The loose ball dropped in the six-yard box, but Johnson and Edun were both a couple of feet away and unable to get on it.

Joe Walsh then had two efforts in quick succession, the first a header from a great Gotts delivery which got deflected over. Within seconds a ball from Scully got nodded back across goal by a defender, and Walsh beat the keeper with his header, only for Tom James to hook the ball off the line.

If it was a boxing match, then Wigan would have been on the ropes, swaying, whilst a sleeping City had woken up and were throwing a flurry of punches. One was bound to lad and with seven minutes left, it landed.

Anthony Scully, who had a superb second half, played a smart ball into Tom Hopper who had his back to goal. The striker, who has come in for criticism recently, turned neatly in the area and slotted the ball between the defender's legs and into the back of the net. 2-1, technical knockout.

There was never a way back for the visitors after that, and the Imps chose not to take chances to get at goal, in favours of heading into the corner. Scully had a cross-cum-shot which the keeper saved, with the loose ball falling to Anderson. He was inside the box, but turned away from goal and went into the corner, eating up a couple of minutes. Deep into injury time, Jones got a shot off at goal which hit a defender's heel and spun up. He took it down, and instead of going again, he went off into the corner. That game management frustrated the visitors, but it ensured no moments towards the end of the game that could cause a wobble.

Michael Appleton was clearly happy with the result, admitting after the game on BBC Radio Lincolnshire that the first half got away from us a bit.

"I thought the first 20 minutes we were really good, but after that, we took our foot off the gas and allowed them to stamp their authority on it. For ten minutes or so of second, it was a bit flat and we gave a really poor goal away.

"I don't think we were as competitive as we needed to be, I don't think our centre-halves were as competitive on the first ball and I made them aware of that regardless of the result."

Tom Hopper is a player who has had a tough time in front of goal, but he turned in a strong performance and capped it with the goal, which delighted the manager.

"Delighted for him, even if he hadn't scored, I think he was definitely our best player by a long shot. He was almost doing my job for me on the pitch, when I was disappointed about our lack of physicality, he was telling the players that."

The Imps now go into the weekend in second place, four points clear of Sunderland just outside the play-off places. It wasn't a classic, but the fact remains that is seven points from nine, and it is three points from a game in which we were expected to win. Wigan are no mugs, Curtis Tilt and Kai Naismith are both seasoned professionals who would fit into our squad, if not first XI, and at times they did look like a strong outfit.

It's weird to be writing this with any negativity, but for 60 minutes I don't think we looked like scoring. However, we keep saying that and yet the collapse you might expect, doesn't happen. All around us, teams lose games, they drop points and we keep ourselves tucked into the promotion race. It seems ridiculous to even say such things if I am brutally honest. Five years ago this week, we were beaten 3-1 at Woking after drawing with Welling. Now, we're above Sunderland, Portsmouth and Ipswich in the Football league and we're still oozing potential and fans think there is much more in the tank.

It's certainly not the position I thought we'd be in six months ago, and however we play for 60 minutes is completely irrelevant if we keep picking up points. I always find living a moment in football is hard – you always think about the next game, other teams, how you have played etc. When you take time to pause and see the bigger picture, things change dramatically. In 2016/17, when we were running away with the National League, every game was judged on individual merits, but who remembers Bromley at home now? Few people bother, it was just a chapter in a great season.

Consider tonight another decent chapter in a belter of a story. Trust me, there are better chapters to come and when you're the 46th best team in the country having been losing to the likes of Woking five years ago, that is saying something.

Are we actual contenders? – Rochdale 0-2 Imps
December 5, 2020

City kept up the pressure on Hull City at the top of League One with a routine 2-0 win against Rochdale at Spotland.

Yup, that's right. Kept up the pressure on the team at the top of League One. Pinch yourself, it isn't a dream. We are a week into the advent calendar and Lincoln City are tucked into the promotion race nicely. Not just the promotion race, the automatic promotion race. We are just about a third of the way through the season and the challenge isn't faltering, we are genuinely pushing for a spot in the Championship. It is just like a dream, a really good dream, that we dare not stir in for fear of waking up and finding we're still on a terrace at North Ferriby.

Michael Appleton made three changes to the side which beat Wigan 1-0. Anthony Scully dropped out of the side, with Harry Anderson making a start on the right. Adam Jackson's injury meant another start for former MK Dons man Joe Walsh, whilst TJ Eyoma returned at right-back, with Robbie Gotts dropping to the bench. Remi Howarth was amongst the subs, returning from an injury sustained against Manchester City Under 21s.

Just as was the case on Tuesday night against Wigan, the Imps were not quite at their best, and the early pressure saw the hosts pressing forward, without too much intent. Rochdale certainly liked to play possession football, with City having to bide their time between passages of play. The first serious chance of the afternoon, or perhaps rather half chance, came from the ingenuity of Jorge Grant.

He had a free-kick 25-yards from goal, away to the attacking left. Instead of whipping it in, as expected, he slipped Johnson down the flank for a smart cross, which was hacked out for a corner. Seconds later Grant against looked to create, sliding in Harry Anderson whose deep cross was good, but behind both Hopper and Johnson who had gambled in the six-yard box.

A moment with ten minutes gone hinted at the end-to-end spectacle many hoped this might be. A nice passage of Imps play saw the lively Johnson get a shot away, but after taking a little too long it was easily telegraphed and blocked. The resulting clearance set Stephen Humphrys away for the hosts, one-on-one with Montsma, who got a foot in the nullify the danger. They were chances, yes, but no more than half-chances at a real push.

Tayo Edun picked up the first booking of the game on 12 minutes, having been adjudged to have handled Alex Newby's cross. Edun went down holding his head, but replays suggested a deliberate block with a hand. The resulting free-kick for Morley lurking on the edge of the area, but his rasping drive was blocked by Montsma, who was having a strong half defensively.

If the Imps main threat came through Johnson's quick breaks, then Rochdale's was down the right with Newby. After two strong outs for Edun, he looked ill at ease with the task of keeping the lively wide man quiet, and Rochdale knew it. On the other flank, former Manchester United man Ollie Rathbone wasn't getting much joy out of Eyoma. For much of the half, nobody got much joy at all, with misplaced passes and scrappy play beginning to take over proceedings. A long-range effort from Rathbone flashed wide, giving Michael Hortin something to raise his voice at, but on iFollow it looked further away than it must have done at Spotland.

Whilst the Imps' threat looked to be coming from Johnson, it was the work of tom Hopper keeping us going up top. He received a pass into feet from James Jones just after the half-hour mark, and after cutting outside the centre half, fired a shot at goal which was deflected for a corner. The set-piece came to nothing, but it was the closest the Imps had come so far in the game.

The acted as a nice precursor to the games most fluid move on 38 minutes. Edun, who had a tough half defensively, got away down the left and smartly pulled the ball back towards the penalty spot. McGrandles ran onto it, but smartly stepped over for Jones to calmly finish for his first league goal of the campaign. It was a rare moment of real quality in a rather stagnant first half, but that didn't matter one bit, 1-0 City.

It was also a degree of vindication for me as a pundit – I think Ben and I called him (or Archibald) to get a goal on the podcast and I suggested he might on Match Day Live too. It's been coming for Jones and the delight on his face told the whole story.

After that, the Imps were able to soak a bit of pressure, nothing too serious, and see out half time. Ollie Rathbone and Jimmy Keohane combined to find space in the area, but the latter's dangerous ball was dealt with well by Walsh, who had a comfortable half on his return to the first team.

If the first half was slow without real threat, then the second more than made up for it. Michael clearly had words at half time about the tempo, with the Imps looking much more fluid and coherent in the opening exchanges. The first real chance of the half, and the second decent shot on target for City, came from Johnson. The Forest man exchanged passes with Grant, then Hopper, before curling an effort at goal which Jay Lynch held with ease.

After a relatively slow hour, Ollie Rathbone was forced off with an injury and, in my opinion, the biggest threat the hosts had went with him. Whilst Rochdale hadn't really threatened, when they did, he looked like making something happen. Whilst their main attacking intent came from one player, ours came from all over the field. Harry Anderson whipped a beautiful cross in as the hour passed by, with Hopper just offside.

Rochdale did begin to go longer to Humphrys, and it almost brought them a leveller on 66 minutes. He drove into the right channel, bullied himself some space and drew a good save from Alex Palmer. The West Brom man didn't have a lot to do, but the one moment he was called on, he was equal to it.

Had he scored, maybe the game would have been different, but a confident City put all fear of that aside to take a 2-0 lead. It started with Edun, breaking down the left before pulling back to Grant. He went further back to Montsma, who only had one thought as he picked up the ball 30-yards out. His low drive should have been saved by Lynch, but it beat the keeper low to his right and ended the game as a contest.

Brennan Johnson had a great chance to make it three with 20 minutes left on the clock, all from a Rochdale free-kick. Their delivery was poor and the clearance found Johnson. He broke at pace, as he does, turning the defence inside and out before drawing a strong save from Lynch.

That brought a good spell of pressure from City, two corners in succession almost brought a third. Both were played short, the second working it's way to Grant who fired narrowly over with lynch confident it wasn't on target. Another corner a couple of minutes later found Joe Walsh with a good header, Lynch making amends for Montsma's goal by scooping the ball away.

There was a brief chance for Dale with ten minutes left, but Kwadwo Bola driving into the side netting. It was nothing and something, a very rare foray in the second period which perhaps typified the game. Rochdale looked like a side in 18th, not terrible but definitely not a top ten prospect, whilst the Imps were exactly the opposite. It could and should have been 3-0 at the end with James Jones lifting a delicious, lofted ball over the area from the right, with Max Melbourne steaming in with a good effort saved again by Lynch.

Michael Appleton, rightly, believed his side dominated. "Absolutely delighted, it is always nice to win away from home in any game. I thought we dominated and controlled the game from the first five minutes or so.

In the second half, it was certainly an easy watch sat here in the office. Across the field, the Imps were comfortable on the ball and never looked like conceding. The opening period smelled a lot like the last couple of weeks, not always perfect but never so bad you thought we'd concede a hatful. Yes, passes were misplaced, but never in key areas and never consistently by one player either. Tayo Edun took a little bit of criticism from Mark Hone on the radio for his defensive positions and there's no doubt he did struggle at times, but equally he had a hand in the goal, winning the ball and claiming the assist. In the second period, he was much better positionally and had a hand in the second goal too.

It was also a great afternoon for the midfield three. Grant played with his usually panache and grace. I think he looks like the kid at school who was just better than everyone, almost like a 21-year-old playing for an Under 15 side for a chuckle. Everything looks easy, even with three players around him he's calm, measured and knows where his out ball is. Around him, Jones and McGrandles were both busy, the former with his usual chances and of course, the goal, whilst McGrandles did exactly what he always does, run.

Talking about running, Tom Hopper must have covered every blade of grass up front. I thought his skillset was evident more in the first half, when maybe the hosts had a foot in the door. Any ball out to him got held up or laid off, and he always seemed to be chasing down a defender when it mattered. He doesn't chase lost causes, we're not talking Kevin Gall running here (if you know, you know). Instead, he chases the right balls, hunts the right player and is clever with his positioning in terms of angles. Watch him next time a keeper has the ball at his feet, he ensures it gets played in a certain direction, by cutting off the other option, even 20-yards away. Clever play and another good outing from him.

The plaudits will obviously go to Montsma and I feel a little too 'on trend' waxing lyrical about him, but if his average rating isn't above 8 for this game, I'll drink a can of my Brewdog Christmas IPA out of a sweaty welly. He plays with an effortless ease, much like Grant I suppose, gliding around the field, spraying passes with utter confidence. At times, I'm sure he thinks he's Dennis Bergkamp, at others, he is Frank Rikjaard. He heads, tackles, chases and harasses like a proper defender, but then strides away with the ball like a slick midfielder. Every Imps fan knew as soon as he got 30-yards out with defenders backing off what was going to happen. The goal settled nerves too and allowed us to be far more expressive and ambitious in the dying minutes.

This was a strong win, routine in that we expect to win games against sides who are 18th in the table, but not a given. No games are easy at this level and one week ago we went to Plymouth and lost 2-0. Remember, Rochdale thumped them 4-0 in midweek, which shows what they do have in the locker. Maybe they didn't show it today, maybe we stopped them showing it. After all, these wins, the incessant cascade of points that we seem to be getting, they're not by accident. We're not second, two points off top, six clear of seventh, by accident. We're not genuine promotion contenders because we have played easy teams. We're not surprising everyone by fluke or error.

We are the real deal. We might well be punching above our weight in terms of budget, stature and all that, but the one thing that rarely lies is the league table. Yes, there might be two-thirds of the season to go, but that is just more time for this team to gel, to improve and to develop.

Dare I ask, but are we actually promotion contenders? Not just for a top-six spot, but for a top-two place? Early indications are that we might just be. Please, don't wake me up from this dream.

Relentless City thrash sorry Salop: Shrewsbury 1-4 Imps
December 8, 2020

The Imps breezed through the second round of the EFL Trophy with a superb performance away at Shrewsbury.

On the back of a fine 2-0 win at Rochdale, City were forced into changes, but that didn't affect the processes one bit. If anything, the players coming into the side rose to the occasion and left Michael Appleton with some nice selection problems going into the busy Christmas period.

As is par for the course in this competition, both teams made changes to their sides, the Imps bringing in six fresh faces from the weekend's win. That included including Zack Elbouzedi for only his third outing of the campaign, and his second start of the season. Remy Howarth also returned, having limped off in the final group game against Manchester City Under 21s. Shrewsbury made ten changes from the side that drew 1-1 with Charlton at the weekend, and it told as they looked completely disjointed.

The Imps started brightly, with the front three causing problems with pace and movement at all times. Shrewsbury struggled to get out and it came as little surprise when the Imps had the best chance of the first ten minutes.

City won the ball at the back and swept forward with a series of slick passes, with Anthony Scully breaking into the right channel. He lofted a ball up, over the defence and onto the head of Zack Elbouzedi, who saw his header saved. He composed himself to pick up the rebound and deliver a cross towards Scully, looking to return the favour, only for Harry Anderson to nip it off the former West Ham forward's head.

Elbouzedi was certainly impressing on his rare start, and he looked to unlock the defence with the next chance. His smart pass towards Scully was cut out, with Remy Howarth picking up the ball. He was felled on the edge of the area, and Scully shaped to take the free kick. His delivery was almost inch perfect, almost. It struck the outside of the keeper's left-hand post.

It was Ireland Under 21 Elbouzedi causing problems again before fifteen minutes had elapsed, cutting in from the left flank and driving a relatively tame shot at the keeper. Across on the right-hand side. Robbie Gotts steamed down the flank, cut into the area and managed to get a shot away after a fortuitous bounce which the keeper saved.

The Imps were utterly dominant and it came as no surprise when we took the lead. It was Elbouzedi again, breaking at pace from inside his own half leaving his defender for dead. He fed a smart ball into Scully, who made no mistake with a first-time finish from inside the left channel. The home side looked shell-shocked as chances had been coming from both sides of the pitch.

When they did get the ball at the back. Salop struggled to play out as City's front three went man for man on the back three. They did manage a rare foray on 22 minutes, Alex Palmer saving Scott High's effort, palming it away and to safety.

Still the chances came for the Imps, with Remy Howarth having two good opportunities. Howarth, like Elbouzedi is on the fringe of the attacking picture, but he drove through the middle on 25 minutes and shot straight at the keeper. Ten minutes before the break, Scully broke in the channel and cut the ball back for Howarth, who took time to control and shape away from his defender, but his effort was easy for the keeper.

In between, Conor McGrandles picked up the most obvious yellow card you'll see, indulging in five-second shirt pulling on Shilow Tracey. The young winger was by far the biggest threat in a lacklustre Salop attack and he had looked to get away from McGrandles, who took one for the team.

The Imps were relentless, with Scully finding space 20-yards out on the left from Roughan's throw. He fired a wonderful shot across goal which the keeper clawed away, another superb save to deny the Imps.

There was no denying us on 40 minutes as the lead got doubled. Brennan Johnson started the attack, driving through the middle of the pitch and finding Harry Anderson. As Scully had at the start of the half, he lifted a delicious ball over the defence for Elbouzedi, who this time made no mistake with a smart header. 2-0, and the Imps were seemingly coasting.

The advantage lasted for just three minutes, as a rare Salop break pulled one back. T was Spurs loanee Tracey who found Eyoma and Melbourne too close in the area, turning both and firing past Alex Palmer. Despite conceding, it wasn't the last chance of the half, with Robbie Gotts getting a shot away which just went over the bar.

Half time saw McGrandles leave the pitch with a knock, which Michael later confirmed we'll know more about on Thursday. In his place, vice-captain and leading scorer Jorge Grant came on. Not a bad change to make, even with Sunderland coming up at the weekend.

The second half saw the home side coming out with much more purpose, in an almost carbon-copy of the win against Rochdale at the weekend. Shrewsbury certainly had more possession and looked to play across the front of the 18-yard area, but with little danger. The only man I felt would do anything for them was Tracey, who is a Spurs youngster I would have no problem with moving to us on loan, as a squad player.

That said, the calibre of squad player at Sincil Bank is high, and Zack Elbouzedi is a prime example of that. He hasn't played 90 minutes yet this season, but he broke on 50 minutes and looked to create a chance. His pull back was cleared, but the Imps pressed hard and got it back to the winger, who found Howarth, with the former Cefn Druids man shooting straight at the keeper.

It was the only decent chance of the opening 25 minutes of the second half, which certainly didn't have the edge of the first period. Although with a single goal lead it was finely balanced as a contest, the Imps will know they never really looked like losing the lead. Eyoma and Melbourne looked assured in the middle of defence, with Roughan and Gotts turning in very different performances at full back – both played well with Gotts perhaps more attack-minded, but Roughan reminding us of his ability throughout the half.

Just before the 70-minute mark, the Imps finished the game off. Brennan Johnson was the architect, winning a slide tackle and then receiving a pass, pirouetting around Dave Edwards before accelerating through the middle. Naturally, he found Elbouzedi who appeared to be involved in everything. He might have been fortunate to deliver the ball to Howarth, who made no mistake with a turn and finish.

That gave the Imps a second wind, and with Jorge Grant on at half time the tricks started coming out. His used his heel to set Elbouzedi away, who curled a lovely effort at goal which was palmed away. After a quieter half, City had come alive and another goal looked likely.

When Salop did break, they didn't look seriously dangerous. They did have a corner nodded across goal which Roughan had to nod out of play, and a couple of Crossfield balls from Donald Love might have been better had they made the right runs. Love did create a half chance for Dave Edwards, but his header was, frankly, rubbish.

With 12 minutes left on the clock, City rounded off a great evening with a fourth. Elbouzedi (again) was involved, picking out Roughan on the overlap. He fed in Johnson who played a lovely one-two with Scully, before being tripped as he shaped to finish in the area. No doubt at all in the decision and with Jorge Grant on the field, there was no doubt around the outcome either. 4-1 City, the perfect night.

Elbouzedi, troubling my spell checker tonight more than any other time since he arrived, almost created a fifth with his running. With the Imps 4-1 up, he might have ben forgiven for not hunting a ball back to the keeper, but his pressure caused the Salop stopper to play the ball straight out to Roughan. He got down the flank and lifted a ball over for Anderson, who was just under the header.

Hayden Cann got a run out with ten minutes to go, his second appearance for the Imps, and that is something this competition is great for. Yes, it has its critics, but Cann got minutes, whilst Elbouzedi and Howarth both sent timely reminders to supporters what they can offer, should the chance arise. Theo Archibald would likely have started had he been fit, but his bad luck was fortunate for Elbouzedi, who for me was Man of the Match (and comfortable at that).

Deep into stoppage time Shrewsbury had their best chances of the second period, both falling to Tracey. He got two shots away, both blocked by Imps. The second was intercepted by Max Melbourne, who started a break. Elbouzedi (obviously) and Johnson crafted a chance with the latter cutting the ball back towards Scully, who was just beaten to the ball by Scott Goldborne.

The final whistle sounded after three minutes of added time, bringing mercy upon the home side who had been toyed with like a cat playing with a half-dead mouse. It wasn't that Salop were atrocious (although they were poor), but the Imps were excellent. There wasn't a bad player on the field, not even one who you could say was 'alright'. Jason Cummings was once a £1m striker, but he never got a sniff. Wherever he went on the pitch, he was marshalled and thwarted by any of the Imps back four. Max Melbourne has to be mentioned, he looked more than comfortable at left centre back, whilst TJ Eyoma makes the game look effortless wherever he plays. Robbie Gotts had Mark Hone purring with delight, whilst Sean Roughan still doesn't look like a teenager making his first foray into senior football.

Michael Appleton was delighted after the game, noting that despite the six changes, the Imps were still recognisable. The boss also heaped praise on duo Zack Elbouzedi and Remy Howarth who both got goals after spells out of the side.

"The changes that we made changed nothing. The way we went about our business, the way we set up, and the areas of the pitch we countered in were the same they would have been if it was our so-called first eleven," he told BBC Radio Lincolnshire.

"To be fair, he's (Elbouzedi) been unfortunate and there have been occasions I wanted to throw him in and he had an injury, or he went away on international duty when he might have played. He came in before Covid and didn't take his opportunity, he'll be the first to admit that. Tonight, he got the chance, took that, got his goal and looked a threat.

"He was starting to look a threat against man City. He'll be delighted, I'll go to him and Zack because they've come in, the fact they got through 90 minutes shows tremendous qualities from their point of view."

From a fan's perspective, much depends how much stock you put in the trophy, but whether you are a Papa John's critic or convert, the performance was still the same. At times, the 'First XI' haven't been clinical, but it appears that is something they're working on hard in training. When you look at our shots and chances ratio, the pessimist might say we should have won by more, but the grounded fan will see we are creating good chances, and taking a few too. Four different players hit the back of the net tonight and whatever the competition, that must be positive.

Shrewsbury will be different next Tuesday, different personnel and maybe even a different approach. However, whatever side we put out, whoever plays in the red and white, we won't be different. That should worry Steve Cotterill's men and it should worry Sunderland too. I think that's three matches in four now where we have been very good, Plymouth, Rochdale and Shrewsbury all away from home. The one home match in the run where we found it difficult in spells brought three points and after a blip in early November, we have one defeat in eight matches.

Every time I turn iFollow on, the pessimist in me believes the bubble is going to burst. The realist in me, the one who watches, observes and formulates opinion, is beginning to wonder if maybe this is not just some run of form. I'm thinking we might be the real deal.

Reality Check – Imps 0-4 Sunderland
December 12, 2020

The Imps were given a sharp reminder of the quality required in League One as Sunderland handed out a thrashing at Sincil Bank.

After winning so comfortably in midweek, hopes were high that we might be in a position to go eleven points clear of Sunderland. Instead, the visitors dominated proceedings and not only bagged four, but also kept a clean sheet, the first team to do so this season.

The Imps made seven changes to the team which beat Shrewsbury on Tuesday night, but just one from the side that got the better of Rochdale. Robbie Gotts came into the midfield, with Conor McGrandles missing out due to the strain he picked up at the New Meadow. The big news pre-match was the inclusion of Gotts he's been impressive in recent weeks at right-back but is thought to prefer the midfield role.

Whilst that might have got fans excited, the actual product sadly did not. It could have been very different, had the Imps been clinical in taking chances early on. It was a scrappy start to the game, Sunderland certainly looking brighter and causing problems down both flanks, with Callum McFadzean looking a real threat. Despite that, the Imps had the best chance of the opening exchanges when Brennan Johnson got away on the counter. Tayo Edun poked the ball through and was pole-axed as he did, but the ref waved paly-on as Johnson went one-on-one with Lee Burge. Sadly, the on-loan striker fired wide.

On 12 minutes Sunderland got the first corner of the game, which ended up of the feet of Max Power who fired straight at Alex Palmer. The keeper bowled the ball out quickly and City went through again, Johnson trying to round Burge when he arrived in the area. The keeper did well, forcing Johnson wide, and he opted to shoot, with the ball ending up in the side netting. It could have been 2-0 City, but not long after that positivity evaporated.

On 15 minutes Sunderland got a penalty for a foul which, on reflection, was not a foul. Jorge Grant was adjudged to have felled Jack Diamond as he broke into the area, when he clearly won the ball. Now, had it been us getting the penalty, as it was against Plymouth, we might have pointed out the tug on diamond a split second before justified a spot-kick. Whatever the ins and outs, it was a penalty and Leadbitter stroked the ball home.

That knocked City off their stride and soon after Michael Appleton got a talking to for his protesting. It seems that he was angry at the decision, but sadly it can't be changed retrospectively. We got a dubious one against Plymouth which turned the game, swings and roundabouts I guess (through gritted teeth).

Sunderland took complete control for a spell after that, with Montsma picking up a yellow card for a soft foul. It did seem a tad inconsistent after Edun's aggressor was let off earlier in the game, but don't all decisions when you're losing at home? The free kick ended up wide and in the side netting, but it was yet another chance. Minutes later, it was 2-0 anyway. The second was poor defensively, with multiple opportunities to clear or get a foot in before Charlie Wyke stabbed home. Whether it was poor or not, there was no doubt that it was fully deserved. City just didn't deal with the threat from out wide, and hadn't taken the two chances presented early doors.

After the second goal Sunderland took their foot off the gas a little, but it didn't mean we got any decent chances. Johnson did fizz a ball over after combining with Edun, but it was neither a cross, nor a shot and never really threatened. After that, Sunderland clearly decided two goals wasn't enough, upping the tempo with ease to bag a third. They broke, Jack Diamond came in off the attacking right and lofted a ball over Palmer and into the net for 3-0. The difference? Sunderland took their chances, City did not.

It should have been four after another break just before half time, but the Black Cats put the ball into the side netting. They had seven first half chances, four on target, three went in. City managed three shots, all off target. At this level, against these sorts of clubs, you cannot afford to waste a single chance. 3-0 certainly flattered the visitors, but 2-0 did not. It was a first half to forget, much the same as the first half at the Stadium of Light back in January.

Maybe, for a brief moment at the start of the second half, there were glimpses the Imps might get back into it, but they were just that – glimpses. It was the visitors who had the first effort of the half, a long-range drive being spilled by Palmer, who recovered and took it at the second attempt.

The Imps best moments of the half came n quick succession. Anderson and Gotts combined to earn a corner, which fell to Edun who drove high and wide. Jorge Grant whipped in a free kick from the attacking left which Burge punched over, and finally James Jones sliced a drive over from a corner. That all came in the space of five minutes and it as the sum total of the Imps' positive work in the second half.

It was, to all intents and purposes, a rubbish second half for Lincoln fans. Sunderland completely dictated the pace of the game, and were able to make four changes from their deep squad. Michael, with Shrewsbury up in midweek, only made two in total, and that showed as City got leggy and disjointed throughout the game.

There were few chances in the second period for the visitors, and not one of note for the Imps. On 71 minutes, Sunderland worked a fourth, Maguire skinning Edun down the attacking right and finding Wyke who poked home. It might be easy to say it wasn't a 4-0 game, but to be honest I can't agree. Sunderland completely controlled the game from the penalty onwards, and could easily have lost by six or seven.

Of course, with a four-point gap between us and the play-off places, it doesn't mean we slip down the table, and with Hull City losing 1-0 to Shrewsbury we don't lose sight of them either, which makes the result almost bearable. Almost.

It isn't bearable though, because it could have been different. Had we taken one of those opening chances, both one-on-one and clear cut, it might have been very different. I can't go on about the penalty, whether it was or wasn't, because we have been on the other side of those moments and benefited. Besides, Sunderland always looked like they were capable of controlling proceedings and were good value for the win away from the penalty. I don't, not for a single second, feel if it hadn't been given the outcome would have been any different.

I do wonder if the games are beginning to take their toll on the Imps. Jones and Montsma both had knocks in midweek and didn't look at their best. Gotts didn't get a chance to impress himself in the midfield and often we looked to lack the running of McGrandles. This was a game won and lost in the middle of the park – control that area and you control the feed of passes out wide. Sunderland won it, we never got a grip and the battle of youth against experience I talked about on Match Day Live was won by the experienced players.

Sometimes, you hold your hands up and say, 'fair play', we were beaten by a better side. I do think we were off form though, lots of passes going astray and a lack of ideas from 55 minutes onwards. Maybe it is the squad tiring, but this was almost as strong as we can be in terms of selection. However, when you have McGrandles, Jackson, Morton and Bridcutt all out, it apparently does show.

I hate the saying 'we go again', but we go again. We are still second and whatever negativity there is in the air after a losing 4-0 at home should be tempered by the fact we are still second and we are massively outperforming expectations. If anything, this should be used as a positive – we might have lost 4-0 but the level of disappointment underlines exactly where we are. This is Sunderland, one of the biggest clubs in the country, and we expected to go into it and get something from it. They've beaten us 4-0 and are still below us, and we have been thrashed and not lost our position in the table.

I'm sure some aspects of social media will implode, but I can also imagine that 75% of the support will understand where we are and keep some perspective. That said, I hate losing and it is never easy to accept.

Sorry City Slapped By Salop – Imps 0-1 Shrewsbury
December 15, 2020 Gary

What a difference a week makes. Seven days ago I sat in this chair writing about an electric Lincoln City performance against an awful Shrewsbury side.

Fast forward a week and I'm here writing about a poor Lincoln performance against an organised and committed Shrewsbury side. If you'd offered me a win tonight and defeat last week, I would have taken it. You didn't, you couldn't and tonight we looked a million miles from the team than left Shropshire elated last week.

The Imps made two changes from the side that lost 4-0 to Sunderland, with Remy Howarth and Anthony Scully coming in. The intent would be for a more positive approach than we saw against the Black Cats, but that really wasn't the case. If anything, it was the visitors who looked more like scoring in the first 15 minutes or so. The Imps looked shaky at the back, with an early cross from the right causing momentary panic two minutes in. Eventually, the ball went out for a corner, but there seemed to be an air of nervousness about the Imps.

The first real foray into enemy territory came on the ten-minute mark, Scully instrumental in working the ball from right to left, only for Brennan Johnson to hit either a cross r a shot up and over the bar. The Imps were edging their way into the game and a quick corner on 15 minutes brought a half-chance, but Grant's flash ball struck James Jones and bounced out for a goal kick.

There was little between the sides heading towards the halfway point, with a tame shot from distance the only work Alex Palmer had to do. Instead of chances, we got a number of niggly fouls, seemingly born of frustration. Watching on, I was frustrated to see two great crosses from the right go across the six-yard area, with Tom Hopper playing both balls and nobody running in to fill the position he vacated. That led to a challenge from behind on Grant which drew the first booking of the game.

The challenges continued, Scully was seemingly taken out on the edge of the area, but the ref played on. Hopper then took out Vela in the same passage of play, which the ref also ignored, before Eyoma was scythed down too. That was a free-kick and briefly, it looked as though tempers might boil over. Jorge Grant fired the dead ball into the wall and things calmed down, briefly.

On 33 minutes Tayo Edun was hit hard in the left-back role with nothing given, and not long after Johnson looked to take a kick to the gut which the referee also chose to ignore. The game threatened to descend into farce with challenges stopping play all over the pitch, but sadly the only farce came in our next passage of defending.

Lewis Montsma, so often the hero, got caught in possession 20 yards out, hitting Daniel Udoh with a nasty challenge as he tried to recover the ball. It failed, and Sean Whalley was able to push the ball home despite Joe Walsh and Alex Palmer blocking his route. It felt to me a bit like Palmer could have done better too, he stayed behind Walsh, unsighted, which gave the striker a better chance to beat both men at the same time. It was an awful goal to concede to a team known for being resolute and hard to break down.

The Imps best chance came on the stroke of half time and it was the Dutchman looking to make amends. Remy Howarth got away down the right and his cross appeared to be handled out for a corner, which the referee once again waved away. Our corners have been poor this season, but Grant's delivery found Montsma who smashed the ball goalward from eight yards out. Somehow, the Shrews keeper got a block in on the line and stopped us clawing back their goal advantage.

Whilst that might have ended the half on a positive for the Imps, the truth is that we witnessed a poor half of football, where a solid Salop were not only hard to break down, but also quick to press and eager to chase every ball. All too often, we took up good positions in wide areas only for the ball to end up at the feet of Alex Palmer sixty seconds later. That is the method and it has worked in the past, but against sides who are compact it is tough to watch. Throw a goal lead in there and it didn't bode well for the second period of play.

I also felt we lacked natural width in a game that might have benefited from runners. That was evident on the right more than the left, where Scully was often found coming inside and the ball not going with him. Two or three times it was Hopper crossing from the right, or Eyoma chasing a lost ball, when our usual approach sees strength in numbers on the flank.

However, Remy Howarth did have a decent half and he was one of the bright spots it what was a laboured and lacklustre opening 45 minutes.

Whilst the first half was lacklustre, there was more in the second half for City, but not the one thing we needed, a goal. The opening chance of the half fell to Daniel Udoh, his strike was cleared by Lewis Montsma. That was almost the sum of Shrewsbury's intentions as an attacking force, as they defended stoically and strongly against what was a laboured and pedestrian Lincoln side.

Brennan Johnson struck a shot over the bar not long after the restart, with referee Craig Hicks then taking centre stage. He hadn't controlled the game in the first half and he turned down two penalty shouts in a matter of seconds. Tom Hopper appeared to have been felled by the keeper, who maybe got a touch on the ball first, but then Eyoma looked to be taken down as the ball broke loose. Instead, a free kick was given against the on-loan Spurs man. Remy Howarth, who wasn't far from being my Man of the Match, hit the post on 59 minutes after Jorge Grant had worked a lovely ball across the field. After another decent passage of play, Johnson got loose to the attacking right but fired into the side netting from an acute angle.

Each bit of good play was punctuated by long periods of nothingness, game management from Shrewsbury which they did well and rather slow build up from City. Too often the ball came across the front of the 18-yard area with players seemingly reticent to shoot. When one did, it was defender TJ Eyoma who sent the ball high into the night sky. On 74 minutes it looked like Wigan Mk II as Joe Walsh was crudely felled on the edge of the area. Up stepped the golden boy, Mr Grant, only to curl his free kick straight into the wall. At that moment it felt like we were destined to get nothing. Being honest, it felt like than the minute they scored their goal.

A snapshot from Whalley reminded us that Salop were still a side to keep an eye out for, but it really wouldn't have mattered if it had gone in, because it was not City's night at all. On 77 minutes Lewis Montsma went down in the area looking for a penalty. Michael Hortin thought it would have been soft, but having watched the replay back, three times, the defender looks to be kicked on the back of the leg as he chases the ball. Still, thems the breaks.

The final ten minutes saw Johnson and Howarth both have shots blocked, but we could still be playing tomorrow morning as we wouldn't have scored. The result saw City fall out of the automatic promotion spots and into the top six, a position still to be proud of. That said, it could and should have been so much more against a Shrewsbury side who only threatened when we gifted them a chance and whose keeper we never really tested, bar the Montsma chance in the first half.

I was very surprised we didn't look to freshen it up in the second period – Robbie Gotts and Zack Elbouzedi have both had good outings in recent weeks and if we are looking to preserve players for the hectic schedule, surely the odd change later on might have gone down well? I know I am a layman and I don't see the lads each week on the training ground, but I felt we needed something different from around 60 minutes. That said, much of our decent play came after the hour mark, but we just couldn't score.

I don't want to moan too much and seeing as I am in an utterly foul mood, I am going to call it there. I may write more tomorrow when I don't feel so angry. I'm not sure what has annoyed me more – the referee bottling a couple of big decisions or the fact we created lots of opportunity around the area, but rarely and an actual opportunity. What I mean by that is we had lots of possession 20 yards from goal, but few chances that looked like going in. In terms of the referee, twice we saw bookable challenges go unpunished by players who had already been booked. The referee wasn't the reason we lost the game, but to the same end, he might just have been the reason we didn't win it. There were three or four penalty shouts and even with my rose-tinted glasses off, I think the handball in the first half and the foul on Eyoma after Hopper had been brought down by the keeper, were both spot kicks. If we get given them, we win. You can't rely on those moments, but when there are four in a game you like to think maybe, just maybe, you get one.

I disagreed with Radio Lincolnshire's Man of the Match, which is unlike me. Yes, Scully looked busy but I didn't feel he warranted the top accolade. For me, he's great centrally in a free role, but as a wide player he drifts too often, leaving Tom Hopper coming out wide. Sadly, for Tom, he was ineffective too and not one of the chances I've written about fell to our striker. If I had to pick a Man of the Match I'd possibly go for Howarth, who looked composed and direct, or Edun who I felt attacked well from full-back. I could argue Tayo didn't move the ball quickly enough at times, but you can only move the ball quickly if there are movement and space, which there wasn't. Maybe that was a credit to Shrewsbury, but if teams have found a blueprint to beat us, then we need to find a plan B. I think that might only come with a couple of new faces to shake things up, offering us something more. An aerial presence in the attacking 18-yard box would be a super start.

It's been a tough few days and the lads will dust themselves down for Saturday, whilst I will feel down that in two winnable matches, we have no goals to show for our endeavour at all. Those injuries, Bridcutt, McGrandles and Morton, do look to be affecting us badly. The sooner one or two make it back, the better we'll be all around.

Resilient City triumph in clash of styles – Northampton Town 0-4 Imps
December 19, 2020

It would be easy to write about a game of contrasting styles here, sitting on some sort of higher ground looking down on a long-ball side, but I'm not a hypocrite.

If you are a Lincoln fan crowing about beating the bruisers today, think long and hard for a moment. A more refined version of that style defined us in 2017/18 and the year after. Almost that exact style got us out of the basement division in the late nineties. 'Long ball' is easy to look down upon when you are not playing it, but as Lincoln City fans we have no place to comment on how Northampton approach the game. i think we let their booing supporters do that, or the ones ironically cheering their first shot on target on 83 minutes.

No, I cannot pass comment on that without feeling grubby and I won't. What I will talk about is the Imps, unchanged from the midweek defeat against Shrewsbury. That's a huge shout by Michael Appleton by the way, a statement to everyone ready to criticise after the game, of which I was, to a degree, guilty. He felt we did enough to win the game against Shrewsbury and he showed that by keeping an unchanged squad. What I will say is even with 15 fit outfield players, we never know quite what the team selection is going to be.

The key in a game like this, a game which could have become a war of attrition, is to strike an early blow and make the landscape very different. This was a game we expected to get a goal in, but the longer the game goes on, the more buoyed the home side become. With fans behind them too and our two recent defeats, we definitely needed to start on the front foot. I'm not sure how much more 'front-footed' grabbing a second-minute lead is.

Brennan Johnson was the creator, breaking at pace after a Northampton attack broke down before feeding in Anthony Scully. He kept up his strong scoring record and showed real composure in doing so, not flashing an instant shot but just snatching a bit of space and finishing coolly. Bear in mind he's only started nine league games, that takes his tally to four in the league and seven in 22 across all competitions. That's a good return in the wider context, but in terms of this game, he couldn't have given us a better start.

With something to defend, you would have to back us and I immediately got a message from my mate Chris, saying he thought we'd go on and score four. I felt that bold, given how tough we found scoring on Tuesday night, but as ever this Lincoln team didn't disappoint. Mind you, the scoreline suggests a rout, but it was far from an easy game.

We picked the right times to attack and the right times to go a little longer. There was little playing out from the back from us, very few passes to defenders from a goal kick, not so much fighting fire with fire than protecting players in possession I felt. Maybe Michael had watched a couple of their previous games and seen some stuff he didn't like because Alex Palmer was quick to deliver the ball forward and take the sting out of any possession they had with prolonged periods holding onto the ball. The natives did not like that, as we wouldn't if it happened at our place.

On ten minutes one such quick ball to Johnson saw him feed in Edun, who put in a teasing cross for birthday boy Jorge Grant to volley over. It was another sniff at goal and a sign the Imps were going for the kill.

It certainly wasn't all one way and a corner on 18 minutes saw a header flashed at goal with Palmer more than a match for the effort. Three minutes later, another set-piece delivery from the home side saw Fraser Horsfall steam in, but his header flew over the bar. The Cobblers got forward quickly at every opportunity, but Montsma and Walsh looked more than a match for the intended targets. On the flanks, both Edun and Eyoma also stood firm whenever chances began to develop.

Remy Howarth, Man of the Match in midweek, was cynically fouled on the edge of the area on 24 minutes, a needless challenge from a naive defender. That gave Grant a chance to do what he does best, but his free-kick was deflected up and over the goal. Another set-piece moments later saw Grant whip a corner under the crossbar which Steve Arnold flapped at, with the ball dropping to montsma at the back stick. He shifted to one side, buying himself some space and powered an effort goalwards which Arnold parried. there were shades of his goal against Swindon in the move, only with a slightly less desirable outcome.

The impact of having fans in the ground was first heard on 28 minutes when a home attack broke down and they went back to Arnold – a chorus of boos rang out around the ground. This is a side with one goal in six homes games going into today, a team with a brand of football which is only pleasing when it brings results. Having 2,000 fans in does help if you're doing well, not so much if you go back to your keeper with less than half-an-hour played, apparently.

The first of several inexplicable referring decisions came on the half-hour mark, as the Imps hunted a second. Some wonderful football saw Scully whip a cross in which was cleared, but he picked up the rebound and drove at goal. As he got into the area he seemed to be fouled, but the referee waved it away. I've watched back three or four times and I fail to see how it wasn't a penalty. Maybe our reputation for 'winning' penalties goes before us, or maybe referee Robert Lewis was warming up for a rough afternoon.

The first yellow card of the game went to Montsma after he hauled his man down on 36 minutes and there can be no complaints. Benny Ashley-Seal had got the better of the Dutchman and he 'took one for the team'. Much of the post-match talk will be about some of Northampton's fouls and the referee decisions, but we did pick up bookings we deserved too.

Remy Howarth had a little rush of blood on 39 minutes which possibly could have given us a second goal. He did well to find space and drive to the edge of the 18-yard area, but he opted to shoot instead of feeding in one of two players in better positions. Johnson looked unhappy after finding all the space in the world on the attacking left, only for Howarth to drag his shot horribly wide of the goal. Three minutes later, all was forgotten.

TJ Eyoma did well to hold up the ball and win a free-kick on the attacking right, which Grant delivered with his usual precision. It spun across the front of the six-yard box, where Hopper bravely stuck his head on it to beat Arnold in the goal. He took a belt in the face for his troubles prompting a break in play, but it was the goal of a poacher, and a brave one at that. Maybe, at 1-0, the home side had a sniff of getting back into the game, but with one goal at Sixfields in 540 minutes or so of football, 2-0 put it beyond doubt. When half time came not long after, the home fans booed their team off. Welcome back.

The second half started with the Imps desperately looking for goal number three on a challenging surface. The reluctance to play out from the back may well have been the state of the turf, and it looked to cut up badly as the game progressed. Within five minutes of the restart City had two decent chances, the second of which was created by the Dutch master. He got away from two players in the attacking right channel and managed to scoop an effort at goal which Arnold was forced to save. The resulting corner fell to Scully, lurking on the edge of the area, but his first-time volley went over.

There was no let-up in the attacking moves from City and on 52 minutes a familiar face escaped a sure-fire booking. Grant did Bolger with a lovely little move, but the former Imps man just cynically stopped our captain from getting away in the area. If Montsma's was a booking in the first half, and it was, Bolger should have got the same. The free-kick from James Jones clipped the wall and deflected away from a corner.

Northampton weren't letting us have it all our own way, Nicky Adams is a player who has troubled us in the past for Bury and he shot over after Montsma's headed clearance fell to his feet. Mark Hone wasn't happy with Montsma's header being down and out of the area rather than up and out, but generally the defenders coped well with the bombardment.

Cian Bolger did get his yellow card on 56 minutes, again flattening Grant in an off-the-ball incident. Okay, if he is on a yellow he probably doesn't make that challenge, but it was the second bookable offence from the Irishman in the space of a few moments. He cut a frustrated figure at times, having to just head the ball out and kick it away rather than do anything meaningful, but he certainly appeared to be targeting Grant.

Another player being targeted was Lewis Montsma and just before the hour mark came a real contentious moment. A flick on saw him challenging Cobblers sub Rocky Korboa, with the latter smashing an elbow into Montsma's face. Unbelievably, the referee waved play on, then stopped the game when the home side had the ball. After lengthy treatment and with Montsma clearly bearing a huge mark on his face, the game resumed with us down to ten men and them able to launch a free ball into our area. Nothing came of it, but it didn't sit well with me at all. I know referees get things wrong, but he was no more than ten yards away. It was brutal too, their lad did seem to glance at Montsma first.

In a bitty and broken passage of play, the next big incident was another foul on Montsma, this time from sub Harry Smith. As Lewis went to clear the ball Smith cynically left his foot on the challenge, taking our central defender out. it enraged Lewis, who went over to the referee asking for some protection. It wasn't coming though, nor was the yellow, although we did pick up two more bookings, both for cynical challenges and both spot on. Sadly, the consistency wasn't quite there from the officials today.

With ten minutes or so left, the Imps ramped up the pressure with a free-kick right on the edge of the area. I thought Korboa was lucky not to go in the book for the challenge, stopping a lively Johnson attack, but the dead ball was just too close to goal. Grant couldn't quite get it up and over, but City smelled blood. Harry Anderson, on as a sub, got away down the right and picked up a lovely ball from Scully, drawing a save from Arnold with a drive across goal.

At the other end, Cian Bolger almost gave his side hope with a close-range header. For the first time in the game, a great free-kick saw him sneak into space, but his effort came back off the underside of the bar in a real let-off for the Imps. The last of Northampton as an attacking force came with their first effort on target on 82 minutes, a Nicky Adams drive saved easily by Palmer. That drew ironic applause from the home fans, clearly directed at manager Keith Curle.

Within seconds of that chance, the Imps killed the game off. James Jones threaded a wonderful ball through to Johnson, who steadied himself before lifting a sumptuous finish over Arnold and into the back of the net. 3-0, game over, can the last one out please turn off the lights.

Michael Appleton will have been keen to see a clean sheet, which is why he looked furious as the game went into injury time. Edun and Palmer got involved in a mix-up which saw Nicky Adams look to lob at goal, only to strike Harry Smith in an offside position. Their two players seemed to exchange views as the Imps were let-off the hook, whilst Edun and Palmer had no such interaction. It's easier to be laid back when you're winning, sure, but I suspect there is no blame culture within the Imps' camp right now.

3-0 didn't flatter the Imps who had been the best side throughout, and maybe 4-0 didn't either. The provider was Robbie Gotts, on as a late sub for Scully. He found himself in acres of space to tee up Johnson, who finished with aplomb to give the scoreline some real gloss. It was the second 4-0 defeat inflicted upon the Cobblers in a week, and it ensured the Imps remain second at Christmas, level on points with leaders Portsmouth and boasting a game in hand.

I enjoyed the game, not just because we won, but because finally, we got to see the Imps against so-called anti-football. There were certain teams that always struggled against us when we played our brand of direct football and there were some who sussed us easily. My fear was this young side might wilt in the face of pressure, relentless long balls and a few of the dark arts. they didn't, they weren't drawn into the tackles or arguing with the referee, they got on with the game in the correct manner, rolling with the punches and making their point with the ball. If pushed for a Man of the Match, I think I'd have to agree with Mark Hone and go for Johnson, but Scully certainly wouldn't be far away, nor would Montsma. The latter proved a point to many today, taking a real battering and standing firm and resolute when he did. I'll be honest, I'm still smarting at Korboa's elbow, although probably not quite as much as Montsma!

It is easy to get drawn into commenting on the style the opposition played, and to a degree, I may have done that through the article, but I won't be heavily critical of it. Some teams approach games in that manner, some even do it relatively well. However, it wasn't hard to see why the Cobblers are struggling this season and of all the teams we have seen, I would have to suggest they were amongst the poorest. That doesn't mean it was the easiest game though, quite the opposite. That's why I enjoyed it, because it wasn't a game of chess, a tippy-tappy exercise in possession or a cagey battle of wills. It was a blood-and-guts lower league game, against a physical side and aerial bombardment, and we came through it. After a tough seven days, it was a lovely way to round the week off and ensured that when the bottom club visit on Boxing Day, we'll be level on points with the top team in the division.

That means a very Merry Christmas indeed, and a New Year where we can still, hope to come out of the third tier, in more ways than one.

Lincoln City SWOT Analysis
December 22, 2020

For anyone who has ever worked in branch management, certainly in a builder's merchant, this will likely raise a smile.

I'm thinking Kev Harris, Simon Barnfield and Paul Bullivant from my Jackson Building Centre days here, but I'm sure anyone who works in middle-management across a range of industry will know exactly what they are about to get. A SWOT analysis is a report that I had to do on numerous occasions about a depot. usually, I found myself doing one when I applied for jobs – the manager roles at Jackson Horncastle, Jewson Bourne and Jewson Huntingdon. As a trainee manager, it was a way of making you aware of market conditions and it is a tool likely used today, not that I have had to write one since I left Jewson in April 2017.

SWOT stands for strengths, weaknesses, opportunities and threats. The idea was you divided a piece of paper into four and came up with a couple of entries for each, which in turn would give your area manager a picture of where your branch was. It is a useful tool for analysis and often when you had to sit and think, it helped shape the direction you took you depot in. Or, in my case, I did it, it got looked at and I filed it in the rounded grey filing cabinet under my desk which also had the Mcdonald's wrappers in.

Still, it makes a change from the usual method of presenting a 'season-so-far' review, doesn't it? I think three items for each will suffice (although if you worked under a certain Mr F at Jewson, that would be six, or nine and if you came in short, you'd be berated, even though he forgot the difference between gross and net in a sales meeting once). So, without further ado, I present to you my SWOT analysis on Lincoln City, December 2020.

STRENGTHS

Versatility

We start with strengths and the first thing that comes to mind when I think of our strengths is our versatility. We have 15 fit outfield players right now, that just about makes up a bench, and yet Michael could play numerous different starting XI's. Jorge Grant can play almost anywhere in the middle third as well as up front on the left, we could field three different players at left-back, yet they could all start in the same team and not one of them actually be at left-back. They say that a squad has strength in depth, but that isn't the case with us. We don't have squad depth and we desperately need McGrandles, Archibald, Jackson, Bridcutt or Morton back from injury (have I forgotten anyone), but it is a strength that even with five players out, all of whom would likely be starting (bar maybe Theo), we are still able to keep opposition managers guessing as to how we will line up.

Management

I remember the day DC left, I had to write an article for Football League World about three managers I felt we should appoint. One of those managers was Michael Appleton and I'm fairly sure I was the first person to suggest him as a possible manager. I'd been impressed with his NTT20 podcast interview and I felt he was prime to come in and do a great job for a club. His record at Oxford stood up against the best in League One and League Two, and I could explain away the other spells in management. I'm delighted to have been proven right, even if it did get a bit worrying up until last Christmas. What we have now, in my opinion, is one of the most exciting managers at this level. he has squeezed miracles out of a threadbare squad on a reduced budget, to such a degree that I genuinely fear for other clubs if he does get a full budget over the coming year or two. There is a philosophy to his play, it is clear and concise and when things don't go well, he sticks to the plan anyway. The players are clearly well-drilled and well-coached and with David Kerslake and Steve Croudson in the background (amongst others), I feel as confident in our management now as I did between 2016 and 2019. Lincoln City fans wait years for exciting, consistent and (hopefully) successful back-to-back management teams and finally, we have just that.

League Position

An obvious strength is our current league position, which has given us a great platform to build upon as we go bravely into 2021. It is fair to say (and I won't mince my words) 2020 has been utter shit in almost all aspects of life, but right here at Sincil Bank, it hasn't. We've evolved and progressed and to go into Christmas second in the league (or joint top, which is what people in second on goal difference say) is not just good, it is unbelievable. 12 months ago there were those who thought we were in a relegation battle, yet here we are with a lower budget and no supporters in the ground, challenging for promotion. Yes, Bristol Rovers dropped from a similar position to relegation candidates last season, but even a pessimist has to admit where we are is a strength. I boldly predicted we could lose four in every five matches between now and May and still stay up. For a club whose fans felt that survival was a reasonable expectation, that is a big strength.

WEAKNESSES

Squad Depth
Writing about weaknesses and threats is not always easy. You can be perceived to be too negative if you are critical when your club is second (joint top) in the table, and I don't want to become an 'Arsenal Fan TV' style platform of overreaction. However, it does not hurt to remember that every situation has elements that are not perfect, the very best teams have areas they could develop. One of the most obvious for me is our squad depth. I don't think it is any secret that the squad needs reinforcements, almost certainly in the central striker role, but probably in the wider squad too. Much does depend on injuries and there will be no huge glut of players given the pandemic and the problems it poses. I think it is interesting that our biggest strength, and possible weakness, are both squad related.

Means
Let's be honest, the budget is a potential weakness. That isn't due to the board being tight as t was back in the early eighties, quite the opposite. What it is down to is us, Lincoln City, a small provincial team battling for promotion with clubs such as Ipswich, Portsmouth, Sunderland and Hull City, all with Premier League experience. The truth is we are the poor relation, the plucky underdog fighting on a smaller budget and winning using guile, craftiness and strategy rather than spending power. Can we go out and spend £2m on a striker? No. We wheel and deal bargain and barter and whilst we are good at it, we are weaker in terms of buying power than some of the clubs around us. Again, this isn't a criticism, it is a stated fact which we succeed in spite of.

Capacity
I did genuinely struggle for a third, and whilst I know some might say 'playing out from the back', long term I wonder if our capacity might be a weakness. I think the club agree, seeing as the proposed development of the Stacey West is going ahead. It isn't even the Lincoln fans not getting in which is a concern, but we could accept 4,000 from Sunderland and Portsmouth all day long at this level. other clubs could bring a bigger allocation too, and for those meaty derbies with Hull City, Doncaster and Mansfield Grimsby Scunthorpe Sheffield Wednesday, we could easily sell 12,000 home tickets. Sincil Bank is a limited ground, it is a wonderful ground, but it might not be currently adequate for the journey the club is on. I can see us looking at further expansion longer term, especially if we did end up in the Championship, where attendances would increase further.

OPPORTUNITIES

Commercial
The opportunities area was always one I struggled with in my businesses because I felt the strengths and weaknesses covered it. I tried to look at the club from a neutral point of view and see where we might be able to continue to expand and grow. One area I think we have done really well in recently is commercial because marketing is a hard sell in times pf a pandemic. That will continue to be the case going into the New Year and beyond, but I do think we have a commercial team who seize on the opportunity and turn it

to their advantage. Take Match Day Live for instance – there have been regular advert slots on there, not too intrusive, but benefitting the club in some way. as we keep winning games and potential rising through the divisions, the income from commercial revenue will keep going up. A jump to the Championship would bring more shirt revenue, potentially better advertising revenue through TV deal and this is a huge opportunity. I saw a post on social media suggesting we didn't want promotion because it would be too costly – utter madness. This isn't 1980 where the costs potentially outweigh the benefits, it is 2020/21 and TV money alone would revolutionise the club.

Youth System

Lots of work has gone into our academy in recent seasons and although he is out of the side at the moment, Sean Roughan is an example of that. To a degree, whilst we didn't get a huge fee for him, Ellis Chapman is too – these are players coming out of our youth team and forging a career in the senior game. I know there will be some criticism we let Ellis go, but that happens – look at Wayne Biggins, Luke Dimech and even Steve Holmes, all former YT prospects who left and became senior players elsewhere. The key is to ensure a steady stream of players, akin to Crewe, with first-team capabilities. They may not all stay, they may not all be a success, but in turning youngsters into professionals, you are exposing that chance, that opportunity. Hayden Cann might be the next Lee Frecklington, the next local boy done good, or he might not. The fact he is around the first team shows what a good setup we do have, a pathway for young players. That's been several years in the making and is a real opportunity the club can hopefully look to exploit.

Player Trading

Player trading is a big opportunity for us, if it is done right. The obvious shout is Lewis Montsma right now, but these chances come along once in a blue moon. Michael made a success of Oxford by trading players, bringing in the likes of Kemar Roofe and seeing the club sell them on for big profit. That works well at times when the market is buoyant, which it isn't now, and when you get the right player. Oxford do it really well, Dickie, Fosu and Baptiste all proof of the model working. The key is to then be able to split the proceeds between players to boost the team and the next big-money sale. Once upon a time, being a 'selling club' was seen as a bad thing in the eyes of supporters, but I think the modern game dictates that it is a method of sustaining and developing. Nobody wants to see Lewis Montsma sold, but if the club got £2m for him and could pay £500,000 for a striker and top the budget up to a normal level, it would be a necessary evil.

THREATS

Player Departures

Whilst player trading is an opportunity, the biggest threat in my eyes is player departures. That could be in the short-term, such as with Brennan Johnson going and leaving a gap in the squad, or it could be the likes of Jorge Grant in the longer term. Nobody wants to see good players come into the side, play well and leave for free and that for me is a huge threat. I think back to the likes of Gary Taylor-Fletcher, Dany N'Guessan and Jeff Hughes, all of whom came in, did well and left for nothing. All of those players were worth £500,000 or more when they left the club and yet thanks to Mr Bosman, we got nothing. Yes, a player such as Jorge Grant can help us get where we want to be in his time contracted to the club, but it would be a crying shame to see him leave for nothing. Sadly, this is a threat the club cannot seriously counteract. Yes, they can offer new deals, but a player doesn't have to sign them. They can offer longer deals in the first instance, but what if a player loses form, gets injured or the manager changes and leaves them in the wilderness? Then you find yourself spiralling back to financial oblivion.

Covid-19

This is fairly obvious and is probably the worst threat of all, but the current pandemic is a big problem for this football club, as it is to many. The lack of fans might be causing Sincil Bank to feel empty and desolate, but that is reflected in the club's bank balance. The longer this goes on, the more likely we are to suffer the effects on the field, especially if we struggle to recruit players, pay the wages required and bring income into the club. The price of testing is a big cost too, I would imagine one the club were hit with post-Sunderland. I know Covid-19 is pretty much a threat to everything, business, leisure and sanity, and the football club is not exempt. Everything you see on the field, everything you hear from Michael and everything you believe we can achieve is currently under the spectre of this bloody virus.

Burnout

The last threat is another which I feel is closer in terms of timelines than most. I fear this squad may suffer burnout. There is talk of a circuit-breaker round of postponements at present (mutterings in the press, not so much officially) and whilst that may help get a few players fit, it would leave serious fixture congestion as we move into 2021. We are still in the Papa John's Trophy too, meaning more games which are financially lucrative to the club. All of this is going on with just 15 fit senior footballers ready to play and there is a lot of pressure on them. Jorge Grant, James Jones and Alex Palmer have started all 18 games in the league, Tom Hopper has played in all 18 and TJ Eyoma has started 16 times, playing 17. This squad is playing two games a week, almost every week, and that presents problems. we have already seen players getting injured and others have been in and out with knocks and strains. If the fixtures do pile up towards the end of the season, one can only imagine burnout is a real possibility.

Zack Elbouzedi bags EFL Trophy award
December 23, 2020

Zack Elbouzedi, who turned in a stunning display as we thrashed Shrewsbury 4-1 in the Papa John's Trophy, has rightly been named Player of the Round by the EFL.

The Irish winger has been forced to wait for his chance, but he seized it with both hands, helping set up a second-round tie with Accrington in the process. Zack bagged one goal and created two with an outing full of power, guile and instinctive finishing.

He has been rewarded for his endeavour by being named Player of the Round, and he expressed his delight in an interview with the EFL.

"I'm delighted to win the award," Elbouzedi said. "It's important for the club to win games and do well, but I had a good performance myself and it helped us get through to the next round which is the most important thing for the club.

"The gaffer made a few changes, but everyone who came in did well and showed that when they're needed they can do a job. It was a good, professional team performance and we really showed what we could do as a team."

Zack also spoke of the club's current form, and was glowing in his praise even though it has sadly kept him on the bench for long spells.

"It's been an unbelievable year so far," Zack added.

"That momentum and the winning mentality has been unbelievable this season and long may it continue. The club want to get promoted but do it in a sustainable way, so that when we do get to the Championship, we can stay there. The management and the way the club is run so professional and I think that's why they've risen up the leagues in the way that they have."

Zack has appeared four times for the club this season, making his first league appearance as a late sub in the 4-0 win at Northampton. After impressing in pre-season, he got 75 minutes of our EFL Trophy game against Scunthorpe, as well as 13 minutes at the end of the Forest Green FA Cup win.

He'll be hoping this award now gives Michael little chance but to give him more time, even at the end of league games, to show exactly what he is all about.

It's a Very Happy New Year – Imps 5-1 Burton Albion
December 27, 2020

When I was a kid, my Dad used to wander around the house singing to himself. Usually, it was one of his favourite songs, such as The Great Pretender (Roy Orbison version), or Billie Don't Be a Hero by Paper Lace.

On matchday, the day before it and the day after, he would usually be singing football songs. Those who know my Dad know he was indiscriminate about the validity of the song, for instance singing 'we are top of the league' when we're not. He did usually keep one back for Christmas though. and the first time I recall hearing this classic was 1987 after we beat Boston – 'Hark now hear, the angels sing, the (insert opposition name here) ran away, and (unintelligible usually), because of Boxing Day'. sometimes the opposition would be 'Grimsby', no matter who we played, and if we lost you wouldn't hear it post 5 pm on the 26th.

Yesterday, I found myself wandering down the stairs singing that exact same song, belting it out, loud and proud. I still don't know the words to the third line, but you can bet your last pound it doesn't matter.

Boxing Day hasn't always been a treat for the Imps, in my mind we lose more than we win (Crewe, Oxford, Guiseley, Halifax and Grimsby have all made the day after Christmas very miserable indeed). It's almost like that post-festive hangover descends on the team and even in our most title-winning seasons we lost on December 26th. I wrapped up Match Day Live predicting a 2-0 win, but secretly I could see the headlines being written, Eardley plonking a cross on Bostwick's head.

Let's face it, that was the narrative, wasn't it? In commentary their names were mentioned as much as Lincoln players and given their exploits with the Imps, it was little surprise they dominated the story before and during the match. It was hard to look beyond them for the headlines unless we wrote our own. Luckily, this Lincoln City side are quite good at finding a new story to tell and within seven minutes of kicking off, the result wasn't in doubt.

I had barely got my pad of paper and pen ready to make notes before James Jone pinged an exquisite 60-yard pass downfield to Anthony Scully. In days gone by, that's a hopeful punt to a winger, but you see in Jones' body shape and Scully's movement it was all intentional. It wasn't a 'danger-alley' hoof, but a perfect ball forward. Scully, who I had struggled to pigeon-hole a few weeks ago, carried on his superb form by getting down the line and teeing up Remy Howarth for his first goal in the Football League. It almost sounds patronising to say 'I was delighted for Remy', because he has got where he is on merit, but genuinely, I was. He's such a down-to-earth lad, he loves life and often they're the sort who maybe just aren't quite good enough (Jake Sheridan anyone?). Remy is proving to have the right balance of groundedness and ability and he'll cherish that moment, with hopefully more to come.

It's the second week in a row we've scored early and immediately we smelled blood against the ageing Burton back four. Scully was involved moments later as he found Tom Hopper, whose ball across the box found Brennan Johnson with an even easier goal than Howarth's. Before the clock had turned to double-digits, the game was over. If Scully had chosen to release Johnson instead of holding on to the ball on eight minutes, it could have ended up a cricket score. I think at 3-0, Burton's heads would have gone completely, but as it was they were let off the hook and slowly looked to make the remaining eighty-odd minutes a contest of sorts.

At the time, we didn't know the game was in the bag, although the commentary team of Mark Hone and Michael Hortin certainly felt that was the case, at first at least. In his post-match interview, Michael hinted at the younger players perhaps taking their foot off the gas, and the half wasn't free of moments where you felt the Brewers might get back into it. Their play was laboured at times and they always looked like conceding on the break, but one or two of their players do have something about them. I liked Charle Vernam, the former Grimsby man, who was a constant threat down the attacking left. He got past Eyoma twice, on 12 minutes and 14, but fired over in both instances. They weren't moments of worry as such, more reminders this was a League One fixture and not a Northern Premier team up against a League One side. With respect, that was the impression the opening ten minutes gave.

On the quarter-hour mark, an engrossing game almost threatened to become a contest again as Tayo Edun's clearance dropped to Akins on the edge of the area. He's a menace, or he could be in the right setup, but he fired over the goal of Alex Palmer to keep the score at 2-0. Before we hit 20 minutes, a quick free-kick routine between Grant, Hopper and Scully presented a chance for Johnson, who got the merest of touches looking to divert it past O'Hara on the Burton goal. It went agonisingly wide and was probably our last good chance of the half.

After that, things went a little off the boil. At times it was scrappy from both sides and we didn't get the flow going again, not properly. There were half-chances for both sides, Vernam the obvious threat for them, although Ciaran Gilligan did have a good run forward resulting in a shot, which was never going to trouble Palmer.

I felt at half time the next goal would be crucial, but that's such a tired cliche. Is anything more obvious at 2-0? Make it 2-1 and the losing team have something to play for, make it 3-0 and it is almost certainly game over (forget Forest Green in 2014), never more so than against this Imps side. The truth is were it not for the goal we gave Shrewsbury, we would have conceded six in nine matches, four of which came in one game against Sunderland. It does seem as if the opposition needs a gift to score, and even Sunderland needed a disputed penalty to get a foothold in that game. Just imagine, if we had bagged one of those opening two chances against them, as we have in the last two games, how different that game might have been.

Football is a game of ifs and buts though, and I'm sure Burton would have been saying 'if we'd been tighter in the first ten minutes' throughout the half time team talk. We hadn't over-awed them the entire half as the opening ten suggested we might, but when you're 2-0 up and top of the league, you don't have to take risks. You just have to be sensible, solid and wait for the opposition to react.

They didn't react, not by making changes nor in terms of coming out and getting at us. The first chance of the second half fell to them, but once again they were aiming for something in the darkening early-evening sky, rather than between the sticks of Alex Palmer. As for us, we just stuck to our ethos, kept passing the ball and eventually, got our rewards. Johnson lashed a shot over after good work from Howarth, and suddenly the Imps clicked back into place.

The killer third goal was a thing of real beauty in terms of build-up. Anthony Scully made a lovely dummy to allow the ball to run out to Eyoma, the sort of skill we have become accustomed too at the Bank. Eyoma's delivery found Howarth who saw his effort saved, but Scully had arrived in the six-yard box for our third tap-in of the game. It's interesting because the criticism a few months ago was we were trying to walk the ball in, and yet the praise on social media last night was raining down. Had anything actually changed? We were still doing the same things, but Burton couldn't cope with it in the way that, say, Accrington or Shrewsbury did. Still, let's not look too deeply for the cloud somewhere in the middle of the thick silver lining, eh? It was 3-0, game over and I was already looking forward to my turkey/beef/ham hybrid leftover dinner.

Burton finally rolled the dice on the hour mark, making three changes in one. Kane Hemmings was one player I thought might cause a few problems, you may recall him being a marquee signing for Mansfield back when we made the play-offs and they didn't. Kieran Wallace came on too, he had six games on loan from Sheffield United back in 2014/15, losing four. Would it make a difference?

No.

Within minutes of the changes it was 4-0, and this time it was like the ghost of Christmas past. Okay, losing 3-1 to Sunderland was just after Christmas, but playing out from the back badly cost us against them and it looked very familiar. O'Hara rolled the ball to Bostwick, under pressure he knocked it to Gilligan and it all went for a Burton (sorry) as Johnson just took the ball off him and slotted it home. Seriously, I find it harder to take the tennis ball from my dog than Johnson found it to retrieve from Burton. I can understand why their fans are angry at their manager – they have a decent squad on paper, but they don't play to their strengths. I always like the saying 'we're a good team, we just struggle in both boxes', and I saw someone comment that about the Brewers. Lads, if you can't defend and can't score, you're not a good team. Sorry.

It all looked like getting on top of the visitors as Robbie Gotts had an effort deflected on 70 minutes, then three minutes after James Jones had an effort saved after Scully's neat backheel. I wondered if we might be looking to get six or seven, such was the fluidity and pace we showed in the attacking third. Unfortunately, a little too much festive spirit led to us giving Burton something to cheer. Lewis Montsma looked to shield a ball back to Palmer, but Palmer had other ideas. Montsma took his eye off the ball and looked over his shoulder to Hemmings, who nipped round and scored. I did hear an expletive or two on the replay and rightly so – there was no complacency because we were 4-0 up. I like to see that, keeping a clean sheet mattered and we didn't manage it.

Montsma made another error on 77 minutes as Burton briefly believed in a Christmas miracle, but this time Hemmings fired over. It was an uncharacteristic display from the Dutchman, but in fairness, he had been spraying some nice passes around and I'd rather we made errors at 4-0 (or 4-1) up with ten minutes to play than make then early doors away at Sunderland. Mind you, after the Shrewsbury goal, there will surely be a few words had on the training ground.

Luckily, any notion of a comeback, however fanciful, was eradicated in the 80th minute as sub Harry Anderson got a goal. He's heading towards 200 appearances for City and has fallen out of favour in recent weeks, but he's a great weapon to have from the bench or the get-go. His shot deflected off Michael Bostwick and into the Burton net. For the record, the other two players in the back four which conceded five were John Brayford and Colin Daniel.

It could and should have been 6-1 before the referee brought things to a premature end. Zack Elbouzedi got his chance after the scintillating Shrewsbury performance and he found himself one-on-one with O'Hara. He just took too long, trying to round the former Manchester United man. In fairness, he did get past the keeper, but by then a defender came back and the chance was gone for Zack. It did fall to Johnson, and sensing his hattrick he got an effort away, but he aimed at whatever Burton had been looking at all afternoon and fired over.

That was that. Maybe I misunderstood the rules, but added time seemed very light. I thought 30 seconds per goal (that would be two minutes) and per sub (with could have been as much as three-and-a-half), but the match official clearly felt it was time to pack up and go home. For the second Saturday in a row, we left the field having won by a four-goal margin.

We also now know that when the god-awful year 2020 is over, and 2021 breaks into its first dawn, we shall be top of League One. We are the best team D3D4 will feature on their podcast and despite a couple of knocks, we have kept ourselves not only in play-off contention but in the hunt for automatic promotion as well. As things stand, we are closer to Arsenal and Chelsea in terms of league position than we are Grimsby and Scunthorpe. Has that ever happened? I don't know, nor do I care too much.

This year has been shit. We haven't been able to go to games, we haven't been able to see our families and in some instances, we haven't been able to walk around the local shops, but in terms of Lincoln City, it has been one of the best ever. We haven't won anything, I get that, but 12 months ago a dynasty was breaking up. Michael Appleton has just lost to Oxford on Boxing Day and although wins against Posh and Ipswich were on the horizon, he had a huge job to do. He had an older squad of players suited to a different style of football, and he had a fanbase to win over who had become drunk on success. You know, as well as I do, not everyone was behind him and even before we got past Christmas I remember a tweet going out from someone questioning whether he was the right man for the job. 12 months later, little remains of that side, a side with success of its own to boast, but needing new direction.

We're top of League One, amongst the favourites for two pieces of silverware this season and we've done it with an injury-ravaged squad on 40% less money than we had last season. I do sometimes lavish praise on little easily but if that doesn't demand a round of applause then nothing will.

What it does demand, even now as I take a toilet break before garnishing this piece with Bubs' pictures, is a quick blast of 'Hark, now hear, the angels sing' as I make my way up the stairs. Merry Christmas Imps, and I barely need to wish you a Happy New Year because Michael Appleton has ensured that until January 2nd at least, it bloody well will be.

Why the achievements of 2020 are so incredible for Lincoln City
December 31, 2020

Another year draws to a close and once again, Lincoln City sit atop of the division in which they compete, proudly looking down on 23 other teams.

In 2016, it was Bromley, Boreham Wood and Guiseley we looked down upon. In 2018, it was Forest Green, Grimsby and Mansfield. In 2020, it is Sunderland, Ipswich and Hull City. That, ladies and gentlemen, is progression. The last two occasions on which we have been top of the pile at New Year, we have gone on to win the division. If that were to happen this season, it would be the culmination of a journey few dared dream about. There is a long way to go and deep down, I think we all know the size of the task is far, far greater than it was in 2016 or 2018, but nonetheless, football is all about hope.

2020 has been a horror of a year in many ways, driving hope from people in every aspect of their lives, but at Lincoln City, it has not. Off the pitch, maybe so with redundancies, cost-cutting and the spectre of financial doom hanging over us, but in terms of the footballing side of the club, things have gone from strength to strength despite the pandemic.

One year ago, we were not in a terrible place in terms of results, with New Year's Eve falling squarely between beating Ipswich 5-3 and Peterborough 2-1. They were good results, but taking the wider context we were in an interesting position. To say we have had five seasons of unabating progression is wrong, and it doesn't do justice to the current management team. Arguably, if ahead of the 2019/20 season, someone had said 'you'll be challenging for promotion in 18 months' time, it wasn't inconceivable, was it? Three trophies in three years, Danny and Nicky seemingly having a method and blueprint that worked – it certainly hinted and a positive future.

However, when 2020 broke into dawn 364 days ago, this club was at a crossroads of sorts. I recall being asked in summer 2019 'what if Danny ever leaves the club'. Naively, I told the person asking it wouldn't happen and moved on. In my gut, I feared it and when he did up sticks and leave, along with Nicky, it hurt. It hurt because we had become so accustomed to the success, to competing, that the end of an era dawned. That isn't always bad, but when that era is the most successful in the club's history in terms of trophies, it left the future as a gaping dark chasm of fear. We all reacted differently, some with anger (some still hold it), so with blind optimism, some sitting on the fence. Even when we made an appointment, nothing could change people's stance, not really. Many fans will readily admit they weren't sold on Michael Appleton at the time, due to a combination of that fear and uncertainty, and his record at Portsmouth, Blackpool and Blackburn. You see, fans don't understand reputation within football, we look at pages like Wikipedia and say, 'he didn't win many at Ewood Park', and the opinion is formed. Go on, how many times have we signed a striker and said, 'he hasn't scored many before?', without knowing anything else about him? That's what fans do.

By the time December 31st arrived, we could see the changes Michael had been making, but results had been patchy. I'd seen some calls for his head, other people hammering the style of play. Which game was it where Cian Bolger got pelters for playing out from the back and reacted angrily at the crowd? Much of that was a manifestation of the uncertainty, of the fear that those 'glory days' under the DC/NC combination had gone. That's where we were 365 days ago – staring at 2020 hoping maybe for consolidation, hoping to become a Gillingham or Rochdale, established as a League One club but understanding that we simply weren't going to be able to compete with the big boys.

Remember that feeling of going into games not expecting to come out as winners? I recall MK Dons at home in February (I think), where I told my Dad I felt a draw would be a decent result. I remember the elation at beating Blackpool 1-0 just after Harry Toffolo left, feeling like we were putting daylight between the bottom three and us. That was the aspiration, to have enough between us and the trapdoor to sleep easy. Don't forget, until we beat Burton in the last game, we could all attend, some still had us down as being in a relegation battle. Indeed, in my post-match analysis, I recall feeling sure after that win that we were safe. That was nine months ago.

Nine months later, where is that fear? Where is that uncertainty? Bar maybe one person, where is the disbelief is Michael Appleton. It has gone. Trust has arrived almost as quickly as it did with Danny and Nicky in 2016, and the job Michael has done has been more overwhelming. Of the players were actually owned one year ago, only four remain at the club and two, Alex Bradley and Aron Lewis, are playing no part. In just 12 months we have undergone a complete overhaul, dismantling a side that had won the League Two title and assembling one which, if the season were to end on PPG now, would win the League One title. I appreciated that is a huge reach, but being top at this stage is no accident. We have more points per game than any of our rivals and whilst that might be challenging to maintain, we all believe that maybe come May, we are still there in the top six, believing.

Where now for the Imps? I think this transfer window is a real test of Michael's skills. The last two have seen him make lots of signings, managing players out of the club and identifying numerous targets to bring in. This will show us another side to his style, the window where we only need a couple of new faces, not wholesale changes. I do expect a big departure, that is a by-product of where we are and how well we're doing, but I have belief Michael can handle that. The trick is keeping players like Anthony Scully and Remy Howarth focused and involved, whilst also adding quality that might help us maintain a serious promotion push. One year ago, we had little to judge Michael on and stepped into a transfer window full of unknowns. It could be argued we came out of that with fans even edgier than they were in December, but hindsight would have us all sleeping a little easier when John Akinde, Harry Toffolo, Bruno Andrade and the rest left the club.

I'm really tempted to use the title 'what a difference a year makes', but to outside observers maybe it doesn't. We got promoted from the National League, took a season to settle, and won promotion. We took a season to settle in League One and are now challenging for promotion. It looks like continuity, it looks like a case of 'same old, same old', but it really isn't. This year has seen us with a higher squad churn than you'd expect from a successful side. It has seen us finally become something other than 'long ball Lincoln' in the eyes of those outside the club. It has seen us take a 40% budget cut and still seemingly have a better drilled, more talented squad of players. It has seen a 12-month evolution which we could barely have imagined possible in December 2019.

It is hard to lavish praise on Michael's achievements without seemingly devaluing those of Danny and the players who left the club this year. I will never look to diminish what those players and the management team achieved, never. That is history now though and, in my eyes, the two achievements are very different. Danny and Nicky took a dying club arguably bigger than the level it was in, breathed new life into it and took us to a level many older supporters feel we belong at. Michael Appleton took a successful club at a peak in their history, took it apart, rebuilt it and has somehow improved it in the process. The fact he has done it in one calendar year (from his first transfer window to now), is remarkable.

If 2021 delivers on the promise that late 2020 has shown, then the Lincoln City trajectory might be even more startling than we could ever have dared to dream of. Whatever happens, I take my hat off to Michael, his staff and players, and those behind the scenes running our football club.

Happy New Year to you all.

January

City in isolation at top of League One – AFC Wimbledon 1-2 Imps
January 2, 2021

Football is a controversial game at the best of times, but in the current climate, it is becoming even more so.

Should today's game have gone ahead? Probably not from a Wimbledon perspective, but then Sunderland might have said the same when they went there minus a handful of first-team players in December. Rightly or wrongly, it did go ahead, without Michael Appleton on the bench. Playing Devil's advocate, would Wimbledon have been so eager to postpone the game just with the Covid problem, as opposed to having five injuries and losing Steve Seddon too? Maybe, maybe not. The mercenary Lincoln City fan will say the game going ahead with them missing more than ten players is a chance to get a relatively easy three points. For the record, that was not the case.

There's one thing you always get with Wimbledon teams – fight. That's probably why Alex Woodyard and Ollie Palmer fit in well there, one is a permanent fighter and the other knows which fights to pick. I'll come to that in a moment because I'm three paragraphs deep and haven't mentioned the fact Lincoln City won and extended the lead at the top of the table. Sure, teams have games in hand, games they have to win. We've won ours, three on the spin, bagging 11 goals in the process. The last two outings were straightforward, this was a little different.

Michael Appleton made one change to the team that bagged five against Burton, Liam Bridcutt came into the side and took the armband, with Remy Howarth the player dropping to the bench. Harry Anderson had shown Covid symptoms and missed out on the squad, but otherwise, it was business as usual. Obviously, Palmer and Woodyard started for Wimbledon.

We have taken the lead early in our last two matches and yet it was the Dons with the first chance of this game. Jack Rudoni got a shot away at Alex Palmer's goal, but fired over. That came on four minutes, whilst the Imps also had a half-chance after a deflected cross fell into the hands of Trueman at the other end, who had to gather at the second attempt.

It looked to be an open contest with Brennan Johnson a real dangerman. He found TJ Eyoma on eight minutes, who saw his cross blocked for a corner. From that corner, the Imps took the lead. Grant's delivery was subtly flicked on by Tom Hopper, with Tayo Edun arriving on the edge of the area to slot home. The ball may have clipped a defender on the way through, but it was a succinct finish from the former Fulham man, scoring his first league goal for the Imps.

City looked to press home that advantage, as we have done in both matches at Christmas, and we could have been home and hosed before the clock struck 15 minutes. Grant was pulling the strings in a more advanced role than in recent games, and he looked a cut above as he always does. It's all about his technique, the little drop of the shoulder or feint one way but moving the other. He found James Jones on 11 minutes, with the former Crewe man shooting tamely at the keeper. On 15 minutes it was Grant again, this time his corner was headed over by Lewis Montsma.

The home side weathered that spell and began to get into the game. They should have been level on 23 minutes, in a scare which foreshadowed later events. Alex Woodyard played a short corner to Shane McLoughlin, and his deep, teasing cross was met by Joe Pigott, who headed wide. Pigott has 12 goals from 24 outings this season and had he not just returned from injury, I've little doubt it would have been 1-1.

From our goal kick, the same player got away down the attacking left, only to see his effort saved by Palmer. Twice in a minute we looked susceptible to Wimbledon's attacks.

The game's first booking came on 28 minutes and almost inevitably it involved a former Imp. I thought Woodyard played like he had a point to prove, and he certainly drew Johnson's yellow card, fouling the attacker but then getting his body over the ball to prevent a free-kick. Stupidly, Johnson gave Woodyard a petulant shove and Lee Swabey flashed a yellow. It was a classic example of trying to rile a key player, something Joe Morrell was good at last year.

Three minutes later the focus shifted to another ex-Imp, Ollie Palmer. I had said on Match Day Live that he was poor in the air for us, so it stands to reason he should score with a header. A carbon-copy deep cross from McLoughlin found Palmer in exactly the same place he found Pigott, but the outcome was a goal for the home side. It was always going to happen, and the only silver lining was there was no away support for Palmer to run towards with a huge smile slapped all over his face. Small mercies.

The pendulum swung back in the Imps' favour after that, with Anthony Scully looking lively, if not as effective as the past couple of games. His cross on 33 minutes was turned back by Grant into the path of Johnson, who slotted the ball just wide of the most. It was Scully again on 37 minutes, this time rushing onto a lofted pass and seemingly going one-on-one with Trueman. The challenge by Daniel Csoka was inch-perfect though, coming from behind Scully to scoop the ball away. Tom Hopper picked up the loose ball but fired over, a real let-off for the home side. I cannot emphasise what a great tackle it was though, Scully was a second away from getting a shot away from 12-yards when the tackle came in. Hats off to Csoka.

There was still time for the game's second booking, this time Woodyard getting the card instead of being the reason one was given out. His foul on Hopper wasn't vicious, but it was cynical and certainly justified. I did see some complaints about referee Lee Swabey online, that a few decisions had gone against us, but I had no complaints as we went in at half time.

The second period was a real test of our resolve. This was a game we should be winning against a side depleted for a couple of reasons and with a solitary point out of the previous fifteen available. They were also very committed and whilst their defence didn't look impenetrable, they were seeing plenty of the ball in the middle of the park. I'd also heard they liked to go quite direct, but they were nowhere near as blatant as Northampton. In fact, with a full-strength side, I can see how they could be comfortable mid-table this season. They were going to be happy with a draw, but we were not. I keep saying points on the board are better than games in hand, and even with Hull leading at Charlton at half time, we were on course to go four points clear of second and six clear of third, but only with a win.

I didn't sense that urgency immediately, and as in the first half, the early chance went the way of the hosts. Johnson played a slack pass on the halfway line, which Joe Pigott seized upon and immediately smashed an effort at goal from the halfway line. It missed, by some distance, but it was an early scare. As it transpired, it was one of only a few in the second period.

Johnson might have let his early pass go astray, but there is no doubt he was our dangerman throughout the second period. Our attacking left looks comfortable at the moment, him and Edun combining with Grant in the middle to play some lovely neat triangles when the opportunity allowed. Within ten minutes of the restart we had two great chances, both courtesy of Johnson crosses. In the first instance, the ball flashed across the six-yard box without a player getting near, whilst the second on 52 minutes went in front of one of our lads and behind Scully at the back stick. It was agonising and if I'm honest, it didn't look like it was going to be our afternoon.

In truth, the game was a bit scrappy at times in the early part of the second half. The Dons did their job well, closing us down quick, pressing high and restricting us to panicked balls forward. I felt we were drawn into a few niggly fouls too, and it was on 60 minutes that the next serious chance arrived. Rudoni, who had the early effort in the first half, broke into the area and opted to go for goal instead of passing to Ollie Palmer. it fell wide and Palmer made his feelings clear. I couldn't help but smile, remembering us beating Chesterfield at home and Palmer doing the same to Matt Green. Karma (I'll leave it now, the whole Palmer thing is becoming obsessive).

Lee Swabey played an important role on 66 minutes and caused me to make my sleeping dog jump up in fear as I yelled obscenities at the TV screen. Johnson (as always) got himself some space in the area, but as he looked to beat his marker he was clearly brought down. Their lad was nowhere near the ball, and yet the official signalled for a corner. Here's the killer – the ball hadn't even gone out. Swabey was so keen to not award a penalty he tried to give us a corner before the ball rolled out of play. From the iFollow angle, it was a clear-cut penalty and I do wonder in recent weeks if the high number we got at the beginning of the season is being held against us.

Still it was the Imps looking more likely to break the deadlock. Johnson got away yet again on 72 minutes, playing another lovely ball across goal which nobody was alive too. This isn't a criticism as such, but on another day (Boxing Day for instance) we could have been 4-1 up with 15 minutes left. Johnson caused utter havoc from start to finish and the despairing Wimbledon right back just couldn't handle the Forest loanee.

Joe Walsh even came close to giving us the lead as we turned on the style for a period. Scully whipped a deep, curling cross towards the back stick which saw the former Crawley man throwing himself at the ball, but a millisecond too late. A minute later, Jorge Grant flicked a wonderful backheel at goal, likened by the home commentary team to Denis Law's for Manchester City in the seventies, but it was read well by the keeper. It did feel like a goal might be coming, but you also felt there might be a sting in the Dons' tail. Last season, we had a one-goal lead against them right until the final minute and I could almost smell the despair of losing a point to them deep into injury time. I felt nervous and hopeful at the same time.

My nerves were settled on 83 minutes, as the Imps grabbed the winning goal. It came from the attacking left following an Edun cross, which had proven to be fruitful all afternoon. That ball fell to the feet of Paul Kalambayi, who sliced his clearance horribly to Grant. He showed real composure to set himself before laying the ball into the path of Tom Hopper, who lashed home his second goal in three games to restore the one-goal advantage. It could prove to be a huge goal, especially with Sunderland dropping points at Northampton, and Hull beating Charlton. As he wheeled away, arm raised in delight, I woke the dog up rather rudely once again in the lounge. I probably cheered louder for that goal than any of those against Burton or Northampton, because the game had built up to a crescendo, rather than exploding early.

That was more or less it in terms of chances, Woodyard almost bagged an assist with a deep cross for sub Roscrow, but he couldn't meet it with a header despite being in a good position. Late on, they tried threading a ball through to Palmer, but Walsh held him off and the former City man fell to the floor, looking a little gutted. I took no delight in that……

Make no mistake, this was a big win against a spirited side. Wimbledon weren't in the same bracket of awfulness as Northampton and Burton, I'd put them more in line with Wigan and Shrewsbury. They undoubtedly have more to offer, I expect more goals from Pigott when he's fit and maybe even some from Palmer now he has settled. To be fair, I thought Ollie actually did well for them, he worked hard and asked a lot of questions of Walsh, which Joe answered. Their Man of the Match, in my eyes, was Woodyard though, he was industrious and tenacious throughout.

On our part, we did what we needed to do to win. On another afternoon we win that game 4-1 and everyone heaps plaudits on Johnson one again, and I'm certainly about to. He provided a lot of ammunition in the second half, with three or four really good crosses that Jones, Scully and Hopper were all close to. Edun had another good game too, although on the other side of the field I felt it didn't quite work. Scully put in a good shift but didn't get the rub of the green, whilst Eyoma perhaps had a rare off day at right back. It was nice to see Liam Bridcutt back in the fold, and he didn't look too rusty either. There are a few heart-in-mouth moments with him, and indeed playing out from the back, but you won't see me questioning it when we're winning games of football.

I seem to recall on the podcast talking to Ben about the run up to the Hull City game on December 29th, saying how we could be on 40 points or more by then. I'm not sure I really believed, deep down, that we could achieve that, but the wheels are still on the promotion bus, despite the fear a couple of defeats caused in late October and early December. We are four points clear at the top of the table, albeit having played a game more than Hull. We are six points clear of the play-offs, albeit having played a game more than Portsmouth and two more than Peterborough and Doncaster. We're NINE clear of the seventh, again with a game or two more than most. Those games must be won by the chasing teams though and some are against each other, so I'll certainly take that. We are in this position not because of Covid, but because we are back to winning matches. I can handle defeats if we win games in response and that 1-0 defeat against Shrewsbury, a game I felt we could have won, feels like a long while ago.

The next couple of weeks see two absolutely huge matches. The first is Peterborough, a side nine points behind us with a game in hand. If we took something from that, it would be a huge statement of our intent. I think the cup game against Accrington is massive too, a chance to progress in the trophy and put more funds in the bank. The more the board can give MA this January, the more chance we have of hosting QPR, Derby and maybe even West Brom next season.

Eyes now turn to the news of a possible new signing this week, and the round of Covid tests sanctioned by the EFL too. We could be looking at a break, we could be adding to our squad, but whatever happens, we will be top of the league this time next week. We could even extend our lead by the way – only Hull, Charlton and Ipswich are scheduled to play next weekend from the top seven, so a win against Peterborough could, realistically, open a gap of nine points in the automatics. In other news, I think we're about three wins from safety. I'd have taken that at the start of the season!

Ridiculous really, isn't it? I guess all we can do is keep our feet on the ground and hoping the points keep on coming. What a time to be a Lincoln City fan.

Lincoln City land loan signing of £4m Premier League prospect
January 4, 2021

The first new face of the January transfer window has landed at Sincil Bank, and it is a cracker.

Manchester City forward Morgan Rogers joins on a loan deal until the end of the season, adding to our attacking options. He is capable of playing across the front three and is on his first senior loan spell. he is a player Michael is likely to know well, having started his career with West Bromwich Albion.

He was with the Baggies from the age of eight, eventually joining Manchester City for a fee believed to be £4m a couple of years ago. One news outlet, whom I will not link to, even had the fee to be around £6m depending on appearances and add ons. He has appeared for Man City in the EFL Trophy, although not against us, scoring once. Whilst at West Brom, he was described by the Birmingham Mail as being a 'tall, rangy, extremely quick attacker who can play anywhere across the front three. He has been likened to England star Dele Alli and certainly shares the Spurs man's eye for goal'.

He is also laden with England youth honours and has scored regularly at every level. He hit five goals in six matches for the Under 15s, five in eight for the Under 16s, nine in 15 for the Under 17s and finally once in eight for the Under 18s which is his current level. There is huge excitement around his capture, as there was when we bagged Brennan Johnson, and rightly so. How many players make a move of between £4m-£6m and are appearing for us 18 months later? He has even been described as the long term successor to Aguero at Manchester City, not wanting to heap pressure on him or anything.

"I'm very happy to have joined this club. I am looking forward to the rest of the season and what it holds for us," he told the club's official site.

"The club is great, I like the style of football that the manager plays and I feel being here will help me develop further as a player. I know a few of the lads here like Alex (Palmer), Max (Melbourne) and Brennan (Johnson) and they have told me how much they are enjoying it here."

"The club are in a good position in the league and we want to keep that momentum going."

Jez George revealed we have been speaking to Manchester City and whilst delighted with the capture of Rogers, he also sees a potential pathway for more young talent to head our way in the future.

"We are absolutely delighted to have signed Morgan on loan until the end of the season to add to Michael's options at the top end of the pitch. He is an extremely talented young player, who we have watched for some time, and he will add quality to the group."

"We initially spoke to Manchester City during the first lockdown and we have been in dialogue with Fergal (Harkin, Football Partnerships & Pathways Manager) and Joe (Shields, Head of Academy Recruitment and Talent Management) ever since. We are really grateful to them for making this possible and look forward to developing our relationship with Manchester City in the future."

I cannot emphasise how exciting this signing is, certainly in terms of potential. Morgan Rogers is very highly-rated indeed and seemed more suited to a loan spell in the Championship than in League One. He has the potential to be a massive acquisition for us, and might just give us the same potent threat on one flank which Johnson delivers on the other.

What I would say is bringing him to the club must have taken an awful lot of work, and once again hats off to the recruitment team. If we get the Rogers I have watched on Wyscout scoring for England and creating for West Brom Under 18s, then we could be in for a real treat. I know there is a genuine buzz around his capture and he will draw parallels with Brennan purely because of the type of player he is. He will certainly add pace to our front line, something few opposition defenders will relish facing.

Dare I say, this has the potential to be the biggest loan signing Lincoln City have ever made.

23-year-old departs Sincil Bank
January 5, 2021

Keeper Ethan Ross has left Sincil bank on loan, joining National League side Weymouth until the end of the season.

The 23-year-old joined the Imps in the summer from Colchester United, having been third-choice in Essex. He played in all of our pre-season fixtures, but was ousted as number one by Alex Palmer's arrival from West Brom.

Ross made two appearances for the club, the last of which was against Manchester City Under 21s in the EFL Trophy, where he made a late mistake to earn the visitors a draw. He did not feature in the victory at Shrewsbury in the same competition, which essentially signalled the end of his first-team chances.

With Alex Palmer the established stopper, the only way Ross would get a chance would have been through injury, and in that event, he would almost certainly be recalled. In recent weeks, Ross has been conspicuous by his absence on the bench, replaced by youngster Sam Long, of whom the management team have spoken very highly recently.

The situation doesn't have to be a closed door for Ross, who I thought looked decent in the early stages of the season. It makes sense for him to be playing regular football, especially if we did see Palmer pick up an injury, as he would come back match ready. In the meantime, Long gets the continued first-team exposure, but without the pressure of needing to prove himself by starting games.

There is an element of sadness on my behalf if I'm honest. Ethan is a genuinely nice lad, grounded and down to earth, and my interview with him for the programme was one of the easiest I'd done at the time. He has a certain character about him which I think would be good around the training ground, but at the same time, he is of an age where he needs to be playing games of football.

Ethan has a lot to prove to Michael now. he must go out and make the keeper position his own at Weymouth, and he must impress sufficiently to earn a contract for next season. The chances are we won't be keeping three stoppers on the books and with Sam's development, that does make it a tall order for Ethan. even if a contract were not forthcoming, his interests are best served by playing games of football.

I hope he gets game time there, having looked at Weymouth's squad and their current run of results, I strongly suspect he will be their first choice. It is up to him to prove his quality, keep them in the National League and use it as a springboard to either return here ready for a new deal or prove his worth to another Football league club who need a decent keeper and a strong, likeable personality in the dressing room.

Oddly this article made me think of my ninth birthday, the only time I ever sat in the old Hunters Stand. My Dad took me to see our 0-0 draw with Weymouth a couple of days after and they had a keeper called Peter Guthrie who played an absolute blinder. I'm sure he signed for Spurs not long after. I hope Ethan can be as strong for the Terras as Guthrie was.

Points Dropped in Top of Table Encounter – Imps 1-1 Peterborough
January 9, 2021

Do not be fooled by my headline. this isn't an article about disappointment, anger or even displeasure.

It is a headline which needs context. Five years ago, we were borrowing youth players from Peterborough. They were the big cousin helping us out, light-years from us in terms of development. They are a club who buy up young talent and sell at a profit, a club who sold a striker for £10m in the summer. They are also a club I am this afternoon disappointed we did not beat. Given that I said I'd be happy with a draw on Match Day Live, given that we had at least three first-team players missing with suspected Covid, and a number of staff members, to say we have dropped two points is actually a reflection on how well we played (at times) and where the expectation is right now. One year ago, beating this lot 2-1 was a huge result, maybe even a highlight of 2020, yet drawing with them 12 months on is disappointing. That is nothing short of exciting.

The preparation for the two sides could not have been different. They haven't kicked a ball in almost a month and, unless I've missed something, have a clean bill of health regarding Covid. In the time they haven't played, we've won three matches, lost our manager from the training ground due to Covid and on today's evidence, at least three first-team players. Harry Anderson, Joe Walsh and Tom Hopper were all absent today, there was no Theo Archibald on the bench and remember we are still without Conor McGrandles and Callum Morton, both injured. That's six players who would be in first-team squad contention, not involved. Michael returned to the training ground yesterday, so had 24 hours to prepare his team for this fixture, whereas Darren Ferguson has had all Christmas to get his troops ready. That's football, or at least that is football in 2020/21, and you have to take the rough with the smooth.

Despite that, the Imps line-up did feel familiar. Adam Jackson returned to the back four, with Remy Howarth returning to the side to replace Tom Hopper. Given Peterborough's lay-off, some felt they'd come out of the blocks all guns blazing, and that is exactly what happened.

Let's not beat around the bush, for the first ten minutes we were beyond woeful. Tayo Edun gave the ball away after five minutes, a feat in itself considering we'd barely had the ball, only for Jack Taylor to drive an effort at goal. Posh got a couple of corners two in a relentless assault on the Imps 18-yard box, and we had no answer. For ten minutes I suspect you could count our meaningful touches on one hand, without using your fingers. Or thumb. Peterborough just played around with the ball and we chased shadows. It was absolutely no shock at all when Posh opened the scoring, Liam Bridcutt's slip giving them a chance to get a shot away. The clearance off the line was the best thing we'd done all day, but it hit Eyoma's ass and went in for 1-0. At that point, I wish I'd overslept this morning by about four hours.

I make notes as I go along ready to do the report and analysis after the game and the sixth note I've made reads as follows: '11 – first meaningful Imps possession, awful game'. We looked like the team that hadn't played for 25 days, in fact we looked like a team who hadn't played together for 25 years. On 15 minutes we got our first booking after Johnson hauled back one of their guys looking to counter and it felt like a long, tedious afternoon was in the offing. My dog moved closer to the door, sensing he might get an inadvertent boot as I got increasingly irate.

Finally, just before the 20-minute mark, we got our first chance. Brennan Johnson got away, firing over when there might have been a square ball on. It was the first glimpse of Lincoln City that we know, but it was also the best chance of the game thus far. 17 minutes in, City had been terrible but also had the best chance. That didn't reflect well on Peterborough and it was the first signs we might be still in the game. Having conceded early, and lost, against Sunderland and Portsmouth, I feared the same was coming here, but the Black Cats and Pompey are way ahead of Peterborough on this showing.

Liam Bridcutt got the game's second yellow on 19 minutes, one of the last I recorded as I began to lose count (eight in total, including two for one player). Looking back, it was not a nice challenge on Szmodics and referee Will Finnie waited patiently before flashing the card. No complaints from me, and sensible officiating too. In fact, I felt Finnie had a superb game, allowing it to flow but also being strict enough with his cards to ensure it didn't boil over. Hats off to him for that, it is easy to lash out at officials when they're bad, but it is important to praise them when they do well.

Posh could have doubled their lead on 25 minutes, a deep cross finding Clarke-Harris who nodded tamely at goal. Lewis Montsma perhaps did enough to put him off and a Sky Sports quality replay showed Clarke-Harris's little finger to be ahead of play. It wasn't offside, but VAR would have ruled it so. Thank heavens we don't have such a hindrance in our game. It was almost the end of a terrible 30 for the Imps, almost. I actually spotted one other thing, just before the 30-minute mark, which had the dog running to the kitchen looking for solace. Bridcutt and one of their lads went in for a 50/50 and Bridcutt let it go out, thinking he'd won a throw. He hadn't, and Posh were awarded it in a decent position. It came to nothing, but it went against an old mantra of my dad's – if in doubt, put it out. Bridcutt wouldn't have needed to put it out, just get the bloody thing downfield if there is any ambiguity. I noticed us concede a corner this way too, maybe against Wimbledon, and it just irks me. It is easy to speak about though when you're sat at home watching.

That saw the half-hour mark slide by and for me, it saw the worst of the game slide by too. Something clicked in City after that and for sixty minutes we grew increasingly more dangerous, inventive and ambitious. Anthony Scully, a constant danger, drove forward and had an effort saved by Pym on 31 minutes, our first chance on goal. On 35 minutes, Johnson fed in Remy Howarth, who really should have done better when in the clear in the right channel. His effort was either high, wide or both, when a shot across goal draws a save, and a cross could create a goal. On 39 minutes Johnson was fouled on the edge of the area, and Grant's free-kick got around the wall and just wide of Pym's left-hand post. Before half time, Adam Jackson had a half-chance from another free-kick too, making it four chances in 15 minutes for City. it wasn't flowing, we weren't completely 'at it', but it was four more than the visitors created. This with a player like Dembele in the team, valued at many millions of pounds, with Reece Brown and Szmodics in the team, both who are creative talents with goals in them, and of course, with Jonson Clarke-Harris who has failed to impress me whenever we have played against him.

As if just to give me a little unease heading into the break, a deep cross from Posh could have caused real problems after Montsma was caught out of position, but Bridcutt got back to stop it reaching the target with a wonderful interception. It is easy to poke players who play badly and for a good half hour, Bridcutt hadn't been his usual self, but he is still vital at times and that underlined why.

I went on social media at half time (always dangerous) and predicted this game was ours to win, adding to my ascertain we were beating ourselves, rather than Posh beating us. What I meant by that was this – they wouldn't have scored had we not dallied in the box on the ball, they never looked like scoring of their own volition and had we been smarter with our decision making, in key creative areas and in a couple of big chances, we could have been home and hosed. That, despite playing poorly, convinced me if we shifted a gear, we'd be in the driving seat. What we needed, was an early goal, akin to Bristol Rovers earlier in the season.

In the same minute, from a similar position to the defeat against the Gas, we got the leveller. It is worth noting James Jones won the corner that led to it through persistence and endeavour, which might get missed. Grant delivered, the ball bounced on the hard surface in front of the South Park end and Scully reacted quickest to slam the ball home. I would say 'cue jubilation', but the honest shout is I knew it was going in, thanks to a text of 'get in' from Pete, who was watching on Sky seemingly a minute or so ahead of my iFollow feed. It didn't mean I enjoyed it any less though, and suddenly the dog felt he could come back into the lounge to chill.

Scully was one of the highlights of the afternoon for me. It's often been said we don't know what his best position is, but I'd argue maybe the correct answer is 'in front of goal'. He's scored three in the last four matches for the Imps, playing out wide and through the centre, and is on nine from 25 for the season. If he keeps this vein up, given that we have 24 games and maybe a cup run to go, he could be a 20-a-season striker without yet defining exactly where he should be playing. Sometimes maybe it is best just to accept a player and not try to label him as something. Maybe. What I would say is aside from his goal against Oxford, he usually scores as part of a big win. His goals have come against Bradford, Forest Green, Burton, Northampton, Shrewsbury and Mansfield, all games we scored three or more in. Today, he didn't chip in on a rout, arguably it was his most important goal for us, maybe aside from the opener against Oxford.

Not long after a Posh free-kick was headed high over Palmer's goal by Clarke-Harris, but the game had shifted. They looked like a side who hadn't played in a month, and we looked like a side top of the league and wanting to remain there. Much of that came courtesy of the first change of the game, and our only

130

change, on 54 minutes. A lot has been said about Morgan Rogers, but it was no surprise to see him get his Football League debut on 54 minutes, replacing Remy Howarth. £4m of somebody else's talent came on the pitch and helped give the Imps real drive to go and win the game, which we really should have done.

Cristy Pym took a bit of a battering for his height from Thommo on his return to the commentary box, but I've always put Pym right up there as a keeper of the highest order, and he proved it with a superb save on 56 minutes from Johnson, after a Grant cross. Pushing Rodgers out wide and seeing Grant drop back into midfield certainly helped us in an attacking sense, as our number ten got much more of the ball than he had whilst playing advanced. Rogers won a free kick on the edge of the area on 63 minutes, which Grant lifted into the side netting. It was almost a carbon-copy of the winner a year ago, and I suspect many imps fans felt the script was written all over again.

On 65 minutes, that script took a familiar turn, as Posh had a player sent off against us for the third game in a row. Nathan Thompson was already on a yellow and he opted to palm Scully's shot away with his hand, which left Finnie with no choice. He pulled out a red, the former Swindon man walked and Jorge Grant got a chance from 12-yards. It seemed a formality, it seemed as though we would move seven points clear of Hull at the top of the table. Instead, inexplicably, Grant missed horribly and the score remained level.

There will be no pile on here. yes, it was a poor penalty, but I think Jorge Grant has enough credit with fans to be excused, don't you? These things happen and besides, we had just under half-an-hour to make our one man advantage count. We almost did that on 72 minutes, when Scully's deep cross saw Morgan Rogers volley it first time back across goal. Sadly, the anticipation wasn't quite there and Pym collected the ball, but in three or four weeks time, (hopefully), Johnson and Rogers will be on the same page and those moves will be yielding results.

Posh were certainly happy with the draw at that point and they looked to get behind the ball and take whatever chances came their way. James Jones had a decent effort for City on 74 minutes, a raking cross from Grant saw him shoot straight at Pym. Two minutes later Rogers won a corner in much the same way Jones had earlier in the game, breaking into the area (and having his shirt pulled by the defender), before cleverly backheeling it into his pursuer when it looked as if he'd gone too far. The delivery saw his shot blocked, then Johnson fired across goal only to be ruled offside. I'm telling you now, if we keep both of them, the next 25 matches are going to be edge-of-your-seat stuff at times.

It is perhaps pertinent to mention a Clarke-Harris free-kick which seemed to be blocked by a hand in the Lincoln wall. Our defender (I think it was Eyoma, commentary didn't pick it up and replays were poor quality on my iFollow feed today) had his hand on his forehead trying to block out the sun as the ball came in, and it hit that hand before bouncing away. Maybe, if it is against us, I have a moan. Maybe. The fact is Clarke-Harris didn't beat the wall, and on 88 minutes he did exactly the same, so more fool him for not being a bit better.

We did push for a winner, but to be fair we didn't really trouble the keeper. A Grant break saw Scully get a half-chance which was saved with ease by Pym, and with eight minutes remaining an Eyoma cross was touched at goal, again by Scully, but it went wide to Pym's right-hand post. Perhaps we didn't taste the blood after the red card, maybe Posh are just better at killing a game than they are at winning one, but four minutes of injury time ebbed away in much the same way my anger had in the first half – slowly and without any real incident.

There we go. Two points lost in a game which looked tricky on paper. We have taken two points from a possible 12 against teams in the top six, which might be cause for concern, but this was the one clash that we really were the better side in. We shared relatively level games with Accrington and Doncaster, we were swept aside by Portsmouth but Peterborough didn't look to be as polished as any of those sides. Maybe that was the lay-off, maybe it is the disruption caused by the likes of Dembele and the transfer request, but they were a shadow of the team I expect us to face. Considering the attacking talent they had on the field, I don't recall a heart-in-mouth moment we didn't hand them in 90 minutes.

What I did recall was the wave of relief washing over me as Scully scored the leveller, because I felt 100% safe from that point on. I felt we'd get the draw, at worst, and that whatever result Sunderland and Hull play out later, we'll be top for yet another week. That's a wonderful position for us to be in and even though we didn't win today, I take huge solace in knowing we are disappointed by that fact.

Four-midable City smell Wembley in the air – Imps 4-0 Accrington
January 13, 2021

Sometimes, waiting a few hours before doing my write up is to let my enthusiasm settle, and for a dose of reality to infect my otherwise success-addled brain.

I do get carried away, as much as I try not to. My tweets and social media posts during a game can often be an exaggeration of what I feel, either way. That's fuelled by watching the events happen, and the emotion of a missed chance or a scored goal making it feel more important at the moment than it really is. For instance, would I come on here this morning and talk about how a thumping win against Accrington is an indication of us being set for the Championship? No, of course not.

Mind you, ten minutes after the game, I might have been tempted. Let's be honest, the Imps were scintillating last night, and not for the first time in a cup competition. We've thumped Forest Green 602, Bradford City 5-0, Shrewsbury 4-1 and even bagged two against Liverpool. We like a cup game, not least when the opposition see fit to make numerous changes. That was Accrington's right and before the game, John Coleman said their players should be well-drilled enough to know the patterns of play and the approach they should take. They didn't.

Now, let us not undermine our own struggles going into this encounter. We had 12 fit outfield players, 10 on the field, with Roughan and Ramirez on the bench, necessitating the first appearance of Freddie Draper amongst the subs. Covid has ravaged the squad and as Michael pointed out before the game, we might have moved to have it called off. Then again, you look at the team we put out and it felt strong. even with no Montsma, Jones, Hopper, McGrandles, Anderson or Joe Walsh (not to mention Archibald, Morton or Rogers), it felt strong. That's nine players (and I'm sure I have omitted someone) who did not feature who might have done. Still, the defence looked competent on paper, the midfield was as good as it gets without everyone fit and upfront, we were certainly hungry and looked so, so quick.

Still, with Covid in mind, should we really have toyed and mauled Stanley as we did?

I did a full watch along and that made it hard at times to keep a note of the chances, but I do know that long before we took our deserved lead, we should have been home and hosed. City were completely different in the first 15 minutes to the weekend with Posh, we played with a purpose and pace which threatened to overawe the Accrington side. It did look like men against boys, as a group stage tie between one of the weaker under 18 sides and the best League One might look.

Two minutes in, Brennan Johnson could have given us the lead as he rounded the keeper but just ran out of pitch, still managing to get a shot away and win a corner. On five minutes it was Zack Elbouzedi, star of the last round, with a golden opportunity to give is the lead. Anthony Scully's delicious ball saw Zack arriving late into the box, but he blazed over with the goal asking to be hit. By the time the clock hit double-digits, there wasn't an Imps' fan watching who felt we'd get beaten. When we hit that sweet spot, you just know, and last night you just knew.

On 17 minutes Scully was the player with a chance to open the scoring, going through one-on-one with Savin in the sticks after a great pass from Johnson. Again, we should have scored, Scully drawing a save from the keeper's feet when he might have felt he should have done better. That's no slur on the former West Ham man, he was covering every blade of grass, Tom Hopper style, and when Hopps is back MA might have a tough shout to make.

Zack also missed a sitter after Scully played a delicious ball between the penalty spot and six-yard box, with the Irish winger arriving perfectly and the ball needing just the simplest of touches. He hit the bar from six yards out and the ball flew over. was it not to be our night? Was Zack to rue those chances missed?

The key to missing chances is to get them in the first place and finally, just after the half-hour, Zack got rewards for a lively opening. He started the move, breaking down the left and cutting inside, before shifting the ball out to Scully. He delivered, again, with Brennan Johnson just touching it into the path of Zack, who had remained on the edge of the 18-yard area. He waltzed into the area, shifted left and finished with aplomb. The dam had broken and the Imps threatened to pour through like a torrent of raging water.

Accrington did get a chance, Alex Palmer spilt a deep ball under pressure and the visitors worked it into a shooting chance, but Mohammed couldn't hit the target from Gary Roberts' ball. It was a let-off, a half-chance which reminded us the tie was precarious at 1-0, for all our chances. Still, when half time did sound, City led 1-0 on goals and 9-2 on shots. Hugely impressive but perhaps not quite home and hosed.

If the first half was good, then the second half was also good. You couldn't say 'better', despite the goal count, because we deserved three in the first half, and we got three in the second. Nobody made any changes at half time, with Accrington players likely to have been given a good going over. As for us, we just started doing what we do best – passing, probing and creating. Tayo Edun, a player I vociferously defend at all corners, almost got a shot away on 52 minutes, shifting feet neatly and displaying the ball control you expect from a central midfielder at left-back, but his shot was blocked. It mattered not, a minute later we doubled the advantage.

It started with the captain (and my Man of the Match) Liam Bridcutt, who put in what might be his best Imps' performance yet. He played a ball into the channel for Scully, then made a run to the byeline to get it back. He looked to have run out of pitch, but instead swivelled and lifted a ball over the area and towards the penalty spot, where Robbie Gotts had made the perfect run. He had enough time to quickly check the other scores on his mobile phone, position himself under the ball and then write next year's Christmas shopping list, before launching a diving header into a gaping net. It was a decent header too, away from Savin who had been caught at his near post, and the delight on the youngster's face was evident. He hasn't played as much as he might like, but he certainly turned in a competent and collected display in midfield.

We continued to push forward, Gotts teeing up Johnson for an effort, and Grant driving one wide, which prompted major changes from Accrington. Off came four of the supporting cast, on came the 'big guns', four first-team players. Remember, this is a first-team with enough games in hand to reel us in at the top of the table, They always say 2-0 is a dangerous score (any score is a dangerous score if you concede more by the way), and as Charles, Pritchard and Bishop joined Butcher as the changes, you wondered if it might be a nervy half-hour for City.

Nope, the first thing we did after they came on was to make it 3-0. Johnson picked up the ball in the middle of the park and fed Elbouzedi, who made a gut-busting run past his marker and into the area. He cut it back to Johnson, who had continued his run, and the Forest striker shifted to move the ball away to the keeper's left with a curling effort. Instead, his body suggested the left, but he quickly drilled it low and hard to the right, fooling everyone with what was a finish of top quality. It is easy to miss the technique in the excitement, but Johnson's body shape fooled the defence and bought him the split second it needed to kill the tie.

It was his last action of the game, he hobbled off afterwards, having struggled after an early knock, and Howarth came on in his place.

The chances kept on coming and to list them all would make this too long. Grant had one, Bridcutt had another, Scully had a decent free-kick and even TJ Eyoma got in on the act of testing the glass on the executive boxes. There was the odd scare here and there, the sort of scare you get from a PG-rated Scooby-Doo cartoon, a little jump when you weren't expecting it, but nothing that would ever have you reaching for the cushions or turning over the channel. For Accrington, the opposite was true, every time we came forward it must have been like a trap from a Saw movie, them wondering what elaborate passing routine or pattern would see them fall into the VAT of boiling acid next. Slick stuff.

The last goal was all about Howarth and he didn't touch the ball. Accrington looked to play out from the back, with a ball going back to Savin. Howarth chased him down and the keeper moved to his left to evade the forward. Howarth did the same and Savin was forced to play a quick ball to his centre half. Instead, he played it to Jorge Grant, who needed no second invitation to round off the scoring with a neat finish from the edge of the box.

Here is the truth about lst night's game – it means nothing in terms of our promotion push. The result is resounding but just as when we played Shrewsbury, it will be a different Stanley we face later in the season. What it does mean though is £40,000 into the bank for a win. It does mean Zack Elbouzedi raises his reputation a little more and has perhaps ousted Theo Archibald as our reserve left-winger. It demonstrated that our patterns, method and approach rely on coaching and application, not individuals. Remember, this was a changed side with players such as Gotts, Elbouzedi and Melbourne coming in after not playing much football, yet they barely put a foot wrong. For me, it was also a great sign that Liam Bridcutt looked as good as he did. He won tackles, played passes and pulled the strings, in much the same way Grant did in his absence. That left Grant to sit further forward, making passes, creating chances and pulling strings. Those two players are the architects of our success on the field, they provide the bullets to fire, they put in the work to break up play and with them in the team, we have two beating hearts driving the beast.

That's not to say the others do not do that when we're good we're very, very good and last night showed that. Sure, it was a weakened Accrington side, but we're talking about the weakened squad of a side genuinely challenging for promotion to the second-tier, not Mark Cooper's cast offs dressed in ridiculous zebra print pyjamas, fearful of being sent to another dressing room if they lose. Accrington wanted the Wembley hoodoo off their back, they came to Sincil Bank and met a squad of just 12 fit outfield players and still went home with their ass roasted, toasted and served up with a four-goal garnish.

It seems, even waiting a few hours, I am still getting carried away, and I make zero apologies for that. Right now, I love being a Lincoln City fan and I'm proud of my club from top to bottom.

Robbie Gotts Leaves – Analysis and Opinion
January 15, 2021

Leeds United have recalled Robbie Gotts from his loan spell at Sincil Bank, sending him out on loan to Salford in League Two.

I was surprised in a way, I didn't expect a loan player to be recalled this winter and in my recent analysis of the loan deals, I rated the prospect of him being recalled at 50% (incidentally, I did call both of our outward loan players correctly too). Well, the 50% of me that thought he could be recalled has been vindicated, and he's now with the Ammies.

Working backwards, I think this is a decent move for Robbie. I interviewed him earlier in the season and found him to be a very professional and grounded young man. I likened him (to friends at least) to Scott Wharton when he was here – displaying a personal maturity beyond his years. When I chat to a young player I expect to find it different to a more experienced professional, such as Neal Eardley or Liam Bridcutt. Some youngsters you feel have maybe had media training, they know what to say and what not to say and Robbie felt very professional in that respect. I don't think his time being cut short here is down to anything he did wrong, but he is a victim of circumstance. I confess I am surprised that Leeds have entrusted his development to Salford, particularly after what I have heard from a couple of their former players directly about infrastructure and club development. Maybe, with Richie Wellens now in there as boss, a manager who wanted Robbie in the summer by the way, they are on the up in that regard.

How was his time at City? I think he suffered a little from being versatile and maybe came here as right-back cover rather than a starting central midfielder. Of the league appearances he made for the club, he only appeared in midfield twice, for 15 minutes at the end of our Northampton win, and for a period in our 4-0 hammering at home against Sunderland. He started at right-back against Portsmouth and had a torrid time, something I don't think he ever really recovered from. He was settling down and looking competent, but that wasn't enough for Leeds, who wanted to see him getting regular game time. The questions are these – is he a better right-back than TJ Eyoma? No. Is he a better central midfielder than any three from Grant, McGrandles, Jones and Bridcutt? Again, no.

I was surprised that he didn't start in midfield against Burton and Peterborough, with Howarth preferred on both occasions, and I do wonder if the club knew at that stage that he might be recalled from his loan. He was almost certainly a box-to-box midfielder, but he was never going to dislodge Jones and Grant and even when a chance did arise, we went with a player arguably a little more attacking in Howarth. Despite that, I still feel there was more to come from Gotts and I expect us to now dip into the transfer market to cover his position, which I'll come to in a bit.

One barometer of a player which is even more subjective than xG is the player ratings the Stacey West readers give the lads after a game. Gotts average rating across his Imps stay was 6.34, which isn't standout, but it isn't terrible either. His stats don't read too badly from Wyscout, a pass accuracy of 72.2% is okay, with 66% accuracy into the final third and 66.9% forward passes. These are decent stats, but again they are not standout and I think that sums up Robbie's stay at Lincoln. He was decent, but he only leapt out of the page on a couple of occasions.

That wasn't his fault though, nobody could accuse him of lacking effort, endeavour or ability. when he did get a game in midfield he looked direct and aggressive on the ball, but sadly for him and for us, the midfield wasn't where we needed him. As a right-back, he adapted and showed good application, but he never screamed 'natural full-back'. He would admit it I'm sure, and I dare bet a good chunk of money that he plays central midfield at Salford, where he should be a huge success.

There is also a small part of me that wonders if the recall was more mutual. There would never be a headline 'Imps send player back', as it reflects badly on the player, but this article with comments from Gotts and Wellens got me thinking. Gotts said it was a priority to move to Salford once they were interested, whilst Wellens hints at him coming highly recommended, possibly by the Imps. Were we already looking to free up a loan space with a different type of player, and therefore agreed a more mutual resolution of the deal? It has certainly been on the cards for a bit by the sounds of it, and I'm sure we would have been involved in that process.

Where do we go now? In terms of cover at right-back, I strongly suspect a new signing at some point in the month. I don't think we'll look to bring in a midfield player to cover if we do go for someone in the centre it would probably have happened anyway. With TJ Eyoma the first-choice right-back, and now only Anderson as cover, we definitely need to recruit. I suppose there is a chance it could help resurrect Aaron Lewis' Imps career, but Michael appears to have been quite clear about that and I don't believe, for a second, that today's events will have been such a shock that he has to go back on his words of a couple of days ago. My feeling is we might accelerate a signing we had planned for the summer. I'm sure Michael and Jez will have identified a right-back that we could target permanently, given that TJ was a loan, and maybe we were waiting for a contract to run down or something like that. It may be we move for a target early, giving them six months to settle in as understudy before stepping up when TJ goes back to Spurs. Either that, or we go to a club willing to loan us a player as cover knowing they might only play six or seven games between now and May. It's a tough call, but I have little doubt there will be a contingency in place.

22-year-old departs Sincil Bank
January 16, 2021

Zack Elbouzedi has left Sincil bank this afternoon, joining Bolton Wanderers on loan for the rest of the season.

The 22-year-old won his second Man of the Match award of the season this week with a scintillating display against Accrington in the EFL Trophy, but his chances have been limited throughout the campaign. Playing on the left side of attack, Zack has had to contend with competition from the likes of Anthony Scully, Brennan Johnson and Theo Archibald, as well as new signing Morgan Rogers. That has led the club to seek football for him elsewhere and to be fair there are no bigger clubs than Bolton in League Two.

Zack signed for the club a little over a year ago, becoming Michael's first signing after taking over as manager. He appeared five times in League One for us during his first six months, the last of which was his first start, away at Southend. That game didn't go well for anyone, and Zack found himself out of the side after being hauled off at half time.

This season, he's done well when given his chances. he looked strong in the pre-season matches and got his first start of the campaign in the EFL Trophy against Scunthorpe. He's had to be patient since, coming off the bench against Forest Green in the FA Cup, before impressing against Shrewsbury, again in the EFL Trophy. Sadly for Zack, that only led to two more League One outings, a brief cameo late on against Northampton and 15 minutes at home against Burton.

Thus far, Zack has made 11 outings for the Imps, with three starts, scoring twice. However, this move is not the same as us finding a club for Aaron Lewis – Zack signed a 'long-term' deal with us when he arrived from Waterford, and it is likely that his loan spell is an attempt to give him the senior football, he needs to kick on as a player and stake a claim in our first-team squad next season. I did mention in a recent look at players incoming and outgoing that I felt Zack might be primed for a loan departure, and I think in terms of his development, this could be a really good move.

The two departures, and the Aaron Lewis situation, do suggest we may be on the verge of bringing a player in, but like Robbie Gotts, I wouldn't expect a direct, like-for-like replacement for Zack. In terms of the squad, our attacking options are still impressive, certainly out wide, and I would imagine that these departures are about freeing up budget for a more targeted incoming player, possibly at full-back.

Obviously, we wish Zack all the best in his loan spell and hope to see him back at the Bank, leaving defenders for dead, next season.

Never in my lifetime – Portsmouth 0-1 Imps
January 26, 2021

The Imps took top spot in League One once again this evening, with a fine 1-0 win against ten-man Portsmouth at Fratton Park, the first victory there since 1977.

In case you missed it and before you read how it happened, Portsmouth had a man sent off. I thought I ought to repeat it as it was all the home commentators went on about for the entire game. I wouldn't want you to forget it.

That aside, the Imps were a completely different side to the one turned over 3-1 at Sincil Bank earlier in the season, even before Pompey were reduced to ten men (which they were). It was a performance that was full of pace and style for 30 minutes, then packed with patience and control for the next 60. It was the performance of a side who believe in what they are doing, who understand their roles and who play for each other week in, week out.

City made one change to the side which beat Northampton at the weekend, as predicted by us earlier Conor McGrandles came in, with Morgan Rogers dropping to the bench. Pompey were unchanged after their humiliating 4-0 defeat at Hull City, meaning Ronan Curtis, John Marquis and Marcus Harness all start, all players who have torn City apart in the past.

The Imps needed a solid start and that is exactly what they produced. Within a minute a neat passage of play saw a ball into the six-yard area for Scully to run onto, but the former West Ham man couldn't quite catch it before it ran through to Craig MacGillivray.

It was all City in the opening five minutes as the game started with real intensity. Brennan Johnson whipped a cross in from the left for Sean Raggett to clear, before an odd moment where a challenge burst the ball. Conor McGrandles launched himself into a 50/50 with Callum Johnson, coming out on top, but as the resulting ball dropped to Jorge Grant, he stopped play pointing out it had burst. There's a first for you – the first Imps player I've seen who bursts a ball with a fierce (but fair) challenge.

Pompey got their first sight on 12 minutes, Tom Naylor shooting wide, but it wasn't as much a half-chance as a quarter, or maybe even an eighth. It seemed as though frustration might have been seeping in just past the quarter-hour mark, as the frenetic start saw Harness go crudely through the back of Johnson to earn the game's first yellow. From the resulting free-kick, City worked the ball to Johnson, who curled an effort narrowly over MacGillivray's goal.

The pace of the game wasn't dipping, and it was City in control. A mistake by Raggett saw Scully nip the ball away, but before he could turn it into an attack he was tugged back for another yellow card. City kept knocking on the door, creating another half-chance through Liam Bridcutt who was having a strong evening. He won possession, with McGrandles using the ball to find Tom Hopper. In a virtual identical chance to the weekend's second goal, he squared for Scully, who saw his shot saved.

Pompey did look effective when they were allowed to put a passage of play together, and a good spell of possession saw them create a half-chance on 26 minutes, but Ryan Williams couldn't use the half-yard he found, seeing his shot blocked by the Imps defence and run harmlessly through to Palmer.

The next major incident was anything but harmless. A ball forward from Eyoma saw Grant pick up possession in the centre circle, but Jack Whatmough leapt into the challenge and seemingly won the ball. On the second watch, he had two feet off the ground and studs showing. The referee took his time to let the situation settle, before flashing a red card.

Instantly, Pompey went into their shell and City looked to press home the advantage. McGrandles latched on to a long ball over the top and nodded at goal, only for MacGillivray to claw the ball away. After Edun picked up the first Imps booking of the game, it was McGrandles who should have put City 1-0 up. A great lofted cross from Johnson saw McGrandles arriving in the area in all sorts of space, but his header was blocked for a corner.

Pompey looked highly susceptible at this stage and it seemed as though an opener was only a matter of time for the Imps. Johnson, who caused problem both out wide and cutting inside, went on a run across the front of the box before feeding in Scully, but his shot was tame.

With just a minute left on the clock at the end of the half, City had another good chance to take the lead. This time it was Tayo Edun, impressive once again, who found space 20-yards from goal to rasp an effort towards MacGillivray. The stopper was at full stretch as he tipped the ball onto the bar and away for another corner. It was the final serious action of the half, which saw City level at half time.

The Imps needed a big second half, playing ten men and in good form themselves. Almost immediately, it was the Imps in the ascendency, Scully curling an effort high and wide after good possession. City were dominating the ball against two solid banks of four, and when Tom Hopper did finally get into the area on the ball on 53 minutes, his effort was crowded out.

Pompey's only real threat came from an odd foray forward, and one moment where Alex Palmer dwelled a little too long on the ball. With Curtis closing down, Palmer shifted and stabbed the ball away with his weaker foot, giving Imps' fans a reminder that it wasn't all going to be one way.

The Imps kept driving forward, Grant had a free-kick from the edge of the area charged down by the wall. The rebound was worked to Scully, who drove a low cross into the area. Grant had made the run into the box, but his deft touch was read by MacGillivray, who was having a strong game in the sticks.

The referee was playing centre stage in the eyes of the home side, with handball shouts at one point before they thought they should have had a free kick on 67 minutes. They hesitated and the Imps used that to sweep forward, with Scully once again curling an effort wide. The youngster was certainly busy all evening, but he just couldn't find the end product.

Pompey didn't properly clear their lines and just a minute later, McGrandles won the ball in the middle of the park. He fed in Edun, who found some space to deliver another dangerous cross, this time MacGillivray saving at the feet of Hopper.

On 70 minutes both teams made a change, with John Marquis coming off the pitch, it signalled the first appearance for him against City in which he didn't score. Scully, lively but not able to find a finish, came off for Morgan Rogers.

Rogers was immediately involved in the action, touching the ball to McGrandles in the box, who rasped an effort at goal. MacGillivray made yet another save, this time the ball ended up hacked away for a corner. Two minutes later, Rogers was involved again, sprinting into the area where he looked to be fouled as he burst past a defender. The referee was having none of it, perhaps it would have been a harsh call to make.

Still City looked to break the deadlock, with the home side almost resigned to fighting for a draw. They dropped deeper and deeper, so deep that Grant was able to amble forward like an old lady browsing an aisle at the supermarket, with walls of blue shirts in front of him on 74 minutes. He eventually found his way to the edge of the area, where a vicious left-footed strike went just wide.

Finally, on 79 minutes, City got the deserved breakthrough. TJ Eyoma, excellent once again on the right, delivered another low cross into the area. It evaded everyone but found McGrandles at the back post who recycled the ball and found Rogers. His first-time strike finally rippled the net, causing my dog to jump out of his skin as I went utterly ballistic.

The goal completely changed the complexion of the game, with Pompey suddenly looking like a proper prospect again. Just two minutes later a deep corner saw Ronan Curtis beat Palmer with a header, only for the ball to be scooped off the line by McGrandles, my Man of the Match. The same Pompey player then curled a free-kick over the bar from 22-yards out, when he should have worked the keeper.

City looked to run the clock down with a couple of changes, the first of which saw Edun replaced by Melbourne, but Pompey rallied. A long free-kick saw Palmer come to claim the ball, only for Raggett to get there first and head the ball up into the air. A deft flick might have brought a goal, but Palmer was able to gather.

Harry Anderson came on for Brennan Johnson, and yet still Pompey showed belief. Sub Ellis Harrison seemed to have got away from McGrandles, but the Scot hauled him down for a free kick in exactly the same place as the one Curtis missed. This time, Jacobs struck the wall and saw the ball bounce out for a corner.

It was a frenetic and fast-paced final few minutes, with Portsmouth looking like creating every time they went forward, unlike the first 80 minutes. Luckily for City, they didn't, and eventually, the referee brought proceedings to a close.

What more is there to say? City beat Portsmouth at Fratton Park for the first time since I was born, Hull lose at Accrington and drop to second, whilst Peterborough cannot break down Bristol rovers and also lose ground. The other big winners were Doncaster, who come to Sincil Bank this weekend knowing they're facing one of the division's in-form sides. Would you bet against us?

I'm going to write more tomorrow, but right now I fear I may drift into inflated hyperbole if I carry on. I have this monologue going around in my head, like the Norwegian commentator from the 80s who went on about Thatcher, but it goes 'Harry Redknapp, Kenny Jackett, James Callaghan, Amanda Holden, your boys took one hell of a beating, etc etc'. It is at that point I know to draw breath, sleep on it and bring you balanced analysis tomorrow, not the insane rambling of a man drunk of the sweet nectar of his once-abysmal football team reaching heights he hasn't experienced in 35-odd years of watching.

Sweet dreams City fans.

Its Official: Jorge Grant Pens New Imps Deal
January 29, 2021

It always happens, I pack up for the day, head off thinking nothing is happening and boom, the Imps make a big announcement.

I have jogged back to cover this – Jorge Grant has penned a new deal with the Imps which keeps him here until the summer of 2023. That's right folks, two-and-a-half more years of that wonderful man spraying balls around the park at will.

It hasn't even been a saga, has it? It has all been conducted in private, with little media coverage and minimal fuss. I spoke to Jorge earlier in December and whilst I would never ask him about the contract situation, I got the impression he was more than happy to be at Lincoln.

"I did feel a bit of a nomad early in my career, I felt like I couldn't really get settled anywhere," he told me. "There were times when I got close to leaving Forest and the move didn't happen and it was tough at times. I came here and I said I wanted Lincoln City to be my home and it has become that. I am really settled now and I'm really happy at the moment too."

That is a sentiment the 11-goal midfielder added to in his comments after penning the new deal.

Speaking to weareimps.com, Jorge said: "I am delighted, there is huge ambition at the club and the whole structure we have is something I am happy to be a part of. I am thankful that the Gaffer has pushed me to make the most out of my potential. It won't stop now because I want to carry on doing what I have been doing this season. I am really happy at the moment."

Michael is also delighted to have secured Jorge's services for the foreseeable future, Imps, saying: "We are delighted to keep Jorge at the club, he has played an important role this season and it is a pleasure to work with him.

"He has really grown in stature as a player and has put in some outstanding performances in a number of positions. Jorge has also shown determination and a high level of maturity in the dressing room and has led by example when given the captain's armband. He is a real asset to this football club, and we will continue to work hard to achieve our goals."

The 26-year-old has appeared 71 times for the Imps, scoring 13 times. This season he has been vice-captain, and netted 11 times from 29 starts in all competitions, including a stunner against Forest Green in the FA Cup, and a trademark free-kick to help turn around a 1-0 deficit against Wigan Athletic.

As a named sponsor of Jorge's home shirt, we're delighted he has agreed to stay with the Imps and help us to push towards our goal of Championship football.

Imps Secure First Permanent Signing of Transfer Window
January 30, 2021

The Imps have made their first permanent signing of the winter window, bringing in MK Dons defender Regan Poole.

As I write this, details of a contract or fee are not available, but I'm sure that will be clearer when the official announcement is made. The reason I can't be clearer is this is being scheduled (correctly) to go out whilst I am on air with Sam Ashoo on Match Day Live, because that is where the announcement is being made. How exciting, the first transfer of the window I announce early by accident and feel a plum, the second I get to be part of the actual live announcement!

Who is Regan Poole? Well, it is usual for me to go on about how much of a good player we're getting, or how I have always rated him, but do you want proof? Check out this match report from earlier this season, or this one from last year. Still not convinced? What about my preview of last season, specifically around MK Dons transfer business? I even dropped his name last season when talking about how Michael could look to utilise the transfer market differently here. I've been aware of Poole ever since Newport beat us 1-0 back at the tail end of our title-winning season, but his story goes back further than that.

Poole was part of the Cardiff City youth setup before moving to Newport, via a trial at Man Utd. His Newport County debut came at the tender age of 16 years and 94 days when he played for the Exiles against Shrewsbury. After 14 League Two starts across two seasons, he was picked up by Man Utd for £100,000, making his debut for them in the Europa League against Danish side Midtjylland. Former United star Mickey Thomas described Poole as an 'international of the future' after that game in February 2016.

He didn't appear anywhere in 2016/17, but during our first campaign in the Football League, he was already playing League One football. He spent a season on loan with Northampton Town, starting 18 league matches. he fell out of favour after Christmas as the Cobblers plunged towards relegation, and went back to Old Trafford in the summer.

This is when I first became aware of him – we were snapping up players in that summer to aid our title challenge, and he was a player that I came across during research. He didn't fit the bill of what we needed, we had the Neal Eardley and a collection of decent central defenders, but it was no surprise to see him sign for Newport on a half-season loan in January. He did really well for his old club, settling quickly and helping them to a 1-0 win against us in the penultimate game of the season, with the title already secured a week prior. His display that afternoon, confident and assured, had me impressed and I felt we could do with someone like him in the summer.

He left United, and at 20-years-old faced an uncertain future. MK Dons picked him up quickly and he's since settled and become a key player for them. He's played 50 times in all competitions with 31 starts in League One, and scored four goals. Poole penned a deal with MK in 2019, a deal which expires this summer according to Transfermarkt. One would imagine Poole is the player Jez Goerge was talking about when he said they'd bring a move forward if they could.

Where does this exciting new signing play? He's a defender, able to operate at right-back, right centre half or right wing-back. My gut feeling is he has come he to replace TJ Eyoma once he returns to Spurs, but in doing so now it ensures he is integrated and ready to go whatever next season brings. That isn't to say you won't see him in the first-team squad, you absolutely will. One would imagine he'll be involved plenty, given that he is an exciting talent maybe even looking to push his international prospects. Poole has been called up to the Wales senior squad, in October 2019, but didn't get to play. Imagine that, Lincoln City signing a player who maybe feels we can enhance his chances of international football, and not with Antigua, Gibraltar or the Never Never Land, but Wales, who seemingly qualify for major tournaments relatively easily now.

It's fair to say, this caps off a great 24 hours for Imps fans in terms of recruitment, with Jorge Grant also penning his new deal. It is something of a watershed moment I feel too, it is the first time I can think where we have gone to a rival club and taken a key player of theirs from them – not a 28-year-old who with very little sell-on potential, nor a 30-something veteran who may or may not be past his best, but a genuine young talent, a player with the potential to play much higher. It is reflective of the wonderful transfer policy the club has right now, and hopefully, one which will stand us in good stead to make a few million and keep turning over really good players.

Now, let's go an make it a thoroughly good 24 hours by winning the game of the afternoon in League One, shall we?

Penalty Woe as City Slip – Imps 0-1 Doncaster
January 30, 2021

City missed the chance to seize the advantage in the League One title race this afternoon, in a frustrating encounter at Sincil Bank.

A moment before I wrote this report, I got a message asking if it was acceptable to simply write a report with just three letters in it – FFS. I toyed with the idea; I really did. City had the better chances, dominated possession and put 23 crosses into the area, which is one every four minutes or so. That alone would usually be enough to leave me wondering how we didn't win, but throw in TWO missed penalties and you get a sense that we were never going to score.

The Imps made one change from the side which beat Portsmouth in midweek, with Anthony Scully dropping to the bench and Morgan Rogers coming into the side. Buoyed by both Jorge Grant's new contract and the capture of Regan Poole, confidence certainly should have been sky-high at a blustery Sincil Bank.

The Imps definitely started the brighter of the two sides, controlling possession and getting into good positions in wide areas. As early as the third minute, Eyoma, Grant and Johnson combined to deliver a ball into the area. It was a weak cross gathered by Balcombe in goal, but it was perhaps the first meaningful touch the visitors had.

Crosses were the main route of City's attack, with both full-backs linking well with the wide players to create space. On six minutes, Tom Hopper started a move on the left, which ended with Eyoma delivering a ball in from the right, which nobody anticipated.

Doncaster are in the top six for a reason and they gave an early suggestion of what that reason was on seven minutes, with Taylor Richards driving forward with real danger. His run wasn't unlike those Tom Lawrence made for Ipswich back in our big FA Cup game, and briefly, City looked vulnerable. Richards' shot was blocked, and the follow up fired high and wide.

City kept pushing for the opener, some good work from Grant and Edun fed in Morgan Rogers, but the on-loan Man City man had a rush of blood and blasted the ball miles over. Shortly after, he worked well with Grant, flicking a backheel into the path of Edun, who again looked to deliver into the area, only for it to be blocked for a corner. Sadly, the Imps excellent play was let down a real lack of presence from corners, with every one dealt with easily by a strong Doncaster defence.

On 15 minutes, Doncaster took the lead. The words 'against the run of play' are easy to band about, but it was part of their plan. Grant looked to have been tugged back in the middle of the park and ended up losing the ball, which found its way to Richards. He drove forward, unchallenged, and hit a shot low to the left of Alex Palmer, who might be disappointed not to have got a touch on it.

The goal certainly shook City and for a brief spell the game looked to be trickling away, but within ten minutes we were back on the attack. Conor McGrandles, who looked back on form, got away and delivered a cross which was blocked. There might have been a shout for handball, but it wasn't given and once again Doncaster cleared their lines.

On the half-hour mark, excellent work from Edun created out best chance. He kept a loose ball in, played a one-two and rushed free on the attacking left. His cross wasn't dealt with, and Johnson strode onto the loose ball, only to fire wide. Five minutes later it was Morgan Rogers going close, this time from the right-hand side. He put yet another cross in (one of 15 from the Imps in the first half), but Balcombe took to off Hopper's toes.

City had dusted themselves down after the goal and enjoyed 70% possession in a busy first half, but the last decent chance of the first period fell to the visitors. Adam Jackson gave away a rash free kick on the edge of the box, but Matt Smith's effort tamely dropped into Palmer's arms with players rushing in.

Oddly, despite what seemed like a one-sided first half, both teams registered seven shots at goal, with not a single one on target for City. Doncaster had two on target, both from Brighton loanee Richards, one of which was the difference heading into the break.

As early as the 46th minute City had a penalty shout, not that it would have mattered based on later events. Edun burst into the area on the left, got to the line and crossed, seemingly being fouled as he did. The referee was having none of it, and just a minute later it was Rogers in the same position, cutting the same ball across the box, only for Balcombe to claim in.

One of the Imps best chances came on 51 minutes, Eyoma got away down the right and delivered a cross which found Rogers. His shot was blocked and fell to McGrandles, who drove an effort at goal. Balcombe, as seems customary, made a super stop to keep the score at 1-0.

The first penalty of the afternoon came just before the hour. Grant played a one-two with Edun and entered the area, only to be fouled right in front of the referee. He pointed to the spot, leaving the vice-captain and new contract hero to surely put City back into the game. His penalty was on target, bot low to the keeper's right and not only did he save it, but he held onto it as well.

That didn't knock City, who kept pressing hard for a leveller. Rogers, who certainly looked livelier than his last start against Posh, picked up a ball wide left, cot across the area and had a pop, only for the defence to once again block.

On a rare foray forward for Doncaster, Tayo Edun committed a foul and drew a booking, but their free-kick was hit well over the stand by Reece James.

With thirteen minutes to go, City turned up the heat, with Grant in the middle of most of our good moves. He waltzed his way into the area before finding Johnson in space 18-yards out, but the on-loan Forest man fired over the bar. Rogers then found space on the left and looked to cut the ball into the area, only for the excellent Balcombe to dive out and make what I can only describe as a cross-save.

Grant, seemingly tired of laying on efforts for everyone else, then had the closest pop of the afternoon for the Imps. He drove an effort at goal from 25-yards out, almost identical to his goal against Forest Green, and finally beat Balcombe. Unfortunately, it struck the bar and bounced out for a goal kick. When it isn't your day….

Even Adam Jackson got in on the act at one point, surging forward, playing a ball into Hopper and then having an effort from the return ball. I suspect if you contact NASA, it is still in orbit somewhere. City were getting desperate.

With three minutes left, desperation turned to elation. A deep cross from Eyoma saw Grant chasing after the ball out towards the left-hand side of the area, with Balcombe rushing after him. The keeper fouled Grant right on the edge of the area and Darren Bond once again pointed to the spot. Was this the moment City finally got the point that they deserved (at the very least).

No. Anthony Scully took over responsibility from Grant, and despite going to Balcombe's right, the big keeper once again saved, and once again held onto the ball. I think those three letters, FFS, are more than applicable here once again. I personally would like to have seen Grant take it, but after successive misses (three if you include Charlton where he bagged the rebound) I guess it was time to change.

I'm not really sure what more I can say. I won't go on social media because I know it will be full of stuff like 'you have to score penalties' or 'we're not clinical enough', but the truth is it wasn't our day. In terms of possession, we were the better side, and we created more chances, but Doncaster were excellent in doing what we are usually good at – putting bodies on the line. The Imps played 23 crosses into the area, four were met by a Lincoln player. Balcombe took more of the crosses than all of the Imps players put together, and often they weren't that close to him either. Their defence was tight and they restricted us to two real chances in the second half, Grant's long-range effort and the McGrandles drive. Other than that, we knocked on the door a lot, but instead of breaking it down we were forced to walk away with it left unanswered.

I thought our wide defenders were excellent, I thought our midfield largely controlled the game and I thought our movement in front of the 18-yard box was strong too. Grant might have missed a penalty, but his contribution was telling all game and most of our positive attacking work came from him. I thought Bridcutt looked composed and aside from their goal, ensured they rarely threatened.

All of that is well and good, but Doncaster scored and we did not, despite having two penalties. The hard truth is we should have won that game, without a shadow of a doubt, and we didn't. I saw nothing that worries me for us going into the next 22 matches, except the fact we will do so without at least one point we should have had from this. Also, assuming you should score penalties, we are now five points behind where we should be, having missed one against Posh too. I'm not sure whether that is frustrating, or whether it makes me look at this young group and just be proud of where we are without those points.

I am frustrated tonight, not with any player in particular, because they put in a decent shift, just with football. It delights us, it angers us and for a few minutes after the game it made me feel sick as a 15-year-old me down Wragby park with a bottle of green Mad Dog 20/20. I felt it rolling around in the pit of my stomach and I wanted to punch something. Then I remembered we're second in League One, not second from bottom in League Two, and things felt better. Then I remembered Jorge Grant signed a new contract, that we signed Regan Poole on a permanent deal and that we have 22 games to go out and get points from.

I also looked at the table and realised that whilst Doncaster would win the league if they won all of their games, meaning that if we did the same, we'd finish second and being honest, if we went up in second place, I wouldn't be lamenting the fact we hadn't won the title. I won't say 'we go again', because I hate that saying, but we have brief respite this week as we face Hull in the cup, before a big match next weekend against Gillingham, where we can quickly get points back on the board.

I just pray we don't get a penalty. Or two.

February

Imps close in on 24-y/o defender
February 1, 2021

Sky Sports are reporting that the Imps are closing in on 24-year-old left-back Cohen Bramall from Colchester United, as we reported last week.

Bramall, who I am told was briefly on trial here in the summer of 2019 (and I somehow missed it) is out of contract in the summer and it is expected the U's would rather take a fee for him now than risk him moving for free in July. Earlier in the window, Championship outfit Reading were also linked with a swoop, which underlines the potential he has going forward, exactly the sort of acquisition Michael is renowned for.

Bramall made headlines back in 2017 when, after spells with Kidsgrove, Market Drayton and Hednesford, he was snatched up by Premier League giants Arsenal for a fee thought to be around £40,000. He spent two-and-a-half years with Arsenal, but he failed to make a senior appearance for them. He did spend time on loan at Birmingham City, where he played five times in the Championship before returning to the Emirates.

Bramall blasted the club when he left after his contract ran out, claiming many of their young players would take the same route in search of regular senior football. One route he took was to join up with us, but after what I believe were a couple of outings in friendly matches, we opted not to sign him. bear in mind, Harry Toffolo joined and we weren't known for loading up on full-backs at the time.

He signed for Colchester at the beginning of the 2019/20 season and has gone on to make 46 League Two starts across last season and this campaign. In total he has made 56 outings, all of them starts, with two goals to his credit. He was heavily linked with another Championship move in the summer, this time Brentford were the expected destination, but that didn't come to fruition either.

Second departure of the day as defender heads out on loan
February 1, 2021

The Imps have seen a second departure this evening, following on from Aaron Lewis leaving the club.

This time, it is fringe defender Max Melbourne who is on his way out, looking for first team experience. Max will join League Two side Walsall on loan until the end of the season.

The Saddlers are currently 11th in League Two, five points outside the play-offs, but they, in turn, have lost Zak Jules to MK Dons, and Max will fill in for him on the left side of their defence. It seems a reasonable move, we haven't seen much of Max this season and given his two-and-a-half-year deal signed a year ago, he needs to get exposure to senior football.

Max has appeared 16 times for City this season, but that doesn't give a true reflection of his first-team exposure – he only averages 23 minutes per outing in the league, and if you were to take away his one start against Accrington, then it would be 12 minutes per outing. Whilst he hasn't directly let us down in any games, he does seem to be one of a couple of players who are perhaps a touch behind the rest. His loan spell with Walsall will give him a chance to catch up.

Max came through the ranks at West Brom, having loan spells with Ross County and Partick Thistle before joining us on loan under previous boss Danny Cowley. Michael Appleton gave him a senior move last January, but the form of Tayo Edun, and early doors that of Sean Roughan, has ensured that 22-year-old Melbourne hasn't seen much action.

That's a left-back gone and we're being linked with a left-back.... I'll be up until 11 pm, but will it be worth it?

City leave it late to bag Premier League prospect
February 1, 2021

This weekend the Imps were undone by a strike from an on-loan Brighton midfielder, so why not go out and get one of our own?

That's certainly the case as we have completed the signing of 22-year-old Max Sanders from the Seagulls, with just two minutes to go. The versatile midfielder has appeared three times for the Premier League side, all in the EFL Trophy, and was earmarked as their top Under 23 talents by 90 Minutes earlier this season. He was reported as 'stealing the show' during their win against Preston, and it was widely reported that a number of Championship clubs had coveted his signature on a loan deal.

Back in the days of Chris Hughton, a man notorious for not naming young players on the bench, Sanders made it twice against Manchester United in the 2017-18 season FA Cup quarter-final and when Liverpool won 1-0 at the Amex in January 2019. He also captained the Brighton's Under 23 side at the age of 20, and was skipper in the 2017-18 season play off final in which saw his side promoted to the top flight of Premier League 2.

The Horsham-born schemer usually sits in front of the back four, but in his time with Brighton has played in a number of positions. In 2018/19 he played LW in one Under 23 game, attacking midfield in another, but usually played in the central role as a traditional '4' or '6 depending on what number scheme you abide by.

He isn't just a wet-behind-the-ears youngster with no senior experience though. Last season he played for AFC Wimbledon on loan, starting 18 League One matches, having originally been with the Wombles as a youngster. In addition, he has also been capped at Under 19 level for England on four occasions, all coming during the 2018 Under-19 European Championships.

This season, his form in those EFL trophy outings piqued the interest of former Chelsea and Aston Villa midfielder Steve Sidwell, who said of Sanders: "In the previous round at Preston, he was probably the man of the match. Nice, neat and tidy on the ball. He puts his foot in. Tries to get forward as well."

He also impressed Portsmouth News reporter Will Rooney, who identified Sanders as the type of player he wanted to see move to Fratton Park this window. Speaking at the beginning of last month, Rooney said: "He had a good season at Wimbledon last season, he played against Pompey in the cup earlier in the season, and then he really impressed against a Championship side in Preston in their subsequent game in the League Cup.

"He's done it at a lower club and now's the time to move up to a Pompey where he can really show how good he is and how far he could go by moving up to a club where there's going to be a lot more pressure on him to perform."

Well, sadly for them, he hasn't chosen to move to Portsmouth but instead dropped into Sincil Bank with a bucket load of potential. This is an eyebrow-raising move for the Imps, and whilst it might not be the striker some hoped for, I have to point out the late deal we secured for Anthony Scully last season around the same time. He was a young player coming from a strong academy, little was known about him and ultimately, he has done very well.

I have a feeling Sanders might well be a player who doesn't get pulses racing reading this, because few know about him at Sincil Bank, but turns out to be yet another very strong acquisition by the club.

Redemption: Hull 1-1 Imps (3-4 on pens)
February 2, 2021

The Imps progressed to the EFL Trophy semi-final this evening, and in doing so found a level of redemption from Saturday's penalty misery against Doncaster.

Both teams made changes from their games at the weekend, but still looked very strong on paper. City welcomed back Lewis Montsma, Harry Anderson and James Jones, whilst Brennan Johnson started through the centre with Howarth coming into the midfield.

Even as the early pictures from the ground came across, it was clear the game wasn't going to be the fine advert for League One teams we hoped to get. The torrential rain was casing huge puddles to gather on the pitch, with the goalmouth area looking particularly treacherous.

It took a while to get the game underway, with a minute's silence for Captain Sir Tom Moore, who passed away today. Eerily, when the whistle blew to end the minutes silence, it continued in the absence of a crowd. The players then took the knee too, as the rain kept coming down in bucketloads.

There was little to shout about in the opening five minutes, with the first chance of the game bringing the first goal. Anthony Scully shifted to his right in the wide position to buy an inch, delivered a cross, and Harry Anderson netted on his return to the side. Anderson timed his run into the area perfectly and got on the blind side of Reece Burke to give the Imps the lead.

The game was both entertaining and a little scrappy at the same time. It is clear to see why Hull are doing well, Keane Lewis-Potter, in particular, looked a real danger, as did Callum Elder. The latter delivered a cute cross into the box on nine minutes, but it bounced in front of the six-yard box and away for a City throw.

Greg Doherty, a former Rangers midfielder, made the first real chance for Hull a minute later. Again, a nice move down the attacking left saw him cut inside and curl and effort over the crossbar and into the empty stands. Hull were beginning to find some good possession, but it was the Imps who narrowly missed out on doubling the lead on the 15-minute mark.

Edun, looking as lively as ever on the left, knocked a nice ball into Johnson, who played it back out of the area to James Jones. Just as he did in the League Cup against Bradford, he looked up and launched a drive at goal, this time narrowly bouncing past the post.

Dan Crowley was the one player who looked very creative, and he fired wide after some neat build up play after 24 minutes. Often, the passages of play seemed stunted and slow because of the pitch, and Hull were certainly handling it better. As the half progressed, City seemed to be penned in, without any serious danger. One shot Hull did manage on target came from Elder, but his mishit ball may have been an attempted cross. Either way, Palmer gathered with ease.

If Hull were going to get a breakthrough, it looked like it might come for Lewis-Potter, who really impressed me. He stripped Joe Walsh for pace in the right channel on 25 minutes, but was forced wide in doing so and his effort was palmed clear by Palmer from a tight angle.

The Imps next chance came from a quick break, all through Johnson. He dispossessed Burke in our defensive half, then stripped the centre back bare for pace as he strode into the area with only the keeper to beat. Sadly, the pitch got the better of him and what should have been a routine touch flew off his boot on the wet surface like a pass, with Matt ingram advancing and dealing with ease.

Despite the increasing pressure, Hull only managed one more decent effort in the first half. Crowley's whipped free kick beat everyone except Lewis-Potter at the far post, but it bounces nastily up on the wet turf and all the youngster could do was lift his effort high and wide.

The quality began to break down in the final 15 minutes, with the Imps passing game clearly hindered by the heavy pitch. In places, the ball stuck, but where the surface was only wet rather than boggy, the ball fizzed at pace. It made the game very unpredictable, but it couldn't be to blame for our final missed chance of the half on 42 minutes. City got a free kick 25 yards out, almost in line with the edge of the box, but Grant's delivery was awful and a low diving header cleared the danger.

Whilst City took a lead into the break, it wasn't a fair reflection of a first half of which Hull deserved to be at least level, and it felt with the pitch cutting up badly, it probably wouldn't be the last of the scoring.

As it turned out, it wasn't. Hull came out looking hungry and should have had a goal within minutes of the restart. Doherty's shot was blocked and fell to Magennis, who Imps defender's thought was offside. For a second, everyone stopped allowing Magennis to get a shot away at Palmer, who saved well.

Our first chance of the half came on 50 minutes, a corner was easily nodded away by the Hull defence, and Edun volleyed the loose ball over the goal, stand and maybe even the Humber. Within minutes, Hull were up the other end, their corner finding Lewis-Potter who headed over, but not quite out of the stand.

The conditions seemed conducive to an end-to-end game, and just before the hour mark it swung towards Hull's end. Doherty got the goal, like Richards for Doncaster on Saturday he was allowed to stride forward into space, before finishing smartly past Palmer. It felt like a crushing blow, our chances had been few and far between and Hull had a raft of subs to bring on, which they did.

The Tigers sensed the game was there for the taking, with Crowley and Lewis-Potter at the centre of their good work. The on-loan Birmingham man found himself in space from a Lewis-Potter cross, but his powerful effort struck the legs of Joe Walsh when it seemed more likely to go in.

On 64 minutes we made our only change, Tom Hopper coming on for Howarth. It felt like a Hopper game, the type where we needed the ball to stick up top for a while. Our wide men started to look leggy, and with the game increasingly stretched and 25 minutes still to play, I did fear the worst, especially as Hull made further changes.

One minute it was Johnson picking up the ball from a corner and having a shot blocked, then it was Lewis-Potter turning this way and that to bamboozle Jones before firing wide. The game ebbed and flowed, clearly high on quality players but on a surface that left the outcome of passes almost totally unpredictable in places.

With just over 15 minutes left, City came alive. Johnson had an effort from 25-yards from a break, but it looked a tired one. Eyoma took the ball 60 yards down the attacking right, then ended the move by collecting a ball from Jones and firing narrowly over the bar. It was Johnson again on 81 minutes, this time Hopper making the quality yards down the left flank, before pulling the ball back. The on-loan Forest man never stopped running, but his contact wasn't great as he looked on the edge of burning out.

It looked as though it might be the home side who would concede as some of our players dragged tired bodies forward on a heavy pitch. Scully hadn't quite got going for much of the game, but clever work from him found Grant, who did a lovely drag to keep possession before curling over the goal of Matt Ingram.

With three minutes left, the pendulum swung again. A deep Hull corner needed punching out by Palmer, but sixty seconds later Billy Chadwick found an inch of space in the middle, but dragged his effort wide of the post. Then, with a minute left on the clock, Doherty should have won it. Lewis-Potter whipped the ball across the area and Doherty needed just a touch to poke home, but the ball rolled under his tired feet.

There was still time for City to have the final words, first Jones went down in the area amidst shouts for a penalty (which it wasn't), but before anyone could react Montsma picked the ball up and drilled a trademark effort at goal, which flashed wide of the post. It seemed a goal was coming at one end or another, and it was almost a shame when Bobby Madeley blew the whistle to signal penalties.

If we'd shown character to concede, leave 10 players on for the full 90 minutes and not collapse, then we would have to show the same again with a penalty shootout. The obvious irony is the two missed penalties from the weekend, helping us to lose a fixture we should have won. This evening, a draw was a fair result from two committed teams in challenging conditions, but it meant that everything came down to spot kicks. 12-yards from progression, five (or more) kicks from £50,000.

James Jones stepped up and netted his with relative ease, almost making me forget the agony of Saturday. When Alex Palmer saved Smallwood's penalty in true Balcombe style, I jumped up and spilt my tea over my desk. I was still mopping up when Montsma quickly reminded me what a missed penalty for the Imps looked like.

Still, it didn't matter as James Scott saw Palmer save his spot kick, handing us the advantage, only for Harry Anderson to reveal he's been watching Italia 90 Semi Final replays and send a ball into Waddle-esque orbit. That meant the Imps had missed five of the last six penalties in all competitions, something I feared as Hull went next. Billy Chadwick smashed his down the middle to restore parity.

Next up, Anthony Scully. His spot kick was saved at the weekend and he had a big task to shrug that off and keep the Imps in the game, and he did just that with great composure. Hull were done missing theirs too, their man of the match 9in my eyes) Lewis potter scoring.

Next up, Jorge Grant. He missed penalties in successive home games, penalties that if they'd gone in would have given us at least three more points than we have right now. Seemingly, without a care in the world, he strode up with absolute balls and made no mistake. He was followed by Elder, who sent the game into sudden death.

I wondered if it might go on all night, especially as a nonchalant Brennan Johnson slotted his home with consummate ease. He showed great character having put in a hard 90-minute shift and made no mistake at all.

That left everything on the shoulders of Jordan Flores and Alex Palmer. The recent signing for Hull hit a half-decent penalty, but on the form Palmer was in, it needed to be full-decent, and it wasn't. He saved, to send the Imps into the semi-finals of the competition.

It was considered a dress rehearsal for the serious business of League One action, but by the time we started taking those spot kicks it turned into so much more. This game, more than any other this season, felt more like 2016/17 than any, with us having our backs to the wall at times, having to dig deep to find reserves of energy and having to show character not just in terms of out team performance, but also with some individuals. Grant and Scully, in particular, stood up to be counted in those penalties and considering they were picked fourth and fifth, it was as if they planned to take extra pressure on their shoulders.

Next week will be different, hopefully we will have got the extra day of rest in and look sharp, we'll have a full bench and maybe the pitch will lose some of the standing water. We know what we'll face though, a side packed with quality such as Crowley, Lewis-Potter and Doherty, but with plenty of faces we haven't seen, such as Honeyman and Wilks. I do feel more at ease though looking ahead, because that was a strong Hull side, as strong as ours, and we matched them. It wasn't always pretty, it wasn't always flowing, but it was entertaining.

We learned a lot about our players tonight, individually and collectively, and we can now look forward to a semi-final and potentially a Wembley appearance, giving Michael the chance to address his own demons in the competition. What price on us to beat Oxford in the final, giving Michael the redemption he surely craves against the team he suffered the double heartbreak with?

Back to the top of the pile: Gillingham 0-3 Imps
February 5, 2021

City returned to the top of the League One table this evening with a resounding looking victory against Steve Evans' Gillingham.

The result ensures a relatively trouble-free Saturday for the Imps, with the hard work already done. We can sit back now and watch our rivals hopefully slip up, knowing a potentially tough tie has been navigated with some success.

City were unchanged from the side which lost 1-0 to Doncaster Rovers last weekend. Lewis Montsma, James Jones, Harry Anderson and Anthony Scully all got starts against Hull in midweek, but all dropped to the bench for this tie. The Gills had former Imp Vadaine Oliver up top, with John Akinde on the bench, and were expected to simply launch long balls forward. That was a simplified version of what they did, and if we expected a battle then we certainly went prepared.

In the first minute, Jorge Grant let Southampton loanee Callum Slattery know he had a battle on with a tough-looking challenge, which set the scene for the rest of the encounter. There were some tough challenges, very few that were outright dirty, and we matched their aggressiveness where we needed to, maybe even instigating some of it ourselves. Let's not be under any illusions, we're not a soft side and there was no repeat of last season, where they stopped us playing and intimidated our young side.

If we expected an easy ride in terms of chances, and by we, I mean supporters, then we soon got a taste of what Gillingham can do. Grant loosely gave the ball away on five minutes, which led to Alex MacDonald driving an effort at goal, which Palmer saved. We began to edge our way into the game, but certainly had less possession in the opening exchanges. Our first half-chance came courtesy of Tom Hopper, who played a decent cross in on 11 minutes, but it evaded Morgan Rogers running in.

Our first shot on target of the half brought the opening goal of the game. It was classic Michael Appleton football, with a nice build up and fancy flick. Grant played a delicious backheel into the path of Rogers, who in turn put the ball in the right area. Brennan Johnson had a go at collecting it but couldn't quite get it out from his feet, allowing Conor McGrandles the space to stride in and stroke the ball into the back of the net. 1-0 City, and perhaps a little against the general run of play.

Despite taking the lead, it couldn't be argued that we were the better side by a long way. Gillingham are good at what they do, and every opportunity they got the ball into the box. Whether it was a long throw, a delivery from one of any number of free kicks they got within fifty yards of the box, or simply through a passage of play, their mandate is simple. Look for the big man, all the time. That put huge emphasis on Adam Jackson and Joe Walsh, but neither shirked their responsibilities. When called upon, they did the sort of defensive work we haven't had to do much of this season, and they did it well. If the ball strayed closer to the six-yard box, Palmer was on it like wasp is on a beer on a warm summer day.

A few typical chances were Olly Lee's header on 20 minutes, following a good free kick from Jordan Graham. I liked the look of Graham, direct and skilful, always wanting to get in behind. I heard a rumour from a Gills fan that we might have looked at home in the winter window and he would certainly suit our style of play, no doubt at all. It was him getting in on goal on the half-hour mark too, a teasing ball found him in the channel with Walsh getting across to block what looked like a certain goal.

When he wasn't looking to get in goal himself, Graham was delivering for other and barely a minute elapsed between his blocked effort and a teasing cross for former Imp Oliver. He has never impressed me when he's played against us, and I didn't want to tempt fate by saying it before the game, but thankfully that run continued as his effort was tame at Palmer.

Lee Hendrie felt Oliver could have been sent off for a challenge on Grant shortly afterwards, but it would have been harsh. It might have looked tasty from the commentary position, but on the television screen there wasn't a hint of a foul, even though he came out of the challenge with his studs showing, they weren't up when he went in. Credit where it is due to referee Sam Barrott, who did get that decision right.

After the goal, we seemed almost intent on sitting back and seeing if the Gills could break us down, but they couldn't. they did manage a flurry of half-chances before half time, a free-kick was sent over the bar, before Kyle Dempsey broke through the centre, saw the ball sit up nicely, and yet he let a weak shot go wide of Palmer's goal.

The general consensus from the people I message during the game was that we had done okay in the first half, we'd made them work, let them have possession that at times they didn't know what to do with and when they did have half a chance, defended well. Despite having more efforts at goal, they hadn't created anything that could be described as clear-cut and it did feel like another solid 45 would see us back to the top of the table.

The second half certainly had incident, with everything but a red card from the referee. It started with the story of the first half being played out again, Jordan Graham getting on the ball, driving at our back four and shooting straight at Alex Palmer. I felt if a goal were coming, he was the man to provide it, but he did fade a little as the game wore on.

We looked to have found our second wind too, and Grant had the first Imps chance of the half on 49 minutes. Johnson was the creator, always looking to get on the ball and drive forward. He delivered from the left, only for Grant to shoot wide.

The next ten minutes were punctuated by a long pair of stoppages, something I felt did help change the game a little. Firstly, Olly Lee got a whack n the nose (Bridcutt I think), which saw him needing treatment. It took a couple of minutes, and barely sixty seconds had passed when Conor Ogilvie took a nasty whack from Tom Hopper. I felt Ogilvie actually tried to foul Hopper in the middle of the park, and in doing so he got a nasty looking wound on his head. He was down for five minutes or so, covered in blood, and yet he somehow passed concussion protocol and came back on. I suspect, if there is such a thing as concussion protocol, it consisted of someone saying to Ogilvie 'are you okay?' and him saying 'yes', before carrying on. He spent the next forty minutes with his head heavily bandaged, and by the end of the game was looking a bit 'Terry Butcher' with claret all over his face.

Before the hour mark struck, the Imps has sealed the points. Rogers and Johnson are beginning to look like they're getting an understanding, and the former teed up the latter on 53 minutes, with his effort coming back off the bar. Shortly after, Johnson entered the area and was tugged back by Jackson, and by tugged back I really am stretching it. The referee pointed to the spot, and although there seemed to be no complaints from Gills players, it looked a little soft to me. Johnson was tugged back, an arm was raised and the referee doesn't have a lot of choice, but if Johnson tries to stay on his feet, it isn't given. Maybe it was a penalty won, but you do have to be in the box and running at players to get it.

Jorge Grant, the victim of saved penalties against Peterborough and Doncaster, stepped up and made no mistake at all. That's three in a week he's taken, and the second in a row he's scored. You could see by his celebration that this one meant more than Tuesday night, being in the league and essentially putting the game almost beyond the hosts.

If that put the Gills on their knees, five minutes later they were on the canvass. Liam Bridcutt found Rogers with a neat pass and the on-loan Manchester City man went on a lovely run, twisting his way into the area and shifting balance to get a shot away. Jack Bonham parried it, straight into the path of Tom Hopper, who nodded home from three yards out. There was a shout for offside from the defence and I think had it been against us, I might have been inclined to agree. Still, it was a nice move by City, and the run from Rogers deserved a goal on its own.

Oddly, having perhaps not played as well as we did against Doncaster, we found ourselves 3-0 up with 25 minutes, plus what turned out to be nine minutes of stoppages remaining.

Gillingham went go for broke, bringing on John Akinde on 66 minutes, and thirty seconds later the big man nearly pulled a goal back for his side. His first involvement was a flick on for Dempsey, who this time struck the ball cleanly and concisely, drawing a good save from Palmer. The passage of play continued and eventually, a deep cross found Akinde, who had taken up a position in the box, only for his header to come back off the bar. It was the closest the hosts went all night and it turned out to be their best chance to get even a consolation from the game.

Vadaine Oliver felt he had something more to say in the game, and yet another ball into the area was headed over by him on 72 minutes. The hosts like a big ball into the box, and yet every time they tried one of three things happened; our defenders dealt with it, Palmer dealt with it or they fluffed their lines under pressure from our defenders, or Palmer. Last year, a young Imps side wilted under the same tactics, this season, it is a very different story indeed.

The 79th minute brought a move which could have come out of a Lincoln City book of old. Good work from Akinde, who did more in his cameo than in many of his Imps outings, saw him get away down the left using pace. He lifted a ball in for Oliver, who saw his effort go wide. Two Imps old boys couldn't combine to undo us, and the footballing Gods finally gave us a break. After all, how many times has a script like that been written? Too many.

City took advantage of the lead to make a couple of changes, bringing off firstly Eyoma, then Johnson. Both had put in a strong shift, but it gave us a chance to blood Regan Poole, with the former MK Dons man handed a debut. Harry Anderson also came on for Johnson, who had been a constant threat with his direct running.

We could have made it four late in the game. Firstly, Morgan Rogers drove a good 35 yards from the middle of the park to the edge of the area, gently teasing in Hopper in the left channel. He took it slightly wide to the left and looked to put the ball across Bonham's goal, but it rolled wide of the post.

Deep into stoppage time, City did score a fourth, and it was certainly less dubious than two of the goal that were allowed. Harry Anderson, on as a sub, played a ball that is now something of an Imps trademark across the front of the six-yard box, and Grant strode from an onside position to stroke the ball home. He was onside, no doubt at all, but the linesman's flag said otherwise. At 0-0, you fume, but at 3-0 with a dubious penalty and maybe an offside too, you shrug your shoulders, mutter 'them's the breaks' and think about Hull away on Tuesday.

152

I haven't seen any post-match reaction, but I imagine Evans has moaned a bit, Michael was more than satisfied and the pundits have done a bit of purring at our slick football. I felt there were a lot of strong performances, starting at the back. Palmer, Walsh and Jackson were all excellent, and Edun carried on his super form too. Bridcutt had a lot of work to do and he did it well, despite a few free-kicks in dangerous areas. I think he gets a rough time from some, because often those free kicks are almost clever. One foul on Graham was calculated and stopped the former Villa man getting around the back, and whilst it meant a chance to deliver, nothing came of it.

Obviously, when we attacked, we looked very good, and I dare even say we're getting better every week. I remember back in November thinking 'where will a goal come from' when we had struggled to score from open play – I genuinely feel now we'll score from a good percentage of our attacks, and never feel we are bereft of ideas. It is ominous for everyone else that we are getting better and better. January was a great month for us, with some strong results, and we did it with a Covid-ravaged squad, with key injuries and against some big opposition. Well, players are coming back and here we are still on top, getting strong each and every week.

Steve Evans is an old adversary, a manager we come up against time and again. I remember chuckling when he was at Mansfield, claiming he wasn't a League Two manager, as if he had lowered to our level. I think this evening, despite not playing badly, we showed that we are probably a level above the Gills in what we do. That shouldn't reflect badly on them by the way, they were far from the worst we've seen this season and actually looked competent and committed, but it was just a ruthless performance from us, showing both sides of our game. when we're good, we're very good, and when we need to be bad, we're able to do just that.

We're into February now, top of League One and gunning for a promotion spot. We bounced back from a defeat against Doncaster in great style, knocking Hull out of the cup and then turning over a big win against a decent side tonight. It's not the first time I've felt we are title challengers, but it is the first time that a part of me truly believed it.

Well, believe it all you want. Lincoln City are 100% in the automatic promotion race and if we keep doing what we're doing, we'll finally be visiting the more illustrious side of the Trent next season.

Clive Nates addresses Imps supporters
February 8, 2021

Imps chairman Clive Nates has penned an open letter to supporters, which dropped on the official club website at 5 pm.

Unlike some clubs, who throw 'club statements' about like free candy, Clive knows the time to address fans, and the time to remain in the shadows. With the effects of Covid still being felt, but the club moving forward on the pitch, he has once again put pen to paper, finger to keyboard. and spoken directly to supporters.

What I like about Clive's communications is that they never pull any punches. He always highlights the positives but has no concern addressing the negatives too. Here we are, in with a genuine promotion chance, challenging at the top of the third tier for the first time since 82/83, and he has no fear about touching upon some of the elements of the season that have caused consternation – fans not being in the stadium being one. He also addresses the fact the Premier League bailout was 40% lower than clubs expected, and that the board have still managed to back Michael going forward. It is easy to applaud the positives, to backslap and self-congratulate, but to reflect on negatives in a manner fans relate too is not all that easy.

I see a lot of comparison between this season and 1982/83. Back then we were a great side, playing decent football and boasting some players with big futures. We set the pace back then, fought bravely and got to Christmas in pole position. Colin Murphy wanted backing financially, he wasn't and the next 40 odd years of history were immediately determined. This season almost everything is the same, except the board have backed the manager, not only in the players who have come in, but in offer Jorge Grant and extended contract. Quite rightly, Clive touches on this.

You may recall I did a SWOT analysis a while ago, looking at strengths, weaknesses, opportunities and threats. Well, here's a big threat that you may not have considered – the credit option on the season tickets. Those of us fortunate enough not to have had to take our money out of the club have been told we can use the credit to get a discount next season, but that is just knocking a big deficit further down the line. In his letter, Clive hints at this and seems to suggest that there might be options for the supporters who can afford to not take that discount next season.

"Behind the scenes, our ticket office team are in the process of uploading season ticket credit to your Ticketmaster accounts, and we aim to have this completed within a week. You will then have a number of options to choose from to redeem against your remaining season ticket balance."

So far, it is as we knew. Those who chose not to take their money back, those lucky enough to not feel they had to, were told money could be carried over to next season. However, that means revenue that the club may have got from full ST sales will be reduced, right? Maybe, but it seems the club have come up with a way to reduce the threat.

"There will be exclusive access to a list of events and merchandise, the opportunity for you to convert to shares once again, as well as spending some outstanding credit on future season ticket purchases. As always, however, I would ask that supporters consider their personal circumstances first."

Now, for a geek like me, words like 'merchandise' and 'events' are exciting. Whatever the club do have planned, it does seem as though they will be offering us something that might just keep a bit of money in the club, but as always, Clive urges you to make choices based on your circumstances. Do you know why he does that? Because he is a decent human being. He might be embarrassed that I'm about to say this, but the letter isn't the only communication he has entered into today. Earlier, when I mentioned my Mum has Covid on Twitter, he took the time to personally message me to wish her all the best. Top guy. Clive does actually care, and he would not want fans putting themselves in peril for the club.

Of course, the letter ends with a thank you for sticking by the club, through iFollow and generally.

As I have always said, a football club is only as strong as its fans – if anything they (we) are all it is. Players, kits, divisions, chairman, grounds and finances all change, but we don't. We are the club, but Clive and the board are the current custodians, the people entrusted to take our club forward. Personally, I have to hold the current board up as perhaps the best we have ever had. They have seized the opportunity of the FA Cup run, National League promotion, Wembley, League Two promotion and that of a manager hunt, They have staved off threats of Covid, losing a manager and a loack of financial clarity the last eight months or so. As a consequence, we are in the best shape that we have been in ever since I first stepped foot in the ground. Clive and the board do all of that whilst remaining approachable, personable and human. We have had some good chairs in the past, we've had boards I respect and who history shine favourably on, but I'm not sure we have ever had a collection of people like we have now.

That leadership and clarity starts at the top and is typified by letters like Clive has penned today. So, whilst Clive has thanked us for our support, I'd like to thank him and the board for theirs. If you want a reflection of what life could be like, go check out Swindon fans relationship with Lee Power, or Grimsby's with Jon Fenty. Both clubs are similar sizes to us and experienced promotions as we did (one before, one after) and yet both are in disarray.

For order, leadership and foresight, thank you Clive and the board.

Investment of £800,000 in Imps Revealed
February 9, 2021

It has been reported today that the club has seen £800,000 put in by the board to help tide us over the Covid crisis.

There is nothing surprising about this investment, I'm told it is the 'Covid-fund', promised by the board to help carry us over the challenging times in which we find ourselves. Whilst I say 'not surprising', I mean it was expected, not that it shouldn't be applauded, or that it is routine.

The truth is we have a superb board of directors and a strong leader in Clive Nates. He alluded to the income in his letter to fans yesterday and this is the physical manifestation of those words. He explained how the board had dug deep to tide the club over, back the manager and help secure the future and there it is: £800,000.

What we must acknowledge is that everything we do on the field is facilitated by a generous, but not a decadent board of directors. These are people who help drive the club forward, who help stabilise us until the new method begins to pay transfer dividends and who can react to a changing climate and ensure our safety during troubling times. They are not rich owners trying to falsely elevate the club by buying success, but when opportunity is there, they have the means to react. When we won League Two, we did so with a decent budget, but also strong crowds and some football fortune too. This season, we have been able to remain solvent and recruit not only through the generosity of the board, but also the clause in Danny and Nicky's contracts and the frugal approach by the manager.

In the past, especially the 82/83 season, the board have been accused of being negligent, of not wanting promotion and a host of other negative points. Maybe those were correct accusations, maybe Gilbert Blades and the rest of the board really didn't have the means to support the club and did what they felt was necessary to keep us afloat. I don't know, I am not privy to the accounts of yesteryear and I can only imagine that the full story was not evident to all. However, the league table at the time doesn't lie – we were storming it going into the winter, and we fell away as a result of upheaval, arguments and a lack of funding. That was the closest we came to promotion to the second tier in 40 years, and the fact the board cost us that promotion is a legend, if not a proven fact.

Today's announcement proves that this board will not be the reason the club is held back. This board is the reason we are where we are and if you doubt that, I have 800,000 reasons why you are wrong.

Stalemate Keeps City on Top: Hull City 0-0 Imps
February 9, 2021

City might not have seized the chance to extend the lead at the top of the table this evening, but a solid and committed display at the KCom ensured a useful point against fellow title challengers Hull City.

The Imps were unchanged from Friday's win against Gillingham, meaning no place for Lewis Montsma, James Jones or Anthony Scully, all of whom featured on the bench. The Tigers featured Josh Magennis, Greg Docherty and Keane Lewis-Potter who all played last Tuesday in the 1-1 draw, but George Honeyman came into the side with Regan Slater not starting as expected. However, with Dan Crowley also in the team, it was certainly a strong-looking home side which took to the turf in snowy conditions.

That was reflected in the opening few minutes, as the hosts came out all guns blazing. Within sixty seconds, they'd hit the bar, Keane Lewis-Potter's effort deflected up and onto the frame of the goal. The Tigers looked hungry and confident in the opening five minutes or so, but didn't have the killer ball.

City's first half-chance fell on five minutes, TJ Eyoma got away on the right-hand side and whipped a lovely cross in towards Hopper, who was just a yard behind it as it flashed in front of goal. That signalled a bit of a spell for City. With Morgan Rogers going close on 14 minutes. He picked up a lovely ball, threaded through the eye of a needle by Jorge Grant, but his effort flashed across goal and wide of Matt Ingram's left-hand post.

City then had a weak penalty shout as Tayo Edun went down in the area, before a moment switched the balance of play again. Conor McGrandles fouled Callum Elder to give away a free-kick and pick up the game's first booking, but as he was being cautioned, we brought off Liam Bridcutt, with James Jones coming on. Bridcutt had been looking in decent form, but after he came off, we seemed to lose our shape a little.

The free-kick was laid off to Lewie Coyle, but he drilled it high and wide, but the pendulum has swung once again. Callum Elder had a vicious drive blocked in the 18-yard box, before Alex Palmer played the ball straight to the feet of Lewis-Potter two minutes later. The youngster suffered a rush of blood to the head as he curled a shot over the bar, by some distance too.

Seven days ago, it was Lewis-Potter on the end of most of their chances and it was the same again tonight. An Elder cross on the half-hour mark saw a diving header from the youngster, which went wide. Six minutes later, he picked up the ball 25-yards and fired at goal, which Grant deflected wide. There were half-hearted calls for a penalty, but it was a weaker shout than ours and that is saying something. Hull's final chance of the half fell to Reece Burke, a free-kick from Elder found the centre half, but his header was well over the bar.

The final five minutes of the half belonged to City. James Jones surging run was ended rather crudely by Coyle, who picked up the game's second booking for his trouble. Grant's delivery was nodded out of play from a corner, and the same player wandered over to take that too, but his ball bounced just in front of Rogers, who stabbed over. In injury time a mix up between Greaves and Burke saw Tom Hopper come clear with the ball, but he didn't have the pace to hold off Burke, who got back and poked the ball off the striker's toes for a corner, which time didn't allow us to take.

As it was a week ago, the second half became a much more open affair without anything clear cut for either side. The first serious action of the half saw Morgan Rogers pick up a yellow card for a foul on Coyle. Shortly after nice work down the attacking left saw Jones deliver a teasing cross which again, nobody was on the end of.

Hull had the better of the play in the middle period of the half, with Docherty one player I'd be happy to see in red and white. He had a drive deflected wide on 60 minutes after we nodded a free-kick away, driving wide two minutes later after picking up the ball 25-yards out.

City were more cohesive in the second period, with not as many passes going astray, but we still didn't get into our passing game. Credit to Hull, they pressed hard and we often found ourselves with possession across the back four, but were rarely able to trouble the hosts. On the occasions we did find a way through the back door, we just lacked the clinical edge that Sky commentators credited us with on Friday night.

Michael made two changes on 62 minutes, looking to freshen up our wide areas, with Cohen Bramall making his debut, and Regan Poole coming on for his second appearance in Imps colours. Whilst it did give us some energy, it didn't change an awful lot – Hull still kept us penned into certain areas and yet we remained stoic and organised too.

On 66 minutes a rare foray from Brennan Johnson saw him break into the area in the attacking left, pulling a little backheel to Jones, but the former Crewe man fired over. It was now City in the ascendency, and on 73 minutes a great chance [presented itself from a corner. Grant's delivery caused some uncharacteristic panic amongst the amber and black shirts, but Tom Hopper couldn't get it out from under his feet, eventually finding Jones, who lost possession for another corner. Sadly, that came to nothing.

Morgan Rogers created the next Imps effort, teeing up Jones who had certainly got into good areas, but once again his effort failed to test Matt Ingram in the Hull goal. The Tigers quickly broke up the other end, with Docherty playing Elder in behind. The full-back looked to pull the ball back to Lewis-Potter, who turned smartly but fired narrowly over. Once again, defence switched to attack and Johnson finally got a decent run at goal, putting the only Imps shot on target at Ingram's goal. The stopper parried the effort, and it dropped just behind the onrushing Hopper.

It was the last meaningful chance for City, and in the final ten minutes if anyone was likely to break the deadlock it was Hull. Their best chance came when Rogers gave away a free kick on the edge of the area, five yards from the touchline, but Honeyman's delivery was easily dealt with by the resolute Imps defence.

Ahead of the game, I would have taken 0-0, I predicted it here on the site too. It always felt like a game which would have a deadlock and nothing during the 90 minutes could convince me otherwise. I think I heard a stat that in 90 minutes there had been 21 efforts at goal with just one on target. Certainly, Alex Palmer didn't have a save to make, which isn't bad considering we were playing a team still packed with Championship talent. Mind you (and I can say this now because I won't curse the game), I felt before the game that Magennis was a striker I'd love to see start, because he offers so little up top in a side that cried out for a proper forward.

To a certain degree, we needed an alternative tonight too. Hopper worked hard, as he always does, but too often he had to come deep to get the ball and at least three decent crosses went begging when a traditional nine might have connected. Callum Morton comes back to the club this week and might be in contention by the end of the month – that's going to be huge because it gives us a viable nine if we need something different. I'm also surprised Michael didn't look to bring on Anderson or Scully late on as Rogers tired, or for Johnson who did drift in and out this evening. That said, securing a point was decent and maybe he felt consistency up top allowed us to be resolute in the final 15.

I thought Rogers looked good tonight, he definitely causes problems and a team not quite as efficient as Hull won't cope with his trickery and pace. I would also point to the pitch as being a reason we didn't quite look sharp, but it was the same for both sides. I suppose the difference is they play on it every week, and thankfully we don't have to.

A word to the centre-halves tonight too, once again they were absolutely excellent. I remember the question being asked of them when Montsma first got injured, how would they play together? I think the answer is there for us all to see – very well. Joe Walsh is an absolute warrior, a man who constantly puts his body on the line, whilst Jackson matches that energy and commitment alongside him. Montsma is a top centre half too, but he is going to have to be patient as the clean sheets keep piling up away from home.

Remember, Doncaster lost at Fleetwood tonight, and whilst Pompey and Peterborough both gained points on us, they did so against opposition they were perhaps expected to beat. Accrington lost, Sunderland lost and the teams coming up from the middle of the pack, Oxford, Plymouth, MK Dons and Shrewsbury all won. This weekend, as we host an Accrington side who haven't won at Sincil bank since 1947, Hull host MK Dons, Doncaster go to Sunderland and Pompey and Peterborough have tricky ties at Crewe and Blackpool respectively. There are no easy games, there are no free hits, and the key to success is not giving up too many points to the teams around you.

Well, we have come through another tough little run with a decent number of points, enough to hold off the challengers for yet another week, so I can go to bed happy.

Stalemate Sunday – Imps 2-2 Accrington Stanley
February 15, 2021

On the face of it, a 2-2 home draw against Accrington might look to be a missed opportunity.

With Hull and Doncaster both losing at the weekend, the real winners are Peterborough and Portsmouth, two sides I think will be our closest rivals for a top-two spot over the coming weeks. However, on the evidence of last night, Accrington are not to be ruled out as genuine contenders for at least a top-six spot. when you consider that, and that Pompey, Hull and Doncaster have to play them twice in the coming weeks, I think we did alright despite the late elation and disappointment. However, on reflection, a draw really was the fairest result.

Thanks to Saturday's postponement, we saw what must be one of the only ever 6 pm Sunday evening kick-offs the Imps have ever been involved in. The desire to get the match on was confirmed by Liam Scully on Match Day Live, as he admitted we only have three free Tuesday evenings between now and the end of the season, with a possible international cancellation against Oxford and a possible EFL Trophy Final too. Not getting ahead of ourselves, obviously, but that necessitated a swift resolution to yesterday's events.

Michael made four changes to the side which drew 0-0 at Hull. New signings Regan Poole and Cohen Bramall came in at full-back, with Tayo Edun and TJ Eyoma dropping to the bench. In the middle of the defence, Lewis Montsma got the nod ahead of Adam Jackson, whilst the injured Liam Bridcutt missed out, James Jones stepping into his role. On the bench, we saw Max Sanders for the first time, a player likely to appear in midweek against Sunderland.

The general disruption caused by the fixture being arranged certainly seemed to affect City, who were way off the pace in the first half. Accrington started at a great tempo, pressing high and forcing errors, which in turn seemed to create unforced errors too. The Imps hadn't had a meaningful touch when the visitors spread the play from right to left, then came back into the box from wide, only for Dion Charles to shoot straight at Palmer.

On six minutes, Charles was again the tormentor, but this time he got his just rewards. A ball back to Palmer put him under a little pressure and he played his clearance straight to Charles, 16-yards out. The striker made no mistake in putting the visitors 1-0 ahead.

In a half of few clear cut chances, gifting an organised side a goal was not what Michael would have wanted, but the best way to respond to such a mistake is by hitting back. Sadly, John Coleman's side were far too efficient in their pressing, not giving us time to get the ball out from under out feet. Time and again we ended up going long, misplacing crosses and even simple passes. In short, it was an awful start to the game.

On the odd occasion we did get forward, it was managed well by the opposition or we just fell short. Morgan Rogers looked to get clear on 14 minutes, but we crudely checked by ben Barclay to draw the first yellow of the encounter. Shortly after, Jorge Grant teased a wonderful ball into the area, where it evaded two Imps at the far post.

On 21 minutes, a Cohen Bramall mistake almost cost the Imps a second. It's fair to say he had a tough first start for City, and he let a ball forward drop over his head. Michael Nottingham nipped in behind, but his cross was wasted. By my notes, and this may be harsh, but the Imps first decent bit of play came on 27 minutes, with a series of passes setting Brennan Johnson free, with the attacker unable to prevent the ball from running out of play as he chased it into the area. The fact that is something I have found space for in the report points at how poor the side were in the first half. It was followed by another good Grant delivery, this time a free-kick from the right, which Joe Walsh got under and lifted high over the goal.

That was the only Imps chance of the first half, and our possession was sporadic in the face of a disciplined Accrington side. They chased when they needed too, throttled our supply lines and saw out the half. At that point, I couldn't see a way that we'd get anything from the game.

Michael said after the game that he made his feelings clear at half time, and it showed as City finally came out with some purpose, and were level before ten minutes had passed. Grant impressed with a 40-yard ball to set Johnson free on 51 minutes, but the winger took one touch before seeing his hopeful shot blocked. However, seeing him getting into the channel was refreshing and he was there again two minutes later.

This time McGrandles was the architect, coming across from the left and playing a one-two with Grant on the edge of the area before spraying the ball into the path of Johnson. His delivery was absolutely delicious, and Morgan Rogers was more than happy to take what was served to him, deftly flicking a header past the despairing Baxter in the Accrington goal.

It had taken eight minutes of the second half to do what we hadn't managed at all in the first, get a shot on target, and yet it didn't knock the resilient visitors. Michael shook things up on 55 minutes, with Bramall an obvious candidate to come off, as well as James Jones who had been quiet by his standards. Scully came on and went attacking right, Johnson seemed to drift into the centre, with Grant looking to have swapped places with McGrandles in the four and eight roles. As for Bramall, I wonder if he might have come off at half time were he an established first-team regular, but Michael gave him ten minutes to avoid the stigma of being hauled off early. He certainly had a stinker of a debut, not rampaging forward enough and too often letting the ball run across him, or bounce over him. He will learn from that though, and doubtless still has a big role to play moving forward.

On 57 minutes a ball from the attacking right found Christian Burgess in acres of space, and he did the right thing heading the ball into the hard ground, but it bounced passed Palmer and up, over the top of the goal. It was a rare lapse in concentration from our defenders, certainly the central pairing, who had up until that point dealt with most balls.

Edun replaced Bramall and instantly looked to make progress down the left. He overlapped Grant on 61 minutes, with the captain having picked up a loose ball out of defence. He slipped it to Edun who delivered a super ball into the area, behind all three of the Imps attackers. All it needed was a McGrandles type run, ambling in a little behind play, for a simple stroke home.

The game began to open up a bit and a misplaced Montsma pass on 65 minutes almost saw the visitors create a chance, but their half effort was deflected and easily dropped into the arms of Palmer. From there City launched a ball forward which appeared to be running through to Baxter, but Tom Hopper chased it down and made the keeper slice it out for a throw. It's fair to say Hopper was excellent, winning more defensive headers than our defenders and still chasing lost causes up top too. The throw-in saw us work a ball across to rogers, who looped an ambitious effort over the goal, stand and maybe even the cathedral.

I had shouted Colby Bishop as a threat pre-match, but Paul Smyth was certainly enjoying himself. He's on loan from QPR and he had two efforts in quick succession on 73 minutes. The first saw a poor clearance from us get picked off by him, but he hurried a shot wide. From the cleared ball Accrington broke, with Smyth carrying the ball down the attacking right, across the edge of the area and into space, but his shot was saved by Palmer.

At that stage it looked as though the visitors might get a winner, and from our corner they sprung a decent counter on 76 minutes. It was almost typical Lincoln, a half-decent delivery was cleared and Smyth broke at pace. He played a ball to sub David Morgan, who appeared a couple of times for City in 2012/13, but his shot was blocked by Regan Poole, who certainly put in the hard yards at full-back. The threat of Smyth even drew a yellow card for McGrandles, who felled him as he got away with ten minutes to go.

It could be argued we had looked better in the second half, but it would be a stretch to say we deserved to win the game, but on 84 minutes it looked as though we might. What we do have is intent, and in attacking areas when we find our flow, it is nice to watch. Jorge Grant seemingly left his studs in on Burgess on 83 minutes, giving away a free-kick and getting a yellow. The visitors gave the ball away rather needlessly, with us sweeping up field. Johnson chased a ball into the corner and earned a corner, but instead of another disappointing set-piece, we took it quickly, Scully finding Grant on the edge of the area. He teased a ball over the defence and in came Hopper, connecting with a header from a couple of yards out to give us the lead.

Briefly, Accrington were shaken at it could have been 3-1 not long after. Tayo Edun, lively as a bag of ferrets when he came on, teed up Rogers beautifully, with the Man City man lashing a volley at Baxter which he parried. Johnson had gambled, but he was just ahead of the rebound and couldn't get it under control when a goal looked possible.

It seemed there was still a sting in the tail of the game, and it came with a minute to spare. Ex-Imps have a habit of haunting the club and whilst we all shudder at Akinde, Palmer and Oliver, few would have batted an eyelid at the thought of playing against David Morgan. The midfielder, who joined us on loan from Forest and made six starts for the club, was making his Accrington debut after signing from Southport for an undisclosed fee on deadline day. He slipped a ball into Dion Charles, who finished with aplomb to level. His vicious effort managed to defy Palmer despite the keeper getting a glove on it, and whilst it was disappointing, it was no less than the visitors deserved from a game they spent at least 45 minutes well in control of.

I said ahead of the fixture that it was just as difficult as Sunderland, Portsmouth or Peterborough, but that because the name on the shirt was Accrington, few would see it that way. I suppose they suffer from that bloody milk advert, from being constant underdogs, but in a way, it works in their favour too. Nobody at this level drops points against Accrington and comes away happy, but plenty have done before us and plenty will do before the season is out.

As for us, there is no hiding the fact we were poor in the first half. I'd go almost as far as to say it was one of the worst halves of football I've seen this season, even including Sunderland and Portsmouth at home. We lacked cohesion and organisation, and that is down to one thing in my eyes – the absence of Liam Bridcutt. It's easy, and a little lazy, to start saying we shouldn't change a winning side, or that Michael shouldn't have dropped Edun and Eyoma, but that wasn't why we were 1-0 down. Yes, Bramall had a tough evening, but I thought Regan Poole looked very good and he featured on a couple of different accounts voting for Man of the Match. As for dropping Jackson for Montsma, the Dutch defender could do no wrong three months ago, so why would him coming in be a disruption?

No, for me the problem hinged on Bridcutt not playing, and McGrandles not being suited to the four role, which is where he seemed to start. I get it, we wanted to keep our attacking flow with a virtually unchanged front five, but sadly that pivot between the defenders and midfield is the most crucial aspect of our game. Take Bridcutt out and we are simply not as good as we are with him in. It's three or four weeks out for him now and my hope is young Max Sanders gets a game on Wednesday and proves to be the heir-apparent in the holding midfield role. Failing that, it has to be Grant, with McGrandles and Jones further forward.

I'm not going to moan about the lads though. We're playing two games a week, all at a high tempo, all against opposition hungry to knock us off our perch. It is mentally draining as well as physically demanding and if we want promotion, we are going to have to use Bramall, Sanders, Scully, Anderson and whoever else we can over the course of the next two months or so. It will be bumpy, no doubt, but let me suggest this before signing off: Accrington have Sunderland to play twice, Doncaster to play twice and Portsmouth to play twice too. Not one of those teams will turn Stanley over with ease because they're tactically aware, organised, disciplined and highly functional. We've got them out of the way, and sure, we have two points from six out of matches against them, but I dare bet they take three from a couple of those big matches. That's what it comes down to now, us relying on others to take points from each other, whilst we pick some up even if we don't play well. Our goals this evening, both well-worked from crosses, proves that when we do function, we are a huge danger.

Last night was a blip, but it isn't a disaster and we're still ahead of everyone else, and nobody can catch us if we match their results like for like. I'd take that moving into the final 18 matches of the season, whether we play on a Friday, Sunday or any other day of the week.

Penalty Agony: Sunderland 1-1 Imps (5-3)
February 18, 2021

I'm going to confess, last night felt like pure agony for me, as it did for probably half of the Imps fans out there.

The other half, those with a wider perspective or no feelings for the Trophy at all are the lucky ones. They're able to shake this off and focus on the great league campaign, but for me, there is a deep pain still in me this morning. It's odd really, I didn't feel excited about the game and had to do a video to gee myself up. It worked, sadly.

Look, I'm going to level with you, there is not going to be a match report in the usual context, because I don't want to relive the game. It really is that simple. I'll cover the basics, pick up on the positives and let's leave it at that, eh?

Firstly, if you are a Sunderland fan coming on to have a read, lets deal with you guys. You're good. That's a fact, every time I have seen Sunderland this season, they have shown why they should be top six and, if it isn't this season, why you'll be top two next season. I do think McGeady is the obvious star, but the patterns of play are decent, your defenders (although makeshift last night) are better than most I've seen and whilst this season other teams have impressed me more, I can see why the corner has been turned under Lee Johnson.

Best of luck in the final, I would much rather you win it that Tranmere Rovers. That's because we have a history with them and hopefully a future coming up against you.

In terms of team selection, I thought Michael put out a strong team, but it was a little forced. Harry Anderson would doubtless have played had he been fit and I do think it would have been of benefit to us if he had. The lads at the back had a decent game, but in terms of form, Walsh and Jackson are our current strongest centre back pairing. I think Montsma will be back on his pedestal within a couple of weeks, but at the moment he does look slightly rusty at times.

It was also nice to see Max Sanders get a runout. Overall, I was hugely impressed with him. I thought he had a slow five or ten minutes but then showed his capability in the holding role. I have just got used to calling the holding midfield a four though, so for him to be wearing the six is going to spin my mind. Which is it, four or six in CDM? Seriously though, he's got a big future with us, he's composed on the ball and showed some technique that I see in Bridcutt, the way he drops a shoulder, the body shape when he opens up for a pass. I'm very excited to see what the future holds for him and I have a strong feeling we might see him this weekend against Wigan.

The game itself wasn't great for 45 minutes. I usually make notes through the game and I managed to make eight for the first half – two of which were around bookings. Being really harsh, Tayo Edun was unlucky to be booked and then fouled twice by Leadbitter and Gooch who got away with the challenges. That's being picky though, generally, Ben Toner had a good game, allowing things to flow. He did get a big decision wrong, which I'll come to.

Chances were few and far between and I don't think either had a shot on target in the first half. I felt it was a training game at times, such a slow-paced affair with no real redeeming features whatsoever. That's positive for us, by the way, because we were away at a very big club and looked arguably the better side on the ball, if not in the 18-yard boxes. Our decision making was very poor in the box though – Montsma didn't get a good connection with a free header, which three months ago would have brought at least a save. Johnson's break on 22 minutes maybe should have fed in Hopper, but instead, he found Scully who lashed a chance very high and wide, and Eyoma got into a good position and didn't hit the target either. All three chances should have been better, but for a short spell, we did look by far the better side, although the hosts ended the half strongly.

In the second half, it was much the same for a short period. 15 minutes elapsed and we finally got a shot on target through Tom Hopper, before Cohen Bramall came on. I thought he had some really nice touches, one in which he teed up Johnson, who saw the ball take a little bobble resulting in a terrible effort from 12-yards.

When we did score, Bramall was the creator again. His ball to McGrandles was superb, a lovely little dink back into the area and arguably the best delivery we saw form us all evening. McGrandles drew a save from Burge and Scully was on hand to stroke the ball home. Genuinely, I felt we were going to Wembley at that point. We'd defended well, kept McGeady quiet and marshalled Wyke excellently (although dubiously at times, they certainly had penalty shouts and had Wyke not tried to stay on his feet, they might have got them).

Of course, in the lead up to the goal the officials got one decision wrong, the throw-in. I'd be hacked off if it were us, it was a clear throw their way, although Scully might have got a free-kick out of the incident. Sad to see Sky Sports completely focused on Sunderland though – Sunderland related guests in the studio and co-commentary and more shots of their new owner than Michael Appleton on the touchline. At least iFollow home commentary is knowingly biased.

162

That should have been the signal for a strong rear-guard action leading to a 1-0 win, but instead, we switched off and let Sunderland dominate. Gooch had a strong drive held, Wyke nodded a header into the floor which Palmer scooped over for a corner and still we let them have space on the right. Another ball came in, again McGeady and again Wyke, but Palmer was equal to it. Finally, McGeady crossed for Wyke to score, simple as. Perhaps he got the wrong side of Montsma, but the fault for the goal begins when we allow McGeady to get a cross over.

After that, there was only one winner and my utter joy at our goal began to sink into the sofa with me. I could feel the disappointment growing inside me, much different to the last time we missed out on Wembley in a cup, against York City. Back then, we had a villain, a disputed penalty to get mad about, but there was no blame here. Sunderland were better in those last 30 minutes, simple as. We had a minimal bench and brought on Remy Howarth and James Jones, both playing as high as they ever have, whilst Sunderland had Chris Maguire, former Championship striker Aiden O'Brien and Conor McLaughlin who has also played in the second tier. I'm not saying Jones or Howarth are bad players, of course, they're not, but we went a bit makeshift in those last 15 minutes. Hopper and Edun, sure to be involved on Saturday, had been our best players and both came off.

After the goal McGeady had a long-range drive saved, then another smart effort from 20-yards which Palmer stopped too. It all looked ominous until we got our big chance. With Sunderland pouring forward, we hit them on the break and Eyoma strode into the area. He was in a better position than his first-half effort but instead looked to find Johnson. By then, Sunderland got back and the Forest loanee saw his shot deflected and over. Game over, 1-1 penalties.

You know what happened next. With each shot, I got more anxious, worried every time we took a spot-kick that it would be saved, disappointed when Palmer got near their first three. Ultimately, it came down to one, Remy Howarth. I'm not commenting on an individual who misses, it is the luck of the draw. Howarth clearly stepped up when I wondered if maybe Jones would, but as he walked to the ball, I felt he might miss. His run-up was short, and his kick crashed against the bar. Sadly, with McGeady and Leadbitter to follow, that really was game over.

I turned off after that and found myself sitting in silence as my excitement fully soaked into my clothes (literally in some areas, liquid excitement….). In a competition I cared little about at kick-off, we'd been beaten in the cruellest manner and had hopes of Wembley raised and dashed within a half-hour period. I couldn't go a tell Fe, my partner, because it would mean her giving me that 'I'm sorry' look, then trying to act normal but in a way that I might find patronising. It wouldn't be, of course, but in the heightened state of emotion generated by a semi-final penalty shoot-out loss, I wasn't really thinking straight.

I'm writing this in the morning, with the benefit of sleep on my side, but the memories are still raw. Yes, I know we're top of the league, I know Doncaster lost again last night and that there are loads of positives to take moving forward, but right now it isn't easy to see those. I'm not disappointed with the lads, they put in a decent shift and if we draw 1-1 there later in the season, it'll be a good result. That doesn't change where we are now though.

One last thing, on Remy. Anyone could have missed that penalty, Scully, Johnson, Grant, anyone. Remy had the balls to take one, and he missed, not the others. Sadly, with the squad we have and the fact he has mainly appeared in the cup, I do fear it could be one of the last kicks he has of a ball in a Lincoln shirt. I hope not, it would be a sad way to remember a likeable and motivated member of the team. However, just spare a thought for him this morning, rather than condemning him. If we hadn't let that cross go in for Wyke, if we'd marshalled him a little bit better, then Remy wouldn't be the so-called villain.

Last night's loss was a team effort, just like the wins are. For now, I'll let this disappointment settle and dissipate and maybe, by the time tomorrow comes, I can focus once again on the positives. Still, it does pay to feel low once in a while, because it makes the highs all the more enjoyable.

Still on top: Wigan Athletic 1-2 Imps
February 20, 2021

Michael Appleton should be beaming tonight after the high-flying Imps picked up three points on the road in a hard-fought encounter.

In our first-ever visit to the DW Stadium, we were left to fight back from 1-0 down with a depleted side, having won just one of six in all competitions. With injuries piling up, there was no Liam Bridcutt, Harry Anderson, Joe Walsh or Theo Archibald, whilst Callum Morton is also not quite match fit.

With those injuries in mind, the Imps made two changes to the side that lost on penalties to Sunderland in midweek. Max Sanders and TJ Eyoma dropped to the bench, with Regan Poole coming in at right back and Morgan Rogers also back in the side. Rogers played as part of a front three with Anthony Scully and Tom Hopper, whilst Brennan Johnson dropped into attacking midfield alongside McGrandles, leaving Grant to fill in for Liam Bridcutt.

As we have seen in recent weeks, the Imps started slowly with a patient, passing out from the back approach. The home side, having been humiliated in midweek, were high tempo, high press and ultimately, looking much livelier than City.

The first half did have chances, but it was also punctuated by missed fouls and silly free kicks. As early as the first minute, Viv Solomon-Otabor seemingly took out McGrandles, with nothing given, but thirty seconds later McGrandles got revenge and Trevor Kettle blew for a free kick. Kettle kept his cards in his pocket, but certainly missed fouls committed by both sides throughout the first period.

The Latics got their first chance of the afternoon on ten minutes, a corner from the attacking right was nodded clear to Funso Ojo. He let a shot go, high and over the goal of Alex Palmer.

City's first chance came just after the 15-minute mark, with Regan Poole rampaging forward. The former MK Dons man found himself in the attacking right channel looking for options, and finding few. Instead, he threaded a shot through the defender's legs and wide of Jamie Jones' right-hand post.

City were misplacing passes with regularity, and one from Jorge Grant led to a chance on 21 minutes for the home side. After the Imps lost possession, Solomon-Otabor moved into the area and looked to curl one to Palmer's left, but got the shot wrong and hit it into the keeper's chest.

Whilst the next chance fell to Lincoln, the game was by no means end-to-end. Regan Poole had a penalty shout turned down after coming together with Tilt, rightly turned down, and the resulting corner almost brought a goal. The delivery swirled in the wind and a touch by Hopper sent it goalward, with Jones having to punch it off the line.

The home side were in control of the game though and had a great chance to go ahead on 28 minutes. A ball from the right was flicked on to Robinson, who had a clear sight of goal eight yards out. On his left foot he made decent contact, but it fell into the grateful arms of Palmer.

Within four minutes, Wigan were finally, and justifiably ahead. Again, Imps possession was wasted, Poole's throw in finding Grant, who was dispossessed. Callum Lang burst from the halfway line, through the middle to around 20-yards out, before launching what could only be described as a thunderbolt into the roof of the net. Palmer could face that shot 100 times and still get nowhere near it.

The home side's joy was luckily short-lived. They say you're most vulnerable after scoring and so it came to pass. Finally, City put a decent run of play together, with McGrandles delivering a high ball in from the left. It again caught the wind, with Jones and Robinson getting into a mess on the goal line. The ball dropped to Scully, three yards out, and he made no mistake.

It was the last of the former West Ham man's involvement though, he went down shortly after, having taken a knock earlier in the game. For three or four minutes he was a passenger, until finally we got Bramall on. City shuffled the pack, Edun moving into midfield and Johnson pushing out on the right. It had been a tough afternoon for Johnson through the centre, he had barely had a kick and when he did, he hadn't been effective.

The injury to Scully is likely to be a big worry for Michael, who is seeing many key players having to spend time on the sidelines. He's bagged six goals in his last 12 matches, and has 12 from 33 all season long – that's already better than Adrian Patulea, a firm fan favourite back in 2008/09, who bagged 11 in 33. It speaks volumes that a player many mention as one of the most exciting at the Bank over the last 15 years has been surpassed by a young lad from West Ham who has been in and out of the side all season. He's had a big influence on games though, and we certainly need his poacher-like instincts in the final 18 matches of the season.

Back in the current season, the final chance of the half fell to Chris Merrie, who picked up a ball in a similar position to Lang's goal, but he blasted over from range. City did end the half brightly, getting a succession of corners which caused panic, but didn't result in a chance.

There is little doubt that Leam Richardson was the happier of the two bosses at half time, not just because of the result, but because his team had been the better of the two.

The second half started better for City, with the wind in our favour. The first chance of the half came on 50 minutes, Brennan Johnson finding space on the right-hand side. He looked to shape for a cross, instead shooting at Jones. The keeper couldn't hold the ball, Hopper stabbed it back to Johnson, but instead of pulling the ball to McGrandles he took another effort which was saved. Wigan broke from that chance, but their surge forward came to nothing.

The second half certainly opened up, as it did in our previous couple of fixtures too, but the wind played a big part. You might be forgiven for thinking the wind played no part in the first half, because the home commentary never mentioned it, but suddenly it came into play in the second as City hunted a winner.

On 54 minutes Bramall used his pace to get into space on the left, but his cross was only touched by McGrandles with Jones waiting to collect with ease. City kept the pressure on though, and should have gone 2-1 up on 56 minutes. Grant delivered a corner into a good area and Montsma had a free header ten yards out, but could only steer the ball into the side netting. It was close though, and Lincoln supporters around the world were doubtless up and out of their seats.

It certainly wasn't all City though, with the home side not looking like a team in danger of relegation. They applied plenty of pressure around the hour mark, getting three corners in succession. The wind certainly made any delivery unpredictable, but finally the third was graciously gathered by Palmer.

One player who impressed me was their right-winger, Viv Solomon-Otabor. I've watched him a bit in the past, when I used to write about Championship football, and he's always impressed me. He asked a lot of questions of Bramall in defensive areas and often came out on top. On 68 minutes, he got the better of our new arrival and fired a wonderful cross in front of the six-yard area, which Lang was inches from stabbing home. The commentary team likened it to Gazza, Euro 96, which I'd also written in my notes. Fine margins.

City did have more attacking intent than in the first half and Grant got a chance to get an effort on goal. Johnson, who is showing signs of fatigue in some of his runs, picked up the ball deep and surged forward, only to be felled as he got to the edge of the area. Grant bagged a great free kick against them at Sincil Bank, but he didn't put this one on target and the scores remained level.

As I suggested on Match Day Live, we got to see 20 minutes of Max Sanders, he replaced Edun who had been solid enough in the middle of the park. The obvious intent was to add some fresh legs in front of the back four, as much of the opposition plan was big balls into the area and looking to pick up seconds. With renewed energy in that area, Michael (who was at the game, by the way) clearly wanted to ensure we had control.

Just two minutes later, City went ahead. Rogers (and Johnson) are easy targets when things don't go well, but both have the ability to make magic happen, as does Jorge Grant. It was the on-loan Manchester City man who started the move, picking up the ball from Alex Palmer and busting forward, before finding Grant. The captain hit a lovely ball through for Tom Hopper, who made up yards into the area before checking onto his right foot and slotting the ball home. It was a wonderful strike, not quite Callum Lang sensational but one that needed teamwork, technique and plenty of energy. I shouted so loud, Fe knew we'd scored despite working at the bottom of the garden.

After taking the lead against Sunderland, a tired City invited pressure and we seemed to do that again, almost gambling on the fact they wouldn't break us down. Sanders showed plenty of tenacity but gave away a free kick in a good area on 81 minutes, which Aasgaard smashed over the bar.

Chances began to come thick and fast for the hosts. A cross from Darikwa from the right-hand side found Proctor in acres of space, he pulled the ball down but made a hash of his volley and sent it over. It was Darikwa again on 86 minutes, providing another good ball from the right into the corner of the six-yard area. Lang got the better of Montsma in the wrestling match, but his diving header went over.

The home commentators were frothing at the mouth for a penalty on 87 minutes, claiming handball and a foul. Watching back, they deserved neither and got neither, but as Palmer dragged his heels taking the goal kick, Trevor Kettle flashed a yellow card. Kettle had a better second half, the game flowed easier but he certainly let a few heavy challenges go, for both sides. He seems to be one who likes a flurry of yellows and then nothing for a few minutes, as he booked Adam Jackson for something I certainly missed, possibly dissent.

I was utterly delighted to see Remy Howarth coming on with three minutes to go. My fear was his lasting legacy would be the penalty miss in midweek, but the shallow nature of our squad means there is a place for him from the bench. I do like Remy, he's a great personality, so to be so wrong about his future pleases me.

From somewhere, Kettle found five minutes of injury time, which was enough for Will Keane to have a couple of chances. Whilst Wigan had been direct all afternoon, they were unashamedly so in the final few minutes, smashing big balls long whenever they could. One, with just a minute or so left on the clock, was flicked on by Proctor to Keane. He twisted onto it, much like Nathan Arnold at Gateshead, but his connection was poor and it lopped up and onto the top of the goal.

With seconds left, another long ball caused panic at the back. We didn't seem to be able to clear our lines and eventually the ball dropped for Keane, five yards out on the angle. He was marshalled by a couple of defenders and his hurried shot hit the side netting. That saw the clock roll towards six minutes of stoppage time, and the big ball forward from Palmer was the last action of an engrossing if not classic encounter.

My Man of the Match was probably Tom Hopper, but I don't think I'm being harsh when I say there wasn't anyone who stood out too much. Regan Poole had a decent enough game at full-back, and Bramall certainly showed his attacking intent. I see a lot of early Harry Toffolo in Bramall, great forward play but occasionally needing some coaching at the back. In terms of defence, it would be remiss not to commend Montsma and Jackson too, a difficult afternoon of high winds and high balls might not be conducive to free-flowing football, but it did give them a fresh challenge I felt they rose to well.

The big wins these days are not just getting three points, but looking elsewhere to see who has not. Three weeks ago, we'd have prayed for Doncaster to lose, but this afternoon their late goal against Hull means two teams behind us drop points. Portsmouth, hit by the absence of Kenny Jackett, also lose ground, and Accrington's advantage in terms of games in hand looks to have slowly evaporated as they were held by a spirited Shrewsbury Town. Peterborough's rise looks ominous, they have won four on the bounce, but Crewe, Ipswich and Wimbledon at home are all winnable for any promotion-chasing side, as is Gillingham away (as we know). In the same period, we face Swindon, Fleetwood and Crewe at home, and Plymouth away, they have just one home game, Wigan, with trips to Plymouth, Oxford and Burton, before Hull visit on March 9th.

The truth is we don't need to worry about anyone else if we keep winning. Today, we won, albeit a game we perhaps deserved to draw. That is what good teams do though, is it not? We won when we played well, at Northampton and at home to Burton, when the pundits purred. The purist might not have enjoyed this afternoon as much, but once again we came out on the right side of the result.

As for Wigan, on that showing, they won't go down. There are worse teams than them, that's for sure, and if they can cut out the silly mistakes they'll be fine. Tilt marshalled Hopper superbly in the first half, and with that, he suffocated our attack. I've mentioned Solomon-Otabor before and Darikwa looked a handful coming down the flank too.

As things stand now, we only play one top-six team in our next 14 matches, that being Sunderland on March 20th. Of the current top six, we only have Hull to come to the Bank, and we have trips to Posh in the penultimate game and that tie back on Wearside. My gut tells me by the time we do travel to Posh, the top two spots will be decided, so we really do have our fate in our hands.

Play badly, play well, injuries or not, this Imps team always show character, spirit and application. Wherever we finish, you can't ask more than that as a fan.

Moving Swiftly On: Imps 2-2 Swindon
February 23, 2021

City dropped two points at home this evening in one of those games which looked like it might go one way on paper, but ended up completely different to what people expected.

It was a game where once again, we beat ourselves at times, but that lesser teams might have ended up losing. We didn't lose, which is a positive to take from an evening where I imagine, social media will be awash with negatives.

Despite the concerns around Adam Jackson, Anthony Scully and Jorge Grant, all three were included in a starting XI which saw two changes. Tayo Edun dropped to the bench with Cohen Bramall selected, whilst Regan Poole and TJ Eyoma also swapped. That meant Brennan Johnson continued in midfield alongside Conor McGrandles, with James Jones on the bench. There was also some positive injury news, as Theo Archibald was once again amongst the subs.

If the Imps were hoping for a good start, they got anything but. It took just two minutes for the visitors to take the lead, a ball from the attacking left was dummied as it came across, and Jordon Garrick finished with ease from 12 yards. It was the worst possible start for the Imps, who looked to bounce back immediately as with the 2-1 win over Wigan at the weekend.

In a frenetic opening exchange, City managed two shots on goal. Conor McGrandles registered the first with five minutes gone, driving forward and firing straight at the keeper from 20-yards out. Two minutes later it was Brennan Johnson breaking through the middle, but his pass to Rogers saw the Manchester City man forced wide, and his shot was weak.

It should have been 2-0 to the visitors before the ten-minute mark had passed, a free kick from deep in the attacking half nodded just wide at the back post. It was a warning for the Imps to tighten up at the back, but it was a warning not heeded, although the game did settle down a little. There was a booking for McGrandles and another for Matty Palmer, neither of which could be argued against. McGrandles miscontrolled a ball and ended up taking out former Imp Jack Payne, whilst Palmer cynical tripped Hopper as our striker surged forward.

On 20 minutes another unforced error almost cost us a goal. Jorge Grant looked to flick the ball back towards his defence but instead found Brett Pitman in space. Luckily, the once-deadly striker couldn't capitalise after making a poor decision with his pick of options.

Scott Twine, something of a long-range specialist, flashed on effort straight at Palmer from 25-yards out on 20 minutes, as Swindon threatened to grab a second. It was Twine again going close on 23 minutes, a mistake by Jackson seeing him given an opportunity, but he shot over the bar.

Against the run of play, City levelled on 25 minutes. Good play by Bramall down the left saw the ball pulled back to Rogers, and he lofted a delicious delivery over the top for Johnson. The on-loan forward burst clear and was cynically tripped for a clear penalty. Grant made no mistake from 12-yards to make it 1-1.

For a spell after the goal, City looked likely to press on and win the game. A corner a minute later found Montsma at the back stick, and he nodded the ball back to Jackson, whose shot was blocked and sent over for another corner. That delivery came to nothing.

Bizarrely, the Imps best chance came from a drop ball on 35 minutes. After striking Declan Bourne, the ball was dropped for Grant who quickly lifted it over the defence for Scully. He went through on keeper Wollacott but scooped his effort over the bar.

That short spell of Imps positivity quickly evaporated as mistakes once again cost the Imps. On 36 minutes, City were carved open from the attacking right, and Pitman found himself free in the area, only to lift his shot onto the bar when it seemed easier to score.

City almost took the lead on 40 minutes through Morgan Rogers, he curled an effort at goal from 20-yards out which the keeper palmed away, but Scully couldn't do anything positive with the rebound, despite reacting quickest.

Just before half time, Swindon were back in the lead in frustrating circumstances. Bramall beat Garrick for pace heading back to goal and laid the ball off the Palmer, but the stopper made a hash of his control and simply flicked the ball up to the Swindon attackers, leaving Brett Pitman with an easy finish. It was a demoralising incident for everyone concerned, players, staff and fans, to see Swindon back in the lead through our own doing, but it was 100% in line with the core themes of the first half.

Both sides could have scored within seconds of the restart. City started with a fine attack, Morgan Rogers delivering a killer ball across the area with nobody arriving. As Swindon cleared their lines, Pitman saw Palmer off his line and lifted a looping ball at goal which saw the stopper scrambling to palm it away for a corner.

Despite a positive start, we still couldn't find a rhythm though, with misplaced passes and bad decisions littering the passages of play. An avoidable corner earned by Jack Payne caused panic at one stage, with Montsma seemingly heading the ball off the line.

The chances stopped flowing for a while after that, the most significant moment coming when Bramall came off for Edun. Tayo's introduction gave City a fresh impetus, and he was involved in a half-chance almost as soon as he stepped on the field. Edun has been the most improved player over the course of the season and doubtless, many will be pointing at him for Man of the Match this evening.

City certainly seemed to get a fresh spring in their step, and Scully had another shot on target on 58 minutes, although it had all the venom of a basket of newborn kittens as it trickled through to Wollacott. The keeper might have been lulled into a false sense of security because a minute later he was picking the ball out of the back of the net. The goal came from nothing, Rogers collecting the ball 30-odd yards from goal and bursting forward, before driving a low shot from range. The keeper should have done better, but he saw it late and couldn't stop it going inside his right-hand post. To be fair to Rogers, he did look dangerous in spells and he's certainly ensuring he is amongst the goals at the moment.

That should have been the catalyst for us to go on and win the game, but a lethargic and tired City continued to beat themselves. Just past the hour mark a back pass by Jackson slipped under Palmer's boot, and instead of busting a gut to keep the ball in, he remonstrated with his defender. The resulting corner saw Payne slice horribly over, but it was another chance of our own making. Maybe Palmer couldn't have got the ball, but it just pointed at frustration on everyone's part. We weren't playing well, and everyone on the field knew it as much as we did at home.

I'm as happy as the next man about our league position, but this was a tired performance with one or two barely looking committed. A couple of times players shirked 50/50 challenges, and when we did string five passes together, the sixth almost inevitably saw the ball given away. Grant had a surprising off-day, and if the player pivoting the midfield doesn't play well, the whole team suffers.

Still, City had a decent chance on 65 minutes, Tom Hopper working hard to play the ball out to Scully, whose delivery was neither a cross nor a shot. Scully has been excellent in recent weeks, but he had a tough time on the right this evening and was often caught making bad decisions or executing poorly.

If it wasn't slack passes from City, it was silly fouls, and twice we gave Swindon the chance to get an effort off from the edge of the area. Firstly, Jack Payne had his standing leg taken 20-yards from goal, and Scott Twine teed up an effort, which Palmer saved superbly.

A minute later, a delivery from the right was flicked on by Jonathon Grounds, only for Pitman to get a weak touch and send the ball wide. The veteran striker thought he should have had a corner, and he might have had a point. From the goal kick, City swept up field and produced a carbon-copy effort, Johnson delivering from the wide area and Hopper getting a deft touch to send the ball wide.

The game certainly picked up pace and within a minute, City gave away another silly free kick in a good area. This time Twine was relieved of his dead-ball duties, Pitman lined up the shot and went for power, not poise. Again, Palmer was equal to it as he looked to make up for his error just before half time.

City have been strong in the last 15 minutes of games, and as James Jones came on for McGrandles, you sensed we might get a late goal, but it wasn't to be. Swindon seemed to be happy with ten minutes to go to slow the game down, and it resulted in few chances. A break on 80 minutes saw Johnson go down in the box, with no penalty given. It was the right decision, and he got to his feet to quickly find Scully, who again played a poor ball into the area. Swindon were incensed they had not been given a free kick on the edge of the area up the other end moments before, again probably the right decision.

Regan Poole came on for Eyoma late on, and he almost had a say in the final result. His delivery has looked good since he has arrived, and he put a great ball over with one minute left on the clock, which Swindon touched wide. The quick corner caught the iFollow replay team out, and it almost caught the visitor out. Grant cut the ball back from the touchline and really, City should have scored, but Jones didn't get a clean strike and the ball went over.

Even with the impetus, we still seemed hellbent on self-destruction. Scully gave the ball away easily late on, which saw Swindon break menacingly and goalscorer Garrick get a dangerous shot away, which an Imps touched out for a corner. Thankfully, they wasted the corner and the game was done.

I have found it hard writing this report, because from start to finish we were poor and yet I don't want to be a bandwagoner saying things must improve, etc, etc. Yes, our goals both came from moments of quality from Morgan Rogers, but it would be hard to say he, or any of his teammates, played particularly well. We looked jaded and tired at times, completely broken at others. Our passing patterns went out of the window, aside from a short spell after Edun came on, and to pick a Man of the Match would be tough. If anyone gets it, I think it would be Hopper, one of the only players who did play a sloppy pass all game that I can recall.

I can't say that I am worried about the performance, but I do think there will be some harsh words from Michael in the dressing room because it was a dysfunctional City lacking purpose. As I alluded to earlier, I think one or two players were at 75% at best, not because of the passes, but pulling out of challenges, not chasing loose balls. Maybe it is fatigue, I certainly don't think it is a lack of desire, but it did show at times.

The lads now have three days to recover, if that is anything like what they need, but these Tuesday/Saturday games are going to keep wearing the squad down. I felt without Bridcutt and Walsh we looked horribly uncertain at the back, and without options on the bench we didn't have a change we could make to impact the game.

I don't want to end on a low though, after all, we are still second in the table and we have to trust in the process and the direction the club is going in. We didn't lose, it is one more point towards our total and as we always say, never too high when we win, never too low when we don't. It is alright talking about home and away form, but in this uncertain season only one type of form matters – all form. In that respect, we are the second-best team in the division.

Nobody ever said this season would be easy, but take away all notion of performance, ask yourself if you'd have taken the position we're in right now at the start of the season. The answer would undoubtedly have been yes, so we just pack this one up and move on to Plymouth away, another tough afternoon which might just suit us more than these so-called straightforward home ties.

Michael Appleton Commits Future To City
February 25, 2021

Fresh off the back of speculation linking him with another job, Michael Appleton has committed his future to Lincoln City, as announced at the club's AGM.

Michael initially joined the club on a three-and-a-half-year deal which ran until summer 2023. He has now penned an extension to that deal which sees him contracted to the club until the summer of 2025.

Predictably, Imps Chairman Clive Nates is delighted to keep Michael at the club, telling the official site: "I am delighted that Michael has signed a new contract through to 2025. "The successful transformation of the squad and a promotion push in his first full season is remarkable, even more so considering the curtailment of last season and a significantly lower pro budget."

Remarkably, Michael has the third-best win ratio of any manager since the Second World War (45.61%), having competed at a higher level than the two managers with slightly better records. With performances on the field looking good, results coming in and a young squad ripe for development, it could be argued he is doing an utterly remarkable job.

Of course, signing a new deal protects us a little from bigger clubs wanting to take our manager, but it isn't the protection it affords that I like, it is the message it sends out. Michael will be very hot property if he keeps doing the job he is doing, but this tells the world he is happy here.

I'll confess, I was worried this weekend. The Bristol City rumour seemed plausible and despite the fake news surrounding the speculation, just felt ill-at-ease. I guess I still feel a little burned by the rumours that grew into a move back in September 2019, and I understand football moves very quickly. I should have taken a step back and a deep breath though because our situation is different now.

Michael is different too. He has been in the Championship and been burned by job-hopping too, and sadly he still gets tarred with that brush, not praised for his work with us and Oxford. If he were to step away from the club, it could be the last chance saloon in terms of the next level. If he takes us into the Championship and maybe even keeps us there, he will be rightly credited with being the strong coach and manager that he is. This deal works well for us as a club, and us as fans, but it works well for Brand Appleton too. It shows commitment, stability and focus, attributes that will eventually take him to the next stage of his career.

The delightful news is that the next stage shouldn't be before 2025, and that makes me a happy man. We've just recorded the podcast and on it we talk about how this news (and any other which might follow), caps off a tough week for the club – a tough week that brought a win against the 2013 FA Cup Winners, an average of two points per game, and saw us remain in the automatic promotion spots at the right end of League One.

The very fact that our expectations have risen to that being a supposedly 'tough' week tells you exactly why each and every Lincoln City fan should be raising a glass to the Big Apple this evening.

Imps Duo Pen Contract Extensions
February 25, 2021

Lincoln City duo Remy Howarth and Anthony Scully have both penned extensions to their existing deals with the club.

Remy Howarth, who joined the Imps from Cefn Druids in the summer, has penned a one-year extension to his current deal. He initially joined City on a short-term deal after impressing in pre-season and has gone on to appear 17 times for City, netting twice. He scored his first professional Football league goal as we defeated Burton 5-1, and suffered penalty agony in the EFL Trophy semi-final.

"I couldn't be happier and prouder to be a part of this football club, I have enjoyed my time so far working under the Gaffer," he told the club's official site. I'm so grateful for the support of the fans and I look forward to feeling their support behind us in the stadium soon."

Michael added his comments too, praising the 23-yeard old. "Remy is a young player who has worked very hard this season. We are delighted to see him commit himself to the club beyond this season."

The second new contract of the day has been handed to former West Ham man Anthony Scully, who is enjoying a strong season. He penned a one-and-a-half-year deal after arriving in February 2019, and it is believed the club had an option to extend that until 2022. Instead, a fresh deal has been negotiated which keeps him at Sincil Bank until the summer of 2023.

"Being a Lincoln player has been the happiest I've felt in football and I look forward to the next few years together and what we can achieve," said Scully, who has 12 goals from 34 outings this season. "Also, I want to say a massive thank you to all of the fans for the support they have shown since I've joined, I can't wait to have them all back in the stadium and enjoy the journey together."

Scully has certainly been in wonderful form, winning the Stacey West Player of the Month for January, and it is little surprise Michael also spoke highly of the forward saying: "We are really pleased to keep Anthony at the club beyond this season. He has developed well over the last 12 months and will help continue to improve and grow the club in the next few years. He's a great lad to have around the place and I'm looking forward to watching him develop."

The fact both players have opted to sign the deals is good news for City. In Remy's case, it sees the continuation of a wonderful story and gives him a chance to firmly establish himself as a key squad player. With Scully, there is an element of him becoming a fan favourite, and to know he is now committed to the squad for the long term is excellent news, especially given how successful his first full season has been so far.

Punched in the Guts – Plymouth 4-3 Imps
February 27, 2021

I'm not sure words can begin to describe exactly how I am feeling this afternoon, after City battled back from two goals down to lead 3-2 at home Park, only to lose in the dying stages of the game.

They call football the beautiful game, but right now it feels like a partner who has cheated on me, who has promised me the world only to roll over and start texting someone else. It has left me feeling alone, a little nauseous and once again trying to focus on the wonderful season we have had so far, rather than the slightly worrying run we are now on.

City made two changes from the side which drew 2-2 with Swindon, Tayo Edun and Regan Poole starting in defence, with Cohen Bramall and TJ Eyoma dropping to the bench. That meant Brennan Johnson started again in midfield, with Anthony Scully celebrating his new deal with a start on the right of Tom Hopper up front.

There were a couple of shocks in the Plymouth line up too, 18-goal Luke Jephcott dropped to the bench in place of Ryan Hardie, whilst Panutche Camara also sat the game out, as did Ben Reeves who scored their second in the FA Cup back in November. Danny Mayor did start though, he's a player we have seen plenty of during his time with Bury as well as Plymouth earlier in the season.

City needed a good start after struggling early on in recent games, but not for the first time it didn't happen. Instead, a frenetic opening exchange saw Plymouth take a two-goal lead. The first came from a cross from the attacking right which bounced in the area and off Adam Jackson to Kelland Watts, who lashed the ball home.

City looked to respond to that quickly, Morgan Rogers getting to the touchline and pulling the ball back only for it to roll harmlessly away. The Imps were playing at a decent pace, but Plymouth looked right on it, slick with their passing and finding space all over the park.

On 13 minutes, it was 2-0 and it felt like it might be a very long afternoon indeed. Mayor had a chance a couple of minutes earlier where he didn't pull the trigger and should have, but he made no mistake from 20-yards out with his second effort, easily beating Alex Palmer with a strong shot.

It looked like it might be a long afternoon for City, who appeared to still be on the coach at times, but Plymouth took their foot off the gas a little and allowed the Imps to build up some steady possession. One such spell eventually saw Tayo Edun lay the ball into the path of Conor McGrandles, who twisted and turned before firing in from 18-yards to make it 2-1.

I felt Plymouth went into their shell a bit after that, more intent on not conceding than scoring, and it meant a good 25 minutes for City without anything to show for it. Tyrese Fornah picked up the game's first yellow for a cynical barge on Johnson as the on-loan midfielder strode forward, but Grant's free-kick was straight at keeper Michael Cooper.

Two minutes later, Fornah committed the same foul of Johnson again, this time on the attacking right, but referee Kevin Johnson chose not to issue a second yellow. In truth, it would have been harsh, and it was sensible from the ref to give the player a chance. Like it or not, a referee should be trying to keep it 11 against 11 where possible and although there were means to send Fornah off, if the shoe was on the other foot, we might have been unhappy.

The Imps were having their best spell of football for a few weeks now, with Jorge Grant beginning to pull the strings, and both Rogers and Morgan causing problems when they got on the ball. We weren't able to get in behind as Plymouth's 3-5-2 fluidly goes to a 5-3-2 when they need it too, but the chances were all ours still. Grant had a pop with a daisy-cutter on 34 minutes which trickled wide, whilst a Johnson's one-two with Scully saw him find space, only for his drive to deflect off Opoku and go over the bar. The resulting corner was delivered to the back post, where Lewis Montsma arrived under the ball to head well over.

Plymouth weren't rolling over and certainly looked dangerous on the break, but City's slow and patient build-up brought more chances than I thought we might see after the lacklustre opening. With just four minutes of the half left, Poole slipped a ball into McGrandles, who let fly with a snappy shot which Cooper palmed away for a corner. Poole and McGrandles both looked composed in possession and able to get plenty of space down the right, which saw Scully able to take up decent positions in the channel, even though he didn't see as much of the ball as he might like.

The halftime whistle ended an engrossing and entertaining half, if you cut off the first ten minutes, in which City had absolutely done enough to be level, apart from the one thing we needed to do to draw level – score a goal. It was now a question as to whether we could go and do what no City team had done in 39 years – score twice at Home Park.

The Imps started the second half in much the same vein as the first, very much on the front foot. A free-kick from the attacking right was cleared on 46 minutes before Scully got away, again down the right. and delivered a great cross which nobody could quite get on the end of. Brennan Johnson was next to try his luck, he tried to slide a ball inside, but it was blocked and fell back to him. He drove a decent shot at goal which Cooper tipped wide of the post.

On 54 minutes, the impressive Regan Poole whipped a delivery in for Scully which was tipped wide of the post by the busy Cooper. The linesman's flag was up anyway, but it was a further sign that City were in the ascendancy. Three mad second-half minutes proved that for a short spell, we were.

Johnson, who I thought had looked strong all game, played a one-two with Scully and burst into the area, only to be felled as he went through on goal. It was a stonewall penalty, and there's only one man for the job in that instance (unless you're playing Doncaster or Peterborough), Jorge Grant. The skipper stepped up and calmly stroked the ball home to level proceedings, although it looked for a moment as though Cooper had saved it.

The Imps ramped it up a gear and broke down a Plymouth attack on the hour mark, springing forward themselves and getting a good effort on goal courtesy of Johnson, whose 25-yard drive was saved. From the cleared corner, Grant picked up the ball on the right, waltzed into the area and was seemingly tripped by Mayor. It looked weaker than the first, but nonetheless, the referee pointed to the spot. Grant does what he does and the score was 3-2 City.

No team should come back from 2-0 down to lead, then lose the game, and for a few moments, it seemed as though we might go on and add another. A lofted pass forward saw Scully pick the ball out of the air magnificently. He slid it neatly across goal to Hopper, who got the faintest of touches. All it needed was an inch or two to the right, but it flashed past the post and wide. I've seen it described online as a 'tap in', which it wasn't, but it was a great chance to kill off the home side. Like in any bad horror movie, if you don't kill off the antagonist when you have the chance, they only come back and get you.

Plymouth made a couple of changes, one of which was Luke Jephcott, and although the youngster didn't get heavily involved, it changed the complexion once again. Ryan Hardie got free on 73 minutes and should have levelled, but Tayo Edun blocked superbly when a goal looked likely. From having such a solid defence, we suddenly look very vulnerable and every time Plymouth got around the 18-yard box, it seemed as though we panicked and expected to capitulate.

That happened on 78 minutes, we failed to clear our lines and Conor Grant lifted a ball over everyone and into the net. It looked like woeful defending and right now, I won't watch it back, but I thought Montsma might have blocked it and Grant could perhaps have nodded it off the line. It was a horrible moment watching the net ripple after we'd played so well elsewhere on the park, but 3-3 felt like it would be a decent result.

What wasn't a decent result was Grant going down on 83 minutes with what looked like a nasty injury. Nobody was close to him as he collapsed in the defensive area, and had to be helped from the field by Mickey Hines. Painfully, it took our holding midfielder out of the game, adding further chaos to the back four. With no Bridcutt or Walsh, and now Grant, getting through the final seven minutes plus stoppages would have been a huge achievement.

Before our hearts were broken, we should have snatched it ourselves. Scully caressed a ball through to Johnson in the right-hand channel, and he had two choices, shoot or square to Rogers. The square ball looked on, the shot was too and he opted for the latter. It was good, on target, but Cooper parried it and behind the onrushing Rogers. The chance was gone and quickly, Plymouth swept up the other end, Mayor playing a one-two into the area and seeing his shot blocked.

In a frenetic final few minutes, much like the first 15, Regan Poole had a half effort saved for a corner although he looked to be offside before Plymouth got their winner. Ryan Edwards saw the ball sit up perfectly for him on the edge of the area and (sadly) a sweeter strike you will not see as he beat Palmer. I can't tell you what happened after that as I turned my iFollow off and shouted obscenities at nobody in particular. In fact, it has taken me all my strength and fortitude not to swear in this report.

Overall, I thought we played really well in the attacking half, looking slick and creating plenty of chances, but at the back, we look in bits. We're certainly missing the organisation of Liam Bridcutt, the back four are not getting the same level of protection he offers at all. We're badly missing Joe Walsh too, sadly Montsma hasn't come back the same player he was before his injury lay off and his partnership with Jackson looks fragile.

If you take away the poor defensive display City were back to their best. Sadly, when you give a good side a two-goal start, you're always going to be up against it. To rally back, score three and still lose is not just a sucker punch, it is a full-on kick in the crotch, maybe even two or three. On 75 minutes, Peterborough were losing and we were winning, meaning us going back to the top of the league. 15 mad minutes later and I feel like I've been given a winning lottery ticket and then had someone burn it whilst I held it in my own hands.

I've even been for a walk to gain some clarity before I write this, and have sat back down with the same anger that I left with. Who am I angry at though? An Imps attack that scored three goals? Nope. An opponent who played nice football but would have been happy if they'd drawn the game? No. A referee who made all the right decisions? No. It was even suggested it should be Hopper for missing one chance, but he worked tirelessly all game and should be no more of a scapegoat than anyone else.

Sadly, I'm just angry at football, and our collective inability to defend. Which, when you consider we have (or had) the best away record in the league, is like saying you're mad at not winning something on the Sky EFL rewards app when you've won something every other week. Incidentally, I haven't ever won anything on Sky Rewards.

My only hope is that we've now got this habit of starting badly and buckling under pressure out of our system, because whilst the lead we have built up in the division means we are still second and still favourites to join Peterborough in the Championship, we have begun to use up that credit. If we keep crumbling like a digestive biscuit every time someone applies pressure, then the next few weeks could be very, very tough indeed.

March

Injuries Threaten Imps Promotion Push
March 1, 2021

I recall sitting back in January thinking 'only one thing can derail us now', as in my head I plotted an away trip to the City Ground next season.

With a great manager, exciting players and a clear pattern of playing, I could only see injuries threatening our charge to the Championship. As we sit right now, that awful issue is becoming a cold, hard reality for the club, and in the wake of our 4-3 defeat at Plymouth, we are now stood on a precipice, looking over at imminent collapse through little fault of our own.

Michael Appleton has said this morning a win tomorrow night would represent one of his best achievements as a manager, and yet the bookies and pundits will be expecting us to beat Fleetwood. If we don't, it won't be the end of our promotion push, but it will be the continuation of a bad run that has started, coincidentally, with one player's injury.

Heading into our 0-0 draw with Hull back in early February, we had won seven in ten. However, Liam Bridcutt limped off against the Tigers and we have since won one in six. The good form over Christmas has ensured we remain in the top two, but failure to take at least four points from the next two games would surely see us drop into the mire of the play-offs. I say 'mire', we would have settled for that ahead of the season starting, but right now it would be a bitter pill to swallow.

Swallow it we may not have to, because we do have a young squad of talented players, but with the latest injuries we have suffered, all experience has been ripped from the heart of our team. If we are to beat Fleetwood tomorrow night, we are going to need one or two players to really stand up and be counted. Bear in mind, Portsmouth play Doncaster and Oxford play Peterborough – a win could really give us a massive boost heading into a critical month.

Who are we going to have to do without? Here is a comprehensive list of who is currently out, and how long for.

Callum Morton
Striker Morton has been out of action since September 19th and will be much like a new signing when he does return. He is back in training with City, which is some good news, but he won't feature tomorrow against Fleetwood. There is a suggestion he could return for the visit of Crewe next weekend, which might offer us another option in attacking areas.

Joe Walsh
Walsh has been a huge miss in recent weeks, and his current lay-off is expected to be 'the longest one' of those we're currently experiencing. MA suggested that Liam Bridcutt would be another three weeks, so Joe Walsh will be longer than that; don't expect to see him until April. It's the third spell on the sidelines for the Welshman this season – he didn't appear until the 0-0 draw with Fleetwood in October, then missed most of November too. His last outing came as we drew 2-2 with Accrington.

Liam Bridcutt
For my money, this is the biggest loss. Bridcutt is a leader on the field and the pivot around which the rest of the team moves. He's struggled a bit with injuries this season, this is his third spell out, and his

presence in the holding midfield role is certainly missed. He is expected to be out for another three weeks, so could miss matches against Fleetwood, Crewe, Ipswich, Gillingham, Rochdale and possibly Sunderland.

Remy Howarth

Remy is a fresh injury worry, and another of our attacking options lost. He's not been injured much before this season but wasn't in the squad for the Swindon game despite appearing as a late sub against Wigan. The duration of his injury is not known and it could be that he appears in the squad against Crewe, but he too is likely to miss tomorrow's game.

Jorge Grant

This is a scary one. Grant has more goals and assists combined than anyone in our squad, and as soon as he hit the deck in the dying stages of Saturday's game, you knew it looked serious. He won't play tomorrow and is likely to have a scan this week, but it looks likely to be a long lay-off. This is a huge blow, he has covered for Bridcutt in the middle of the park, but now we have lost both holding midfielders for a key period. From what I can tell, it would be a huge surprise if we see Grant at all in March, and beyond that is unclear.

Harry Anderson

Harry would be a great option at present, but he too is still out. Michael suggested this morning it could be ten days, which means he will miss Fleetwood, Crewe and Ipswich, perhaps making it back for Rochdale a week on Saturday. Harry appeared upbeat on Match Day Live this weekend, explaining how this was the first injury of its type he has had, and therefore it was unclear how long he might be out. Of the injured senior players, expect him back first.

Adam Jackson

Last, and perhaps as damaging as any right now, is Adam Jackson. He is due to go for a scan this week after picking up an injury against Plymouth and that means we're down to one senior centre back – the out-of-form Lewis Montsma. Jackson is unlikely to appear tomorrow, which almost certainly means an Eyoma and Montsma centre-back pairing. It seems that a recall of Max Melbourne is not possible either, the obvious shout in terms of our thin squad, so losing another central defender is a huge blow.

Into the play-offs: Imps 1-2 Fleetwood Town
March 2, 2021

City slumped to another defeat this evening, going down 2-1 to a spirited Fleetwood side at Sincil Bank.

There was a surprise in the starting XI, with Adam Jackson thought to be unfit, be he ruled himself in to Michael Appleton's side. James Jones came in to replace the injured Jorge Grant, with the Imps reverting to a 4-2-3-1, offering protection to the central defensive pairing.

The game started at a decent pace, both sides having a bit of the ball without any real threat. Jackson did have to be alert with a header early doors to keep Vassell from getting a scoring chance, but the best chance of the opening exchanges fell to Lincoln. Anthony Scully bought a foul close to the touchline almost in line with the corner flag, which James Jones took. His delivery had power and that perhaps caught the onrushing Regan Poole by surprise, as he flashed a free header over from eight yards out.

The Imps enjoyed a decent spell of pressure and the next to have a pop was Brennan Johnson. He was still in central midfield as he has been in recent week, and after good work by Rogers, he raced forward 50 yards before fizzing a shot wide of the keeper's left-hand post. That ushered in a spell of Fleetwood pressure, with a deep cross from Wes Burns causing a bit of panic. Poole was able to head it up into the air, with Palmer grabbing it as it dropped with Vassell lurking.

Fleetwood certainly had plenty of promise in possession, and good work from Vassell and Batty saw Camps have a good effort from the edge of the area, which Palmer saved. City kept pressing though and on 22 minutes another good chance went begging. A ball into the channel from Edun found Johnson, who flicked it back to Hopper. The captain for the evening stroked it into the path of Scully, who could only curl over the goal from 18 yards out.

That marked the end of the clear-cut chances for City, and the visitors began to edge into the game as the Imps early promise faded. Burns, causing Edun plenty of problems on the left, looked to be offside as he got away on 26 minutes, but the flag stayed down and Palmer was forced into a save. The resulting corner landed on the head of former Imp Callum Connolly, but his header wasn't accurate.

Johnson was certainly putting in the hard yards, looking to pressure Fleetwood high up the pitch, and he almost bought a goal on 30 minutes. He chased down three players as the visitors played out from the back, and the eventual clearance cannoned off him and drew something of a save from the keeper.

The Imps might have done better with a chance on 37 minutes. A quick free-kick played McGrandles into trouble, but he shifted his way around three players to find James Jones. The recalled midfielder had lots of options, the worst of which was to shoot wildly and inaccurately at goal. Sadly, that was the option he took.

Fleetwood exposed the Imps' defensive frailties on 38 minutes when a ball straight down the middle found Vassell in space. He took it slightly wide of Palmer's goal, but still drew a save from the West Brom man. On 42 minutes, despite an even first half, City went behind. A high boot by Jones was punished, rightly, by a free kick, and City didn't deal with the delivery, leaving Gerard Garner to smartly volley home from the edge of the area. It was a dismal end to a decent first half for City, although we were far from our free-flowing best.

It might be fair to point out Edun, Scully and Rogers all looked off the pace, and as we know if one or two cogs don't work in the Imps machine, then it can be a forced, laboured performance. It wouldn't be fair to say the first half was terrible, but we did look more like top ten hopefuls than Championship contenders.

City needed a big performance in the second half, but with tired legs, we got the opposite. We did get the first chance of the half, a quick free-kick worked its way to Edun, but his powerful cross was controlled back to the keeper by Scully. sadly, the Imps just couldn't get out in the early period of second half, and leggy players started playing tired balls once again. On 51 minutes it was all too easy for the visitors as they got into the area and fired over, but it was a warning of what was to come a minute later. Callum Camps bagged the second, an easy strike from play which simply carved open the home defence.

After that, the game just seemed to collapse for City, Wes Burn getting a free-kick and curling it straight into the chest of Palmer, who held well. Breaks forward were rare and easily snuffed out, whilst the opposition seemed to be a yard quicker and sharper than we were. it made a frustrating watch, something that feels like a recurring theme over the last few weeks as we struggle to get to grips with two games every week, and the injury crisis.

On 62 minutes, City made a triple change, Poole, Edun and Scully coming off, with Cohen Bramall, TJ Eyoma and Callum Morton coming on. Morton, a surprise inclusion amongst the subs, made his first appearance since we beat MK Dons in September. Whilst the subs did have a part to play in a decent final thirty minutes, City didn't immediately react to the changes. we did look fresher though and it felt like we might get back into the game, but instead Vassell was the player creating a chance to make it 3-0, he found space in the right channel but nobody picked up his deep cross.

The Imps made another change with 67 minutes gone as Max Sanders replaced James Jones and if anything, that finally changed the game in the Imps favour. Sadly, the lax defending early in the second half meant we had a mountain to climb. On 71 minutes, the Imps were handed a lifeline. Palmer plucked a ball out of the air at the back and quickly delivered it forward for Morton. A Fleetwood defender slipped affording Morton the chance, and he pulled the ball to the right before slotting past Cairns in goal.

After that, if anyone was going to score, it was the Imps. Bramall looked lively after coming on and he knocked a ball into Rogers on the left flank. The Man City man cut back inside and opted to shoot, rather than find a pass. It didn't trouble the keeper. On 78 minutes Fleetwood hit us on the counter, but a super tackle from Jackson set City away. McGrandles burst down the right and after a blocked pass he found Eyoma. The sub delivered a sharp cross into the six-yard box, which Cairns collected.

With just six minutes left, City got the best chance of the closing period, courtesy of Max Sanders. He whipped a cross in from a quick corner, and Montsma lurked to head home but was just beaten to it by the defender. It was frantic from Fleetwood, with the Imps in the ascendency. Rogers had time for another weak long-range drive that should have been better before a late corner saw Alex Palmer. Clever game management from the visitors meant there was little of the five minutes injury time that could be exploited, and eventually the referee ended the game with Fleetwood winning 2-1, probably the right result.

I despair a little because, despite the injuries we have, I still think we could have been better. We certainly seemed more at ease with Sanders in the holding role and Morton helping out Hopper, but I'm not sure Michael will go two up top in future games, and Morton is likely to be a late sub again this weekend.

This is the Imps slump, the loss of form that everyone else has had, but we have not. The key is bouncing back, which I keep saying at the start of each game, but we needed a reaction after drawing with Swindon and instead, we have lost two on the spin. If anything, the side looks tired but the changes do suggest in Morton and Sanders, we may have a couple of players who can step up in the coming weeks.

I won't write too much more right now, mainly because again I feel the pain of defeat. It's easier to take than Saturday, because we got what we deserved after a poor spell either side of half time. We went into the game with low expectations as well, but we do need to find form, quickly, if our automatic promotion charge is to be maintained.

I will finish with this, as a bit of perspective. If someone had told you we'd be heading into the play-off places on March 2nd, with games in hand that could put us in the top two, then I think we'd have taken that. Well, if we can address the run of form over the next couple of matches, there is no reason why we can't get back to where we were before kick-off and keep up the pressure on the teams above us. 15 games to go, 15 massive games in this club's history.

This one, we'll just have to forget.

Three-sy does it: Imps 3-0 Crewe
March 6, 2021

One year ago, three home goals for City saw us move into a position that you felt might be safety in League One.

A year on, we've seen no live football but another three goals for the Imps once again brought a win. This time, City kept the pressure up on the promotion hunting sides, namely Hull, Doncaster, Sunderland and Peterborough. Three won, but our fate is in our hands and after a tough spell, confidence should have been restored ahead of a crucial week. Three goals, a clean sheet and a fully composed and accomplished, professional performance kept the Imps in the hunt for Championship football.

This was the first time since 2016/17 we have played a team three times in a single season and won all three matches. In the Football League, (this might be wrong) but it looks like the first time since we beat Port Vale three times in the 1983/84 season. Whatever the stats, it is a big achievement in my eyes to play a good side three times and win all three matches.

The Imps made two changes from the side beaten by Fleetwood in midweek, with Callum Morton and Cohen Bramall replacing Tom Hopper and Anthony Scully. It meant a major reshuffle with Tayo Edun dropping into midfield and Brennan Johnson moving back out on the right-hand flank.

City's inability to start a game well has hampered efforts in recent weeks, going behind in the last five league matches. A decent start was needed, and to be fair, I thought we did start brightly Crewe dominated possession, but we looked more composed than in recent weeks and certainly felt a little more direct in our attacking play. It was a frenetic opening, with Crewe clearly not only comfortable in possession, but also with quick counter-attacks.

The first chances of the half fell to the visitors on eight minutes. Chris Porter got a shot away after finding space, which the Imps dealt with, but then poor distribution from Alex Palmer brought the chance around again. This time, as a dangerous ball looked to worry the back four, Lewis Montsma strode in with a challenge and it has to be said Montsma looked much more composed than in recent weeks in the early exchanges. The deep resulting corner found Nathan Wood at the back stick, but his header was poor and City were off the hook.

After that, it was the Imps turn to threaten, with Bramall looking a particular menace on the left flank. Crewe were playing left-footed full-back Rio Adebisi, on the right, and Bramall looked to take advantage with some strong attacking intent. On ten minutes, his wicked cross found James Jones, who drew a save from Dave Richards, only for Morton to stab home from an offside position.

It was the first sign of the Imps as an attacking force though, something that continued through the half. Two minutes later Johnson picked up a loose ball in the centre of the park and broke forward. He had Morton ahead of him, trying to find space, but instead, he drew defenders away from Johnson, who eventually pulled a shot wide of Richards' left-hand post, but it was another good chance.

I couldn't make my mind up about Edun in midfield at this point. The chance for Johnson had almost been one at the other end as Edun gave the ball away first, but then he also seemed to have that composure in possession we see from Bridcutt, as well as the tenacity to cover the back four. He'll split opinion, again, but I thought he looked alright in there for the first half and especially strong in the second.

Just past the 20-minute mark, City grabbed the lead. It was a typical sweeping move up front, with Rogers cutting in from the left and spreading a Crossfield ball to Johnson. He held it for a second, and with Poole overlapping sent it back into the path of Rogers, who struck first time from the edge of the area to beat Richards. It was a typically confident goal from the Man City forward, who already has four in his two months at the club.

It was also probably deserved after the Imps showed more attacking intent early doors. Bramall and Rogers were seemingly getting round Adebisi and on the other flank, Johnson wasn't just outpacing Harry Pickering, but also tracking him every time he roamed forward. Both Johnson and Rogers have had their critics in recent weeks, rightly or wrongly, but nobody could knock either on their first-half showing.

Crewe got a decent chance just before the half-hour mark, when a free-kick was cleared by City, but came back quickly to centre half Beckles in space. He turned and volleyed at goal in a manner you expect a centre half too, and somebody living on Brant Road will find a football in their garden when it comes down from orbit next month.

Very quickly, City were back at it, Johnson again running at their back four. They weren't comfortable at all with the on-loan Forest man getting forward, and as space opened up, so did he, rifling a shot at goal. It took a deflection which lessened the ferocity and Richards gathered comfortably.

Johnson certainly looked lively and he had two more chances either side of a Crewe effort from Adebisi on 41 minutes. Firstly, a move started by Edun saw the Imps move the ball through the lines neatly, ending with Johnson coming in the channel and shooting into the side netting. Then, on the stroke of half time, the lively Bramall again found space down the right, and he delivered a wicked ball across the front of the six-yard box which just evaded a despairing Johnson at the back stick.

With that, referee John Busby brought the half to a close, with the Imps leading 1-0. On the balance of play, despite having less possession, I think it was a fair reflection of the first half.

A 1-0 lead is precarious, but City rarely lose games from winning positions. The issue we have as Imps fans is fear, and the fear of this 'bad run' dragging on makes a 1-0 lead look slender, not commanding. What we wanted to see was a desire to make it 2-0, maybe more, as we came out for the second half. Too often, we have played well for one half and not the other, but luckily this energised Imps side din't disappoint.

Within a minute, the Imps could have taken that all-important 2-0 lead. Regan Poole, who had a really solid game, found Johnson on the overlap, and his cross looked for Morton. The striker was so close to scoring, with Richards spilling the ball but Crewe managing to clear their lines.

The visitors always looked good in possession, but rarely dangerous, whereas City saw less of the ball but seemed likely to do more with it. On 51 minutes, Poole received Palmer's clearance on the right touchline, nodding it into the path of Jones. He strode forward with real purpose, making up yards before finding McGrandles on the edge of the area. It's hard to put into words how good he's been since coming back into the side, and he only raised his profile more by controlling, cutting inside and finishing with aplomb to make it 2-0.

The game was in real danger of running away from Crewe as the Imps quickly hunted a third. Edun, who controlled midfield once he found his stride, spread a ball out to Poole. His cross was instinctive and accurate, with Morton getting ahead of his defender to stab at goal from six yards out. Somehow, Richards pulled off a super stop to keep it as 2-0.

Before the hour mark, the visitors had a fine chance to make it 2-1. You couldn't say they folded and after bringing on Daniel Powell, who I thought was excellent at their place, and Mikel Mandron, they got the chance they wanted. A free kick from the left was cleared as far as Charlie Kirk, who fired a volley past Palmer and off the post. The rebound dropped to Powell, who caught his half-volley sweetly only for Palmer to parry to away from goal.

That shook the Imps a little, and for the next ten minutes or so, they went into game management mode. There was less of the forced attacking of recent weeks, and a return to the patient and measured build-up play we have become accustomed too. At 2-0, we needed no risks, no scares, and the players delivered. We did get one chance, Rogers finding Johnson in the channel with a neat ball. Morton looked a good option for a cross, but as he got crowded out Johnson just neatly touched the ball to Jones, who blasted over.

Adam Jackson picked up the Imps' first yellow card of the game not long after for a rather crude challenge Tom Lowery, before Callum Morton was withdrawn for Tom Hopper. Morton had put in a decent shift and should definitely have had a goal for his endeavour, drawing the fine save from Richards. He's going to be a big asset in the coming weeks for the Imps and his return is a big bright beacon of hope emerging from the injury gloom we continue to suffer.

We got a glimpse of Bramall's good and bad side on 71 minutes. He tried to shepherd the ball out with Powell in attendance, only to lose out to the wide man. However, as Powell's delivery came back, the tenacious former Colchester man got the challenge in to clear. It's taken Bramall longer to settle than it has Poole, but he certainly impressed me throughout this afternoon's fixture. Yes, it helped having a left-back at right-back for him to face, but going forward his pace was a real menace and it doesn't matter what foot you kick with if you can't catch the player you're up against.

Crewe had a half=decent chance to get one back on 75 minutes. Edun was lucky not to be booked for a high boot on Kirk, but when the ball got placed for the free-kick, it had migrated to a good right central position, and a yard or two back from the 18-yard box too. Antony Evans, a player we were linked with in the winter window, stepped up and stroked the ball over Palmer's goal.

With ten minutes to go, a great Imps move killed the game off. Tom Hopper won a challenge in his own half and broke down the attacking left. H caught a glimpse of Johnson in space and pinged a wonderful cross field ball to the winger. He controlled it in a single touched, stepped inside and smashed the ball into the roof of the net with power and purpose. 3-0, game over.

After that the attacking fizzled out from both sides. I was heartened to see Theo Archibald come on, and put in a good ten-minute shift on the left. He is very much a forgotten man this season, but I still believe there is a diamond in there if he gets a run of games.

The win keeps the Imps third, but it was the manner of the performance which should have people smiling. It has been a really tough week or three for City, drawing matches, making errors and being the architects of our own downfall. Today, against a side who have been playing well, we looked more like the Lincoln we have grown accustomed to seeing.

Despite a shaky start, Edun looked decent in the holding midfield role, and having two proper midfielders ahead of him gave us a solidity that I feel we didn't have with Johnson there. As for the Forest man, he was sensational and I much prefer him on the flanks, teasing and taunting a full back. He worked so hard all game, tracking back and grafting for the team, he was a good pick for Man of the Match. On the other wing, Morgan Rogers looked slick and dangerous too, and he too put in a good shift without a hint of fatigue.

Even across the back, an area that has been problematic in recent weeks, I felt we looked strong again. Montsma had his best game for months, Jackson was a great captain and put his body on the line, whilst Poole and Bramall did their best impressions of Eyoma and Edun circa December with rampaging attacking displays and gutsy defensive outings too.

Overall, it was a massive win for us. If we'd lost, we'd be fourth now, but looking like play-off hopefuls and not top two candidates. With everyone else winning, it was vital we did too to keep the dream alive, and we did. Sure, Sunderland are within touching distance now, but above us the top two are being reeled in. Hull have still played two games more than us, Posh faltered and are now within two points too. Everything is boiling nicely for the last 14 matches.

It was at this stage last season everything stopped, and it is worth noting that if the same were to happen now, we'd be second on PPG and we'd go up. That's how far we have come in 365 days – we beat Burton 3-2 a year ago with us looking at the teams below us, and a year on we beat Crewe 3-0 and are definitely looking up. It's three goals, three points, Imps in third and the third time we have beaten a side three times as a Football league team since (you guessed it) 1982/83. All the threes, lucky Lincoln.

If we play as we did today in the next 14 matches, as well as getting Bridcutt, Grant and Walsh back, we might just take this hunt for Championship football right to the wire.

Reflections On a Year In Sincil Bank Exile
March 7, 2021

One year ago, at around 9am in the morning, I rang my Dad to see if he fancied meeting for breakfast at the Corn Dolly in Wragby before the Burton game.

"I can't Gaz," was his reply. "We'll do it in a fortnight." If only we knew.

Breakfast with my Dad is just one part of the whole matchday experience that I have missed, and one year on, I still haven't had a bacon, egg and hash brown session with my old man. We've chatted, we've drunk in my bar and we see each other when we are allowed, but we haven't ordered a nice fry up and chatted the Imps. I'm sure you all have the same feelings about your routine.

At first, I'll be honest, I didn't mind the break. I missed being at the ground, but I'm not one of these hysterical 'football day is all I'm about' types. I enjoyed having a Saturday at home in the garden with Fe. I enjoyed not having the pressure of worrying about other team's results as we dropped down the table. At first, it was perhaps even light relief from a season that had been a challenge at times.

After maybe two weeks, I began to miss the little things. I missed the breakfasts, sure, but also the walk to the ground, just nodding at familiar faces. Being a little conceited, I missed people I knew only by sight coming up and saying something like; "you don't know me, but I read your site…" before we chatted a bit about the club. I missed people, and for someone who was given an 'I Hate People' badge for Christmas, that says a lot. Yes, I don't like the general public, but I do like the Lincoln City public. There is a difference.

I began to miss standing in our little huddle by the TP Suite with the other armchair managers, discussing tactics and approach, arguing about why one player was better than the other. I miss Jimbo's nuggets of wisdom, and just being around the other fans. At first, I didn't entirely miss the football. I sometimes don't like the actual games, because I'm so emotionally invested in them, and knowing relegation was still possible had meant I hadn't really enjoyed a game of football at the Bank for a while, not for 90 minutes.

After all, football is everywhere, isn't it? We got a chance in those first few months to relive classic matches, to enjoy some of our previous achievements and it distracted from the uncertainty of our future direction. I could play FIFA for a football fix, or turn to the internet to talk football. I had grown a little apathetic towards our future prospects, genuinely settling into a 'fifth from bottom will do' mindset over the summer. It is fair to say by the time August arrived, my feelings of detachment were about the experience, not the football itself. Yes, I missed Gav, Stan, Matt and the others who sit around me, I missed the half time scrum for the toilet, Alan's 'make some noise for the boys', but part of me hadn't missed the actual games. Maybe, because I talk and write so much about them, I still felt connected to the action. Maybe I had just made myself believe we were heading in the wrong direction and any delay to the comments of 'wheels have come off' was some sort of relief.

The first time I felt a desperate longing for an actual game was as late as Forest Green in the FA Cup. We ran some video clips on Match Day Live of the previous games against them, and the FA Cup matches, and hearing that roar as a goal went in just got me. Off-camera, I felt a little emotional as I realised, I did miss the football, I did miss the ecstasy of a goal going in. I don't mean just the big ones either, I miss celebrating pulling one back in a dire game we still end up losing as much as I do the third in a rout of a relegation-haunted side.

Since then, the longing for a return has built inside me. I was lucky enough to attend the Liverpool game, but it wasn't the football experience I know and love. What I longed for was everything, from breakfast to the bar, from checking team news on Twitter to hearing it read out against a backdrop of signing before kick-off. I miss questioning the referee's parentage when he gives a foul against us that was totally justified, only to sit down a second later knowing I was wrong. I miss that simmering excitement as we get down the wing into the attacking third, that expectation of something happening which, 90% of the time, it doesn't.

Most of all, I miss that moment the net ripples and whatever happened in your week up to that point just goes away. Whether 1-0 up, 2-1 down or drawing 6-6, when a goal goes in it fires something, like turning a key in an engine or lighting a firework. Emotion, desire, passion, whatever it is, you don't get in watching iFollow. Sure, you cheer and you feel happy, but is it the same? Cheering in your living room with a dog looking bemused from the corner? Does that really compare with 8,000 other people all in a stadium feeling exactly the same as you? All different ages, sexes, religions, professions and personalities united in that split second because a goal is scored? No. Nothing compares to that. Only that shared delight can erase memories of a bad week at work, a dying relationship, a dodgy ankle or whatever else has dogged your thoughts for seven days prior.

So, that is where I am now. I miss it all, from the minute I open my eyes, knowing Fe will walk the dog because I have to meet Dad for breakfast, right through to the moment I step back through the door at night to an excited pooch with an article to write, a programme to toss on the pile and either a win to celebrate or sorrows to drown. Yes, we still have some elements of that experience, and yes, Michael's wonderful squad have done their best to ensure our season has been better than that of many other teams, but it still isn't the same.

365 days ago, it all felt very routine, expected and (perhaps) taken for granted. Right now, as we look forward to another game on iFollow on Tuesday, it feels anything but.

Here's to finally getting back to where we belong, cheering those goals, sharing the agony and the joy together. Here's to moaning that people are heading in the exit of the Coop toilets, here's to having the cap taken off your bottle of pop. Here's to Jimbo, the crew by the TP bins, people whose face I recognise and to the programme sellers to.

Most of all, here's to my next Corn Dolly breakfast with my Dad.

City survive terrific Tuesday in third: Ipswich Town 1-1 Imps
March 9, 2021

The Imps earned a point this evening away at Ipswich, in a game that keeps us in touch with the top two.

On an evening where six of the top eight played each other, it was good to see the other two, Doncaster and Accrington lose. In fact, only two of the top eight won (Hull and I assume Sunderland who lead 2-0 at Fratton Park as I write this), meaning the gap between the top four is five points, but Hull have played two matches more. The gap between us and the final place outside the play-offs is now ten points and looking like becoming a chasm.

Michael Appleton made two changes from the side that beat Crewe 3-0 at the weekend, Callum Morton dropped to the bench, with Tom Hopper coming in, whilst Regan Poole also lost his place, replaced by TJ Eyoma. On paper, it looked a big challenge with an Ipswich squad packed with talent but not quite firing on all cylinders. Paul Cook will get them playing, but City hoped it wouldn't be before the 90 minutes were up.

One thing the Imps have been guilty of is poor starts of late, but there was no fear of that in a confident opening 15 minutes. Both sides certainly had their moments without any clear cut chances, but it was certainly a good advert for League One. Both teams tried to play out from the back, and Ipswich had seemingly identified Cohen Bramall as a good weak spot to attack, switching Edwards from his usual left wing spot to match up.

If that was the plan, they vastly underestimated the former Colchester man, who looked to cause problem in the attacking third from the get-go. One moment saw him started a good five yards behind Luke Chambers, but knock the ball beyond on him glide past like a Audi overtaking a transit van on the A14. It was Bramall who had the first serious Imps chance of the game, a corner was cleared to Edun, who teed him up on the edge of the area. His shot was high and wide, but it was a warning for the home team.

City had a strong spell in the middle period of the half, with Morgan Rogers looking lively too. He was often found tucking into the channel with Bramall going down the outside, but he got his first sight of goal after a corner dropped to him 12-yards out. It took him by surprise a little, but his shot was well blocked anyhow.

I felt referee James Oldham was having a bit of a tough game, but it could be the rose-tinted glasses. He did miss a blatant handball in the area, not deliberate, but I have seen them given. Then Alex Palmer seemed to be fouled as he contested a ball, but the officials gave a corner. Finally, from an Ipswich corner, City broke with Johnson and I thought he was brought down as he made up the yards, with the referee giving a corner. They weren't horrendous decisions, but they were enough to have me muttering bad words under my breath.

On 22 minutes, City hit the post through the unfortunately Nsiala. This time it was an attack down the right hand side doing the damage, Brennan Johnson finding Eyoma on the overlaps. His ball was sent to the near post, and with Hopper lurking Nsiala turned it onto the post, before it surprised Jones and his header came to nothing. As the ball came back out, Montsma picked it up and let fly with one of his ambitious, but worrying drives which had the keeper beat, but also the goal.

City were turning the screw and on 27 minutes, James Jones had an effort blocked. The former Crewe man has struggled of late, but impressed against his former employers at the weekend and looked strong in the first half here. Bramall was the initial creator, with his ball finding Hopper, who worked it to Jones for the effort.

Just before the hour mark, City took a deserved lead. It was all the work of Morgan Rogers, confidently and dare I say nonchalantly swaggering forward with the ball, looking for options. Bramall drew a runner and a bit of space opened up for the young winger to curl a lovely effort to the left of Tomas Holy, and into the net. It capped a good opening half hour and a dominant quarter of an hour for City, and was certainly just reward for Rogers who had their back line petrified.

The game tailed off a bit after that, with Ipswich finding their footing. Mile Kenlock impressed me with his forward intent, but often fans watching were treated to slow and patient build up from both teams with little penetration. Of course, that suited us as we had the lead, but just before half time we got reminded of how narrow that lead was.

Both times the architect was Andre Dozzell, courtesy of Tayo Edun fouls. The first saw a free kick from the attacking left, on the edge of the area from 18 yards out. Dozzell lifted a neat ball over the top for Nsiala, who got under it and could only head wide. Within minutes, Dozzell had another free kick, this time to the attacking right after a rather cynical Edun challenge, which drew a yellow card. This time Dozzell, son of Ipswich legend Jason, curled his free kick to Palmer's right, with the keeper at first parrying, then catching the delivery.

It was the final effort of an engrossing first half which saw us have six effort, with only one on target. The home side, for some decent possession, mustered just two, with one on target. It wasn't a great return for them, and it felt as thought there must be more to come from Paul Cook's men.

There wasn't an awful lot more to come from them, but there was even less from the Imps in a tepid and unentertaining second period. In fact, my notes for the second half start on 57 minutes, which shows what seemed like a lack of ambition according to Ipswich commentator Mick Mills, but what might have been as much about energy conservation as anything, given that we have played eight more games than the home side.

I felt the referee continued his rather odd interpretation of the rules, but this time favouring us. Edun got away with a couple of 'fouls', but then we were punished for far softer challenges. There was nothing game changing, but it felt a little inconsistent at times, for both teams.

Up until the hour mark, the best 'chance' of the half fell to Miles Kenlock, and by chance I mean he got free on the left and hit a cross-cum-shot which was neither into the waiting arms of Alex Palmer.

The home side looked to shake it up on 60 minutes with a triple substitution, and that prompted the Imps to have a decent chance. Montsma hit one of his typical Crossfield balls to Bramall, who knocked it into Tom Hopper. He may have lost his bearing a little, because he hit a shot high from the sort of angle Marco Van Basten might have shied away from. A minute later, Montsma introduced himself to sub Troy Parrott with a foul apparently worthy of a booking and to be fair, it was hard to disagree.

I thought Johnson put in a decent shift, he was certainly tracking back into the full back position, and I noticed on the other flank Rogers doing the same. The pair of them have come in for some criticism recently, but they have certainly been working themselves hard in the past couple of weeks.

On 71 minutes, the home side got their only real clear-cut chance of the game, and scored from it. Edun gave away a bit of a silly free kick in the middle of the park after losing possession. A long, straight ball into the area was headed on by Chambers, and typically James Wilson found space to nod past Palmer to level things. It was probably coming and against better opposition, we might have been punished for how much we sat off them, but this isn't a great Ipswich side. That said, they took a chance and we were back to all square.

After that they didn't really press on for a winner and we looked happy with a draw too. Callum Morton, Anthony Scully and Regan Poole all came on at different points, but none could really affect the outcome of the game. We had the better chances, two of them, but wasted both. The first saw Nsiala make a mistake (shock), which Johnson looked to seize upon. He took the ball wide of the defender, rather than across him and at goal then fired at Holy from a tight angle when a pass to Morton might have brought a better opportunity.

As we entered injury time the Imps got another half chance, a wicked Crossfield switch from Scully for Rogers, when jinked into the area, but saw Nsiala block his shot at goal. Despite much more possession, even in the final fifteen minutes, Ipswich didn't threaten at all after their goal.

I have to say, I called a draw before the game and once again, I was spot on. It was a game of tight margins, one I felt we could have killed off in the first half and one I felt we had little desire to finish in the second. I feel if we had doubled our lead, the game would have opened up like a royal couple on patio furniture with Oprah, but instead it remained a closed shop, stuffy, boring and unentertaining. Mind you, this was a free hit in my eyes, and you can only judge a game after 90 minutes, not 70, 45 or 30. Over 90 minutes Mick Mills felt a draw was fair, but personally I think we did enough to win the game, even if we didn't seem like that was our primary intention in the final 45. Of course, it was what we wanted, but I know

Michael won't be disappointed at going to Portman Road and bagging a point, because a win this weekend will make it seven from three, a good haul indeed.

The second half might draw some comments, but with so many fixtures it really doesn't surprise me we weren't able to maintain the high pressing, fast pace of the first half. It was a weak goal we conceded and despite a decent enough showing Edun just doesn't do the job Liam Bridcutt does. However, the continued emergence of Cohen Bramall is promising and that leaves Edun our only seriously viable option in the defensive midfield role, especially as I noted Max Sanders wasn't on the bench.

The lads can take a day off tomorrow, nurse a few knocks and strains and hopefully head into the weekend with the firm intention of getting three points and keeping the pressure up on the other three teams I feel we are fighting with for the top two place – Hull City, Peterborough and Sunderland.

Woeful City Slain at Home: Imps 1-2 Rochdale
March 13, 2021

Before I start today, let me ask a question. What is my role as fan-driven media?

To show balance and an understanding of the wider picture? Yes. To find the bright spots in the dark, and highlight the dark ones in the light? Maybe. To be fair, reasoned and informed? I'd say so. I'd hope so, at least.

So, I think to myself as I walk around the Wolds with my dog after today's debacle, how do I write that up? Genuinely, how would you approach it? I could sum it up in four words, two of which you wouldn't want to hear your ten-year-old say, but what good is that? I could try to gloss over some of it and point to the good parts, but in heart of hearts, I cannot. Today, I cannot talk about positives, about the hunt for automatic promotion and all of that, because if I did, I would be lying to myself.

I said at the start of the week, six points from the three games was a minimum. Anything else, and we're play-off material, not automatic promotion candidates. I'm not a hypocrite and sadly, four from the three games is not good enough to challenge for the top two. We could have moved back into contention this evening, instead, in my opinion, we showed why top six will now be an achievement.

Look, in the grand scheme of things, it would be an achievement, a huge one at that. I keep seeing comparisons to 2006/07, but there's a difference. Back then, we were surrounded by teams of our size and we had no reason to feel inferior. This season, we're competing against teams who have played in the Championship and above. I'm afraid the last few weeks are not us collapsing, they are us finding our level this season. If that level is sixth or higher, then we've done bloody well, even if we did look likely to top the league at one point.

You can point to many reasons for the recent form. Liam Bridcutt being out is the main driver for me, we had begun to fall off when Jorge got injured, and even when Joe did, but Liam is the key for me. He allows us to play any central defensive pairing and not feel like we did today, that every break might result in a goal. He ensures that we have a moment on the ball in the middle of the park and he calms down some of the younger, more talented players we have on the field. Once he is back, we might just do enough to finish third or fourth, but my honest assessment is that we're not quite top two standard yet. To be so close is a huge achievement, but not because 'four years ago we were playing Boreham Wood', because that context is not applicable here. By the same rationale, we could say 'two months ago we were top' and make our current position look poor. It isn't poor, we're still doing incredibly well, but one thing I will not shy away from is today's performance.

For me, it was the worst of the season by a country mile. This was our Southend from last year, the one game where we could have played for six hours and still been beaten. I haven't said this much this season, but I felt we were poor all over the pitch, and not against a side who are doing anything at all. Rochdale won one in 17 going into today, and hadn't scored since early February. Against us, they looked like scoring every time they got the ball.

I make notes through the game and usually do a full match report, but I can't bring myself to write that up today. I don't want to relive what felt like a relentless and utterly futile grind against a side we should have brushed aside. We can talk about injuries all we want, but they have lost key players too, not least 11-goal leading scorer Matty Lund. Today, all of the usual things that I feel apply in terms of squad quality, games played, injuries etc, do not apply. There are no excuses, there is nowhere to go and hide. We lost to a team that (and I'm sorry for this Rochdale fans) I believe will be playing League Two football next season, and we didn't just lose, but we deserved to lose.

I am upset, because from the fourth or fifth minute you could see the way the game was going. I'd write down a chance in my notes, with Alex Palmer going to take a goal kick, and when I looked up, Rochdale would have possession. We gave the ball away easily, when we had it, we had no real zest or imagination and when they had it, we shrunk away like scared children hiding from playground bullies. Often, when a nice meaty 50/50 looked likely, I saw our players shy away from the challenges and as far as I'm concerned that wasn't acceptable.

For 36 minutes it was a bad performance, but one you felt we could still win. If we get the first goal in that game, we go on and win 3-0. That's my opinion, I feel Rochdale were a side low on confidence, but high on character and with a degree of self-belief. A goal for them would always give them something to believe in, and that is why the first goal was crucial. Let's be honest, they could have had it three or four times over, were it not for Alex Palmer in the first half. Dare I say that if any player other than Palmer gets Man of the Match from the SW readers this weekend, I'll be tempted to take down the player rater. He was the difference between a 2-1 defeat today and a much more embarrassing outcome altogether.

The goal wasn't actually as bad as some of the other chances we conceded. I counted eight Rochdale corners, and seven first contacts I think, which is really bad, but when the goal came it had shades of Plymouth. Nobody seemed to want to challenge Rathbone and his finish was enough to beat Palmer, who saw it late through a crowd. It's not the first we've conceded like that, no bodies were being put on the line and we paid the price.

Rochdale should have scored two or three before that, and before the half ended, they should have scored one more. It came from our attacking free kick, which was poor, cleared quickly and Humphrys' ended up with a chance. It summed up the first half for me, and whilst I always try to find some bright spots, I couldn't. We had one shot, off target in the first half and Rochdale and 11 shots, three on target. They started the day bottom, remember that.

Look, before you stop reading because of the negativity, I can accept us being third. Hell, if we finish third it'll be the best finish in my lifetime, and it will represent and wonderful job from Michael and the squad. If we finish in the top six, I'll class that as success, I'm not a moaner who will point to being top earlier in the season. I can accept bad performances too, but I won't hide away from calling a spade a spade and that first half was, I'm afraid to say, as bad as anything I witnessed last season. Michael will have been fuming, no doubt at all, and he will have wanted a second half response from his players.

If Michael wanted a response, he didn't get it. Sadly, we came out and played exactly the same as we did in the first, at least in the opening stages. Take nothing away from Rochdale by the way, they were a committed bunch who scrapped for everything and in most instances, got what they deserved. They were quicker in the tackle, sharper cutting out balls and they definitely attacked with purpose and desire. Yes, I am disappointed, but we must also acknowledge when a side puts in a good shift. They won't be accepting of us saying how bad we were without praising their own team and rightly so. If I was a Rochdale supporter tonight, I'd be proud of my team, but if you gave me the chance to swap places with them, I wouldn't. I've been proud of this Lincoln team too many times to mention, and I haven't felt this let down by them all season.

Anyway, the second half went off like the first, although I felt we did begin to show a bit more promise. We still looked easily penetrated though, and why we can't win a defensive header is beyond me. They should have been 2-0 up on 55 minutes when McGrandles, one of three players I felt could take a little solace from his performance, headed off the line. Four minutes later Rochdale were mugged off by the referee when they should have had a stonewall penalty. I've watched it back, Edun on Humphrys (I think) and the foul is akin to a wrestling move, with no contact on the ball at all. It seemed like the 'luck' we needed to kick on, and within a minute or so we had at least something to cheer.

I've been critical, as you'll already know, but there cannot be anything other than superlatives laid at the feet of young Morgan Rogers, the only other outfield player I think can take credit from his performance. His goal illuminated a dull and dire afternoon, the wonderful combination with Callum Morton leading to yet another finish which may trouble the goal of the season awards. He's making a habit of it and whilst his trickery and inventiveness doesn't always pay dividends, when it does, it is lovely to watch.

I got the customary 'get in' text from my Dad, him doubtless hoping that we could go on and win the game as I was. For five minutes, I felt we were in with a chance too. A quick break saw Johnson get a little space and his thunderous drive drew a wonder save from the Rochdale keeper. Many supporters probably smelled blood at that point, but rather pessimistically I text Dad back with 'I still think we'll lose', because we just were not at it at all.

I can't even describe the action after their goal, because as yet another sloppy bit of defending cost us, I pelted my notepad and pen across the room and went into a sulk I haven't come out of. Sure, we pressed forward late on and could have maybe pulled level, but did we deserve it? Not a chance. We got what we deserved from that game, nothing at all. I'm not going to talk about our late spell, because it is an illusion. A tired Rochdale had to sit back and let us have the ball, but we didn't pour into them, did we? Instead, on 87 minutes, I saw a midfield player turn in his attacking half and start that long, arduous journey of going all the way back to the keeper.

From today's outing, I felt Rogers had some credit, McGrandles too, and Alex Palmer was outstanding. His saves kept the score away from the realms of 5-1, and that is no exaggeration. Other than that, not one player can claim to have had a good game. Bramall was the scapegoat at half time, coming off for Scully, but he wasn't the worst player on the pitch, not by some way. For periods, we looked like nine or ten strangers trying hard to work out where each other would be. As I said, credit to Rochdale for forcing that to a degree, but if we'd played half as well as we did against Crewe last weekend, we would have won the game. It's that simple.

I'm told after the game, Michael has said more or less the same, we deserved nothing and Liam Bridcutt will likely play on Tuesday. That's a big plus for us, I keep saying how we have lost just two league games with him in the side and I think he'll firm us up, offer that porous defence some respite and help us to cement a play-off place, but as Michael said (before anyone jumps on me for being negative), we're not an automatic promotion side and I don't think the captain coming back is going to be enough to see us snatch a spot in the top two.

Doubtless, some will have stopped reading by now, probably upset with my seemingly negative outlook on the afternoon's proceedings. I have to stress I have been cutting in terms of this game, not the whole team. Not one of those players has regularly let us down and some have been a cornerstone of the form which has seen us rise to where we are. I wouldn't hide behind the injuries, but we have lost Walsh, Bridcutt and Grant at a time when we needed the key players fit. We have lost the experience and leadership, something I don't think was evident today, and of course that isn't ideal, but it isn't why we lost today. I don't even think this is 'the slump' continuing either, because Ipswich first half and Crewe were both very good performances.

I'm proud of my football team this season and I will remain so if we finish second six or tenth. When the first ball was kicked, I felt anything top half would be a massive achievement and I stand by that right now. It would be disappointing if we finished below seventh, which when you consider it is ridiculous given where we were a year ago. The progress the team has made is incredible and as a fanbase, we must stay focused on the bigger picture. Today was awful, I won't shy away from saying that, but the season as a whole has still been incredible and I'd rather have awful performances when we're third and definitely moving forward than I would have a plucky win with 12 games left and still being adrift at the bottom of the table.

This isn't '82/83' all over again, because that was a lack of ambition in the board, something we don't have. It isn't '06/07' all over again because that was a side fighting teams of similar stature in the basement division. This season is without comparison, because of what has come before and how we have been forced to adapt and when the dust settles in May, wherever we happen to be, we can be proud of the team and confident we're heading in the right direction.

It might just take a few IPA's and a night's sleep to see that clearly again.

Gifted Goals Are City's Grumble – Imps 0-3 Gillingham
March 16, 2021

It was another utterly abysmal night at Sincil Bank as Steve Evans got his biggest win against the Imps.

It wasn't actually a terrible performance across the park, we had a few chances and certainly played better than we did at Rochdale at the weekend, but it doesn't matter if you gift the visitors the game within minutes of kick-off. That's what happened and I'm afraid once you shoot yourself in the foot, you're never going to walk far afterwards, no matter how much you try.

The Imps made two changes to the personnel that lost against Rochdale, but shuffled the pack to accommodate a 4-4-2. That saw Edun back in the left-back role, captain Liam Bridcutt partnering Conor McGrandles in midfield and a two-pronged attacked with Hopper and Morton alongside each other.

To be fair, and I do try to be, we started quite brightly, finding space on the right for Regan Poole to create the game's first chance. His wicked delivery flashed across the front of goal and despite doubling up on the number of centre forwards, we still couldn't force the ball into the net. The problem hasn't been scoring though, it has been conceding, and as the clock hit double figures the same ugly problem reared its head.

What is angering, and I do mean that as aggressively as it sounds, s any good work we do is always likely to be undone by absolutely awful defending at the minute. Quite how Vadaine Oliver got such a free header is beyond me, and whoever is doing the defensive coaching might want to go back to the Ladybird books, rather than advanced stuff when the players are next in. It was just so simple, ball into the box, free header, 1-0.

I thought the return of Liam Bridcutt would change things at the back, but it hasn't, not at all. Suddenly, at 1-0 down, everything changed. Gillingham had a lead to defend and when they want to be, they're compact and organised, and we just looked laboured. I thought Morgan Rogers had a decent first half, spreading some nice balls across the field and making positive runs when he got the chance, but we didn't create anything clear cut before it went to 2-0.

Again, it was such a sloppy goal, with City not clearing their lines properly from a set piece and being punished. You have to give credit to Gillingham, of course, but where are the bodies on the line? Where are the blocks, the last-ditch tackles? As Dempsey strode into the area, I saw a powder-puff challenge that never looked like winning the ball, the complete opposite of at least two from their midfield in the first three minutes. It's so, so sad to watch us do this to ourselves, but without playing badly we were 2-0 down.

Passes weren't going astray like they did on Saturday, but we just never got a decent ball into a decent area. We had efforts, mostly from range from Rogers and one from McGrandles, but nothing that had Jack Bonham needing to warm his hands. At half time, it was seven shots from us, none on target. On the other hand, Gillingham had six, four on target, and but for Alex Palmer's heroics, then a little rush of blood, it could have been more. He pulled of a great save to stop it going to 3-0, then committed too early and had to be bailed out not long after.

The sad fact is there was little between the teams in terms of play, but when Gillingham attacked, they looked hungry and we looked absolutely terrified. When we attacked, they looked organised and solid, whilst we just didn't have the tools to break the wall down. It meant a first half that had me considering turning iFollow off and going away from my computer, which is how the last month has been making me feel. After all the excitement and pomp of earlier in the season, we look in serious danger of dropping out of the top six. I know that being safe from relegation was the first target, but it isn't easy to watch what was a good football team capitulate when a bit of pressure is applied.

What more can I say about the first half? There is no blame; we're not looking tired, we haven't got six or seven players out, we're missing one from the back, Joe Walsh. He didn't play until Fleetwood away earlier in the season, and we had been top before that, so is him missing really the problem? I don't know, I really don't know what is, but if we keep defending that badly, then don't worry too much about booking a holiday play-off final week, because Charlton, Blackpool, Sunderland, MK Dons and Oxford will all be taking advantage.

Normally, you'll get a two-page, second half analysis but what can I really say that covers the second period? Yes, it was attack against defence, but why not? Gillingham were 2-0 up and needed us to break them down. Sadly, we never really looked like we'd got the right tools to do it. We had lots of possession, and we did create the occasional chance, but it was never a case of looking like we were actually going to get back into the game. If anything, Edun moving into midfield gave us a bit of an impetus, and that isn't a sleight on Bridcutt who I thought had a decent game.

Edun probably came closest to giving the Imps a lifeline, his long-range strike was tipped onto the bar by Bonham, but it was probably the only save the stopper had to make. Regan Poole had a decent chance too, a decent delivery into the area fell to him 18-yards out, but he fired wide. Those were the pick of the chances, but not the major talking point.

Brennan Johnson got a booking, possibly for a dive, maybe for dissent, it isn't clear, but it was a soft yellow. If it was for a dive, then it is safe to say Steve Evans' antics before the game worked, as he got into Ross Joyce's head. Edun then got one too, literally being told by Adam Jackson to stop talking to the ref, which he didn't, and that saw him go into the book. Bizarrely, John Akinde then got the same punishment for a studs-up challenge on Alex Palmer. I wasn't convinced by Ross Joyce when he last came here to officiate the 2-2 draw with Notts County, and I wasn't impressed with him tonight.

Not that anything he did would have affected the result, because we simply weren't good enough, yet again. We manufactured our own problems, giving the visitors a two-goal lead and then never looking likely to claw it back. The game ended on an even more sour note for the Imps, Cohen Bramall shoving Jordan Graham over in the area to give the visitors a chance from 12-yards. The same player picked himself up and fired into the roof of the net.

"It's been a disappointing night in the end," Michael Hortin said on the radio. I concur. In fact, it was an utterly demoralising defeat, one that simply makes me sick to my stomach. Dreams of the Championship are beginning to look just like that, for this season at least.

To take any positives, and I'm afraid I don't mean from tonight, but we're still going in the right direction, we just spiked when perhaps we shouldn't have earlier in the season. I know this was said jokingly a long while ago, but we're not going down and if we take this disappointment and accept that promotion is slipping away, we can almost take the pressure off ourselves for the last few games.

What I will say is we must be better than we were tonight, and much better than we were Saturday, if we're to finish in the top six. However, if the worst thing that happens this season is we finish eighth, then whilst it will be disappointing, it really isn't the end of the world.

Solid City Secure Stalemate: Sunderland 1-1 Imps
March 20, 2021

The Imps claimed a strong point this afternoon against the division's in-form team and took another step towards assuring a spot in the play-offs at the end of the season.

There's no doubt Sunderland are on a roll, and as they brush aside other teams I think they'll be in the top two come May, but we're proving that despite the run of poor form, we have some attributes that cannot be lost. We've been woeful over the past 180 minutes, maybe even 225, but this afternoon we went toe to toe with a very good side, and came out feeling that we could have won the game.

Draws are only good if you pepper your record with wins, and in the context of a four-game run, two points are not great, but Sunderland away is as tough as it gets in this division, and we've now been there twice in a month and avoided defeat both times. It wasn't all about the result though today, it was the performance, once of resilience, commitment and, apart from one mad moment, defensive stability.

The Imps made one change to the team that were humbled by Gillingham on Tuesday. Cohen Bramall came in for the injured Tom Hopper, with us reverting back to a 4-3-3 and Tayo Edun pushing up into the attacking midfield role for what I think might be the first time this season. He finished the Gillingham game brightly and I certainly feel the eight role is the one he shows the most composure in.

In a game that few fancied us to get anything from anyway, we started relatively brightly. As expected the home side had lots of possession, but without creating anything of note before the ten-minute mark. In fact, the only noteworthy aspect of the first ten minutes came from referee Carl Boyeson, who managed to check two corners and blow his whistle more often that a 90s raver at the Pleasuredome.

Cohen Bramall certainly had a decent start to the game showing his pace on one occasion, but it was Sunderland who got the first chance in, Max Power driving wide from distance. Within seconds, the Imps had faced another shot, weak playing out from the back saw the ball quickly turned over, with Grant Leadbitter smashing in an effort form 30-yards, which Palmer saved.

City responded to that with a couple of half-chances of our own. Bramall once again had his full-back on toast, but nobody got the end of his cross. There was a weak shout for handball, which shouldn't have been given, and wasn't. The Imps best chance of the opening 20 minutes fell to Rogers. The lively Edun combined with Bramall to set up Rogers, who let fly with a shot from 18-yards, but didn't hit the target. Sadly, as proved to be the case against Gillingham, we only really looked like having shots from range as we struggled to carve open Sunderland's resolute defence.

Regan Poole had kept Aiden McGeady quiet for the first 20 minutes, but as the clock ticked over to 21, the Eire man got his chance. He worked space and got a shot at Palmer's goal, which the on-loan stopper saved. Within minutes, City got their best chance of the first half. Poole showed tenacity to harass O'Nien on the right flank, winning the ball and breaking two-on-one. The former MK Dons man opted to take the ball to a tight angle and shoot, when Callum Morton was in a better position, and Lee Burge was equal to it.

The game settled a little after that and to be fair, we looked like we were in it. Tayo Edun was getting quite advanced, but Morton was largely ineffective up front, starved off the ball. He chased a couple of lost causes, but not with complete conviction, and it seemed as though we'd try to frustrate the home side. Indeed, when Wyke cynically tripped Lewis Montsma for a booking on 33 minutes, it did seem like it was working.

On 38 minutes Morgan Rogers lost possession deep in the Sunderland half, but a quick and clever ball by Max Power found McGeady in space. He cut inside and lashed a shot over the goal, but it proved that we couldn't switch off, not for a second. Sadly, a minute later, we did.

It wasn't as bad as the goals against Gillingham, but after doing well in the corner to win the ball, Bramall's clearance dropped straight at the feet of Power, who dropped a delicious cross onto the head of the unmarked McFadzean at the far post. Johnson had seemingly lost his runner, and with Poole coming infield to man-mark McGeady, it left the back stick undefended and McFadzean unopposed.

It felt like a real kick in the balls after a decent first half. We hadn't really looked like scoring, but we had contained Sunderland, and there isn't a fan reading this who wouldn't have taken a draw before the game kicked off. However, once again City conceded the first goal, and with Hopper and Grant, we didn't really look like scoring one, unless there was a moment of magic to be had.

Max Power did pick up a booking for a foul on Edun, giving us a great chance from a set-piece, but without Grant, we may as well have just been given a goal kick. The half finished 1-0 to Sunderland, a tough one to take after a decent 45, but probably fair on the balance of chances created.

If the first half was solid, but ultimately disappointing, then the second was certainly worth the iFollow fee alone. Lincoln weren't exceptional, but it was the sort of performance we became accustomed to in the early parts of the year, matching our opponents and looking dangerous at time, rather than the last few weeks where we have shrunk away.

I wonder what Michael said at half time, because within a minute of the restart we'd won our third corner of the game. It was wasted, as most of our corners were, but I did feel we made an early statement. This was a game few expected us to get anything from, especially not when we had gone 1-0 down, but we showed the same commitment as we did in the first half. In the past, conceding first against Sunderland and Portsmouth, as well as Fleetwood, Rochdale and Swindon, has shaken our confidence and the football became hurried. Not this time, and dare I say, I think Liam Bridcutt is the reason why.

Praise should also go to Montsma and Jackson, both of whom have struggled in recent weeks, whether for injury or form, but both were solid today. Montsma took a whack from Charlie Wyke early in the half, leading to a five-minute break in play, and for a short period after that, Sunderland seized the initiative.

There were few clear cut chances in the first 15 minutes of the half, Adam Jackson had to get behind a McGeady cross on 56 minutes in a moment of danger, but the game exploded on the hour mark. Firstly, Rogers was penalised for pulling one of their attackers and a free-kick was awarded in a great position. It was one of the numerous decisions I thought the referee got wrong, for both sides I might add, and it could have cost us. Palmer was forced to parry McGeady's effort and eventually, the Imps lines were cleared and the pressure alleviated.

Three minutes later, we got back into the game. Bramall found some space on the left-hand flank and delivered a ball into the area, which was nodded out, and then back into Morton in a quick game of head tennis. The on-loan striker, anonymous for the opening 60 minutes, controlled well, held off his defender and slid the ball past Burge with consummate confidence. From nowhere, the Imps were back in it.

I get the feeling we're a side that thrives on belief and confidence because the goal changed the complexion of our play. Just three minutes later a free-kick for Sunderland was cut out, Morton nicked the ball off McGeady's toe and ran the length of the pitch, earning us a corner. Of course, the corner came to nothing, but the wind was certainly behind us. Suddenly, from looking shot-shy and a little apprehensive, the old Lincoln began to show a little.

With 20 minutes left on the clock, City should have led 201. Morgan Rogers, frustrating and brilliant in equal measure, skinned Dion Sanderson and pulled a superb ball back for Bramall, arriving from the left. The full-back had a gaping goal to shoot at, but went for power over placement and put it back towards Burge, who pulled off a really good stop. Bramall made it saveable, but hat's off to the former Colchester man as I thought he had a solid game.

Charlie Wyke should really have seen red on 71 minutes, already on a booking he went in late again and had a long talking to from the referee. For an official who seemed fussy in the first half, it was a let off. Boyeson just annoyed me throughout the game, he gave one free-kick against Morton after O'Nien held on to the striker's shirt and both went down, and he missed Bridcutt being completely taken out on an attack too. I'm sure Sunderland fans will have moments they shook their head, but my rose-tinted spectacles didn't pick those moments up. I know how bad Boyeson was though, so I know there will be something we did that he missed.

The Black cats are no mugs and despite us getting back into the game, they threatened. They brought on Ross Stewart, a £300,000 buy from Ross County in January, and his first touch was a free header at goal. It was a rare lapse at the back (rare in the second half, not any other time) which saw him free to nod up into the air and watch as the ball dropped into Palmer's waiting gloves.

Palmer earned his wages this afternoon, that's for sure. On 76 minutes McGeady sent a defence-splitting pass through to Wyke. The striker had dropped off the shoulder of his marker and turned to go in on goal, but hadn't banked on Palmer who came diving out and claimed the ball almost on the edge of the area. Palmer was almost beaten with 12 minutes remaining. Sunderland's deep free kick dropped back on to the edge of the area, but Maguire's volley was deflected up and over the goal. From the camera angle, I briefly thought our hard work had been undone, but no, we stayed level. It impressed me, not only how quickly we shrugged off the one moment the concentration dipped, but how against the most potent attacking force in the division, we kept our calm, even with two patched up defenders and two new signings still feeling their way in. Dare I say, Bridcutt is the difference.

Before I go into the last ten minutes, I take my hat off to the skipper, who I saw filling in for Bramall after the full-back chased Gooch across the field, who I saw drop into the centre back when Montsma strode out and who popped up in attacking moves too. Say what you want on social media, but if the midfield didn't have Bridcutt in today, my gut feeling is we don't get a draw. He's a top player and brings real calm to the midfield. He freed Edun up too, and he turned in a really solid performance, getting forward and backwards with consummate ease. Until Grant is back, Bridcutt, Edun and McGrandles is my midfield trio.

In the last ten minutes, we looked likely to go on and win the game. Anthony Scully came on as a sub, and his tenacity saw him keep a bad ball in on the right hand side, then snatch it away from his defender and lay it back for Poole. His delivery was snatched at first time by Rogers, drawing a wonderful save from Burge. After a first 60 minutes where we barely troubled the keeper, he'd now made tow great saves to stop us going ahead. If Sunderland deserved to win the first half, and they did, then we certainly deserved the second period.

It could have been worse for the home side on 86 minutes as Bramall put his foot to the floor and left Mclaughlin for dead in the middle of the park. The defender had to cynically trip our man from behind, drawing a yellow card. Whilst it was no more than a yellow, it was a tackle from a rattled and worried defender, one you might call a necessity.

The game ebbed and flowed in the final stages, but we could have snatched it just as the clock ticked over into injury time. The excellent Edun found Scully, he took his time before slotting the ball into the feet of Rogers, and his vicious effort was blocked with Burge committed to the dive.

It was an exciting end to the game, one in which I always felt we might concede, probably because it is what we do of late, but in the end it wasn't the case. Instead, we came back from a goal down against arguably the best squad in the division (albeit one decimated by injury too), and a game we probably should have won on the balance of second-half chances. What was nice is both keepers had saves to make, and although Palmer made more than Burge, I think our two second-half chances were better than the efforts they had from range. However, a draw was certainly a fair result.

We have proven, time and again, we can go away to the big clubs of the division and get a point, or more (Hull, Ipswich, Sunderland, Portsmouth). What we now have to do over four games is try to pick up two wins, hopefully against Oxford and Charlton, which would go some way to cemented our place in the top six. We're still in there, still fighting hard and hopefully, after what can only be described as a bloody horrible week, today's draw is the platform we can build upon and move forward. Only one team in the top ten won, and whilst we match the results of others, we'll stay where we are and ensure we are still in the mix for a Championship spot going into the final couple of matches.

Battered and Beaten: Oxford United 2-1 Imps
March 27, 2021

Last night, as the final whistle rang out around my living room, I turned the TV off and sat in silence.

I genuinely feel like I could have cried. That is how much this season has got to me. Every defeat has felt like a punch or a kick and it is made worse by the experts on Twitter. It's made worse by the blind optimism of some, claiming 'we can still do this', and then on the other hand by the usual suspects with their 'not good enough' rhetoric. It feels like they're talking about my family, passing their judgement when I feel like the only one who can see the truth.

Of course, that's not the case. They have opinions they have every right to express, as I do. Lincoln City is not my family, I just spend most of my waking life doing something related to them. The way I take defeat is probably usual, but it feels very unique for me. Honestly, after last night's game, I felt very alone.

This man could fall into a barrel of tenners and come out skint at the minute – Courtesy Graham Burrell

I could pick it over, ball by ball, assessing and commenting, but it almost feels wrong to do so. The fact is, Lincoln City are broken, Michael Appleton's exciting squad has been stretched to a point where a huge tear has appeared in the middle and last night, circumstances beyond our control meant we were a carcass going into battle. If we had three players called up for international duty, the game wouldn't have gone ahead. If a couple more had covid, the game wouldn't have gone ahead. Earlier this season, Grimsby postponed a game because of one covid case, and last year Bolton didn't fulfil a fixture because of player safety. I know those circumstances are different, and I wasn't complaining when Wimbledon had the same problems earlier in the season, but I do wonder if this had been a bog-standard Saturday match, not on Sky, if we might have gone to the FA given the covid stuff?

I don't know. What I do know is that anyone passing judgement on us right now needs to understand and accept the context of our recent demise. Yes, we have been poor, but what do you expect? We're a small squad, 40% down on last year's budget with our best central defender out, the captain missing 50% of our games and only completing 90 minutes once since his comeback, our leading scorer out, or number nine out, our marquee summer loan signing out, and our exciting Premier League capture from January out. Throw two covid cases in there too, our only other recognised forward and the other experienced central defender and what do we have? A team broken and battered, fighting on despite clearly being past the point of no return.

I looked at all the comment last night about how it wasn't good enough, how our passing was poor etc and it infuriated me. They were right, those people had called it right, but calling the game at all felt wrong. I used to have this old Mazda 323F, 1.5L, and it sat in a work car park packed with decent, more expensive cars. Mine cost £295 and it was a wreck, but sometimes we'd do little laps around the car park, seeing how fast our cars would go. The Mazda held its own alright, it wasn't the fastest, but for the money, it did well. One day, on the way to work, I got a puncture and had to put one of those Fisher-Price Noddy wheels on, you know the ones I mean? Guess what? It still had four wheels but it didn't go as fast or as smoothly as it had done before. Now, imagine you have four of those toy wheels on. The car is the same, it still drives, but you lose four key components and you cannot be expected to maintain performance.

It doesn't help when what I thought was a decent referee has a bit of a shocker either, does it?

Ok, let's go to the match, because I know I have to talk about it. We started brightly, but I expected that because Liam Bridcutt was in the team. When he is in, 90% of the time we play well, and although Scully's finish wasn't clean or concise, it was enough to give us a lead to defend. In recent months, when defending a lead, we have had Tom Hopper up top to run tirelessly, hold the ball up and take away the pressure, but we didn't have that last night and it showed. Scully gets goals, no doubt, but is he a lone nine? Not a chance and that meant our attacking prowess was weakened. Harry took time to get into the game, it was his first league start since December 9th. It meant we looked a little shaky after the goal, and Oxford are a decent side with players who can hurt you, and they did.

Mark Sykes and Brandon Barker both impressed and in fairness, a goal was coming from them as they began to pour forward. They should have had a free-kick in a good area when Shodipo was fouled cutting in from the right, but it wasn't given. Then, they should have had a penalty when Harry caught Rob Atkinson in the box, not given. At that point, I thought our luck was in. Two decisions went our way, Alex Palmer making good saves and a couple of defenders putting bodies on the line. At the other end, whenever we broke we looked dangerous without creating anything too clear cut, and I firmly believed we could make a game of it, even if we conceded.

When we did concede, it was a gut punch. Yeah, I get it, these things even themselves out and all that, but it shouldn't be like that. I'm sure Scott Oldham hasn't done it deliberately, but Matty Tylor has handled the ball in the area before teeing up their goal. It's a foul, that's the end of the discussion. If they had got the penalty, they might have missed it, but if we had also got the free-kick we would have still been winning the game. It's a huge error and all I want to believe is that it wasn't done to even things up. I suppose these things happen, but when your squad is broken into pieces and you get a lead that is crucial to a promotion push, you just want a bit of luck.

After 40 minutes, Liam Bridcutt went off with a hamstring injury and looks like he might be out for another couple of games. Call me a defeatist, but as far as I see it, that could be the end of our top six dreams. If we lose our captain, as well as all the other players, how can we function? My Mazda might have got around that car park with four toy wheels on, but take the petrol tank out and it's going nowhere.

That exasperated my anger and upset and I'm not sure I called the rest of the game clearly, I just sank deeper into wallowing self-pity. When Harry went through on their keeper and he was crudely taken out, I screamed for a red card. Okay, the keeper was the last man, but Harry was heading wide, should that matter? It is a deliberate attempt to stop a player with no thought of playing the ball. In fact, if it had been a defender, the keeper had been in the sticks and Harry had been straight at goal, the defender would have been the last man, so surely a keeper doing it with an unguarded goal behind him deserves a red? Scott Oldham doesn't do reds, I praised him for that before the game, now I've got a picture of him on my dartboard because I don't have anyone else to blame.

I didn't like the tackle on Harry just before half time either, another nasty late one, an Achilles' snapper if ever I saw one. Yeah, to the letter of the law it is yellow and only a fool would say it should be a red, but if you're going to stop a player cynically just drag him back, don't risk his safety with that sort of challenge. It looked snidey and a bit reckless. Maybe it was just me protecting my team in my mind, but those two incidents felt unsavoury.

After half time, our play fell apart and Oxford didn't need to be decent, which is good because they weren't. The referee continued in his inconsistent vein, booking Edun for the faintest of pull backs on their player, but then ignoring a worse infringement from Hanson on Harry, again, not long after. If one is a yellow ref, the other has to be, it shouldn't matter if you have already booked the player. There was another blatant handball in a move by Sykes which was missed, but then Scully offended in the same way and it was caught. I'm not saying those incidents changed the game, but they just poured more sand into the side of my scales marked 'injustice'.

Am I calling the game fairly? Maybe. Maybe I'm seeing it through the eyes of a hurt and disappointed child, the young lad who has seen his Dad dream of promotion for the last 40 years. My Dad rang me the other night, after one of the poorer defeats, and his voice was just so low and soft. 'I guess I won't see second-tier football again in my lifetime' he said, and it really upset me. He went to his first game as a really young kid in the early 60s, once watching us in the Second Division. The fact my Dad, a 68-year-old (or 69, I'm not sure), sounded like an upset boy, got to me. They are the eyes I'm seeing this through, not the ones of a fan wanting to be critical. Criticism isn't my go-to place when things fall apart. If things go bad in my life I don't lash out at those around me, I look for blame. Last night I looked for blame in a yellow shirt, or through the man with a whistle in his hand, or Covid, or whatever. I just don't want to blame the players and I won't.

They were to blame for the goal though, and that is even more galling. We could have drawn that game 1-1, if we'd played our football in our way with concentration and application, we take a point. Instead, Lewis Montsma plays a suicide ball to McGrandles and rightly gets panned for it. McGrandles got let off the hook a bit for being outmuscled and Oxford score. 2-1, probably the right score on the balance of chances, but a smack in the chops, a kick in the crotch and a spit in the eye for good measure. I wanted to scream at Montsma, I wanted to call McGrandles, but actually, neither had a bad game. I know you lot will be pulling them down on the player rater, but not many of our players actually had bad games last night. They did what they could, but it's square pegs in round holes, three trainer wheels on a four-wheeled car with a gaping hole in the exhaust and petrol tank. Were stuttering and I'm not going to start calling players under those circumstances.

That said, if Bridcutt is on the field, he makes that bad ball into a decent one and clears his lines. That's what he does.

We had chances after the goal. Harry got in down the left but shot with his right and saw a save. James Jones had a good chance for a header which he just nodded up into the air too. I'm not sure what has happened with Jones, he was really good earlier in the season, but since his lay-off, with covid, he has been a shadow of the player he was. Are there effects of Long Covid there? I hope not, I hope it is just form and nothing else, but the drop off has been remarkable. He isn't the only one, not by a long shot, and sadly because of the crippling circumstances we have to keep turning to players who are struggling.

The game just petered out after that. Oxford were happy to defend their lead, and rightly so. I saw some quality in them, but I can also see why they have been inconsistent this season. Sadly, my counterparts at Oxford won't be writing positives about us, they'll be asking how we got where we were, and if we'll stay in the top six. Actually, I saw a lot of 'experts' on social media last night, podcasts and bloggers covering League One, all questioning our form, that sort of thing. Nobody seemed to mention the injury-ravaged squad as part of the reasoning, it is just a cursory glance at results and comments of 'Lincoln have dropped off'.

Yeah, we have. We've dropped off for a reason and I'd ask you to take the time to acknowledge that. Same goes for our fans saying 'injuries aside' before saying it wasn't good enough etc. No, it wasn't good enough, but saying 'injuries aside' is like saying 'putting asides you ran out of milk and eggs, your cake is a disaster'. Would it have been a disaster with full ingredients? No. Would we have lost last night's game with Hopper, Grant, Walsh, Bridcutt (for 90 minutes), Johnson and Jackson in the side? I suspect not. So please, do not dismiss the situation around the club as 'no excuse', because it is a better one than blaming the referee, Michael Appleton or whatever else you hide behind when trying not to let the hurt and disappointment ruin your weekend.

As for me, my weekend is already ruined. I've watched another Lincoln performance that upsets me without anyone really to blame and that makes them all the harder to digest and process. Plus, I've got to go to Tesco in Cleethorpes now to choose new glasses, and if there's one thing I hate almost as much as feeling desolate and empty about my brave football team, it is Cleethorpes.

April

Comeback Kings: Imps 2-2 Blackpool
April 11, 2021

The Imps showed courage and resilience in the clash with Blackpool, coming from two goals down to secure an unlikely point.

On a lovely, sunny afternoon at the Bank, City enjoyed going into a game as firm underdogs. In the past few weeks, we've almost always been favourites to win our home matches, and almost always failed to do so. Blackpool are one of the division's in-form teams, with a 20-goal striker leading the line and they started the day above City. That certainly eased some of the pressure on the players as they lined up for kick off.

Bearing in mind we are still without our captain, leading scorer and number nine, the odds were firmly stacked against City. Joe Walsh returned to the squad, but not the starting XI, whilst Max Sanders got his first league start of the campaign in holding midfield. Brennan Johnson and Callum Morton both missed the defeat at Oxford, but both returned to the starting line-up, with Anthony Scully and Harry Anderson dropping back onto the bench. In defence, Adam Jackson also returned, with TJ Eyoma losing his place.

City started on the front foot, with a backpass to Blackpool keeper Chris Maxwell causing early problems. Callum Morton challenged for the ball and drew possibly the fastest booking of the season with under two minutes on the clock. Initially, the trio of McGrandles, Edun and Sanders looked to have the upper hand in midfield, and City enjoyed a lion's share of possession in the first quarter of an hour or so.

It was, sadly, possession without a purpose, and before long the visitors began to ease into the game. Just for Richard Cross (I saw the comment on MDL), I tipped them as contenders at the beginning of the season, and that is how they began to look. Instead of Jerry Yates being the dangerman, the lad they have from Everton, Ellis Simms, looked likely to score.

I saw lots of comments later in the day about our poor defending, but I thought we did very well for much of the first half. We lacked a spark in the final third, I don't think we had a shot on goal in the first 45, but we did look relatively solid at the back. I thought Montsma showed some nice touches at the back, and Adam Jackson seemed solid too. They had to be – this slick and organised Blackpool side often looked dangerous, with Sulley Kaikai one player I thought could turn the game on its head with his individual flair. He had a good chance from a free kick, a move partly of our making. We broke up field, but instead of being able to find the front three, we came backwards to start again, overplaying and losing the ball. That led to the free kick and whilst it might have been seen as playing out from the back, it wasn't, it was playing into the back from the front. Credit to Blackpool though, they throttled space up top and forced us into the error. Anyhow, Kaikai's free kick drew a decent save from Alex Palmer.

Our best chance of the half fell to McGrandles. He was fed in nicely by Morton, making a great run to enter the box, but rounding the keeper left him at a tight angle and he could only fire into the side netting. It was a half chance, but not one you expected us to score. A little later, Brennan Johnson ran across the area and couldn't find time or space to shoot, but other than that our attack looked toothless.

On the other hand, everytime the visitors went up they looked threatening. I felt we did a decent job of keeping them quiet, lots of hard work from the likes of Jackson and Montsma, as well as the improving Bramall and steady Poole, but the back four do still look shaky. When you consider Michael's skill is as a coach, and he hasn't had much time to actually coach given the schedule and then the EPC closure, it is no surprise the team are coming together slowly. We're building for the future with Bramall and Poole and both will be much better next year, not that they're poor now.

As has often been the case this season, City went behind through a seemingly poor goal on 37 minutes. I have a fundamental issue with the laws of the game which allowed this though. Blackpool played a ball forward with yates (I think) in an offside position. He was 100% offside, but the assistant referee now cannot put the flag up until he moves to the ball. However, his presence forced us to put the ball out, rather than just let the move run its course. How is the player therefore not interfering with play? His presence meant instead of a free kick, or calmly collecting the ball and playing on, we gave away a throw in a decent position. If the flag goes up the minute he steps offside, our lad leaves the ball and the threat goes.

I know there is opportunity to stop the goal after that, but the next phase of play, from the throw we shouldn't have had to concede, leads to a goal. Might I say, a well-taken and fully deserved goal, but a goal nonetheless? I don't buy the player down with a head injury argument either, I know some of our lads wanted play stopped, but there wasn't reason to in my opinion. Mind you, I don't buy into it being shocking defending either; poor maybe, but there wasn't a standout error which led to the goal.

That saw us through until half time, where the visitors held a justified lead. They'd been the better side, no doubt, they held the ball better, created more and looked the likeliest to win the game.

My halftime was made a little better by seeing the scenes from Grimsby. I don't wish relegation on anyone, but I've never really liked Stefan Payne and to see him headbutt his own player and get sent off whilst stood in the door of a portacabin just had me howling. When your luck is out, right?

I did feel like perhaps our luck was out early in the second half. Michael Appleton turned to his bench early, bringing on Joe Walsh and Harry Anderson with Sanders and Montsma the two withdrawn. That meant the Imps seemed to go 4-4-2, with Johnson joining Morton in attack, with Edun and McGrandles the midfield pairing. It resulted in us being a like-for-like match with the visitors as we attempted to restore parity.

Blackpool dealt what felt like a hammer blow just minutes into the second half. A ball forward from City seemed to result in Morton being bundled over, but the referee was having none of it, and as play came back at us, Kaikai was quickest to react. He strode through the gap where a holding midfielder might have stood, and confidently slotted past Palmer for 2-0. I don't think there was an error from us in the goal, it was a swift moment of football from the visitors, who I must say impressed me up to that point. At 2-0, I felt there was little way back for City.

The Tangerines then began to lay siege a little. City did get the odd attack, but when we went forward it looked like we'd need a moment of madness to let us in, whilst only dogged defending from red shirts prevented a massacre. It might have been different, had Maxwell not pulled off a super save from Jackson's header after Bramall's wicked delivery from wide left, but he did and we remained two goals down.

Jerry Yates had an effort cleared off the line by Jackson, who had a solid outing, and that would have ended to game as a contest, then the same player had another goalward bound effort blocked after Palmer saved from Simms. City were on the ropes, but sandwiched between those two moments was Michael Appleton's big play. For the first time in a Football League game, he used all five subs, bringing on James Jones, TJ Eyoma and Anthony Scully. Off went Adam Jackson, Tayo Edun and Morgan Rogers.

The change was probably made with one eye on Tuesday against MK Dons, a case of necessity over and above anything else, but City suddenly came to life. Within minutes of Yates' second effort being blocked, the game came alive. Harry Anderson found space to cross on the right, Maxwell tried to punch clear only for the ball to fall to leading scorer (from open play) Anthony Scully, who volleyed home from a tight angle. From nowhere, City were back in it.

What I like about Harry, making his 200th appearance for the Imps, is he will go and look for the ball, whereas the likes of Johnson and Rogers want it played to them. I'm not criticising either loanee, both have been superb at times this season, but I do wonder if our attack looks a little less potent when we have both of them wanting the ball given to them. With Harry, and to a degree Anthony Scully, there is perhaps a little less flair, but a little more forcing themselves into the game. Is our best approach to play one of Johnson or Rogers with one of Scully or Anderson? Maybe.

The goal brought a little confidence back to the Imps' play but it was still a huge surprise to me when we bagged the leveller. Bramall and Scully worked a little space on the left flank and the latter's lovely through ball was seized upon by Johnson in a perfect example of what happens when we can get the ball to him in the right area. He finished with aplomb to level the scores and ultimately give the Imps what might have seemed like an unlikely draw. The stats on the BBC claim we had seven shots to their 17, three on target to their seven, so you could argue it was even a little undeserved, certainly if you were a Blackpool fan.

In the final moments, the visitors felt they had a shout for a penalty. I'm not convinced, either way. I think the anger would have been felt more significantly had it been given than if it wasn't, but there might have been just cause for a handball. I wasn't utterly convinced by the official if I'm honest, he let a few tough tackles from either side go and was happy for Morton to be knocked about like a rag doll, but his decisions didn't really impact the game. Yes, there was a foul in the build up to their goal, but it was a soft one only highlighted by this writer because I'm a Lincoln fan, not a Blackpool one.

I was delighted with the result and I see this as the building block of our last push towards the top six. Very few Imps fans will have had this down as anything other than a defeat, I bet even the fountain of unsubstantiated optimism Cornell would have been happy with a draw. At 2-0 down with 20 minutes left, there seemed no way back, and that in itself is a great motivator for the players. We showed huge character to keep plugging away when things weren't working for us, and we showed a degree of adaptability to change it up at half time, take the blow of a goal on the chin and still stay in with a chance.

I do wonder now if the accepted 'first XI', the one you all pick on the Fan Hub app prior to the game, is actually due for a change. I like Rogers, when he's good he's very good, but without being harsh he was anonymous yesterday. If we go 4-3-3 I feel we must look to have one of Scully or Anderson on one flank to force the issue, to push for turnovers instead of expecting the football to flow. I saw a couple of arguments as to why it didn't work in the first half yesterday, with one train of thought being that Rogers and Johnson didn't work to get on the ball. Another argument was the midfield didn't work to get the ball to them. I can see the justification for both, and someone sent me a video of the McGrandles' chance which demonstrated perfectly what they bring off the ball.

Morton broke in the left channel and had two defenders to deal with. When the move started, McGrandles was in the centre circle and the attacker providing support, Johnson, drifted wide. As Morton looks up, Johnson wants the ball switched big, across the area, out to the right flank. You can see him point as he runs out there, but there's a huge gap developing in the middle of the park for McGrandles, who motors through and gets the chance. Now, was that naïve from Johnson, expecting the ball played big? Not for me, no. He was drawing the defender away from the centre of the pitch, creating the space for McGrandles.

It was our only real chance of the first half, but it did show why Johnson, and Rogers at times, are so useful. Writing them off on social media is easy and sloppy, but we also have to accept that sometimes, having two players of their ilk, flair and speed doesn't always work. Blackpool were organised at the back, their centre-halves were strong, well-positioned and aware. They were happy to be deep enough to thwart our attacks too, cutting out the danger of our pace. That's why Rogers was frozen out and that's why the change, bringing Anderson and Scully on, paid dividends.

Horses for courses, I think they say.

I also want to point to the return of Joe Walsh as being big for the side. I thought Montsma had a decent first 45, and both Jackson and Walsh did well too. To have all three back and ready is going to be huge, especially with dips in form. It was encouraging to see TJ come off the bench too. Michael is going to have more players at his disposal over the coming weeks and he'll need that with a punishing schedule ahead.

That's it from me for now. I started this at 6pm last night and it's not 10.45am and sadly, I'm still full of cold. I'm going to rest, recuperate and have some time believing once again. You see, in my weekly conversation with Pete I said that I felt anything less than four points from these two matches would be a blow to the Imps play-off hopes. I said that something against Blackpool, anything, would be a stopper on the poor form. Personally, I think we did that against Sunderland; I don't count the Oxford result because we had so many players out there was only ever going to be one outcome. I've seen enough in the last three fixtures to convince me we can hang on to sixth, and with Hopper, Bridcutt and Grant back in the squad, I'd be happy to back us against anyone in this division, anywhere, at any time.

As for Blackpool, they'll be in the mix too. Something tells me we might not have seen the last of Neil Critchley's side, and with nine goals across our two matches, neutrals will be delighted with that outcome! Remember, they're depleted by injury too, so both of these sides could be very different prospects when the 46 games are completed.

Also, in an odd quirk of fate, we have take four points from two games against them, but only been leading for two minutes across the 180!

Double Century For Imps Wing Wizard
April 11, 2021

Harry Anderson's appearance from the bench yesterday saw him rack up his 200th appearance for the club.

24-year-old Anderson has been around since the days of the National League and is in his third spell with City. He initially joined on loan early in the 2016/17 campaign, returning to Peterborough before joining for a second time on loan in the run-in. That summer, he made his final move to the imps, joining on the same day as Michael Bostwick for a combined fee which was thought to break the previous club record.

Since then, the likeable right-winger has appeared 200 times, scoring 32 times including five this season. He is one of only a couple of Imps to appear at three different levels at Sincil Bank, as well as scoring in three different divisions. The last player to achieve that feat was John McGinley, back in the late eighties. However, McGinley achieved his feat whilst the club were on the slide, making Harry Anderson unique in Imps' circles as the only player to play in, and score in three different divisions starting at the lowest point and heading up.

The 200th outing has been a while coming for Harry. In the 22 matches we have played in 2021, injury has restricted him to just six outings, but he finally made it yesterday and celebrated with an assist of sorts. His cross was palmed out by Chris Maxwell, only for Anthony Scully to seize on it and give us a lifeline to get back into the game. The stats people might not consider it an assist, but anyone watching will. Officially, according to Wyscout at least, he has 18 assists during his Imps career, but has had a hand in far more goals than that.

202

Is he a legend? He is probably the most decorated Imps player with two league titles and the EFL Trophy triumph, and I doubt very much any other player has appeared for the Imps whilst top of three different divisions, so he certainly has to be up there. The fascinating aspect of his career is his tender age — he has played more professional matches than Adam Jackson, for instance, and yet is still young and learning. This season, he started well, won the second Stacey West Player of the Month award and has proven himself to be more than comfortable in League One.

Everyone connected with the site would like to congratulate him on his achievement and obviously, raise a glass to the next century!

Four-midable City back in the hunt: Imps 4-0 MK Dons
April 13, 2021

City's stuttering assault on Championship football got a kickstart this evening, as MK Dons were brushed aside in a sensational second half of football at Sincil Bank.

I boldly said the other day that four points from the two home matches would be a signal to me that we were genuine play-off contenders, and that is the return we have got. Not only that, but results went our way and we're back up in fourth, looking to maybe even reel in one of the runaway top three. It would be a big ask, but little 'ol Lincoln City are back in the race and holding our heads high.

Mind you, for the first 45 minutes, I didn't just forget we were chasing a top-six place, I almost forgot what it meant to love football. MK Dons football is lauded when it comes off, but we found a way to stop it, resulting in a solid, but uninspiring first-half of football. MK certainly like to have possession, and I wouldn't go as far as to say it has no purpose, but it can be rather laboured if they are unable to find the spaces. Sadly, for the neutral at least, they were unable to find the spaces.

The Imps made two changes to the side which started the game against Blackpool. Predictably, Joe Walsh started in place of Lewis Montsma, whilst Anthony Scully's goal and assist earned him a start at the expense of Max Sanders.

As early as the second minute, City showed some attacking intent. Cohen Bramall, perhaps freed by the experience of Walsh alongside him, got in on the overlap using his pace and earned a corner. The delivery was poor though and the chance gone.

MK's best effort of the half came on seven minutes, the tricky Sorinola getting a good cross into Grigg, who headed down into the turf and over the bar. Referee Bobby Madley caught a deflection in the move which led to a corner, but little came of it.

On ten minutes Bramall's pace was causing problems again. This time he left veteran Dean Lewington in his wake, before fizzing a ball into the area. Morton looked to have been bundled over in the build-up, but to MK's credit they defended well through Darling. The resulting throw in caught them by surprise and Johnson whipped a wicked ball across the six-yard box, but Morton was blocked off and Scully not alert enough to capitalise.

Regan Poole picked up the game's first booking, justifiably, with a foul on Sorinola, before Brennan Johnson picked up the second, and perhaps should have been sent off. He penalised for a soft foul on 20 minutes and petulantly kicked the ball away, resulting in a yellow card. Within seconds, he ploughed into Ethan Laird and should, by rights, have been sent off. Instead, Madley did his best to keep it at 11v11, and whilst we would have been fuming if it had been against us, it was a let off.

If City were going to score in the first half, it would come from an unforced error more than likely. On the half hour mark, MK let us in yet again, lax passing resulting in a chance for Rogers, who saw his effort deflected up and over the bar. The corner, as was seemingly the case all first half, came to nothing.

MK rarely threatened Alex Palmer's goal, a Sorinola header which I think was meant to be on target ended up being a nice ball out to the flank, and a free kick dropped into Palmer's arms, but that was about it. However, by the time half time arrived, City really should have had two.

On 39 minutes, a moment of class from Edun saw him shift the ball past a couple of players before finding Bramall. His delivery was decent, landing at the feet of Regan Poole, who saw his effort blocked on the line. As the ball bounced out, Bramall lay prone on the turf after a late challenge by Laird, who was booked.

On the stroke of halftime, City were given another route into the game. Johnson seized on the error, but he tried to feed Morton in the channel and got it all wrong, with the striker having to work to keep the ball in. He recycled the chance, finding Poole, but his effort was poor and easily blocked.

Despite the handful of chances, the half couldn't be described as entertaining, which was as much down to the amount of possession out of key areas as the Imps wastefulness when gifted a chance. Anthony Scully, whom Michael Appleton wanted to see more of from the off, barely had a touch, and our best opportunities were created by MK Dons' back three, rather than our own endeavours. Despite me trying to make the report as interesting as possible, neither keeper had a save to make the whole half.

If the first half brought little joy for fans and neutrals alike, then the second half was the polar opposite. Within just a few minutes, City had sounded the excitement klaxon. A wonderful ball from Bramall found Scully, who should probably have done better than he did.

The Imps didn't have to rue the missed chance for long. Rogers pressured McEachran as MK played out from the back, winning the ball confidently. He then switched a lovely ball through the defence, splitting them like a warm knife through soft cheese, leaving Johnson to lift a lofted finish over the keeper.

With that, the Dons imploded, and their possession-based football began to look fruitless and fragile. On 52 minutes the Imps launched an attack in numbers. From the right Scully found Morton, he laid it off to Rogers who in turn laid it off to Johnson. He strode in from the angle on the right-hand side and finished with aplomb for 2-0. Within seven second half minutes, the game had gone from sterile to teeming with life.

The visitors made a double change, Dan Harvie one of the players coming on for McEachran who was probably at fault partly for the first goal. Within seconds, the sub was at fault himself. Johnson was the creator, of sorts, getting away down the right and lifting a teasing cross into the area. Harvie had hold of Rogers and as the Manchester City man tried to wriggle free, the infringement was spotted. Bobby Madley had no hesitation in pointing to the spot.

William Robertson scored a six-minute hat-trick for City in 1929 (thanks Gary Parle for that), with Clive Ford doing the same in 1967. Had the first penalty from Johnson been allowed to stand, his hattrick would have stood at around nine minutes. There was never any doubt as to who was getting the chance from 12-yards, he had the ball on the spot ready and finished with aplomb. Scully had timed his run badly though, and encroached in the area, so a retake was ordered. That puts Johnson's hattrick at eleven minutes, but a hattrick it was as he stroked the ball home with consummate coolness.

After that City went into preparation mode for the weekend's encounter with Bristol Rovers. TJ Eyoma came on for Adam Jackson, but little changed. MK still had their possession, but rarely looked like putting the ball in the net. Instead, it was the Imps looking to improve the goal difference, with a decent chance on 66 minutes.

Morton, who ploughed something of a lone furrow up top at times, chased a ball into a blind alley and saw it cleared. It fell to Tayo Edun, who fed Morton in, for a cross to be nodded behind for a corner. For the first time all evening, the corner even caused panic, dropping invitingly on the edge of the six-yard box before being hacked clear. The visitors were bloodied and on the ropes, whilst City grew in confidence.

Johnson's night ended on 66 minutes. It could have ended on 20 minutes, MK will wish it had, but it will be the eleven minutes after half time which will be talked about most. He got rapturous applause, even from an empty stadium, and Harry Anderson moved onto 201 outings.

On 71 minutes the game was put to bed, tucked in and kissed goodnight. MK's defence once again folded like a bad poker hand, with Rogers coming away with the ball. He looked to open his legs but was scythed down as he moved towards goal. From the left-hand channel, 20-yards out, the Imps had a free-kick and whilst a right-footer should have been over it, Bramall stepped up instead. Showing frankly awesome technique, he curled it left-footed around the wall and against the post, with the rebound bouncing off the keeper's back and in. Regan Poole slammed it home from close range to make sure, so the dubious goals panel at least have something in their inbox tomorrow.

After that, the game petered out. MK kept passing sideways and looking for a chance, we brought Walsh and Bramall off for Montsma and Jones to save some legs. Not that it mattered, the game was over and done with long before Mr Madley blew on his whistle to finally put MK out of their misery, in a game that their fan Jonathan Harries described as their 'worst performance of the season', Delighted it came against us, thank you for that.

It will be hard to look beyond Johnson for Man of the Match, for obvious reasons, but McGrandles, Edun, Bramall and Walsh all turned in strong performances as well. I'm such a huge Tayo fan, he's grown into a fine player this season, so confident in possession and with great close control. I think Bramall's contribution was excellent this evening, and I've no doubt having Joe Walsh just to his right will help him from a defensive point of view. In terms of an attacking threat, he turns average balls into good ones with his electric pace. He's so fast, he could outrun my car over the first 20 yards or so, and as he works on his final ball, hell go from an exciting prospect to a first-team favourite.

We've been here before, a big win, a confident performance and lots of hope, but isn't it nice to finally have something to feel great about. Blackpool and Portsmouth drew, Sunderland and Ipswich lost, and we won. Have we put our poor form behind us, and are we the team finding our feet at just the right time? Possibly, we'll see, but what I do know is anyone saying that we need to ride these next few matches out, that it is all about next season, is missing what is right in front of their nose. We might be in a play-off battle now, but rest assured we are in the battle, we are well-placed to be involved once again and if we get players back and can keep the form going, who knows?

The season ain't over yet chaps (and ladies), hold on to your hats.

Brennan Johnson Hat Trick Facts
Fastest in the EFL since the war (joint with Clive Ford)
First since Lee Angol at Braintree in 2016/17
First at Sincil Bank since Jonny Margetts against North Ferriby in 2016/17
First in the EFL since Ashley Grimes, away at Stockport, 2010/11
First at Sincil Bank in the league since Jamie Forrester v Rochdale, 2006/07
First in the third tier at Sincil Bank since John Thomas v Port Vale 83/84

Triumph in the Battle Royale – Bristol Rovers 0-1 Imps
April 17, 2021

City's play-off dreams took another step towards becoming reality this afternoon with a hard-fought win against a tough and tenacious Bristol Rovers side.

The Imps were once again hit by injuries, both Adam Jackson and Joe Walsh missing out through injury. Such as been the Imps luck this season that as we take a step forward in welcoming Walsh back, we take two back losing both centre-halves. It meant Eyoma and Montsma partnered in the middle of the back four, with Bramall and Poole at full-back. Conor McGrandles picked up the armband, joining Bridcutt, Grant, Anderson, Jackson and Hopper (and I'm sure there are more) in captaining the side at some point during the campaign. I believe it's my turn next week.

The supposition was this would be a straightforward game for the Imps. Joey Barton's pre-match press conference saw him telling people he'd turned over during our 4-0 win against MK Dons to see how football should be played, then he described our game plan of four years ago as our current approach. They seemed ill-prepared in terms of knowledge, but like Steve Evans it did a great job of deflecting the attention away from his players, who had four points from two matches and a real chance of doing a job on us with two centre-halves, our captain, vice-captain and number nine all out.

That certainly looked like being the case as early as the second minute, when the first corner of the game saw Alfie Kilgour send a looping header over our defence and off the bar, although McGrandles appeared to be on the line in attendance had it dipped anymore. It was an early let-off for the Imps in an opening ten minutes which might have had you questioning which side were gunning for promotion.

Luke McCormick was the next to have a pop, Poole and McGrandles getting in a bit of a mix up which allowed the Chelsea man a shot which he hit wildly over. Just past the ten-minute mark, the lively Johan Ayunga won a ball in the air, turned smartly and also fired over. I liked Ayunga, I hadn't seen much of him before the game, but if he were our Tom Hopper back up, I think we'd be happy. He was big, strong, used his body well and perhaps just lacks the finesse in the area that some Michael Appleton focused training might bring.

It had been a pretty average opening quarter of an hour for City, but with our first serious chance, we got the goal we needed so desperately. We've slipped behind early in too many games this season, and when we chased games, we make errors. In fact, one of the few I recall us scoring first in and losing was against Bristol Rovers earlier in the season, so it was nice to get ahead. It was a typical City goal too, starting with Regan Poole. He knocked a little ball into Rogers who in turn found Scully. He nudged it out wide right to Johnson, then made his way into the area as Brennan did what he does, jinxing in past a defender before teeing up Scully for the finish. Arguably, it was the first nice passage of play from the Imps, and it brought the vital goal.

It didn't deter the home side though, and the troublesome McCormick tested his sights once again on 25 minutes. Poole headed clear a free-kick from the left, and the midfielder shot wide. It was Rovers again knocking on the door on the half-hour mark, McGrandles losing out on the edge of the area and committing a foul. Luckily, the free-kick was driven straight into the wall.

On 35 minutes, what had been a bit of a lacklustre encounter exploded into life without reason. What seemed like an innocent tussle between Upson and Johnson saw the latter held down by the former, seemingly with an arm across the neck. Some have said a punch was thrown, I didn't see that, but I did see a melee immediately after, which suggests Upson's actions angered some. Tayo Edun, never one to back down when a teammate is in trouble, got into Upson and was grabbed around the throat for his troubles. I have seen people claiming Upson eye-gouged Johnson, others thinking it was something and nothing all at once.

Once things had calmed down (at least on the pitch), Upson was sent off, whilst Johnson and Edun were booked. Personally, if the red card had gone against us, I might have been disappointed. I've watched it back a couple of times and whilst it looks unsavoury it didn't have the serious intent of, say, a challenge in the last minute of the game which got a booking. Still, Will Finnie flashed the second red card in games involving us this season, and again it went against the opposition. I'm not committing, the iFollow feed is not entirely conclusive, but I will say that Finnie is not a man who flashes red cards like an M5 speed camera flashes BMW drivers (one got me once actually, but I was in a Vectra).

The game broke down a bit after that, Bristol Rovers clearly wanted to get to halftime to regroup, whilst we didn't press the advantage as some might have liked. The only real half chance fell to Luke Leahy, another player who really caught the eye, but his effort was saved with ease by Palmer.

After the whistle, it seemed a few individuals were keen to have words after the red card. Oddly, David Kerslake headed for Joey Barton. Now, I didn't watch the touchline and I don't know what was said, but having spoken to Kers I don't think he is the confrontational type. I did notice as we waited for the whistle, at least three of our bench were up and waiting to go to get in their manager's ear. In the end, as things began to heat up, a Rovers staff member got in front of Kers and stopped him from getting a response from Barton. I guess when this incident draws more words than any Lincoln chance other than the goal, it tells you everything about the half

The home side shook it up in the second half, bringing on Brandon Hanlan who has previously troubled us with both them and Gillingham, as they pushed for the points they so desperately needed. City had to work phenomenally hard to stay in the game at times, but work hard we did. As in the first half, the opening chance fell to the Gas, Rogers losing the ball on the break and Zain Westbrooke finding himself with half a chance, which Palmer held on to with relative ease once again.

Edun began to dice with death a little, throwing a ball away in frustration at one point, which I'm not sure the ref spotted. Michael Appleton did, he hooked the midfielder for James Jones, who came on and did add some composure to the side. Edun is a fiery player, fiercely protective of his teammates and not one to rile, but he has been close to a red on a couple of occasions this season (Ipswich away I seem to think), so perhaps was best spending a bit of time watching on.

I can't say we looked like we had more men on the field, and that is a testament to the Bristol player's work rate. They did match us across the park and only really allowed us to play football on rare occasions. However, when you consider the players we had out injured, you have to doff your caps to our lads too. This was very much a patched-up City going at it with a wounded animal, and doing well. Of course, 11v11 would have been different, but even so, City's players didn't let the guard drop once. I thought both Montsma and Eyoma were excellent, dealing with the very physical threat of Ayunga and Hanlan.

City should have scored just before the hour mark. A lovely sweeping move, the sort we have become accustomed to this season, saw Johnson and Rogers links up on the left. The former looked like making it 2-0, but Jaakkola pulled off a super stop, parrying the ball away. It fell to Callum Morton, who blasted over the bar from a tight angle. It felt like it might be a key moment, a big missed chance against a side fighting hard for their survival, but it did not come to pass.

The home side were back on the attack shortly after. Cohen Bramall fired a free-kick into the wall after Rogers was fouled, and then Rovers delivered one of their own into the area not long after. It did cause a panic, and eventually, the ball was headed over, but as it was, Poole slammed into the post trying to get back and keep it out. It sounded awful, looked uncomfortable and contributed to the seven minutes of stoppage time we had to endure later in the game.

Still, Poole played on, but City did introduce Max Sanders for Scully. I felt Sanders settled in nicely and we looked likely to add a second. One incident, on 72 minutes, saw us cause trouble from a corner. Eyoma was involved in winning the ball and Morton got a good effort at goal, which Jaakkola blocked for another corner. It was a golden chance once again to make it two, but certainly not the last we'd have.

There was little in terms of real chances, but the game had a frenetic, hurried feel to it. Bristol Rovers began to go back to front very quickly, and for a while City looked penned in, but the rear-guard held firm, and as we moved towards the final minutes, we really should have put the game beyond doubt. Blue and white shirts were so committed forward that every clearance could have brought a chance, and just before the 90, Morgan Rogers wasted a great opportunity. City broke, two on one, and all he had to do was square to an unmarked Harry Anderson, six yards out with an open goal. Instead, he fired high and wide. I could feel the anger in Anderson, especially as a second after the assistant flashed seven minutes of injury time. Was that the chance we'd rue missing?

The Gas piled forward, not getting anything clear cut, but causing plenty of panic, but the final goal of the game should have come with 96 on the clock. Again, City broke and this time it was Morton who was through, one on one with Jaakkola. The big Finn made himself a formidable figure to beat, and a tired Morton lashed a wild ball over, when a delicate finish across the keeper might have been better. Easy for me to say though, sat here in the sunshine in the Wolds, judging a player who had worked tirelessly for 96 minutes without any real joy at all.

There was still time for controversy, with City once again trying to break at pace with seconds left. As we did, McGrandles and Harries had a bit of a wrestle, which saw both spoken to by Will Finnie. From that moment City got a throw-in, and when the ball came back to McGrandles, he was poleaxed by a nasty challenge from Jack Baldwin. It looked like a frustrated, last-ditch tackle by a player resigned to his team's fate, although Leahy apparently wandered off telling McGrandles 'you dive because you're shit'. Nice.

That was the end of the game and as the curtain came down on a real battle, Joey Barton made his way across to the Imps dugout and made sure he shook everyone's hand, including Kers. It was a break in kayfabe as they say in the wrestling world, a moment when the curtain comes down and the actors drop their charade. Barton is the villain of the piece with Imps' fans, but actually, he is a caricature of a football manager, painted by himself to fool you into not looking at his team. Who spoke about their misfiring strikers in the build-up to the game? Nobody, because we were laughing at him 'naively' watching the Champions League. Still, his side were in this game right up until the end, so never write him off as a bad manager, just a 'heel' playing a role for the cameras. I bet when he goes home at night, him and Mrs Barton give to charity and play music low as to not annoy the neighbours. I bet he even orders sushi and tips the delivery boy whether the order is right or wrong. Still, I'm afraid both him and our friends at Gas Cast will be visiting Scunthorpe next season.

Forgetting Bristol Rovers, what does this mean for the Imps? A draw between Charlton and Ipswich means we are in a stronger position than we were when things kicked off, whilst Blackpool beating Sunderland hauls the Mackems closer to us once again. Portsmouth were beaten at MK Dons by a Scott Fraser penalty, so one assumes the home side took the lead then kept the ball for the remaining hour, but it did us a favour too. Our spot in the top six is not cemented, but teams are running out of games, and points to catch us. A win for Hull, after going one-nil down, does seem to confirm them and Posh in the Championship next season, but after a horrible time from Valentine's to Easter, we're back in the mix. Seven points from three games is a super return and just a single point at Burton would still leave things wonderfully poised heading into the final five. Yes, we have Posh, Charlton and Hull to play, but my gut tells me a win at Charlton and four or six elsewhere is going to be enough.

That is where we are, but how we got there today was by fighting hard. It wasn't a great performance, only on occasion did we show the class we have in the side. What we did do was contest every ball, and players, like Poole, put their body on the line. We blocked, we tackled and we chased every single ball. I likened it to the Eastleigh away game in my earlier article, mainly because it was sunny and I had a shed to paint, but by the end of the game, the similarities were stronger. A hard-fought 1-0 away win against a team who made it difficult for us has boosted our chances of promotion. Like Michael and Rob said in the commentary, if we end up in the same way we did five years ago, then I'm sure everyone will be happy.

If that happens, and we go into the post-season play-offs with Walsh, Jackson, Bridcutt, Hopper and Grant back, then there is still every chance that come the middle of August, we could be visiting Sheffield United, Nottingham Forest and Middlesbrough as equals, despite many writing us off over Easter.

Football, it's a funny old game, as someone once said. I doubt Joey Barton and Bristol Rovers are laughing after losing a game they turned into a real battle, but the smiles right here in the Wolds are real and genuine. Bring on Burton Albion.

Advantage City in play-off hunt: Burton Albion 0-1 Imps
April 20, 2021

Michael Appleton's excellent Imps made it three wins from three as the play-off push got firmly back on track with a fourth successive win against Burton Albion.

With other results going our way, it would take a monumental collapse for City to not make the top six now, and with players coming back and confidence seemingly high, few would want to face this side in the end-of-season lottery. We don't want to get ahead of ourselves, but a fine performance with half of the team still missing underlines the potential this squad has, be it this season or the next.

The Imps were forced into a change, with Cohen Bramall succumbing to an injury he picked up against MK Dons. James Jones came into midfield, with the versatile Tayo Edun dropping into the left-back slot. Regan Poole, who clattered a post in the win against Bristol Rovers, passed a late fitness test. Burton boasted several ex-Imps, or players with Imps connections. Michael Bostwick and Danny Rowe both started for them, veterans of our EFL Trophy and League Two triumphs, whilst Michael Mancienne also started after spending time training with the club earlier in the year.

The home side started very brightly, with Ryan Edwards one player who caught my eye. Their midfield three certainly looked comfortable in possession, and with the long throw on Tom Hamer that had a real threat from anywhere in range of the 18-yard box. The best chance of the opening ten minutes or so fell to the Imps with Brennan Johnson surging forward and driving a shot at goal, which was deflected wide. Sadly, two early Imps corners came to nothing, one under hit and the other given too much power.

As the game wore on, the Imps began to settle and play some lovely possession football. Just before the quarter hour mark, Morgan Rogers fed the ball out wide to Scully, who in turn pulled it back to the edge of the area for McGrandles to strike. His effort was blocked and went out for a corner, which came to little.

Burton certainly began to go from back to front quickly, with Hemmings doing plenty of running but with little reward. They still looked dangerous on the break though, and Alex Palmer had to be smart of dive at the feet of the onrushing Akins on 18 minutes.

With Rogers and Johnson both a constant thorn in Burton's side, it didn't come as a huge surprise when City scored. The goal came from a sustained spell of pressure, Scully seizing on the ball in the area, shifting his balance and shooting at the goal of Ben Garratt. The former Crewe man didn't get a chance to save as the Brewers blocked it for a corner. The first corner was taken quickly, with Edun reacting to win another corner.

This time, City made the home team pay. Another quick corner found Edun on the edge of the area, and his weighted ball evaded Hayden Carter, with TJ Eyoma arriving with a superb diving header to give the Imps the lead. It was Eyoma's first goal of the season, his first in the professional game and it gave a lively City side something to defend.

Defending wasn't seemingly a problem for the Imps, with Eyoma and Montsma both looking assured against the Brewers' attack. Poole and Edun played a part too, with very few scary moments to report on after the goal. Edwards did lash over from range on 28 minutes, but it wasn't any real danger.

City could have extended the lead as the half wore on. On 34 minutes, a good spell of passing saw City go from side to side, forward and backwards, before Poole's smart ball found Rogers just around the centre circle. He turned and spread the ball to Edun, revelling in his role at left back. The former Fulham man pulled the ball back to Johnson, who saw his shot once again blocked by a dogged Burton back line.

The Brewers suffered a further blow just before half time, when Mancienne pulled up with what appeared to be a hamstring injury. It was a huge blow for them to deal with, the former Forest man was labelled a key player for them during Match Day live by Jack from Brewers TV and it had been easy to see why. Terry Taylor, a former Grimsby loanee, replaced him.

City could have bagged just before half time, when Johnson broke away at pace down the left. He had acres of space, and rolled a gentle ball to Jones. He shifted to one side and struck an effort with his right foot, which once again was deflected over for a corner. The half time lead looked very good in the context of other results, particularly at Swindon, where Brett Pitman's double gave them a surprise 3-1 win against play-off hopefuls Portsmouth.

Burton upped the ante in the second period, looking to play more football, and with the likes of Danny Rowe looking lively there was a few worrying periods for the Imps. Within minutes of the restart, Bostwick hit a cross which was cleared by City, with Carter volleying back at goal. His effort was blocked, but two minutes later Sean Clare's was not. He picked up a clearance from the long throw and blasted wide of Alex Palmer's goal.

The Brewers were invigorated, if not entirely convincing, and Taylor perhaps summed that up on 51 minutes. They broke after a bit of Imps possession, but his eventual effort sliced horribly off his booted and looped away, amounting to nothing.

City's first chance came eight minutes after the restart. Edun found space on the left, as he did all evening, and checked back before looking for Jones. He appeared to be running onto the ball, but instead the impressive Poole came across from full back and neatly struck an effort at Garratt, which the keeper saved. Both Edun and Poole had excellent evenings for the Imps, with the latter looking better and better with each passing encounter.

Burton weren't done though, not by a long shot. As the booming voice of manager Jimmy Floyd Hasselbaink rang out around the empty stadium, Rowe probed down the right-hand flank. They worked the ball across to Akins, a player I've always thought should was dangerous, but after cutting inside he could only curl over the top of the goal to Palmer's left.

John Brayford was the next to have an effort as Burton applied more pressure. It was never heart in mouth stuff, but they were knocking on the door. In truth, it was an engrossing encounter, because for all their huffing and puffing, it was almost City who blew their house down on 57 minutes.

Two efforts in the space of 60 seconds should have brought a goal. The first came after a lovely ball from Eyoma found Edun, who in turn fed in Johnson who saw his shot blocked. The Imps recycled the move quickly on the left-hand side, with Jones eventually trying his luck, only for it to bounce wide of Garratt's goal.

The game ebbed and flowed and for a while, that flow was towards the Burton goal. Morton had a tough time trying to evade the clutches of Bostwick, literally at times, but he did superbly well under pressure to knock a ball out to Scully on 60 minutes. Scully found Morton in space with the return ball, but as seemed par for the course, his shot was blocked.

How many times have I written 'shot blocked'? Many, and I think that was a testament to the dogged resilience of the Burton backline, and the creative influences City had up top. One thing I have not mentioned is referee Josh Smith, a man who I thought had a calm and collected game. there were a few tackles that a more whistle-happy man might have gone for, but Smith lets the game flow. I Like him.

Burton made a couple of changes trying to affect the game, but Rowe and Akins came off, both of whom I felt had done well. Ryan Broom and Joe Powell came on, two players I would be happy to have in our squad, and to be fair the patterns of play didn't change a huge amount. It didn't swing the game back in their favour either, as the Imps had another good chance. This time, Montsma's delicious ball found Edun, again, in space, again, and he in turn created a chance for a teammate. For me, Edun was the Man of the Match, and this time Jones was the benefactor, his shot held by Garratt.

Almost immediately City were back, Rogers surging forward with that electric turn of pace he has, but lashing an effort wide. It was a good spell for City, but good spells come into play because good players do good things. I've spoken plenty about Edun, but McGrandles was often at the heart of moves. He has been superb in recent weeks and he played what we now term 'the Bridcutt role', an Achilles Hell of sorts, and he did so with aplomb.

Another player who can play the Bridcutt role is Jorge Grant, out since we lost 4-3 at Plymouth, and much to everyone's joy at Lincoln, he came on with 20 minutes to go. To see the vice-captain joint leading scorer sprint on was delightful, although watching him get caught minutes later in a confrontation with Sean Clare was not. It seemed there might be bad blood between him and Clare, as it wouldn't be the last time they had words.

The change ushered in a spell for Burton, who might have felt they should have had a penalty. Powell looked to bring a loose ball under control in the area, and was seemingly felled by an arm in the back from Montsma. It would have been soft, but as Rob Makepeace said in commentary, we have seen them given. Shortly after, Kane Hemmings held the ball up well in the corner, and although the resulting cross was cleared, Clare picked up the loose ball, but his shot was a daisy cutter and saved by Palmer.

Burton were back in the ascendency and for a while, it looked like they may get back into the game. Harry Anderson came on for Morgan Rogers as City looked to wind down the clock and take the sting out of the game. Often, I don't think that has happened this season, but there was definitely a feeling that Michael was using his subs wisely. The last real chance of the game came on 84 minutes, Clare again picking up a cleared cross and again testing Palmer, but a test that wasn't that hard for a keeper with two arms and hands to pass. The big stopper held the ball and with it, he held Burton's chances of a point too.

Sure, there was action after that. Grant was felled late by sub Fondop-Talum, drawing the first booking of the game. As Grant went down, Clare blasted the ball into his chest, causing our man to get up and have a few words, and he was again pulled away. Any history there? Maybe, or maybe Clare was just on Grant from the start. It was a yellow for the foul, but the referee sensibly dealt with the little incident after.

Remy Howarth came on for Johnson as the clock wound down some more, before a frustrated Taylor stopped a Lincoln counter by pulling back Scully for another booking, but that was more or less your lot. The three minutes of injury time was branded 'embarrassing' by their manager, something we all heard on the iFollow feed, but it was about right. 30 seconds per sub, no injuries in the half and no goals, where was he getting any more from?

As is customary with so few games left, the final whistle was greeted by me quickly flicking over to the BBC Sports website for the latest results. Doncaster: lost. Oxford: lost. Ipswich: Lost. Blackpool: lost. All supposed play-off contenders, all beaten. Could things have gone any better? Probably not, this was a big night for us, make no mistake.

I like it when Lincoln win, obviously, but I like it when we win and have played well. This wasn't a game in which we rode our luck, nor one in which people will say we played badly but still won. We had a certain verve in attack which I felt made us dangerous, whilst that makeshift pairing of Montsma and Eyoma actually looks very good. Eyoma is a really special young man, controlled and strong with great passing and application. It almost makes me wish he'd played in the middle more when we had Walsh out in the spell before Easter, because he looks like a player with 200 career games under his belt. Poole has settled on the right, and putting Tayo at left back was like welcoming back a key player. He fitted in with ease and as I said, was Man of the Match for me.

Nobody had a bad game, and whilst Burton might not have the league position to suggest this was a challenge, it was a challenge. They are completely different to the side we hammered 5-1, they work the ball well and have play-off form since Hasselbaink went in. Make no mistake at all, this was a super result and dare I say, the best of our three recent wins. Yes, better than 4-0 against MK Dons, because we played better, we created more and we had more to deal with.

We go into a huge match this weekend with a seven-point cushion into the top six, with 15 points to play for. However, the team we have the seven-point advantage over only have nine to play for. Below them, Portsmouth do have a game in hand, but seven points is still the gap. You would think one more win and one draw from the final matches secures a play-off spot, but what about that last automatic? s it a dream? At the time of writing, Peterborough are seven points ahead of us, but we have a game in hand. Win that, it's four points and we still have to go there. Could we?

Probably not, but I'll tell you this. To come through the spell before Easter, the injuries, the Covid and the loss of form and still be sitting here with five games to go talking about the outside chance of automatic promotion is amazing. Remember the saying: form is temporary, class is permanent and Lincoln City have certainly got class.

Now, did someone say some Tigers needed taming?

No Shame in Defeat: Imps 1-2 Hull City
April 25, 2021

Yesterday's 2-1 defeat at home against Hull City was an odd one for me personally, and I think that's where I have to start.

You know full well had that been a normal afternoon, with 10,000 in the Bank, the atmosphere would have been utter madness. I think the result might well have been different too, but these are 'Covid times' we live in meaning an empty stadium. Sadly, Covid also ruled me out of action yesterday, albeit in job form.

I missed Match Day Live, something that was very tough as I have done every one with Sam since the start of the season. By the time it went on air, I was in bed and I emerged only at 3pm to watch the game, before scurrying back to my pit afterwards. There was no report, no reflection, I didn't even change the player rater on the site. Hell, you know things are not good when I don't even think about writing on here.

I've woken up this morning still a little groggy, but certainly better. However, I'm not going to go on a blow-by-blow account of the game, it's too late when most proper outlets already have their full report out there. Instead, I'll pick up on a few key points and my overall observations of the game. I haven't been on social media since the final whistle so I don't know if these thoughts align with those of others, but then I suppose that's the point of the site, right? You don't want me to just rehash what everyone else says.

Personally, I was proud of our team yesterday, Hull were the most organised side we have come up against and I felt we deserved to win the game. The early goal was really disappointing and if I'm being harsh, I thought it might have been defended better. Magennis isn't a good striker (he's not the best at Hull, let alone in League One) and maybe Montsma could have come and met the ball a little quicker when it was delivered. Maybe we could have stopped the cross too, but hats off to the Hull players it was a decent delivery and Magennis did finish well. I was worried a bit at that stage, Hull looked bang up for it, and it felt a bit like the Peterborough game earlier in the season.

After that, we got a grip on the encounter and certainly enjoyed more possession, but without any really telling play. I don't think we were bad, not at all, but I do think they knew how to stop us. We went from side to side, we went down the flanks and back, but did we really create anything of note? Conor McGrandles, a shining light in recent weeks, miskicked our best opportunity. That's no slur by the way, he was excellent again and has a knack of arriving in the box at just the right time. The point is Hull kept us quiet, but they didn't really threatened much themselves. It felt to me as if they thought one goal was enough, and were happy to shut up shop.

There was a bit of talk about George Honeyman too, a player who certainly wound up our supporters watching on iFollow. There's a train of thought he could have been sent off, but not for me. Remember MK Dons a few weeks ago, when Brennan Johnson could have been sent off and wasn't? This was the same sort of thing, only it went for the opponent not our lad. I didn't think Sam Purkiss was a poor ref, he let things go which others might have punished, but if it goes in our favour then we'd be raving about him. Yes, Callum Morton got a battering at times, and maybe Magennis's boot was high for the goal, but flip the teams around, put us as the scorers and their centre froward as the one getting roughed up a bit and nobody complains. As for Honeyman, he was trying to referee the game, as Bridcutt does when he is on. It is what influential players do, and we might not like it against us, but I don't have any complaints. My only gripe was the shoulder challenge with Edun, never a free kick, not that it came to anything.

Right before half time we could, and should have made it 1-1, but again I'm not going to moan about the chance being missed, I thought we kept to our game plan and got the opportunity our play deserved. It didn't go in, but we are consistent and approach the game the same every time.

At half time, whilst I knocked back the paracetamol and a pint of water, I pondered on the fact Hull would be promoted if the score stayed the same. We were, in my opinion, matching a side destined to play second-tier football next season, probably with much the same squad as they have now. Remember, that is without arguably our two strongest centre backs, without our captain and our number nine, and with a semi-fit Jorge Grant making his first start.

It is easy to say 'if', but if we had kept all those players fit and functioning, then in my eyes, yesterday is simply a title decider between two teams already on the verge of promotion. You can talk to me about too many home defeats all you want, but had this team not been ravaged by injury, we don't lose to Fleetwood and Rochdale at home, we don't draw with Swindon and I'm almost certain we beat Accrington too. I know it is an 'if', but genuinely if your first thought after yesterday's game is one of negativity, then you astound me.

Hull didn't seem to want it in the second half, and we certainly did. For 20 minutes, we controlled the flow of the game, putting pressure on but getting no luck. It was a bit like the three little pigs and the wolf, we huffed and we puffed but the house wasn't coming down. Then, on 65 minutes, Lewis Montsma did what he was once known for doing. One corner, finally delivered perfectly after weeks of trying, saw him sneak in with a tremendous volley to level proceedings.

I have heard after the match Michael Appleton revealed there is a lot of interest in Lewis and I'm both surprised and not at the same time. Since being out with Covid I don't think he's been as good as he was, and sometimes defensively he is a little naïve, but there's no doubt he is a talent too. He strolls out of defence with ease and when his sixty-yard balls hit the mark, he's a joy to watch. I get a sense of him getting back on form after a tough winter, and with both Walsh and Jackson struggling, that's great news.

I have to take my hat off to him and TJ, forced together in a makeshift defence that few thought would be effective, I felt both were strong yesterday. Yes, I thought Lewis could do better for the goal, but on the whole both kept Magennis quiet, and when you consider the other players around that attack, I felt they did remarkably well. Same goes for Tayo and Regan Poole.

I'll come on to Regan in a second, but after the goal I felt there was only one winner, the team in red and white (not that you could tell who was who on iFollow, what a woeful kit clash that was). The problem was we didn't create anything clear cut, but neither did Hull. I watched the whole game, and I never noticed Gavin Whyte and Dan Crowley come on for Hull, which tells you how effective they were. Hull's squad is laden with good players, a Championship squad in the making, and yet even with the chances, I didn't feel we looked out of our depth. We took Edun and McGrandles off, both MoM candidates, which should have affected our performance. It didn't.

Look, I know football is about goals and I know we didn't threatened as much as we should have done, but Michael used the game to bring some faces back as much as he made tactical changes to win it. Grant starting, Bridcutt and Hopper coming on, these were moments that weren't intended to change the game, but rather the rest of the season. It was still makeshift to a degree, shuffling Tayo from left back to midfield, then taking him off too, just continually having to remodel to get the injured players a few minutes. This, against a full-strength Hull City, and we still looked more likely to win the game.

A word on Tayo: brilliant. That's the word. I'm so impressed by him, his flexibility, he versatility and his dogged determination and strength. He's a proper little terrier and that charge on Honeyman was, in my opinion, fair. It demonstrated Tayo's strength, his raw aggression, but the boy can play a bit too. I know in the past, fans have asked if one of this squad might be Lincoln's first £1m player, and I don't think anyone suggested Tayo might be, but if he keeps developing as he is now, he's going to be hot property in no time at all.

I suppose we then move on to the penalty. I was disappointed to see Poole labelled things such as 'brainless', and called a 'fucking idiot' on social media. That pains me because I think he had a decent game, marshalling Wilks well and helping us control much of the play. It was a penalty, 100%, and it wasn't the best of challenges, but Tom Eaves used his body well to make it look much worse than it was. I find it disappointing that a player can be lambasted so openly on social media without any real reason. Footballers give penalties away, it happens, and to see Poole hammered as he was really did disappoint me. I think he's getting better and better, he's been with us for just 85 days, played 18 matches and doesn't look out of place. Give him a pre-season with Michael where we can work on shape, patterns of play and the like without game after game after game to cloud things, and I think he'll be huge for us.

I even rated out character after the goal, Johnson hitting the post and City pressing hard for a leveller. I didn't feel Hull would give up a winning position twice, but at least the heads didn't drop and we kept on pushing and pressing hard. Sure, we got beat, but there is no shame in losing to the Champions when, on the balance of play, a draw might have been a fair result.

The win meant Hull were promoted and got to celebrate that on the pitch at our place, which makes the pandemic a bit of a saving grace, doesn't it? Their fans don't get a moment of glory at our ground, which I would have found tough. I know plenty have congratulated Hull and over our three matches, I think they are the best team we have played, but I won't be lavishing too much praise on them. I am chuffed for the fans of theirs that I know, but I wouldn't have stayed to clap if we'd been in the ground. I didn't when Accrington were crowned champions in 2017/18, it's just me. I'm not bitter, I can acknowledge a decent team and an achievement, but I support Lincoln City and if we're not the ones celebrating, I'll give it a miss!

Who knows, maybe this isn't the same game you watched. Maybe you think we didn't create enough, or maybe you think another home defeat is a sign of weakness, but the whole 'home and away' dynamic has changed this season. I just look at 42 games, or 46 by the end of the season, and judge us on that. If we're top six at that stage, then we've done well, no matter where we won or lost along the way.

As for the play-offs, we're still looking good for those and I firmly feel we'll be a big prospect for anyone at all. If Hopps, Bridcutt and Grant keep their rehabilitation going, and hopefully one of Jackson or Walsh get back too, then we'll be as strong as anyone else. Imagine, 46 games, City are top six and that would be at half-strength at times. Nobody, not Blackpool, not Sunderland, Portsmouth or Charlton would want to face a Lincoln City side at full strength, not a chance.

The Championship dream is still alive. We might have to do it via the top six and Wembley, but don't rule out getting a chance to see Hull at Sincil Bank next season, and with 10,000 in the ground to enjoy it, what an occasion it will be. Just as long as I don't have to have another bloody jab that makes me feel like I'm knocking on heaven's door.

Edging Closer: Shrewsbury Town 0-1 Imps
April 27, 2021

There are many types of football match, and as a fan you'll know what I mean when I say that.

There are games you are worried about, but your team do well in (Pompey away). There are those that look tough, and end up being bloody tough (Pompey at home). There are ones you can't call (Posh at home), ones that have 0-0 written all over them from the day the fixtures come out (Fleetwood away). Some surprise you (MK Dons home), amaze you (Burton at home), disappoint you (Doncaster home) and leave you distraught (Rochdale at home). Tonight, up and down the country, we saw them all. Rochdale fans, doubtless elated at the prospect of the great escape, left shattered in injury time. Pompey fans, broken at half time, joyous with minutes left, damaged at the end. Grimsby fans, crying, broken-hearted and ultimately inconsolable. There, for the grace of God, go I. Or rather, go us.

Then, there are matches where you break longstanding club records for the number of away wins in a season. They're quite rare, don't ya know.

I knew what the Imps' game would be like this evening, from when I woke up until I write this now. I called it on Match Day Live, exactly as it went off. A cagey affair, one of few clear cut chances, that we'd edge 1-0 and bag that record. I'm not claiming to be Nostradamus, although I do have a great record on MDL this season, but you could see what was going to happen from kick-off. We needed a win, but not a win at all costs, and that's crucial. If we'd drawn tonight, no biggie, we're still in the best position for the play-offs, meaning we'd go for a result, but wouldn't take risks in doing so. Shrewsbury needed nothing, other than pride, but I suspected they'd want a result for their gaffer. Of all our rivals, they've been most affected by Covid and if that hadn't happened, I think they'd have been tucked in with Accrington and Ipswich in that 'just outside the play-offs' area.

Also, with our returning players, I expected a rhythm and flow in the early stages, then some nice game management and maybe a more fractured second period as we made changes and swapped things about a bit. I didn't say that out loud on MDL, but it was the vision of the game I had in my head.

Not that you could tell that in the first 20 minutes. we came out of the blocks quicker than normal and looked to be well placed to hand out a three or four-goal thrashing. There was space in behind for us to exploit, and with our first choice midfield and maybe one player shy of our first choice attack, we had a fluidity and sharpness about our play which reminded me very much of November. I've said it a million times if I've said it once: this squad, fully fit for 46 games, wins the league. Honestly, it's that simple. In fact, even this squad with no more than two players out injured at any time, as long as Grant and Bridcutt play, wins the league. Bold, maybe so, but I defy anyone to disagree with me when you think about what might have been, even with injuries, Covid and all that guff.

That's what we looked like in the first part of the game. Johnson glided around the pitch like an adult playing kids football, a Dad in the Under 16s messing around at training, faster and sharper than the players he was up against. Jorge Grant was back to being Jorge Grant, twisting, turning and pinging balls effortlessly around the field. Bridcutt was there taking the ball from Palmer, pivoting the side, making the game look easy with a drop of the shoulder, and stealing yards by thinking one step ahead. Edun, McGrandles and Rogers just did what they have been doing, whilst Montsma and Eyoma's partnership grows stronger by the day.

Our goal came as no surprise at all: a dead set-piece was recycled cleverly with swift football before the two key components of our season combined, Bridcutt crossed for Grant's header, to throw one shoe, containing one foot, into the play-off race. There was something poetic and satisfying about those two combining, although the goal was as much about the play before their involvement as anything. Bridcutt, the captain and talisman, landing the ball on his vice-captain and leading scorer's head to settle early nerves. Wonderful stuff, so much so that Fe (forced to watch the game on the big screen as I opted to relax on the sofa for the game) cheered as I did. She didn't even know the permutations for the play-offs.

Shrewsbury played their role well early on, the patsy merely there to make up the narrative as the Imps' unlikely season gets an extended run into May. Ollie Norwood got an early booking, rightly so, for a challenge on Grant and generally, I thought the scorer was unfairly targeted on a few occasions. It felt much like we'd go on and score three or four, maybe even with them not having a full set of players by the end. Settle in Fe, this is going to get tasty.

It didn't though, not really. When Johnson came off, hopefully as a precaution, we lost part of the vajazzle (yes, I know what that means) that glistened whenever we previously tried to penetrate. Shrewsbury reverted to three central defenders, either three or five at the back depending on where you place your full backs in the scheme of things, and closed the doors in front of us. That is our kryptonite, 3-5-2, the formation we can struggle against if implemented right. We've seen teams do it badly, I think possibly even Shrewsbury in the EFL Trophy, but generally against a back three, we struggle to prise them open. Morton had to work harder for his corn, but got far less reward than his endeavour deserved.

At the other end, the home side came alive, and Josh Vela could have easily sent his side in leading 2-1, hitting the post with one effort and firing wide when it seemed easy to hit the target just before half time. The balance of play swung against us and although many would say we deserved to lead at the break, that would only tell half the story. In truth, Shrewsbury's management rescued the half in terms of play, and although we did edge it, I did feel a little pleased when the half time whistle blew. We hadn't been under the cosh, but with Johnson going off and Salop switching it around, it began to resemble the game I expected, not the one the first 20 minutes hinted at.

A word of referee Ollie Yates: average. He did try to let the game flow, but I thought he missed a couple of tasty tackles, for both sides. Another ref might have flashed a few cards, and whilst I admire one who keeps them in his pocket, poor Callum Morton must have been wondering what he needed to do to get a free kick. I fear if a ginger limb had come off, Yates might have seen it as part of the game and waved it on. He didn't get any big calls wrong, there weren't really any big calls to make in a bruising but relatively fair encounter, but I'd hate to see Yates in a game that required a big call or two. I thought he got worse in the second half, swayed by a home crowd that wasn't there, but maybe it's my red and white tinted glasses. We've had some good refs in the past and whilst this one wasn't bad, I couldn't mark him down as 'good' either. So, back to the start of the 198-word paragraph and one word on the ref: average. Why didn't I just leave it there, eh?

The home side certainly had the best of the opening exchanges of the second half, as we made another change. Liam Brdicutt got his 45 minutes, and Tom Hopper came on for another 45 too. It meant a reshuffle for City, one I don't think we were comfortable with at first. it showed too, as Salop edged further into the game. They were a little quicker to balls in the middle of the park for a period, but I didn't ever feel as if we'd concede. I thought the back four, untouched by the formation swap, looked comfortable all evening. Regan Poole shrugged off the disappointment of giving the penalty away on Saturday to deliver a solid outing, and neither Eyoma nor Montsma looked to have a problem with anything Shrewsbury had. In truth, it was a damp squib of a second half, chances were at a premium with very little for either team to shout about.

Salop did get a couple of free-kicks which barely troubled Palmer, Whilst a few passages of play later in the half saw us knock on the door, but with all the conviction of a Jehovah's Witness's child sent out reluctantly to canvass doorsteps. Sure, we knocked, but there was never going to be an answer and both parties were pretty happy with that. Literally, I'm three paragraphs in on the second period and that has more or less summed it up. It wasn't poor, not by a long shot, both teams played some decent football at a good pace, but there wasn't quite the edge that you'd expect from the game. I found myself spending as much time scrolling through the BBC website looking at the latest scores, a veritable soap opera of football that thrilled me because it didn't really bother me. After all, if we win games, nobody stops us going up, so with us winning and in no real danger of throwing it away, I felt comfortable looking elsewhere for saga and intrigue.

Grimsby were relegated after going 2-1 up at Exeter, having a man sent off and losing 3-2. Honestly, I don't take a lot of pleasure in it because I have time for Luke Waterfall, Sam Habergham and Matt Green, but I won't shed a tear for the club closest geographically to my house. Scunthorpe hammered away at a

Newport side containing Aaron Lewis, could still go down as well, although it would have to be some set of results that made that happen.

In our league, goals kept flying in and yet over at the New Meadow, I never felt like it would happen to us. I did quite like the look of the boy Salop brought on, Harry Chapman, and if anyone was going to score for them he was, but he didn't. Towards the end we looked like we might get another too, Morgan Rogers came to life in the last 15 and threatened to bag another worldie as he did against Rochdale and Ipswich. He hasn't always impressed fans with his rather languid style, but his capture was incredibly important in the winter window and if we do make the play-offs, which we will, none of the teams we face will be happy trying to stop him. He's a player who could explode at any minute, who might be quiet for ten, but only needs a yard and a partial sight of goal to turn a game on its head. I like him, can we have him back next season please Manchester City? You won't play him and we promise to look after him. Cheers.

What plusses do we take from tonight? Obviously, the result, especially as those goals kept going in around the grounds. Accrington and Crewe did us (and Sunderland, Oxford and Blackpool) a favour with late goals to damage Charlton and Pompey's hopes. Sunderland should make the play-offs, but they're in horrible form (no wins in seven), look shaky at the back, and I wouldn't mind facing them. Blackpool are still a side I'd not be comfortable facing, but we're unbeaten in three against them. Whichever of the other sides manage not to throw away sixth place wouldn't scare me either. We're the side in form and another win tonight underlines that.

Getting those injured bodies back is massive too. 45 for Hopper and Bridcutt suggests they'll be ready for 60 or 90 on Saturday, but don't expect them to be risked. We're in a unique position now of needing one point, or other results, to 100% secure our spot in the top six, then you plan. Do we go hell for leather in the last three games, risk injury, but keep the level right up there? Do we shuffle the pack, lose momentum but have a fitter, leaner squad? I've seen both approaches fail: in 2004/05 we secured the play-offs early, but then went three without a win as we stumbled into the semi-finals, starting the likes of Aron Wilford and Ritchie Hanlon and resting key players – did it backfire? We were lacklustre against Macclesfield over two legs and could have beaten Southend in the final. In 2006/07, we were the side out of form and were beaten by Bristol Rovers despite having barely been out of the top three all season. In 2017/18, injuries and squad depth left us short against Exeter at a crucial time. You only know the right way after the play-off final. If you go up, it was the right way to do it. If you don't, you got it wrong. Probably.

The thing is, I trust Michael Appleton and the staff to get it right, because I don't see anything they got wrong at all this season. I don't think he'll risk the form, nor will he risk the players, but he'll manage the three games sensibly. We're getting to a point where the squad looks more or less complete, and if Joe Walsh comes back this weekend, then bar maybe one face, we're full strength. Have we been in that position at all this season? Maybe on a handful of occasions. It's frightening to think that we let the top two slip from our grasp, but as we now head into a play off campaign (all being well), we've rescued the season and now look as good as we did at any other point. Tonight proved it, we won a game against a decent side without any real threat after we took the lead. That's not to say Shrewsbury didn't maybe deserve a point, perhaps they did, but they didn't get one. We saw the game out, managed it well and always posed a danger, the third 1-0 away win in a row. On Saturday, we deserved a point against the Champions-elect, another huge positive.

In fact, since Easter, all I've seen are positives. Players coming back, results ground out, results in games we've dominated, massive tests of character (2-0 down against Blackpool) and a return to what I believe is the 'norm' under Michael Appleton, a well-honed, tactically aware side willing to fight and scrap, but easy on the eye as they do. Operation Championship is still very much alive and kicking, so strap in folks, it's going to be an interesting two weeks for this football club, and hopefully an engrossing and exciting month.

May

Robbed City Confirm Play-Off Spot: Peterborough 3-3 Imps
May 2, 2021

Due to the social media blackout, there was nothing from the Stacey West online yesterday.

That was probably for the best to be honest, because for a couple of hours my judgement and clarity were clouded by a refereeing decision so bad, it can be mention in the same breath as George Cain's interpretation of the offside rule in 2005. There is so much to talk about from yesterday's game, but the main talking point happen five minutes into five minutes of injury time at the end of a game Lincoln City should have won.

I'm not unhappy at missing out on automatic promotion; we didn't finish outside the top two because of John Busby's woefully bad split-second choice in the final minute of the game. We finished outside the top two because we suffered horrible injuries through the season and lost with half a squad at Oxford, plus those home matches against Rochdale and Fleetwood. John Busby might have cost you and I a little excitement going into Tuesday's clash at Charlton, but he didn't cost us a Championship place and, being brutal (and this pains me) Peterborough didn't go up because of it either. They went up because they have been consistent in winning matches, three more than us over the course of this season so far.

That's not to say he didn't cost us three points against Posh yesterday, he did. 100%. Without his awful choice, we win the game 3-2. Do we go on and beat Charlton and Wimbledon? Maybe, maybe not. Do Doncaster subsequently beat Posh next weekend? Maybe, maybe not. If those results happen now, we still cannot say John Busby cost us, because things may have been different. That said, it doesn't mean I wasn't raging with injustice and anger throughout the early part of yesterday evening. On my personal Twitter account I kept seeing the replay and every time I did, I got angrier. To relax, Fe and I chose a comedy on Netflix, Thunder Force, which turned out to be as funny as finding a dead baby owl in your garden, twice, which only worsened my mood. It's only now, in the rather brisk Sunday morning sun, I can be truly objective.

Ok, from the top: City played some brilliant football, from starts to 65 minutes. We came out of the traps hungry for it, and this on what I considered to be a weaker side. No McGrandles or Edun, which given their form of late was a big, big call. With Walsh, Jackson and Johnson all out, Lincoln City went to a future Championship side with (arguably) five first-team players out of the squad. In came Harry Anderson against his old club (as I suggested on the radio last night) and Cohen Bramall at left-back. Of course, the two most vital players in our functioning side, Liam Bridcutt and Jorge Grant, both started.

I've got to say it and I don't care if you think I'm blowing smoke up his arse, but Liam Bridcutt is a class above. He's just so calm, when he plays well, we play well. He exudes confidence on the ball and he organises so well. He's a Championship-quality midfielder, even into his thirties, and with him in the side I genuinely believe we can beat anybody. With Grant looking back on top form too, it was prime Appleton-Lincoln, playing neat passing, holding on to the ball and probing away. Peterborough looked a little shell-shocked in the opening exchanges, struggling to create anything really meaningful, and it was the Imps who took the deserved lead.

I was delighted Harry Anderson was involved. It's been tough for him, post-Covid, and whilst we all talk about Jones and Montsma losing a little form, Harry has seemingly lost what was a nailed-on starting place in the side as a result of his injury and spell out. On a truly rotten pitch, his tenacity and skill saw Scully sneak in unmarked and head home from six yards out. There will be serious questions asked by Peterborough's defender, or there would if it mattered, as to how Scully found the space. If they want the answer, I have it – he's a clever player. He makes the right runs in the box, the right decisions when on form. How many times has he snuck in like that? He did it for the season's opening goal and he did it again yesterday.

Instead of spurring Posh on, we kept the pressure up. I cannot enthuse enough about our performance yesterday, for me it was the best of the season. Peterborough had very little to cheer and never really looked like scoring against us. We put bodies on the lines whenever it was asked, with TJ Eyoma in particular on super form. In fact, the highlights do not show it, but it was his solid, certain tackle that led to Anderson's cross and Scully's goal. With Bridcutt in front of the back four, the potent attacking force of Clarke-Harris, Szmodics, Brown and Dembele looked unnervingly quiet to me.

Before half time we were in dreamland, studying those permutations carefully. Brennan Johnson usually wins our penalties, but as he say out it was up to Morgan Rogers. I imagine Nathan Thompson will have had enough of the Imps this season, he's given two penalties away in as many games, and been sent off. He went down a little easily under Rogers' challenge and Busby waved play-on, correctly, leaving Rogers to streak free. The defender clumsily got back to his feet, fouled Johnson, and Grant stepped up to add another to his tally. 2-0 City, and the chanting outside London Road stopped.

At this stage, I'm going to praise John Busby, because so far I've done everything but. I thought he let the game flow well for 90 minutes, yes he let a few fouls go but there was a real pace to proceedings that would have had a neutral purring. He could have given a foul against Rogers in the run up to the penalty, some would, be he just let it go. I genuinely wonder if, after giving that, someone got in his ear about it being soft, because his eagerness to level things up and hour later was appalling. The issue is, Rogers was fouled, it was a penalty and, as you may have gleaned, Szmodics was not.

It was a tense half time for me because, for the first time since March, I actually did believe we might be back in with a shout of automatic promotion. I made my peace with the play-offs, acknowledged what a huge achievement it was, only to have two goals make me wonder once again. As my mate Chris said to me after Tuesday's result, it is the hope that kills you. That, and John Busby's eager whistle.

Into the second half and for 20 minutes, City were just as good as the first 45. That's not to say dominant, Peterborough have good players and always looked dangerous even if that didn't manifest itself in many clear-cut chances. Instead, we got the third of the game, and it might just be one of the best of the season. It started with Eyoma, his ball out from the back was dummied by Scully to allow Bramall the space to run onto. He pulled it back for Grant, who found Scully. The former West Ham man then produced a finish of such utter class that, had we been there, it would have been talked about in the same breath as Charlie Adam against Grimsby. It was exquisite, a curling effort from the edge of the box which even had me silent for a second as I pondered whether he had actually pulled it off. So often this season, we have tried the spectacular and in Scully's case, he hasn't always got the execution right. My goodness, he was certainly bang on yesterday, giving the Imps a 3-0 lead. Unassailable? Yes, without a little helping hand.

City had played with clarity and purpose, making a very good Posh side look ordinary and pedestrian. Jonson Clarke-Harris was named League One Player of the Season earlier in the week, but a little Irish lad we got from West Brom would have been the player scouts were scribbling about. His endeavour, combined with the tireless hard work of Hopper and the magical boots of teenager Morgan Rogers gave us a real attacking purpose. Grant and Anderson were superb, the full backs were both solid and we blocked everything the home side had, with Montsma and Eyoma looking like 9/10's every bloody week now. All of this pivoted around Liam Bridcutt, the heartbeat of the team, the foundation upon which the side is built. We need him in the team and just after the hour mark, with the score 3-0, he went off the field, conserved for any possible play-off matches. It was the right choice at the time, it was the right choice with hindsight, but it changed the complexion of the game.

Within a minute, Peterborough levelled. They made their own change too, it would be remiss to say 'we drew because Bridcutt came off. They brought on Ethan Hamilton, a former Man Utd youngster who has played against us for both Southend and Bolton, and his driving run led to a cross for Dembele to sneak in and make it 3-1. No complaints, a good goal from a good attacking team.

I think John Busby's error has perhaps made some fans miss the fact we could have been 4-1 up not long after. Posh committed players forward, looking for the goals to send them up, and that allowed us to break at will. Rogers, creative and full of ideas all game, broke away in the left channel and found Tom Hopper. Hopper has had a good season, he had a solid game yesterday, but he will be watching his miss through his fingers, just as Busby will be watching his error. Hopps took his time, steadied himself and with all of the goal to shoot at from eight yards out, fired over. That chance kills the game. That chance leaves us on tenterhooks for one more week. That goal, wasn't a goal, it was a miss.

After that the game was just utterly barmy, going from one end to the other. Posh hit the bar, and began to put more and more pressure on us. Their second goal had a real troke of luck about it. They got a free kick on the edge of the area, the right decision, and instead of blocking the effort the wall deflected it horribly past Palmer and into the net. 3-2, with plenty of time left for them to get the leveller.

I thought our play got a bit panicky, Posh had the wind in their sails and were desperate to get the leveller. That said, if we played ninety minutes, plus five stoppages, in fair and equal conditions with fair and equal decisions, City win the game. I do say things like 'these things even themselves out all season', and they do. We have had penalties which have been soft (not quite that soft though), and if this happened in our game earlier in the season, then we wouldn't be quite as bitter about it. I thought we killed the game a little towards the end, managing to block and cut out their threat whilst maybe not quite hitting our levels when Bridcutt was on the field. Still, with thirty seconds of play left, a ball into our area brought the moment I keep alluding to.

I don't need to tell you what has happened, but I will, Szmodics has tried to turn with the ball in the box and with his back to goal, failing to control the ball properly, he bumps into Scully and goes down. Scully has done nothing wrong, if anything it is him fouled. Busy has a great position and instantly points to the spot, no hesitation. This, from a referee who had been cautious with his free-kicks and who had let the game flow, but he pointed to the spot in a moment that left me incredulous. How on earth is it a penalty? I did see across social media fans of other clubs baffled, and rightly so. Still, it is what it is, Clarke-Harris scored and we were left in the play-offs.

Imagine, getting to this stage of the season and believing the League One play-offs are the consolation prize. They're not, a season is 46 games long, not one minute of added time in a crucial game. It was in our hands at other stages of the season and circumstances contrived to see us fall away. In recent weeks, we have battled back bravely, and yesterday put a rather sour twist on a wonderful run of form.

Here's the take away story for you – on successive Saturdays, Lincoln City have matched teams heading into the Championship. Yesterday, all things being equal, we win 3-2 at Peterborough with three of the five players I shouted as possible Player of the Season out of the side. We have been tremendous at times, never more so than the first 65 minutes at London Road yesterday. This team is far better than any Lincoln

City team I have ever had the pleasure of watching, and whilst the play-offs might be a tough route to take (given how we have a record of six failures from six attempts), it is a gift that few fans expected to be handed back at the start of September.

If Peterborough had taken a three-goal lead yesterday, and we'd come back to draw 3-3 with Scully's goal the winner, we'd be purring about our achievements, about how we have secured the play-offs when it looked likely we'd fall out of them at Easter. That's how we should be looking at it, not soaking up the blind injustice of an awful decision that didn't even get a mention in the BBC write up.

We now have two warm-up matches in my eyes, two games to keep giving Grant and Bridcutt 60/70 minutes, two matches to ease Joe Walsh back in (hopefully), two matches to ensure that when the 46-game season finishes and the play-offs start, that for a third time this season one of the Championship promotion places is sealed in a game featuring Lincoln City, only this time I don't want to be watching the celebrations of other teams. Come the end of May, I want to be at Wembley, watching us celebrate promotion for real. If we play like we did for 65 minutes yesterday, I've no doubt we will be.

Why John Busby's Bad Decision Should Be Forgotten
May 4, 2021

I know, I'm carrying it on myself, but I've been pondering on John Busby's decision that has robbed us of our slim automatic promotion chances, and I just wanted to get something out there defending him.

Yes, you heard it right. I'm the man who is on Huxtable's back before a ball has been kicked, who shivers at the name Stockbridge even if it doesn't apply to Seb, and who still occasionally wakes up furious with Ben Toner for his woeful handling of our FA Trophy semi-final against York City. Mind you, at least he waved that penalty away three times before giving it, John Busby didn't hesitate, and Saturday's was far easier to call.

Since the weekend I have seen plenty about the standard of officiating in our division, with shouts of it not being good enough, of refs bottling big decisions and the like, but on reflection, I don't think the referees we have had have been too bad. I think it is important to remember that when a referee has a good game, nobody notices him. When he has a bad game, he gets called out, but I'll go on record as saying in the 180 odd minutes John Busby has refereed Imps' games this season, he's had a split second that was woeful, and barely raised a moan from me the rest of the time.

Then consider the likes of Kevin Johnson, Josh Smith, Will Finnie, Bobby Madley, Declan Bourne, the list goes on. Can you tell me the games they officiated? No. You know why? Because they all had good outings. Madley, Smith and Finnie in recent weeks have been great, and all try to let the game flow and keep it 11v11. It's really important to remain grounded when criticising referees because one mistake is under the microscope.

It is perhaps wise to consider this: in a typical game, a referee makes around 245 decisions (unless George Honeyman is playing, because he seems to make quite a few on behalf of the officials). Assuming that Busby made that many at the weekend, how many did he get wrong that you noticed? Two? Four? Sure, the penalty was a big one, but he made that decision with the aid of a dive, some appealing players who knew it wasn't a foul and what seemed like pressure coming from the home bench (remember Ferguson's little tantrum halfway through the second half? A lot changed after that). Maybe, John Busby got 1% of his decisions wrong. Tops. Bear in mind, a so-called 'wrong decision' in your eyes might be the right one from the opposition side of things, so perhaps he got fewer than 0.5% of his decisions wrong. Yes, it was a big call, but it is not an easy job. Now, if he put in a performance like Toner against York, maybe he could be slated as a bad referee, but this is a man who was (or maybe still is) closing in on the Select Group

2, a referee widely touted for one of the play-off matches. Just think on this, if you were asked how many mistakes you make at work, could you, hand on heart, say fewer than 1 in every 245 tasks you carry out?

With that in mind, do you really think he was a cheat, or keen to even it up? I don't, I think he just made a split-second decision that was wrong. If it happens in the 60th minute of a game in December, you barely talk about it a month later. If it happens in a game that decides promotion, or indeed a semi-final with a Wembley place on the line, then you talk about it all day long. The truth is this: John Busby will be feeling almost as bad as anyone this weekend. We've heard the referee's body had apologised for the decision (something that apparently happened in games against Gillingham and Plymouth earlier in the season when we got the decisions), with Michael saying in this morning's press conference: "The referees have apologised for the decision. It doesn't change anything just that it wasn't a good day for the ref or for us as a club. There's another very good opportunity coming up for us soon and we need to make sure we're in the right mindset for them. It's as bad decision as you've ever seen, but it's done now and there's nothing you can do about it. It's potentially cost the club a lot of money but we've got an opportunity to make sure that isn't the case."

Exactly – we can still make sure the decision doesn't cost us, we have our fate in our hands. The same applied when Gillingham, Fleetwood and Rochdale tickled our bellies at home, didn't it? Or when we threw away the 3-2 lead at Plymouth, or drew with an awful Swindon side. If we'd scored penalties against Posh and Doncaster earlier in the season, it wouldn't matter either. The point is this: John Busby made a bad choice, but it was one single second of a 46-game season and I'm afraid when all those games are played, you finish where you deserve to. We could have been top two, but a season isn't just what happens on the field, it is about injuries, squad management and all sorts. There have been so many moments that have affected that, it is wrong to point the finger at one man's choice.

On the other hand, we could have been seventh, or tenth. We could have been relegated, we could be Grimsby Town who seemingly enjoyed the National League so much they wanted to go back. This has been a wonderful season, a rebirth of the club from last year's upheaval, and a new direction and era that few thought possible after Danny Cowley left the club. That should be what we are all talking about, not one decision. The focus now, around the club, the fanbase and here on the site is going to be on Charlton, Wimbledon and then the two huge matches coming up after that. I ask you this; has there ever been two (hopefully three) bigger games, in terms of success, in the club's history? I doubt it and that is something to focus on, not the one poor decision from a man who I have no doubt feels much sicker than you about it, even if he can't come out and say it.

John Busby isn't the enemy. Referees are not the enemy and whilst they are easy targets, now the dust has settled let's focus on the real enemy – whichever side we face in the two enormous, history-defining matches coming up in May.

Failed Auditions: Charlton 3-1 Imps
May 5, 2021

The Imps have never won at the Valley, and one wonders had we come through Saturday's game at Peterborough with a win, if that would no longer be the case.

We didn't, we drew and that means the play-offs are guaranteed. Last night, that gave Michael Appleton the chance to shuffle the pack a bit, preparing the squad for the headline games later in May. The result was a tough watch for those at home, maybe even the worst £10 I've spent on iFollow all season. Mind you, with no Johnson, Rogers, McGrandles, Bridcutt or Hopper in the starting line up and Joe Walsh only just coming back into the side, it was a makeshift lincoln City team that took to the field looking to end the hoodoo.

I'm not going to come on here and start throwing out such lines as 'not good enough', 'lost momentum' or any of the other overreactions I've seen around social media this morning. I hate losing just as much as anyone, it stains me like coffee on a white table cloth and is often tough to get out even after a win the following weekend, but I had an element of not caring too much last night. When Charlton scored I didn't feel that sick in my stomach I did when Rochdale, Fleetwood or Swindon scored against us earlier in the season. there was more a feeling of 'okay, that's happened, what next?'. Next, well, that was two more goals, leading me to want to turn off the television and walk away. Lincoln City have better things to do than exert too much effort in a meaningless game against Charlton and after 80 minutes, I felt I had better things to do than watch them do it.

I still paid my £10, knowing what was coming. I still sat through their goals, because that is what fans do. I didn't even feel bitter when I heard Sky Bet were showing the Imps game for free on their website because I've paid for every game this season and I'm not about to moan about the club having a tenner of my money. If I moan about the performance, it is because I've watched it, not listened on the radio or got a two-minute collection of clips from Sky Sports News. We lost 3-1, but am I moaning? No, I'm not. I'm pragmatic and I understand where this fits in relation to the season.

What I did find disappointing, to a certain degree, was the assertion by Michael after the game that players who were auditioning for the play-offs failed their audition. It wasn't Michael assertion I found disappointing, he's right, they did struggle, but I fear it may lead to a backlash against certain players who I feel have plenty of reason for their recent form. I think rather than try to take you through a trying 90 minutes of football, I'd look at those players, and why they may have struggled of late.

The main one I think has really struggled post-Christmas is James Jones. He came under fire on social media after last night's game and I can see why, like eight or nine of the others on the pitch, he wasn't great. The problem for Jones is he hasn't been involved in the games where we've done well, so fans simply do a quick subtraction, players who played Saturday from those who did not, and the ones left get a bit of a kicking. Actually, if you watch Jones' performance, it wasn't bad, it just wasn't match-winning either. His passing stats, according to Wyscout, were 47 attempted, 35 completed, an average of 74%. His average for the whole season is 36.11 per game with 79.5% of those completed, so he was about average. Of his total actions, 47 from 82 were successful, 57%, only marginally down on his average of 59.5%. That might be stat heavy for you, but the fact is he wasn't as bad as some have made out.

Also, I think he has to be cut some slack given what happened to him over the winter. We're under the impression he was one of the players affected by Covid and since his return, he's been a little off the pace. Unless you've had Covid and suffered the effects afterwards, it really isn't your place to tell him he's 'not good enough', as I saw on social media. I do think after last night he might only be seen as a late sub in the play-off matches, if at all, but I back him to come back fitter and stronger next season.

Callum Morton didn't start at the weekend but did start last night, and of course, that has led to a bit of stick online too. I'd be lying if I said I thought he played well last night, his touch looked awry at times and he was shackled by the Charlton defenders well. The Callum Morton we saw for Northampton bags one, if not both of his glorious chances last night, and if that happens then it is a different result altogether. The first goal was utterly crucial against the Addicks, if we got it, I think they panic and we maybe go on to win. If they got it, then confidence grows and the result goes their way.

Actually, Morton's efforts showed an improvement on recent matches: since scoring against Sunderland he's had seven shots, with just one on target against Bristol Rovers. In the 2-2 draw with Blackpool and the 4-0 win against MK Dons, he didn't get a single effort at goal, and he got just one off target against Shrewsbury and two off-target against Burton. In the Burton game, he was given Man of the Match by Michael Hortin (I think) for the way he fought their centre-halves, so it isn't always about shots.

However, I concede he could have finished one of his chances last night, on target on not, and I think he is a bench warmer for the play-offs. Again, in his defence, he missed five months of the season with injury, and he's playing out of his normal position. He isn't a hold-up striker like Tom Hopper, he isn't a false nine and yet he has been put there during Tom's spell out and again last night. Granted, it hasn't always worked and last night he didn't have a good game, but again labelling him 'not good enough' is a fallacy. In the right system, he is comfortably a League One striker, but I fear that system is not the one we play.

Who else do I think was auditioning for a place in the starting XI post-Wimbledon? Almost certainly Harry Anderson, who got a goal and an assist at the weekend, so to say he failed would be tough. I think he is yet another who has really struggled to get up to pace since being out injured, again someone who will benefit from the break over the summer. Harry was one of our best players before Christmas, he tore Crewe apart at their place and did the same against Forest Green. I think he's been unlucky, getting injured and seeing Rogers come in and do well making those cherished wide positions even harder to claim, but he will be useful from the bench in the play-offs, no doubt at all. Did he play well last night? Not especially, no, not many did, but he did get a shot on target to score, and he did complete five of his eight dribbles. He didn't get much into the box, but our crosses weren't great all night. That's as much down to some good defending from the opposition as it was our own wastefulness.

I think the other player who was looking to send a message was Anthony Scully. He seems to go from hot to cold quicker than the mixer tap on my bath, he was sensational against Peterborough and yet very quiet indeed last night. He made a point in his pre-match interview I found interesting, he said he doesn't feel he struggles from the start of matches, but that in some games it is harder to get on the ball and affect play. Actually, whilst I was inclined not to agree at the time, his stats from last night do back that up. He made 17 accurate passes from 20, that's 85% accuracy and well above his season average of 77.7%. He got one cross in, which was accurate, made two dribbles, one successful and his only long pass was also accurate. What he did, he did well, but he just didn't do enough. Maybe he didn't get the ball enough, maybe he was crowded out, but rather than play badly, he just wasn't able to get on the ball. I think it still leaves him outside the XI for the play-offs though.

I saw a bit of stick for Regan Poole too, and I often see stuff directed at newer players. I always refer to Tom Pett when talking about January signings, he wasn't popular at all after he arrived from Stevenage, until he bagged against Yeovil. The following season, with the benefit of a full pre-season, he was excellent. Now, I don't think Poole has played badly at all, I think there is a perception from some he has struggled, which is wrong. I saw him make one or two crucial interceptions last night (he made four in total by the way) but sometimes play happens so fast you don't see who cleared the ball. Even in commentary, one clearance of his, a stinging header away, was called as Montsma by Michael, and I thought it as too. It was only by me looking back now at the Wyscout actions that I saw it was Poole. His crossing was also fairly consistent too, he made six crosses (more than both starting wide players combined), two of which were successful. On the other flank, Cohen Bramall is showing great pace which is winning him admirers, but he only delivered one cross, which was unsuccessful. Regan Poole put more balls into the box than all three of the other wide players combined, but he still had a bad game? Perception is an interesting thing.

My point with this rambling defence of a team I readily acknowledge did not play well is intended to show two things. Firstly, all is not always as t seems and whilst opinion is all part of the game, to lazily described a player as 'no good enough' fails to tell the whole story. If the players who auditioned for the play-offs (and even those who failed) are not good enough, how have they formed part of a top six League One squad this season? Secondly, I want to underline that even those players stepping into the side have plenty to offer a squad, if not the first team, and whilst last night's defeat stings, it is not the world-ending, play-off threatening result many feel it is.

As for positives, Joe Walsh coming back is huge. I think coming up against Sunderland, Blackpool, Charlton or Portsmouth could be tough, all have experienced strikers happy to leave in an elbow or able to show awareness to peel off a defender and find space. Our recent run has been good, Eyoma and Montsma have done well, but Mageniss, Stockley and Clarke-Harris have all scored against us. When it comes to big-name strikers, we do tend to struggle, with Wyke and Marquis also putting the ball into our net. I think the back four needs Joe Walsh, a defender with a little more know-how and a willingness to indulge in the dark arts. At times, I thought Stockley bossed Montsma last night, albeit with a nasty elbow shot at one point, but that is what he does. Having an older head in there might serve us well come mid-May.

I also think it is a bonus Rogers, Johnson and Bridcutt did not play. I think all will play some part against Wimbledon but look at it like this: Michael knew Charlton were going to be at it last night. They had to win, so tackles would fly in (they did), and there would be scraps and battles all over the pitch. Was it worth risking players who could turn a play-off game on its head for us? No, not in my opinion. It was disappointing to lose, but there is no cause for concern around momentum. We have been excellent in recent weeks and as long as we turn in a decent performance against a Wimbledon side with little to play for, we can put the Charlton game behind us as the last seconds of the Peterborough game.

Don't panic, it is all part of Michael's plan and right now, there is no reason to think he's doesn't know what he is doing, is there? Who knows, we might even get that elusive win at the Valley in mid-May, and I firmly believe a full-strength Lincoln City has little to fear based on what I saw last night, even though we were soundly beaten.

Into The Unknown: Imps 0-0 AFC Wimbledon
May 9, 2021

I've said a few times that the bigger picture has to be the focus after tough afternoons, and from what I can gather, a lot of people thought this was a tough afternoon.

I didn't. Maybe I watched a different game, maybe the perspective from the stadium was a bit different, but I actually enjoyed much of the football on show.

Much like the Charlton game, good honest analysis isn't really applicable. We were playing for home advantage in the play-offs, something already established as nothing more than a minor advantage, if at all. I suppose there are a few people who would have liked us to avoid Sunderland, but when all is said and done I think we're as good as they are. Yes, them having 10,000 in the SoL for the second leg could be an advantage, but it could be the opposite. Charlton's fans turned on them when they returned for test events earlier in the season, how will those Sunderland fans react if their side is trailing from the first leg and start slowly? The weight of expectation is one them, not us. Frankly, we're here for the ride and to see how far it takes us.

Rewinding a bit, today's game didn't serve up the sort of spectacle I hoped it might. It did open with a poignant minutes silence for the 56 who lost their lives at Bradford in 1985, impeccably observed. It was eerie as the whistle rang out around the ground to signal the end, only to be met with virtual silence. Usually, a big roar goes up, and it often feels as though it is a cheer for Bill Stacey, Jim West and those 54 souls from Bradford, but it just didn't feel right having a handful of fans only to lift the roof immediately afterwards.

Once the action got underway, one or two looked to be in preservation mode, keen not to pick up an injury or red card which might impact our chances of facing Forest and Sheffield Utd next season. That said, I felt we started well and controlled much of the opening 25 minutes. I was lucky enough to be in a box for the game, having filmed the last Match Day Live of the regular season there. It was a treat, seeing these boys in action, and maybe the experience has made the game seem more lively to me. From where I was sitting, Brennan Johnson has their left-back on toast for 25 minutes and realistically, we could have been 3-0 up. Before you say you think I'm deluded, Sam felt the same (sorry Sam). Johnson certainly had one good chance saved, and Morgan Rogers' saw an effort parried too. It then shocked me to see Twitter awash with anger, although I understand that was something to do with the Charlatans. My Dad wasn't impressed by the game though, he texted me something to that effect, but for me, we looked decent without getting out of second gear.

Perhaps Conor McGrandles looked a little rusty after a couple of games out of the starting XI, Tayo took a while to get going at left back and whilst Tom Hopper worked hard there wasn't a lot of joy, but they didn't play badly, they just took time to get into the game. I don't think this was a bad Lincoln performance and had there been anything on the line other than a negligible advantage, I think we had one or two more gears to cruise through before we hit our peak. I know some will say we should have been treating this as a dress rehearsal for the play-offs, but I also see the benefit in not overstretching and picking up injuries.

I tell you who was playing at 100%, full throttle, no prisoners: Liam Bridcutt. He was into everything and having seen him play in daylight for the first time in a year or more, I have got to say the lad has thighs that I'm sure could crack a brick open. He's looking in superb shape and as he rattled into challenges and contested every decision, I got the feeling he was right at his peak. If we get him at 100% against Sunderland, we're in with a big shout of getting a result over two legs. I did wince a couple of times as he launched himself into challenges with real gusto, praying he didn't stay down. In terms of results, 0-0 might not be the one many wanted, but '0 Injuries' is. Thank the good lord that is how we seemingly came out of the game.

As the half went on, we looked more likely to get a goal. Brennan obviously did score, and I think if Jorge hasn't had a touch when he did, Brennan is actually onside, but the assistant called it right. We had a big shout for a penalty at the end of the half too, but Scott Oldham doesn't award penalties. He didn't when we played Oxford earlier in the season, but back then it was us committing the foul. From my angle, and I haven't seen it back, I thought Morgan was felled, but the referee didn't give it. Overall, he did let the game flow, but once or twice I scratched my head as clear fouls went unpunished for both sides. When I've been at home watching on iFollow I've often thought that a good thing, but watching a player pick himself up after a clear foul does cloud your view somewhat. On iFollow, if a player stays down for even a couple of seconds, clearly fouled, you don't see it. In the ground, you do.

From halftime onwards my experience of the game changed. Firstly, from a vantage point behind the goal it is hard to see exactly what happens up the other end of the field, and I began to follow the other games with keen interest. I knew it was unlikely we'd face the team finishing in sixth, but even so, it was fascinating with Danny Cowley involved. Everyone kept going on about the narrative of us against the

Cowleys, but I've had my eye on another one: us and Oxford at Wembley. I felt it inevitable in the EFL Trophy, but Sunderland scuppered that. Could it really be Appleton v Oxford, both with two defeats from two at Wembley, in the final? There's a long way to go for that, but it smells like a real story.

It didn't help that we chopped things about in the second half and the rhythm of the game felt disrupted. They had the better play early on, but they never really threatened. At no point during the game did I think Joe Pigott, 22 goals this season and six from seven going into the game, would score. Nor did I feel Ollie Palmer, almost nailed on to do something against us, would get a goal either. I never felt, not for a fleeting second, that we'd lose the game. It might be over confidence on my part, but they played like a side not wanting to lose, obviously, but also aware they didn't need a win. This lot stuck five past Accrington away a couple of weeks ago, did Ipswich 3-0 and beat Oxford United. Did you see any of the threat that suggests they have? Not really.

In the flesh, watching Rogers and Johnson is something special. I know ow both drift in and out of games, but a moment sometime around 65 minutes from Rogers looked brilliant. He got away from four Wimbledon players, and chipped the keeper, only for play to be pulled back. That sort of magic is driven by having a crowd, that sort of flair, and that of Johnson, feeds on 9,000 home fans all having a sharp intake of breath in anticipation as they burst forward. One of Brennan Johnson's best games came away at Northampton, when there was a home crowd to silence. I think both could be key men in the play-offs, and not just in front of our fans. Genuinely, I think some players almost thrive as much on silencing opposition fans as they do thrilling their own. My instinct tells me Johnson, certainly, is one of those.

I genuinely thought we'd scored with ten minutes left, Johnson's blocked shot eventually finding Grant who hit a great drive. We were right behind it and it had venom and trajectory, drawing a super save from their keeper. It was a rare moment of absolute quality from City in a slower second half. Another move, which didn't bring a chance, certainly impressed both Sam and me. It was a flowing move of about thirty passes, probing down one flank, coming back, across the field, down the other flank, lots of crips balls and nice movement. It didn't bring a goal, but it was great to watch and again, in the flesh, it was even better. Watching the movement of players on one side of the field as action unwinds on the other gives you an idea of what an oiled machine this team is. There is always a runner, always space to exploit. There's nobody will want to play us as we stretch the opposition and ask serious questions. We are wasteful at times, Hopper, Johnson and Rogers could all have scored, but I'd rather we waste chances than not create at all, because eventually, a team will take a proper good hiding. If we were to get to Wembley, the big open spaces of that field will definitely suit us. If we get to Wembley.

One moment late on had me chuckling. It was the last minute or so, and Liam Bridcutt came together with Shane McLoughlin right in front of me. It was a nothing challenge, a shoulder barge the like of which had been let go all afternoon. The assistant's flag went up, and I heard as clear as day the reaction from the player. Liam asked her what the decision was for, a couple of times, whilst another player, who shall remain nameless, yelled from the penalty spot 'what was that for? Learn the ******* game, man!'. I guess it goes on all game, every game, but for some reason it tickled me immensely.

That was that. After heading in around a silent ground and into the box, I did the same journey in reverse, only briefly seeing Paul Owen on my way out. I felt honoured to have been at the game, delighted to be able to see the team in league action, and also a little sad that there wasn't 10,000 other fans there to see it too. Sincil Bank without fans is like Red Bull without Vodka, bacon without eggs, beans, hash browns, fried tomatoes and a nice fat sausage. It just isn't right. Luckily, that should be the last time the ground doesn't ring out to the sound of a thousand or so Imps fans, at least.

We now head into unchartered territory, the League One play-offs. In all but one of our last six play-off campaigns, we have expected some degree of success. Only once have we gone into the end of season spectacle with freedom and no pressure, 2002/03, when we hammered Scunthorpe 6-3 on aggregate. Make no mistake, all the pressure is on Sunderland, all the expectation is on them too. If we were to get past them, Oxford and Blackpool will expect to be a big challenge, they're both sides with extensive League One pedigree. Us? We're just the new kids on the block, the aspiration squad that, at the start of the season, even the manager said 'might surprise a few' with what sounded like hope, rather than absolute, certainty.

Well, we have surprised a few, myself included. What a season it has been and whatever happens through the course of May, the future at this football club is very, very bright indeed.

"We do know what it will take" – Michael Appleton on Sunderland and the season's turning points
May 17, 2021

I was fortunate enough to catch up with Michael Appleton yesterday, ahead of the week's play-off semi-final with Sunderland.

Michael is the subject of the final programme piece of the season, a programme you can order here if you are not lucky enough to be going to the game. Michael is a great talker and I was lucky enough to get some bits from him for the site as well.

It is well publicised that he felt we might surprise a few this season, and it is fair to say we did. I was interested to know if there were any moments in the season where he stood on the sidelines and thought that we might actually be on to something.

"Not necessarily an individual games as such, but more groups of games," he told me over the weekend. "Not the memorable ones either, there was a couple where we didn't play well and did enough to get over the line. Wigan at home is an obvious one, it's taken something a bit special from Granty (Jorge Grant) to get us back into the game from a free-kick, then for twenty minutes it looked like we might score five or six. With a different group, on a different day or a different season, that game might get away from you and you end up losing 1-0."

For the manager, it is not always the wins that stand out, but how the team bounces back when faced with adversity or challenges. He feels there is as much to learn from playing well and losing as there is playing badly and winning.

"There's been a few times this year when we've lost a couple on the bounce or haven't played well and there have been questions asked of the group and they have bounced back very well. I remember earlier in the season where we lost a couple at home, Shrewsbury sticks in my mind. We lost 1-0 but I thought we were excellent and the message was very clear; continue to perform like that and results will come back quickly.

"Another that springs to mind is Doncaster at home, where we lose 1-0 but we completely dominated them. After that game, we knew very well that there were wins around the corner and again the group answered any questions people had."

The group now face the biggest question of all: do they have what it takes to finally defeat Sunderland? We've met four times this season, lost 4-0 in a game we should have led 2-0 after ten minutes, then battled to a pair of 1-1 draws at the Stadium of Light. Some think the play-offs offer a chance for a tactical approach, maybe get ahead and defend a lead or with our away form, hold them at our place and look to make it third time lucky in the north east.

Michael doesn't feel and for the avoidance of doubt, he clarified exactly what Lincoln City will be looking to do on Wednesday and Saturday.

"We are going into these matches wanting to win both games, just to take doubts out of it about what results might be enough. If we go to the Stadium of Light all square, or behind, fair enough, we know we need to win the game to go through. Ultimately, our attitude will be to set up and win both games.

"That's easier said than done though as we haven't managed it in three games this season. We do know what it will take to beat them, I thought in the previous two we played we did enough to nick result, rather than draw. A little bit of quality, a little bit of rub of the green on the two evenings and we can get the wins."

With a place in the showpiece final at Wembley, and possibly a spot in the same division at Nottingham Forest, Derby County and Sheffield United up for grabs, the stakes really could not be higher. Roll on Wednesday.

Imps Prospect Set For Chelsea Trial Spell
May 17, 2021

It seems young Sean Roughan is really catching the eye, with Chelsea the latest to be linked with a move for him.

Earlier this month, the 17-year-old spent time on trial with Southampton, and with the Saints yet to make a move, it seems Chelsea are now having a serious look. This all bodes well for me by the way, I have a signed pair of his boots!

Seriously though, whilst he didn't feature as much for the first team as he might have liked, there's little doubt he has a big future ahead of him. he didn't look out of place during his stint in the first team and his outings for the Under 18s have been mature and composed. He's definitely a big talent and the level of club watching him is a testament to that.

The 42 reports that Roughan is set to have a week-long trial with the Blues ahead of their final Premier League games of the season, and is likely to feature for their Under 23 side. That will give Technical Mentor Claude Makélélé a chance to cast his eye over Roughan, although it is more likely to be Andy Myers, the development squad manager at Stamford Bridge, who has a look. Either way, it is something that reflects well on our club's setup and recruitment.

The young Irish defender is seen as an exciting prospect, having started the season in the first team. He made 11 starts for City, six in the league, but disappeared from view as the season progressed. That hasn't stopped him helping the Under 18s to the FA Cup 4th Round, and there was a deep belief he would be around the first team next season, having signed a professional deal at the age of 16 last summer.

n response to his trial at Southampton, Michael Appleton said: "It was an opportunity for them to have a look at Sean. They've shown an interest for a while now. We were more than happy for that to happen. He's our player until someone makes an offer, it's as simple as that."

We wait with baited breath to see if the £750,000 we received for Jack Hobbs is to be beaten for another young defender, but with interest heating up it does look unlikely that we'll see him in a City shirt again.

90 Minutes From Wembley: Imps 2-0 Sunderland

May 20, 2021

Last night was a great night for Lincoln City, but to hear suggestions of celebrations flying around this morning does baffle me.

As yet, we have nothing to celebrate, not really. It is halftime of a game and only a fool will celebrate a win at half time. We can feel good (bloody good), we can feel hope and genuine expectation to a degree, but there is no cause for cracking open the cans of IPA and throwing a few back. the job is half done, but it half done very well indeed.

It's funny, as I sat in the pub (like a normal person) listening to my Dad's pessimism, I felt quietly confident. Having been in the Third Tier podcast and had all the pundits bar one back us, I did feel we were the underestimated side. Yes, Sunderland have players that can hurt you, but so do we. It's easy to look lovingly at the likes of McGeady, only to forget Johnson, Grant and Rogers in terms of attacking prowess. Sure, Wyke can score goals, but Tom Hopper makes them and apparently, scores a few too. Football is all-too-often a game of subtle jealousy, praising other team's players based on a few clips or seeing their name in the top scorer's charts, whilst underappreciating your own lads because you see every kick, misplaced pass and stumble as well as the highlights.

Dad fell into the trap of seeing McGeady and Wyke and believing they had too much for us. I wouldn't commit on a score, but with Walsh and Jackson back and the first-choice midfield of McGrandles, Grant and Bridcutt, I felt we could get something. My optimism, not something I'm renowned for, quickly changed when I saw the teamsheet. No Joe Walsh and no Conor McGrandles soon had me reverting to type – "It could be a long evening Dad". Oh ye of little faith.

Much of that was displaced by being back in the ground. I did feel emotional, I'm not the teary sort (although the end of Unforgotten did get close to prompting a few), but the feeling of hearing the fans roar as the lads came out to train before the game. It was like opening a pressure valve and the steam rushing out, 18 months of pent-up frustration pouring out. If you were there and you thought that was loud, imagine what next season will be like, whether it is Sheffield United or Sheffield Wednesday on the fixture list.

180 minutes will define which of the Sheffield clubs we face in the league. For the record, the last time either were at the Bank in the league was 1984, with the Owls last meeting city eight days before I was born in 1978. Right now, the bookies are probably thinking that we're favourites to face the Blades, or at least get a chance to square off against either Blackpool (likely) or Oxford (need a miracle) for the right. I'll be confident if we're still two goals to the good with a couple of minutes remaining on Saturday, until then, I'll reserve judgement!

I thought we were excellent from start to finish last night. I said before the game we needed to play well and win, two elements we hadn't always managed to pull together at the same time, and yet we managed it against a Sunderland side I think get more stick from their fans on social media than they should. Remember, they're at their lowest point ever, so when they watch this team they have expectation and memories of far better times. We are at the highest point we've been at for forty years, and so when our fans see the boys in action they see one of the best-ever sides. The truth is, take away the expectation and perception, and you have two very similar teams.

The neutral watching at home certainly had their fill of excitement, with more than 30 attempts at goal between the two sides. We had the best of those in an exciting opening period, showcasing the best of our football at the same time. I thought Regan Poole was outstanding from first kick to last, with Tayo on the other flank quickly getting into the rhythm as well. They were key, overlapping where they could, and with Scully getting in more open spaces than household dust, we looked a real danger. His curling effort was definitely a corner, tipped over excellently by Burge, but the referee didn't spot it. When Johnson struck the post not long after, I wondered if we'd had our chance.

I've seen in some places our first half performance was described as the weaker of the two, but I disagree. We put a proper marker out early on, Michael's bold·team selection paying dividends. When we lost Adam Jackson early I felt their attacking players might capitalise, but Lewis Montsma came on and was excellent as well. Eyoma is a proper gem, he's going to the Championship next season and my only hope is that he can do it with us. He's been a revelation since filling in at centre back, leaving me a little sorry we didn't get Regan Poole earlier, freeing TJ up to play his natural position. In truth, their most dangerous effort of the first half was Gooch's long-range drive, but that is what we seemed to be reducing them too – speculation, rather than any serious threat.

My only other comment on the first half has to be towards Liam Bridcutt. he is such a good player and with the benefit of being able to see the whole pitch, you get a real grasp of what he does. When the ball is miles away from him, he is coaching players around him, directing traffic so to speak, nad it is clear he has a big influence. At one stage Joe Bursik, a keeper thrown in at the deep end, made a catch and dropped onto the ball, and the first to shout to him was Bridcutt. He is a true leader of men and I have no doubt at all that in ten year's time, he will be a manager.

I ought to have a word for Bursik too. It wasn't easy for him, coming in late and having such minimal time to train and get into the rhythm of the squad, but he was excellent. He made some crucial saves in the second half, which I'll come onto, but his general demeanour was just so assured and competent. Not once did I think 'stand-in keeper' when he went for a ball and I'll tell you this for free – if Alex Palmer goes back to West Brom, as expected, and we need a new number one, I'd take that boy all day long for a year. My only worry is if we go up, Stoke won't lend him to us!

The second half started worryingly for City, as Sunderland turned the screw. Dad and I were in a great position to see Jordan Jones' effort which Bursik tipped onto the bar, a wonderful save that kept us in the game. As McGeady came across to take the corner he got a round of boos and abuse, but I stayed silent. I've seen it too many times, you call a player and immediately his delivery leads to a goal. McGeady is a player who can deliver, and he did, whipping in a lovely corner for Bailey Wright to head against the crossbar. The big bad wolf was huffing and puffing, but even if the ball went in, I don't think anything was blowing Sincil Bank down last night. Had they scored, the noise would have kept on coming, the fans would have stayed focused on supporting the team. As it was, rattling the bar only served to crank the volume up another notch.

When the first goal came, it was hard to see from our vantage point. Scully and Johnson, both excellent all night, combined to serve up Grant who saw his shot saved. Then the captain grabbed the game by the scruff of the neck, hauled it up to face level and screamed 'we are Imps' in its face, rampaging through the Sunderland back four and getting the ball to Grant. He delivers, more punctually than DPD, and at the back stick was the goal poacher Tom Hopper moving into double figures. I found it ironic, all the talk before the play-off was of Jerry Yates, Charlie Wyke and Matty Taylor, and the fact we didn't have that fox in the box. Right on cue, Hopps delivers. I had a chat with someone before the game about us being more clinical, and with the greatest of respect, Hopps hasn't always been that, but cometh the hour, cometh the man.

At first, I celebrated like the rest of the crowd, it felt second-nature. It was only after a split second I realised the gravity of that goal. It was the first we'd celebrated in 15 months or so, the first time I'd heard that roar which, over the years, has been a refuge for me and many other fans. If your life is shit, it doesn't matter for a few seconds after a Lincoln City goal. If you are rich, poor, healthy or sick, you forget it as the net ripples and 3,000 (or 10,000) fans unite in unbridled joy. As Hopps wheeled away to celebrate and I stopped hugging my Dad, I got a familiar feeling. I'd missed this. It is my drug, my 'just one more' issue that I can't shake off. I've had addictions in the past, I've smoked, I've been hooked on painkillers and even computer games, but this is the one that will always keep me coming back. Again, I don't cry, but I could have done. Oh yes, I could have done and writing this now, I've got goosebumps. In the moment the goal was what it was, an opener against Sunderland in a play-off semi-final, a huge goal, but in the context of the wider world, it was so much more and always will be. Cheers Hopps.

Putting the emotion to one side, there was still a game of football to be won and Sunderland thought they could do it. They could too, they're a decent side and when McGeady is in your team, you have a fighting chance. He really is the main threat, the go-to man whenever they need a moment's magic. Regan Poole had him marshalled well, but he's like a Jack-in-the-Box, you can't keep him quiet all of the time. When he did deliver, the threat of Mr Wyke loomed large.

I was pleased to see tackles flying in, a few that were a bit tastier than you see on iFollow. The crowd definitely added needle and a pace that might not have been seen all season. I tell you something – I wouldn't want my car to collide with a Bridcutt slide tackle, because I think it would come off worse. He's fearless and more than once I saw him fouled, only to get retribution a little while after. His booking, for an off-the-ball block on Wyke (I think) seemed to come after the Sunderland striker had left an elbow in on one of ours a few moments before. Bridcutt is like a big brother, if you pick on any of his siblings he's going to smash you. It was a physical encounter at times and both teams gave as good as they got.

Sunderland had their chances and every single Imps' player put his body on the line, TJ Eyoma took more blows than I care to count (there is a simile there but even I draw the line somewhere), and when the defence was breached, the excellent Bursik pulled off the saves needed to keep us in the tie. On 77 (ish) minutes, we did look a little tired and I had only remarked to my Dad that it had 1-1 written all over it seconds before the keeper launched a big boot downfield. How ironic, after a season of wonderful football and slick passing, the goal that seals the first leg comes from a big punt down the middle. You all know what happened, their semi-fit defender Tom Flanagan lazily pushed it back to Burge and Johnson, doubtless fuelled by the adrenalin of a loud cheer, chased the ball down. 99 times out of a hundred he doesn't get the ball, or it cannons off for a throw-in or a goal kick, but this was the one-in-a-hundred chance, in the 59th game of an epic season. On this occasion, God smiled down and the ball dropped to his feet yards from goal. Apparently, he said afterwards as he saw events unfold he was already planning his celebration. Me too Brennan, me too.

I rushed to the loo after that and as I found my seat again, I heard Alan Long announce the time of the goal and I was convinced he said 67 minutes. That's how quickly the evening flashed by, everything seemed so new and exciting that it was over in an instant. There were no nerves as the clock wound down, after Brennan's goal it only seemed like seconds before the board went up. Even in injury time, which was agonising and protracted at London Road, the seconds flew by, and I was shocked to see we went over by a minute or two. It was a great match though, why wouldn't the referee want to see it go on?

The final whistle brought a big cheer, not the biggest of the night. In fact, one of the best moments was right at the end when Harry Anderson came on. The stadium erupted into his song, probably because he is the only player who even has his own song this season, but also because he is a proper City icon, a player who has been here through the whole rise. There is some discussion over whether he stays or not, but I sincerely hope he does and by the sounds of it, 3,000 other fans feel the same.

Nothing is won at half time and last night's game will feel very different after Saturday. Right now, it is the first series of a great show, think Game of Thrones or Breaking Bad. It is the brilliant opening, the curtain-raiser which has us all excited about what is to come. Saturday, at the Stadium of Light, will either provide the suitable ending Breaking Bad got, or disappointment which tarnishes, to some degree, last night's result.

What will never be tarnished, not by defeat at the SoL, by the passing of time or anything else, is finally being back at the Bank. Nothing will ever take away that roar as Hopper's goal went in and the realisation that we are heading back towards normality. In fact, the only noise that will ever better that, aside from 4,000 fans in London celebrating a winning play-off final goal, is the roar of 10,000 supporters when the Imps run out for next season's opener when we're all back and together, Imps As One.

Speechless: Sunderland 2-1 Imps (2-3 agg)
May 22, 2021

Whenever I sit down to write something like this, I usually have a plan.

I have a clever start, or I relate to a previous game or feeling. I find an angle or a hook on which I can hang a few killer paragraphs, or form a message in my mind I want to convey with a few similes, metaphors and clever observations. That's my usual plan, but a couple of hours after this afternoon's game, I don't have that. I don't know what to write or what I can tell you, because as Imps fans you have lived that too.

I could make observations about a terrible first half in which we looked timid, exposed and weary. They got the crucial early goal they wanted, from a City error, and never looked like they were going to struggle. Wyke should have scored, 100%, then he did, and it seemed a matter of time. If it were a boxing match, we had gone into full of hope and taken a good battering. Sunderland, in full flow, are a hell of a side and they pressed that advantage on us with real pressure. Every ball fell to them, if it didn't they just won it and relentless waves swept upfield, leaving me a complete and utter wreck.

I said games in the play-offs turn on single moments, on a lucky bounce or a blow of the whistle, but this one wasn't going to. It turned on 45 relentless minutes of red and white pressure, and eleven Lincoln City players looking dumbstruck in the onslaught. Is that too strong? It is what it felt like to me. I was watching on a mobile phone, leant up against my laptop screen with Twitter in the background, and the general gist seems to be everyone agreed with me. The difference is how fans react to that at half time.

Inwardly, I was broken. Sunderland were at full throttle, completely in control of the game with us mere bit-part players in their romance tale. 'No team has come back from two goals down to win a play-off semi-final since....' said the commentators. '10,000 fans sound more like 30,000' they dribbled excitedly down the microphones as they willed the big club on. I don't moan about partisan commentary anymore, but Sky did take the biscuit today – at one point I'm pretty sure Keith Andrews even referred to Alex Palmer as 'the Lincoln keeper' as if we were the faceless henchmen being brushed aside by the superhero down on their luck in League One. I felt Sky wanted the narrative to favour the home side, but maybe that is just 'little club' syndrome on my part. I had that fed a bit when I went on Talk Sport earlier in the day – Max Rushden, a top presenter by the way, said that 'Lincoln haven't had a lot of media coverage'. It made me think – actually, we don't do bad. We've been on Sky what, four times this season? Michael is a story everyone loves and under Danny, we were never out of the paper. Maybe, it is time we shrugged off this 'little Lincoln' title.

The only way you do that is on the field, and with 45 minutes of this semi-final remaining, we had played into the role ourselves. Sky seemingly wanted the patsy, the fall guy to roll over and let McGeady (who they mentioned more than I mention xG on a podcast) and Sunderland write the headline. I stress this isn't an attack on Sunderland, nor their fans, but on the way certain games are presented.

I think with hindsight, Michael might even feel now that the team selection, a bold and attacking option, didn't work properly. Scully, excellent in the first leg, didn't get the ball anywhere near as much as he would like, and the secret weapon which stunned Sunderland Wednesday just didn't have the element of surprise anymore. Mind you, if we're being fair, there wasn't a strong outfield performance from anyone. Regan Poole kept McGeady quiet on Wednesday, be he will doubtless feel disappointed with his first half performance. Nothing stuck to our players and as they traipsed out for the second half, I was fearful.

Up until kick off, I felt no nerves. I didn't think Sunderland would get their early goal and I felt the game would be tight, but after the second, it felt like my world was caving in. There was no context, no reasoning, just me getting incredibly upset. Did I lose confidence? I don't know, I felt outwardly I said the right things about belief, about the squad, but the balance had left me. All I could see was a 3-0 or 4-0 defeat and it hurt, a lot. I just knew that the Imps were capable of playing better and that gave me a sliver of hope.

The changes Michael made were obvious to most observers, Joe Walsh is our best central defender and with him coming on I felt we might be a bit stronger. I might have considered shifting Eyoma over to the right and taking Poole off, but Montsma made way instead. McGrandles is one of our strongest performers of late and when he came on, we looked more solid. Scully just hadn't seen the ball and he cannot be blamed for that, but if you need pace and a desperate counter attack, Brennan is a better choice on the right. It is fair to say that roll of the dice, as well as the half time message, paid dividends.

What was the half time message? 'Turn up', that was what Tom Hopper said after the game. Michael told the team to turn up, in a game we'd already effectively thrown away the advantage we had. It would have been so easy to come out and fold like a napkin, but it was not easy to go out and turn the game on its head. Sky had told us, our players were young, the 10,000 could affect them massively, so for us to come out and be the better side showed such character, I wept with pride at the end.

We all watched the second half, I don't need to tell you what happened, but it was Appleton's Lincoln City, not that pale first-half imitation we'd been subjected to in the first half. Led by the excellent Liam Bridcutt, we were back with vengeance. We passed with accuracy, moved with a little more purpose and we exposed the Sunderland that lurks beneath the veneer of the big club with top players. I know they saw the 4-0 against us as the benchmark which they rarely met through the season and I feel the first half of this game was the same. They can do it, but we're every bit as good if we do our thing. In the second half, we did our thing.

The goal still shocked me though, a goal from a corner! We haven't been great at corners, but Jorge's delivery was superb and Tom Hopper, the modern-day Simon Yeo, stepped up to be the hero. Remember, Yeo made his name by scoring four goals in three games in a play-off battle, and Hopper has now bagged two in two to win us matches. One, the first in front of fans back at the Bank, was crucial, but this one was more than that. What words can you use that mean even more crucial than crucial? Critical? Absolutely f*cking critical? Season-defining? Who knows, it might even be history-defining. It was somewhat fitting that he shook off the attention of Charlie Wyke, the player Sky raved about as a danger, to do just that. In an article ahead of the play-offs I heard that number nines could be crucial and guess what? Ours was.

I woke up the sleepy Cornwall hamlet of Widemouth Bay with my celebration, and yet the drama didn't end there. I checked my BPM on my smart watch as the half went on – I got up to 130. I've felt nerves before, but for some reason this game, this bloody tie, finally grabbed me and wouldn't let go. Every kick had me either wincing our cheering and one kick, in particular, drew me big cheer – the kick that felled McGrandles in the area. That was the moment, and as Jorge placed the ball on the spot I prepared to crack open the cans and toast Wembley. Lee Burge put me back in my box with a good save.

After that the game went from one end to the other, both sides should have done better with the chances they had. My phone kept going off, people from all walks of life messaging me about the game, some I barely know. It felt like an England game, with friends who have no interest in football messaging me and asking questions like 'are you nervous?'. There are 15 minutes between us and a place in Wembley, a possible place in the Championship for the first time in a lifetime... what do you think? I didn't answer in that manner though, but I felt like I should. Of course, I'm nervous, every bloody kick is raising my heartbeat, I'm sweating like Ghislaine Maxwell every time she hears footsteps outside her cell after hours and even the Sky commentators seem like they want them to score. I'm beyond nervous, I'm bloody terrified.

Maybe I shouldn't have been. McGrandles introduction gave us stability in the midfield and as a consequence, everyone stepped up their game. I felt Poole had a great second half, Eyoma and Bridcutt were perhaps the only two who played well over the full 90, but both certainly excelled late one. To a man, e were bang on it again and that should have left me feeling calm, but it didn't. I was on the edge and a bag of fear.

Those seconds dripped away, one after the other and into injury time. We missed chances, they missed chances and with each one my pulse went up and up. Six minutes into the five minutes of injury time, Michael Salisbury (who had a good game, by the way), blew his whistle. The game was over and we were through to the play-off final.

Fe was sat opposite me at a table and she looked at me knowing we'd got through, knowing that I should be celebrating, and for some reason, I just cried. I could feel it coming up for a few seconds, but I just covered my face and cried. As you know, it had been 115 minutes (including half time and injury time) of pure desolation and joy mixed into one. I hate the saying 'a rollercoaster of emotion', but what else was it like? It was a rollercoaster, like no other game I have ever experienced. If I had to draw a comparison, it would be the 5-3 with Scunthorpe back in 2003, with the lead, being pegged back and then finally smashing it.

I still can't believe it. I'm filled with pride (and chicken and satay sauce too), I even text Michael Appleton and said thank you. I haven't thought rationally since the final whistle went, I've been singing songs about players that I've made up. I've not spoken to Dad yet, but I've text him, my phone has barely stopped buzzing and I'm just taking it all in. Tomorrow, I shall put it on the shelf and think about next week, but right now, I'm going to enjoy this. This tie isn't the achievement in itself, there's a big game still to go, but it has to be savoured and enjoyed, it has to be appreciated and absorbed without prejudice, without clouding the issue with fears over Blackpool's players or what might happen at Wembley. I won't even think tickets or anything, I just want to enjoy this moment.

In one week's time, we have a date with destiny, but right now, I'm going to enjoy today's defeat for what it is, a moment in Lincoln City history that can never, ever be taken away.

I love football.

Lincoln City On The Cusp Of History, Once Again

May 29, 2021

I started this site (and the books) more than five years ago now. When I did, we were languishing in the National League, backed by a group of hard-working people dreaming of restoring the club to former glories.

Since then, I have written 3615 articles, give or take, charting our rise from the ashes as I did. I have had the pleasure of writing words such as these (if you don't want to read a load of hyperbole from years gone by, skip the quotes. I wouldn't though....), which I'd like to replicate before I jump into this article.

"To all my fellow Imps, enjoy tomorrow. Enjoy making your memories, maybe you'll watch it on the big screen at the ground, or at a mates house. Maybe you'll be chatting to those mates in twenty years team recalling the day...." Burnley away.

"Usually dreams are reserved for situations that you wouldn't get in real life. Often after sleeping you wake up and realise although you've been dreaming about something so fantastic and unimaginable, it briefly feels real when you open your eyes. That sensation usually wears off as you adjust to the surrounding of your bedroom, but for me this week it hasn't gone, it hasn't worn off." Arsenal Away.

"Tomorrow is what being a football fan is all about, it is what we dream about and what we dare not dream about at the same time. It is what we watch others achieve year after year knowing one day, if the gods all line up and Pluto enters Uranus at the right angle, if the right blend of managers, players and luck can be brought together, if the fans get behind the club and we all push on as one, then one day it could be us. Tomorrow it is us. Tomorrow it is our time." Macclesfield Home.

"Whatever the score, however the game goes down, words cannot of justice the pride I will feel at watching my beloved Lincoln City take to the Wembley turf to compete in a Cup Final. I'm a little choked writing this right now and only now am I truly allowing myself to get a little bit excited. We're the famous Lincoln City, and we're going to Wembley." Shrewsbury 2018

"Whatever it meant to you, whether you celebrated in a pub with friends or like me, with a glass of Cherry Pepsi Max and a beef dinner with your partner, you'll always remember it. What occurred today was history, to be written about, talked about and toasted for years to come. Who knows, with three trophies in three seasons we might not have to wait 43 years for the next." Tranmere 2019.

Of course, there are more where they came from, more moments where I have sat in my office, looking out the window wondering how I can ever sum up what it means to see the success we have seen of late. Each time I do I think to myself I can't get better, it can't be topped, and yet here we are, on the cusp of a Wembley return, a potential promotion and yet another benchmark and another chance for me to wax lyrical about a football club that rarely afforded me the chance in the past. Often, supporting Lincoln City felt like punishment for a bad deed, the agony of just missing out on play-offs, battling relegation or having promises broken by inept managers. Success was something others enjoyed, not us. No, we were the nearly men, happy when a season was over in March because we knew we were safe. Okay, Keith's side banished that a little, but we never got promoted, and our victories were small compared to others.

Today, things are so very different. Today, as we lay on the cusp of genuine club history, I can't help but glance back over my shoulder at those quotes above, the moments that have defined the site, the Imps' recent history and which have left an indelible mark on our culture and the club as a whole. They feel applicable to today as they did four years ago, three years ago or whenever I wrote them.

Five years ago to the day I wrote about Matt Rhead handing in a transfer request as Danny Cowley looked to build a squad capable of getting out of the National League, and I looked forward to a European Championship where a former Imp was likely to feature. Today, we look ahead to a potential promotion unmatched in 70 years, and to a European Championship in which one of our current players might appear. Five years in real-time, but five years which have contained a lifetime of trophies, promotions and excitement.

I say 70 years because that is (almost) the period of time that has elapsed between our last promotion from the third tier and today. It was April 23rd 1952 when more than 21000 fans were in Sincil Bank to see us beat Stockport 2-1 and clinch the Division Three (North) title, sealing enough points to ensure Grimsby could not catch us. Johnny Garvie hit both goals and doubtless, fans dreamed of promotion to Division One the season after. Nine seasons of Second Division football followed before we finally slipped back out in 1961. Very few fans alive today will recall that promotion, which only serves to underline this really is a once-in-a-lifetime occurrence.

Is it though? It is once in the last lifetime, but what of the next sixty years? Already, in just five, there have been more moments to savour than at any time in history, more promotions in a short space of time, more Wembley appearances and more silverware. The success and rise of this football club has been astonishing, galvanising and nothing short of a fairy tale. Little Lincoln City, getting beaten 3-2 at home by Woking a little over five years ago, are 90 minutes (or maybe 120) from going toe to toe with Nottingham Forest, Middlesbrough, Fulham and Queens Park Rangers. All week I've done media bits and have spoken about how great the rise has been, what a ride we've experienced and yet only now, as I sit here and properly contemplate the possibilities, that it has really hit me.

In terms of tomorrow, I'm not overly excited, nor am I nervous. I just feel quite calm and relaxed, a feeling I know will go once we get underway, but I think all the success and big occasions of the last few years have left me at ease with our future. When you have watched your team get beaten by Bradford Park Avenue, Salisbury and North Ferriby, it really is hard to feel anything other than positivity towards a game for a place in the Championship. I shall thoroughly enjoy the day and I know I'll be crapping myself when the game kicks off, but right now I'm just looking forward to it. Maybe I'm suppressing my nervous energy, maybe I'm burying the fear of losing the game, I don't know. Maybe I'm just aware that other fans are more expressive of their excitement or easier to hype up than me, perhaps at 42 I've just become more stoic and grounded than at any other time in my life.

What I do know is a win tomorrow will be life-changing for the football club and a result just as big as any of those I wrote about above. We can look for hints as to how we might do in the past, we can talk about their great play-off record, our failures and even the league matches. The truth is, none of that matters. All that matters is 90 minutes on the Wembley turf, between two teams who may wear the same colours as players of the past, bear the same badge and name, but are not in any way affected by what has gone before. Keith's sides and this team are different in every way, it's a different game in 2021, a different level and for fans it will be a different experience.

That doesn't mean if we lose I'll feel any different though, I will have that desolation deep inside, the empty feeling you get when you get so close, but are so far away. If we win..... I don't know. I can remember looking to the skies in March 2017 and wondering what it might feel like to be promoted from the National League. I couldn't fathom what that joy would feel like in real terms and to a degree, the same has to be said of now. The difference is that now we stand on the cusp of something never done before. There is no GMVC/National League comparison to be had, not really. Victory tomorrow would be the first promotion we experienced from a national, merged third tier and it is into a division unlike any we have ever been in, where million-pound transfers are the norm and occasional, tens of millions are spent. It would be a brave new world for Lincoln City, stepping into unknown territory the like of which we have never stepped into before. The Championship was the third most popular division in Europe in 2016/17 in terms of attendances and is currently fifth. Next season, Lincoln City could be a part of that and I find it terrifying, exciting and unbelievable in equal measure.

I'll tell you something, I bloody love football and I love my club even more. Let's go to Wembley, make some noise for the boys, and celebrate their achievements this season whatever happens. Hopefully, tomorrow we witness more history being made by this truly amazing football club. Up the Imps.

Always The Bridesmaid: Blackpool 2-1 Imps
May 31, 2021

I don't want to write the game up yesterday, but I have to.

I write up every game, sometimes a little reluctantly, but very rarely with every sinew of my body not wanting to. That's how I feel right now. If I were to describe it in any way, I feel a bit like a junkie who has just had too much – yesterday I didn't get the excitement or the nerves, the high wasn't there, but the lows are as bad as ever. If you are a junkie (which I hope you're not), that is the time to stop. I won't stop supporting this club, ever, but right now I do feel like I'm on a massive comedown without having had the pay-off.

Of course, I have had the pay-off, when we beat Portsmouth, Sunderland and even Blackpool earlier in the season. Over 46 matches I've seen a new, rejuvenated Lincoln City doing things we only dreamed of, not just five years ago, but ten, 15, 20 and right back as far as I can remember. It has been the best season since I started attending matches and that is the pay-off, isn't it? That should be the focus, not what I can only describe as a rubbish day at Wembley.

It was rubbish too, I'm sorry for those who didn't go and couldn't enjoy it, but it was. The journey in was crap, I had a Burger King which was stale and gave me indigestion, which was the start of a terrible experience. There was some poor lad killed on a motorcycle on the North Circular, and he lay dying as we drove past. People were desperately trying to save his life, with a crowd of morbid pedestrians watching every moment, but those battling to save him were doing so in vain. We didn't know that at the time, but it put much into perspective later in the day. When we got parked up, pubs wouldn't admit us, nobody around the ground seemed to know where Lincoln fans should be and when we did get to Wembley way, the lack of supporters made it feel like two village teams coming together in the FA Vase final. That might even be detrimental to the FA Vase, because I'm sure that game would have more than a paltry 9,700 there.

Seeing the likes of Terry Hibberd before the game did perk me up. You might know Terry as the former Media Manager at the club, who left the role in December. He is a lovely bloke and I was personally gutted when he left the club as he started out like me, writing a fan blog for Sheffield Wednesday, before getting a job in football. We were both eager to meet up and doing so did add enjoyment to those early hours. The same goes for Bubs, Ben, Rick and a host of other faces I've not seen for months, even a full year or more. It was normality, to a degree, or at least it had the veneer of normality until you lifted up and looked underneath.

Underneath it was 'Football Lite', a version of the game and experience we love with a few features cut down. Inside Wembley was muted, stifled if you like. Getting in was no problem, but as soon as you did it was 'mask up', and I find that ridiculous. It's nobody's fault, but how can I sit in a pub with my mask off, but be forced to sit in open-air stands with my mask across my face? It didn't help I forgot my usual mask, a neck-gaiter and had to wear one kindly supplied by my mate Matt. It covered half my beard, but whenever I exhaled my sunglasses steamed up – prescription sunglasses without which I can't properly see the game. When I did pull my mask down to get a decent view a steward told me off – rightly so, it's his job, but there was nobody doing that at the Brit Awards, was there? I spent 90 minutes adjusting the mask, wiping my glasses and getting increasingly hacked off.

Around the ground, City fans stuck to the rules, remained distanced and the stewards at our end certainly jumped on those who did not, but at the other end of the ground there appeared to be no problem with large groups congregating together, and that did affect the atmosphere. Blackpool had two big groups singing, whilst we had one, behind me, of around 100, whilst everyone else remained where they were meant to be. It did make them louder than us and I'm not blaming their fans for doing what they did, nor the stewards in our end for stopping it, but it just made the day more rubbish than it was. It felt like there was an imbalance, and I don't know why it was. Should we just have been more forceful in telling stewards to get lost? How did Blackpool achieve that and we did not? These are questions that will never be answered and probably not even asked after this article is finished.

After the game (yes, I've skipped the game for now), we got stuck in traffic for almost two hours thanks to that accident and ended up on a tour of the less than salubrious parts of Wembley, the St Raphael's Estate, Ikea and then eventually, thanks to a mix up between myself and my navigator, a Wembley car park. We eventually had to take the M4 out to the M25 and come right back around, all thoroughly annoyed, tired, thirsty and down in the dumps. Then, on the way home, Matt scrolled social media and found lots of angry fans at home blaming those at the ground for not making enough noise. Madness, utter madness. That's like accusing Michael of not being animated enough because Sky showed three shots of him looking pensive, but nothing after that.

Our last trip to Wembley was loud, exciting and even though it rained, it felt like a celebration. Yesterday did not, at all, and I'll be honest, I feel empty and cheated. It's not the club's fault, nor Blackpool's, but the situation as a whole isn't one I think I'll look back on fondly. Of course, it would all be very different had we won the actual game, which I guess I'll discuss a little further. It's my duty, I suppose.

We were beaten by the better team on the day.

Is that enough? It does sum it up I think and I wish that I could stop there. We didn't play badly, but a better team played well and won the game. I said on the way home we could go back today, play the game again and we might win it, whereas the day we played Bournemouth back in 2003, we could have played for the next six weeks and lost every game. It was always going to balance on the edge of a knife and so it came to pass.

If anything, the early goal was a bad thing, certainly from a fan's point of view. The ball hit the net, we all went mental and for a short moment, all you could hear were City fans. I sang (all game, by the way, in case someone out there is keeping score), I cheered and I hugged my Dad. I looked up at the scoreboard and realised there was still 89 minutes to go. That in itself was a bit deflating, knowing that although we had the advantage, there was still a whole game to go. From only leading for a single minute across two matches in the regular season, we'd have to lead for a full game.

This was a game of small margins. Had that curling effort later in the half not struck the crossbar, we might be a Championship side now. I seem to think we hit the post in the first period too, again, small margins. Sadly, a slip by Grant saw them break and net, levelling the tie, and I felt there would only be one winner after that. They controlled possession better, they stopped us playing our game more effectively and when they got a shot away, it was usually on target. In 90 minutes, we didn't make Chris Maxwell make a save and that's why we're going to Cambridge and Cheltenham next season, not Fulham and West Brom.

There are no excuses either. Sure, the referee seemed below par from a red and white perspective, and I felt there was a good shout for a penalty in the second half, but did his decisions change the game as John Busby's did at the start of the month? Nope. I wouldn't want Mr Harrington in charge if we made this stage again in the future, he did seem to have a Blackpool bias, but so did Wembley. Before their team got read out they had a rousing speech about play-off games past, whereas Alan Long got to read out the teams and thank us for our support. Accidental? Maybe, but everything felt weighted towards Blackpool.

For a long while, we have been the story wherever we go, but these last few weeks have proven us not to be a good enough tale for anyone. Peterborough were a good story after they were 'cheated' out of promotion (in their eyes) last season. Sunderland were a bigger story, certainly for Sky, in the EFL Trophy and the play-offs and post-Oyston Blackpool seemed to be the darlings of the media yesterday. Each time, we have rolled up simply to play the opposition, the Big Ger Cafferty to their Rebus, the Moriarty to their Sherlock, the Baron Greenback to their Dangermouse. I'm not getting a complex, by the way, it's just the way it is and of all the clubs in the EFL, Blackpool are one I begrudge it to the least because their fans went through hell. Remember, they didn't see a home game for ages, not because of Covid, but because a convicted rapist and poisonous ownership were tearing their club apart and they stayed away in protest. We had redemption in 2017, our current situation is evolution and progression, but for Blackpool, they're just getting back to where they feel they probably belong. Fair play to them too, as painful as it was to watch.

The second half was good and bad from our point of view. They scored a carbon-copy goal which sealed the tie, and after that I felt we were the better side, but we lacked a cutting edge. Tom Hopper has been superb these last few weeks, but he was lost in the game yesterday and sadly his replacement, Callum Morton, looked less likely to affect the game than 3,000 people singing. You can make all the noise you like, it doesn't put the ball in the net and since his return from injury, neither does Morton. He tried, he worked hard, but his attributes and our style are not aligned and it really showed. When we made our first change, I was a bit gutted it wasn't Harry Anderson coming on. Harry on the right, Johnson in the middle and Tom Hopper kept up top for ten might have given us more potency, but Michael is paid to make these decisions, not I, and his choices have got us to within 90 minutes of the Championship. However much it stings, I'll take that.

We huffed, we puffed, but we got nowhere. I don't think any player was particularly bad, but there wasn't anyone who was great either. It was the biggest game of the season, we had our full first team to pick from (give or take the odd body) and we came up short. That's the fact of the matter, we lost because we didn't put the performance in on the day, we were managed by a very good side and the right team won the game. I find that harder to take than anything. There is no blame. It wasn't the supporter's fault, it wasn't the referee's fault, no one player was to blame and the team selection wasn't wrong. We lost, and that's the bottom line. I hate losing fair and square because there is no solace, no shelter and no protection from the searing disappointment and cutting pain.

That's it. In terms of this season, that's all she wrote. I tipped Blackpool, Hull and Peterborough to go up this season and I've never been as gutted to get it right. All three celebrated their promotion against us, three times our players have been forced to watch on as someone else has their big day. It is the third time we have been forced to hear a final whistle and the roar of delight, be it from the bench, players or fans, as someone else has their moment. Alas, not us, but we've had a few ourselves over the last five years and I guess we have to grit our teeth, look ahead and be happy at the progress and achievements of the season.

If anything, I only have one thought in my head today anyway, or at least one that overrides all others: I came home alive yesterday, and I saw the final moments of a poor soul who did not. With that in mind, does it really matter which division we're in tonight? We have a future, we have plenty to look forward to and be thankful for and that is the solace, protection and shelter that I need from the sting of a play-off final defeat.

Stacey West End of Season Awards
June 1, 2021

It is time for the Stacey West End of Season Awards, mainly chosen by you, the readers of this site.

It's been a long season, one full of drama, excitement, elation and occasionally, disappointment. One thing is for certain – Lincoln City fans have not been disappointed overall. Losing at Wembley stung, getting denied the chance to face Tranmere in the EFL Trophy final because of a penalty hurt a lot, but on the whole, we have to be happy with our achievements. This was the best season since the early eighties, one which I'm sure will live in the memory for many years, even if we did not take any silverware.

Over the course of the season, you have been rating each player, week by week, giving me the chance to do an awards article based not only on my interpretations but that of a collective of Imps fans everywhere. Without further ado, why not sit back, relax and check out the six awards we're giving out this season, which are:

Young Player of the Year – TJ Eyoma
The Young Player of the Year Award really was between two players – TJ Eyoma and Brennan Johnson. Had the season finished in the middle of April, Johnson would have taken the SW award as he did the club's official award, but TJ has been sensational since coming back into the side during the injury crisis. I really like this lad, I think he has a super future ahead of him as he's proven himself to be adaptable, powerful and able to cut it with some very tough strikers. His block in the play-off final second leg helped send us to Wembley, but across the whole season, he has been excellent. He did save a couple of his best performances for last too, with his 8.9 from the play-off first leg his season highlight according to you. A worthy winner of the first-ever Stacey West Young Player of the Year Award.

Loan Player of the Year – Alex Palmer
I thought I'd do an award for loan player of the season, because it does seem that clubs like us have a good number through and they often have a big say in our season. This year, three really stood out. One has won Young Player of the Year, the other (Brennan Johnson) was a close second, but both were just bested by Alex Palmer. It would be hard not to award this to Palmer, he played 46 league games for us and despite one or two mistakes mid-season, he was largely dependable and a commanding presence in the box. Oddly, as you'll find out later, he isn't the only keeper to win an award in our series!

Jack Mulhall xG Award – Anthony Scully

I've been looking forward to this one – it's the Jack Mulhall Award for xG. We've worked this out by taking a player's goal tally from the season and subtracting their xG. The higher the number that remains, the more clinical they were in front of goal. A player outperforming his xG significantly scored more goals than the stats believed he should. Three players had a total more than a single goal – Tayo Edun was third and Lewis Montsma a close second. The winner though, who up until the cut off point (Wimbledon) has three goals more than his xG suggested he should, is Anthony Scully. We'll be sending a trophy, and an explanation, to Anthony over the coming days!

Best Team Display – Sunderland POSF (H)

Every week (bar September) you were rating the Imps' performances and that gave a picture of exactly which games you thought were the best we took part in. Unsurprisingly, the winner came after the 46-game season, namely Sunderland at home in the play-off semi-final. It seems we did save the big performance for our return to Sincil Bank, and despite riding our luck somewhat, it snatches the prize away from other big outings, such as Shrewsbury away in the EFL Trophy and Gillingham away live on Sky. Both of those scored highly, but you enjoyed the win against the Mackems the most. I guess that's a good thing, seeing as though we'll have to do it all again next season!

Best Individual Display – Joe Bursik

Joe Bursik carved himself out a little slice of Lincoln City history this month when he not only appeared for one solitary game but had a stormer. Alex Palmer would have won this award for his performance against Hull City in the EFL Trophy, but instead, Bursik nicks it with an average rating of 9.30. It's astounding that a young keeper can come in, have a day or two with the squad, and then turn in such a committed and competent display. I do hope that Stoke decide to loan him out next season because he would be a wonderful addition to this club over 46 games.

Player of the Year – Conor McGrandles

Your Stacey West Player of the Year differs from the official club vote. Jorge Grant took the accolade in the official count, and with good reason, but you lot see a different game at times and have given it to midfield maestro Conor McGrandles. Before I go on, a couple of points.

Firstly, two other players would have been there or thereabouts but did not feature in enough games. Joe Walsh actually outscored everybody over the course of the season, grabbing an average rating of 7.16, but he only appeared 25 times and therefore didn't qualify for the award. Zack Elbouzedi had a great average too, 7.77, but only appeared six times. Finally, Liam Bridcutt finished just behind McGrandles and made the exact amount of appearances to qualify, 30 in league and cup. He enjoyed a great finish to the season too, and we might have been further up the table had he managed 40 or more.

Instead, Jorge Grant finished third, Tayo Edun fourth, and the summer signing from MK Dons took the top accolade in your eyes. He did have a super season, bagging eight Man of the Match awards, two more than Tayo Edun, three more than Harry Anderson and Jorge Grant and double anyone else. Seven of those awards came after the turn of the year, proving McGrandles to have been a massive influence since coming back into the side after his layoff. In fact, if his average rating for before New Year was taken, he would be behind Grant, Edun, Palmer, Eyoma, Jackson, Johnson, Anderson Hopper and Lewis Montsma. How's that for having an impact late in the season?

Without further ado, all that remains is for me to crown Conor McGrandles the Stacey West Player of the Season for 2020/21. Well done Conor, all the players who won awards and the whole squad for delivering such an exciting season.

Squad Details

	L1 Apps	L1 Gls	FA App	FA Gls	LC App	LC Gls	EFT App	EFT Gls
Harry Anderson	14 (15)	3	2 (0)	0	2 (0)	0	5 (1)	3
Theo Archibald	0 (7)	0	2 (0)	0	0 (1)	0	2 (0)	1
Alex Bradley	0 (0)	0	0 (0)	0	2 (0)	0	1 (0)	0
Cohen Bramall	12 (5)	0	0 (0)	0	0 (0)	0	0 (1)	0
Liam Bridcutt	22 (1)	0	0 (0)	0	1 (1)	0	5 (0)	0
Josef Bursik	0 (0)	0	0 (0)	0	0 (0)	0	1 (0)	0
Hayden Cann	0 (0)	0	0 (0)	0	0 (0)	0	0 (2)	0
Tayo Edun	36 (5)	1	2 (0)	0	2 (0)	1	9 (0)	0
Zak Elbouzedi	0 (2)	0	0 (1)	0	0 (0)	0	3 (0)	2
Timothy Eyoma	34 (5)	1	1 (0)	0	3 (0)	0	10 (0)	0
Robbie Gotts	4 (3)	0	2 (0)	0	0 (0)	0	3 (0)	1
Jorge Grant	35 (1)	13	1 (1)	2	3 (0)	0	7 (3)	2
Tom Hopper	33 (6)	8	0 (0)	0	1 (2)	1	5 (1)	2
Ramirez Howarth	4 (7)	1	0 (0)	0	0 (2)	0	5 (2)	1
Adam Jackson	27 (1)	1	1 (0)	0	1 (0)	0	4 (0)	0
Brennan Johnson	38 (2)	10	2 (0)	1	0 (0)	0	7 (0)	2
James Jones	28 (8)	1	0 (2)	1	3 (0)	1	1 (3)	0
Conor McGrandles	35 (4)	4	1 (1)	0	2 (1)	0	4 (3)	0
Max Melbourne	1 (7)	0	2 (0)	0	2 (0)	0	4 (0)	0
Lewis Montsma	38 (2)	6	0 (0)	0	3 (0)	3	4 (2)	0
Callum Morton	11 (6)	2	0 (0)	0	1 (1)	1	1 (1)	0
Alex Palmer	46 (0)	0	2 (0)	0	3 (0)	0	7 (0)	0
Regan Poole	18 (4)	0	0 (0)	0	0 (0)	0	3 (0)	0
Morgan Rogers	23 (2)	6	0 (0)	0	0 (0)	0	3 (0)	0
Ethan Ross	0 (0)	0	0 (0)	0	0 (0)	0	2 (0)	0
Sean Roughan	6 (0)	0	1 (0)	0	1 (0)	0	3 (0)	0
Max Sanders	1 (4)	0	0 (0)	0	0 (0)	0	1 (0)	0
Anthony Scully	22 (18)	11	2 (0)	2	3 (0)	1	7 (2)	3
Jamie Soule	0 (1)	0	0 (0)	0	0 (0)	0	1 (0)	1
Joe Walsh	18 (3)	0	1 (0)	0	0 (0)	0	2 (1)	0

League Table

	P		Home					Away					GD	PTS
		W	D	L	F	A	W	D	L	F	A		
Hull	46	14	4	5	32	14	13	4	6	48	24	42	89
Peterborough	46	15	5	3	52	22	11	4	8	31	24	37	87
Blackpool	46	12	7	4	30	18	11	4	8	30	19	23	80
Sunderland	46	9	8	6	32	25	11	9	3	38	17	28	77
Lincoln	46	9	5	9	35	30	13	6	4	34	20	19	77
Oxford	46	13	4	6	39	21	9	4	10	38	35	21	74
Charlton	46	8	7	8	36	37	12	7	4	34	19	14	74
Portsmouth	46	9	5	9	29	24	12	4	7	36	27	14	72
Ipswich	46	12	5	6	25	18	7	7	9	21	28	0	69
Gillingham	46	10	5	8	31	30	9	5	9	32	30	3	67
Accrington	46	10	7	6	31	26	8	6	9	32	42	-5	67
Crewe	46	10	7	6	32	30	8	5	10	24	31	-5	66
MK Dons	46	10	7	6	36	28	8	4	11	28	34	2	65
Doncaster	46	11	4	8	34	32	8	3	12	29	35	-4	64
Fleetwood	46	9	8	6	26	17	7	4	12	23	29	3	60
Burton	46	7	4	12	32	42	8	8	7	29	31	-12	57
Shrewsbury	46	5	8	10	28	31	8	7	8	22	26	-7	54
Plymouth	46	11	4	8	31	39	3	7	13	22	41	-27	53
AFC W'bledon	46	7	5	11	32	39	5	10	8	22	31	-16	51
Wigan	46	5	6	12	26	42	8	3	12	28	35	-23	48
Rochdale	46	4	9	10	27	42	7	5	11	34	36	-17	47
Northampton	46	8	5	10	20	26	3	7	13	21	41	-26	45
Swindon	46	8	1	14	25	38	5	3	15	30	51	-34	43
Bristol R	46	7	2	14	23	32	3	6	14	17	38	-30	38

Printed in Great Britain
by Amazon